AF575676

CAST-IRON COOKING

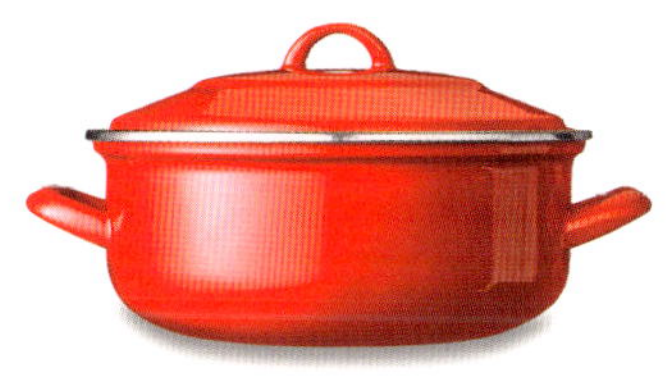

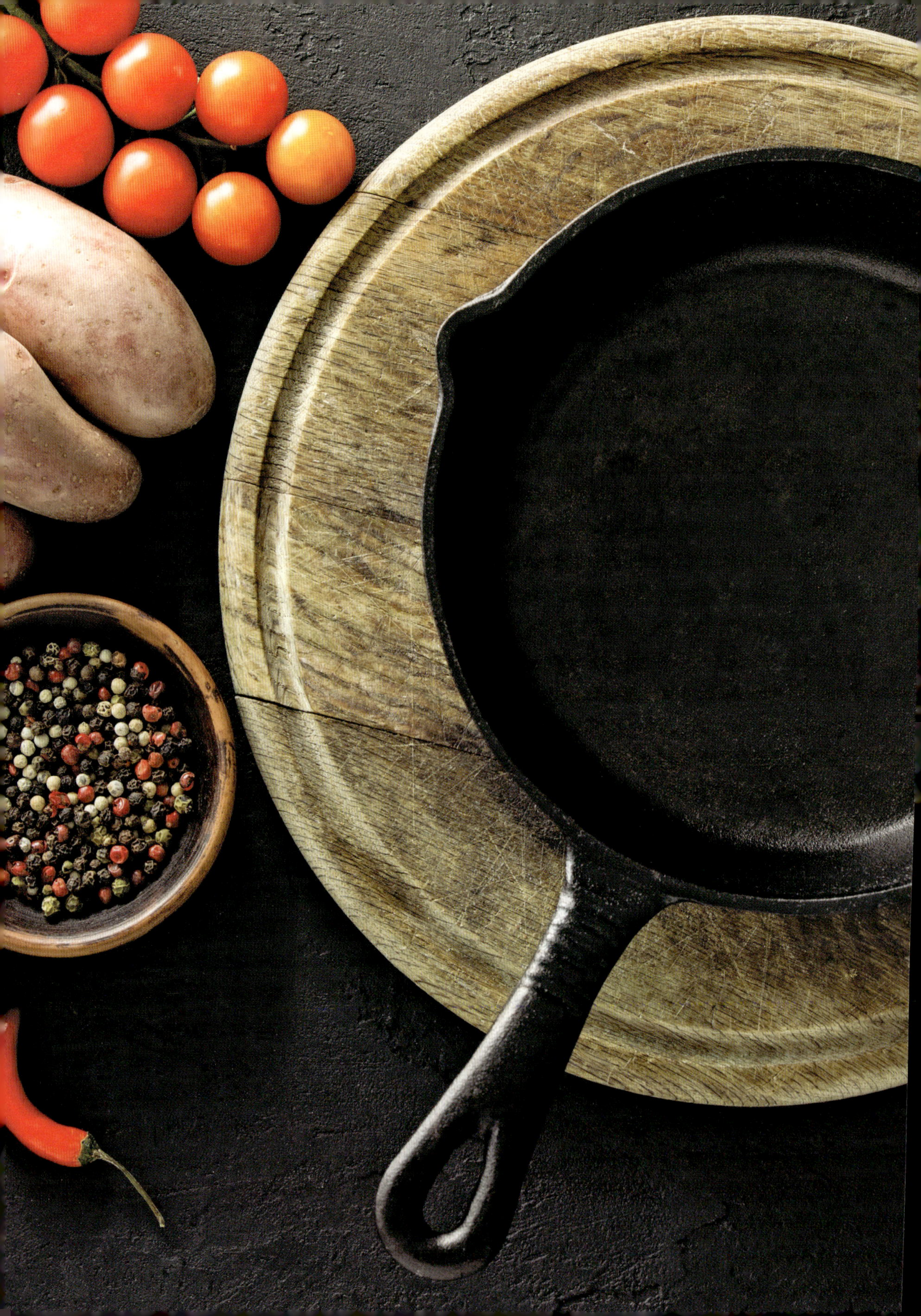

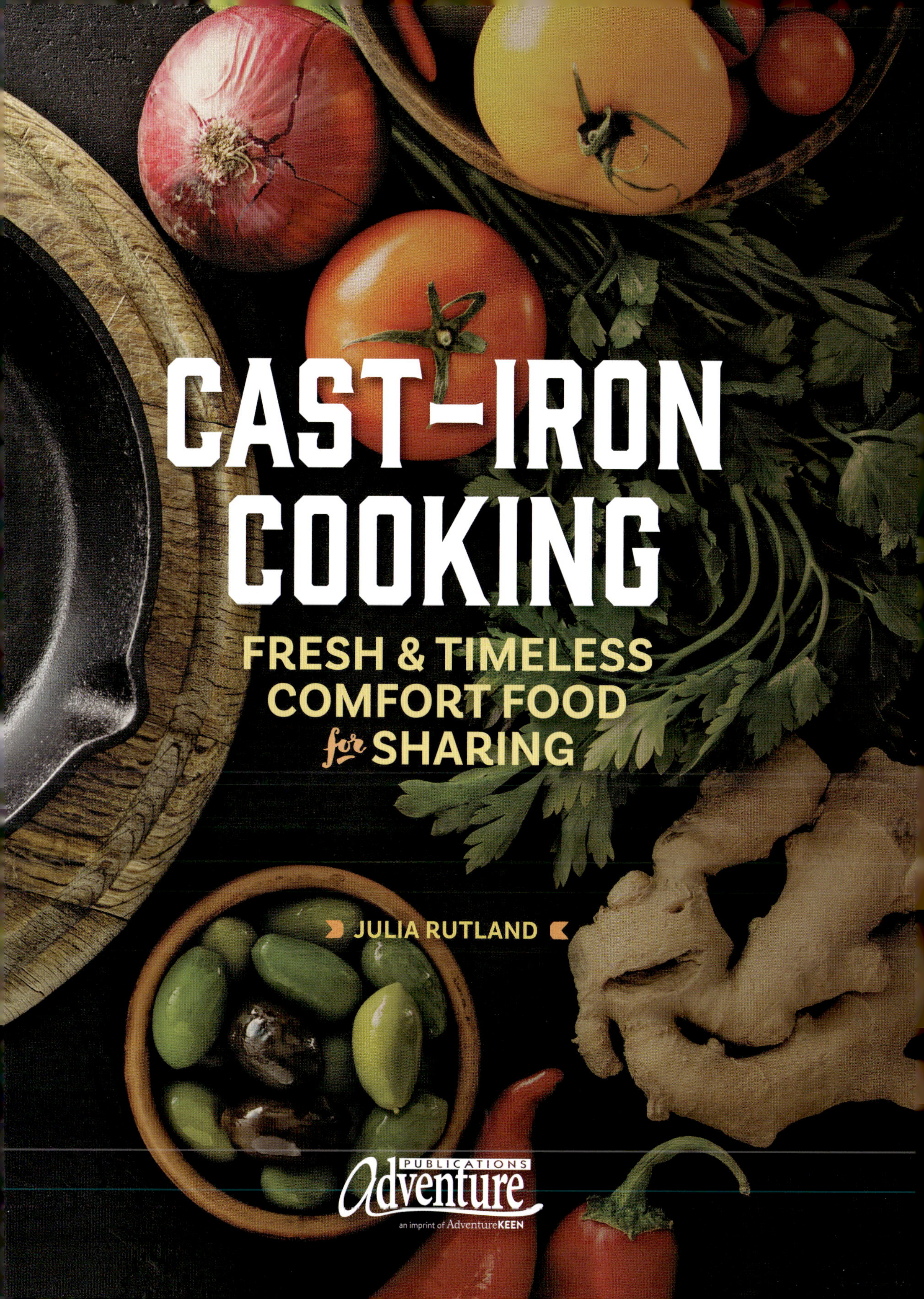
CAST-IRON COOKING
FRESH & TIMELESS COMFORT FOOD for SHARING
JULIA RUTLAND
PUBLICATIONS
Adventure
an imprint of AdventureKEEN

TABLE OF CONTENTS

ACKNOWLEDGMENTS

I am sincerely grateful to all those who have supported me in the creation of *Cast-Iron Cooking*. To my family: Dit, Corinne, Bishop, and Nick, whose encouragement and agreeableness to try all types of culinary experiments are greatly appreciated. A heartfelt thank-you to the incredible team at AdventureKEEN—Molly, Brett, Emily, Hilary, and Liliane—for their professional guidance, dedication, and tireless efforts in bringing this project to your kitchen. I am also immensely grateful to my friends who generously offered their time and taste buds to test the recipes. Your honest feedback and enthusiastic participation made this journey not only successful but also incredibly enjoyable. A special shoutout to Mark Kelly, formerly at Lodge, for giving me my first piece of cast iron many years ago. Additional thanks to Field Company, Staub, and Le Creuset. This book would not have been possible without each and every one of you.

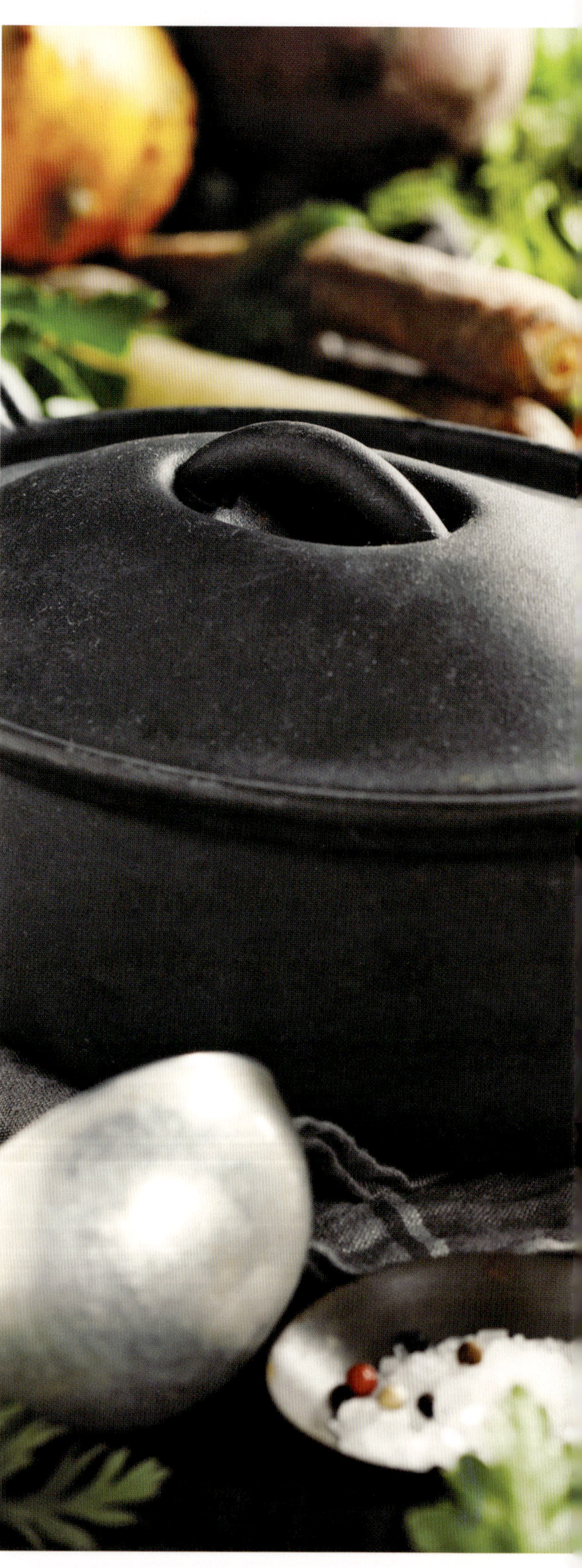

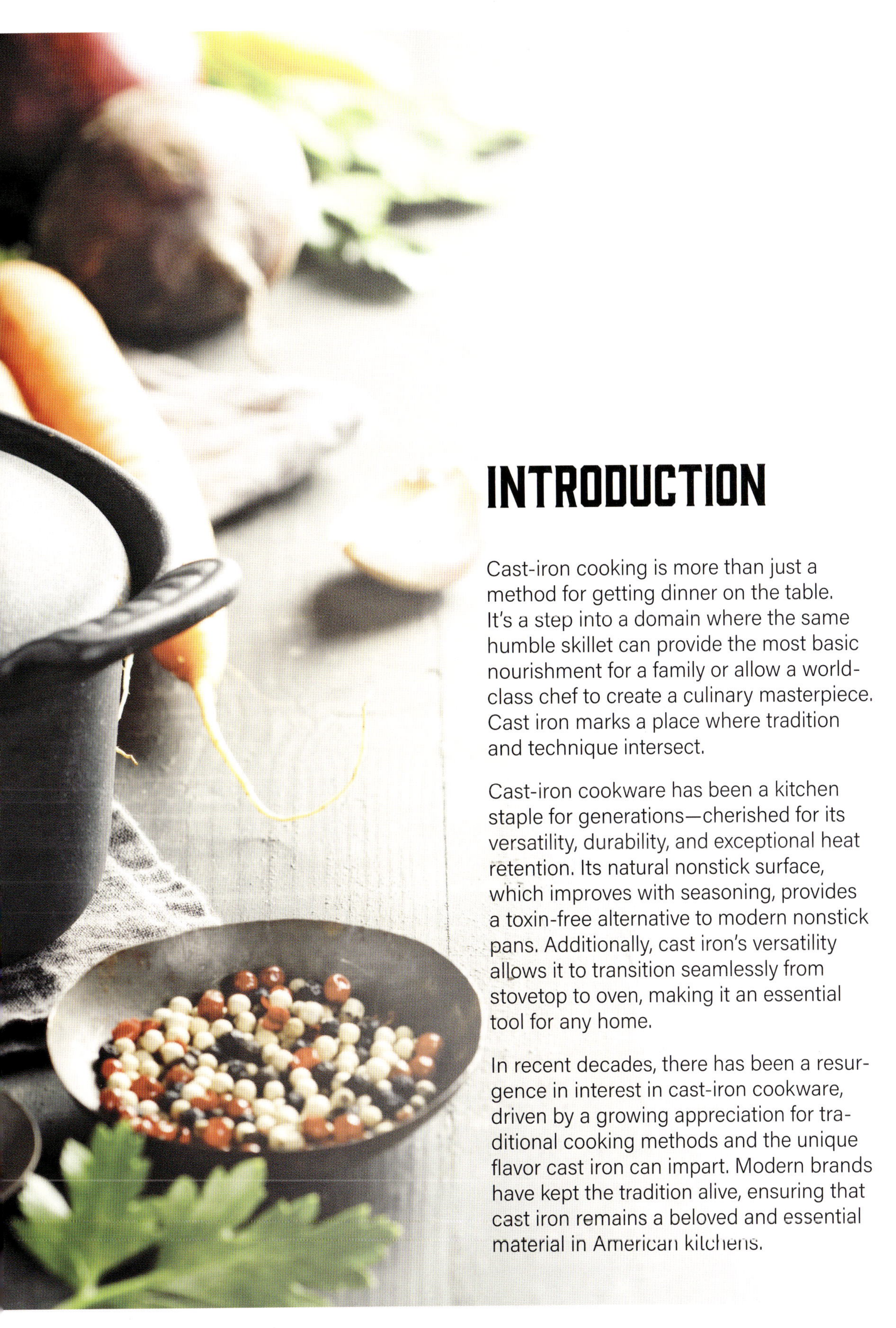

INTRODUCTION

Cast-iron cooking is more than just a method for getting dinner on the table. It's a step into a domain where the same humble skillet can provide the most basic nourishment for a family or allow a world-class chef to create a culinary masterpiece. Cast iron marks a place where tradition and technique intersect.

Cast-iron cookware has been a kitchen staple for generations—cherished for its versatility, durability, and exceptional heat retention. Its natural nonstick surface, which improves with seasoning, provides a toxin-free alternative to modern nonstick pans. Additionally, cast iron's versatility allows it to transition seamlessly from stovetop to oven, making it an essential tool for any home.

In recent decades, there has been a resurgence in interest in cast-iron cookware, driven by a growing appreciation for traditional cooking methods and the unique flavor cast iron can impart. Modern brands have kept the tradition alive, ensuring that cast iron remains a beloved and essential material in American kitchens.

HOW CAST IRON IS MADE

As a technology, cast iron has existed for several thousand years. The basics are simple: Wrought iron consists of nearly pure iron, which is heated and then struck—think of what an old-timey blacksmith does—to remove impurities and produce the desired shape. Cast iron, in comparison, is less pure—it's a combination of iron and a small percentage of carbon and silicon; it's then poured (or cast) into a mold, often made of sand, that produces the desired shape. Once the metal cools, the sand mold is removed, and the piece of cookware is polished. The particular processes and materials used by each individual manufacturer are proprietary, but the general method is the same. Once a piece of cookware is created, it's often "pre-seasoned" before being sold: oil is heated in the pan, creating a reasonably nonstick surface. Further seasoning (upon purchase) is almost universally recommended by manufacturers.

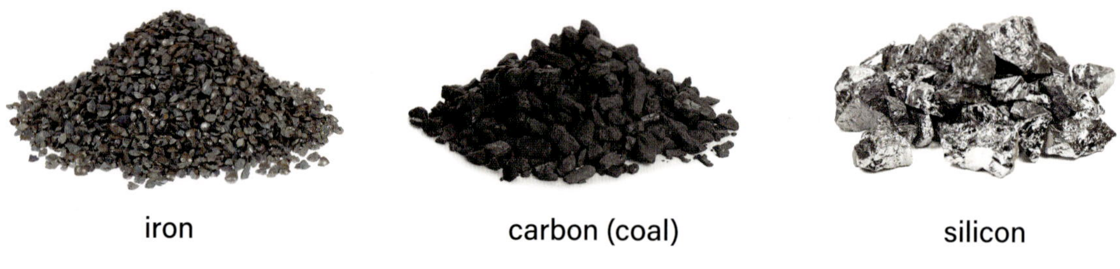

iron carbon (coal) silicon

HISTORY OF CAST IRON IN THE UNITED STATES

European settlers brought cast-iron pots and pans with them when they traveled to the colonies and early states. Pieces were thick, heavy, and designed with "feet" to be used over an open fire. Similar pieces are sold today for camping. As indoor residential stoves became the norm, cast-iron pots and pans evolved to be lighter with flat bottoms. Three American foundries—Griswold, Wagner, and Lodge—created a demand for the practical cookware. Today, only Lodge is still in operation. Founded in 1896, it is one of the oldest cookware manufacturers still in business.

In the mid-20th century, cast iron fell out of favor as inexpensive pans with nonstick coatings arrived on the market. A few decades later, cast iron has become popular again, as PFAS (aka "forever chemicals") and other compounds used to make nonstick skillets have been linked to health hazards.

Today, a number of domestic companies produce high-quality cast-iron cookware. Many of the new companies are small and family owned. Examples include Field, Smithey, FINEX, and others. They devote extra time to their products, especially in terms of processing, which makes their pans lighter and gives them more of a nonstick surface than economy options. It also makes them more expensive.

COLLECTIBLES

For many fans of cast iron, a single skillet or Dutch oven isn't enough, and devotees often amass large collections of unique cast-iron pieces as a hobby. Vintage cast iron, in particular, is quite popular. Older cast-iron cookware is renowned for its quality and durability, often outperforming its modern counterparts. Over time, a skillet that's properly cared for will develop a naturally slick surface that many argue is superior to modern nonstick pans. Charming designs and distinct markings make vintage cast iron highly coveted and often a valuable investment for collectors and enthusiasts. Griswold and Wagner brands are particularly desired by collectors; skillets and pans can sell for eye-popping amounts. Communities of collectors are active online, increasing the knowledge base and availability of all types of cast-iron pieces.

BENEFITS

Cast-iron cookware offers numerous advantages that make it a favorite among both professional chefs and home cooks.

- **Durability and longevity:** Cast-iron cookware is incredibly durable and can last for generations with proper care. It's resistant to wear and tear, making it a worthwhile investment.
- **Even heat distribution:** Cast iron heats evenly and retains heat for a long time, which helps in cooking food uniformly. This is particularly useful for dishes that require consistent heat.
- **Versatility:** Cast-iron cookware can be used on various heat sources, including stovetops, ovens, grills, and even campfires. It's suitable for a wide range of cooking methods, including frying, baking, roasting, and sautéing.
- **Natural nonstick surface:** When properly seasoned, cast-iron cookware develops a natural nonstick surface. This makes cooking and cleaning easier and reduces the need for excess oil.
- **High heat tolerance:** Cast iron can withstand very high temperatures, making it ideal for searing, frying, and baking. It can go from stovetop to oven without any issues.
- **Adds iron to your diet:** Cooking with cast iron can increase the iron content of your food, which can be beneficial for those with iron deficiencies or those interested in increasing their dietary iron intake naturally.
- **Synthetic-free cooking:** Unlike some nonstick cookware that can release harmful chemicals at high temperatures, cast iron is free from synthetic coatings and chemicals.
- **Cost-effectiveness:** While the initial cost of high-quality cast-iron cookware can be higher, its longevity and versatility make it a cost-effective choice in the long run.
- **Aesthetics:** Cast-iron cookware has a classic, rustic appearance that can add charm to your kitchen. Enamel-coated pieces are particularly attractive as serving pieces and can go from oven and cooktop to serving table.

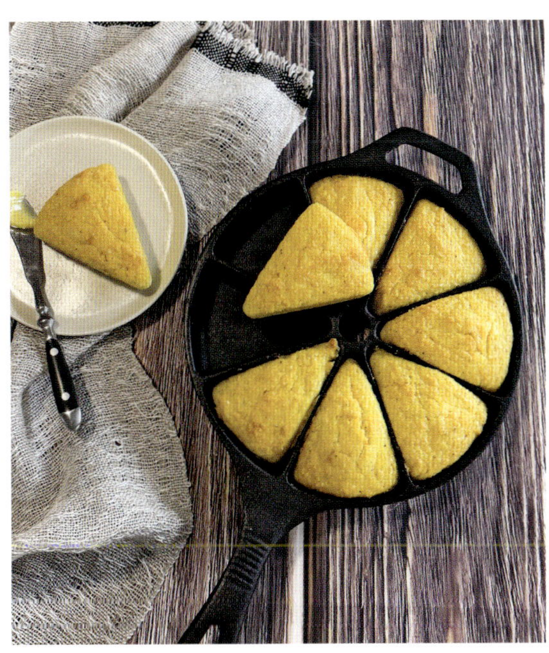

CATEGORIES OF CAST IRON

If you count novelty pans, cast iron comes in hundreds of different shapes, but all pieces fall into one of three categories: bare cast iron, seasoned cast iron, and enamel-coated cast iron. The differences are primarily in the surfaces and maintenance requirements.

- **Bare cast iron:** This is cast iron in its most raw, untreated state. It requires seasoning to create a nonstick surface and, importantly, to prevent rust. Bare cast iron can rust quite easily if it's not properly cared for, and it is typically more prone to sticking initially.
- **Seasoned cast iron:** Much of the modern cast-iron cookware purchased new has been lightly treated to give the home cook a bit of a head start on a well-seasoned pan. Seasoned cast iron has been treated at the foundry with a layer of oil that has been heated to create a protective, nonstick coating. This process (known as polymerization) improves cooking performance and helps prevent rust. Over time, the seasoning can build up, enhancing both the nonstick properties and durability of the cookware. After many uses, a well-seasoned cast-iron pan will develop a dark-black patina.
- **Enamel-coated cast iron:** This type of cast-iron cookware is coated with a layer of enamel, a glass-like substance that eliminates the need for seasoning. The enamel provides a smooth, non-reactive surface that is easier to clean and maintain. Enamel-coated cast iron offers the benefits of cast iron, such as heat retention and even cooking, along with resistantance to rust and suitability for cooking acidic foods. However, it is generally more expensive and can be more susceptible to chipping if mishandled.

STYLES

Different types of cast-iron cookware are suited for various cooking methods. Some popular styles include the following.

Long-handled skillet: This iconic pan is round; it's flat-bottomed with high sides, a long handle, and a short "helper handle" on the opposite side for easier lifting. It's extremely versatile and used for searing, frying, and baking because the entire piece is oven-safe.

Double-handled frying pan or baker's skillet: This type of skillet is specifically designed for baking. It typically features high, straight sides and a flat bottom, making it ideal for baking bread, cakes, casseroles, and other baked goods. The cast-iron construction ensures even heat distribution and excellent heat retention, resulting in well-baked and evenly browned dishes. It can also be used for cooking on the stovetop.

Grill pan: Designed to mimic the grates of an outdoor grill, this pan's ridges allow fat and juices to drain away from food, creating sear marks and a grilled flavor. Cast-iron grill pans can be used on various cooking surfaces, including stovetops, ovens, and even campfires. They are ideal for grilling meats, vegetables, and sandwiches indoors.

Griddle: A cast-iron griddle has a flat, rectangular or round cooking surface, typically with a low lip—or none at all—around the edges. It is designed for cooking foods that require a large, even surface area, such as pancakes, bacon, eggs, and grilled sandwiches.

Dutch oven: This heavy-duty, versatile cooking pot with thick walls and a tight-fitting lid is designed for slow-cooking methods, such as braising, stewing, roasting, and baking. The cast-iron construction ensures excellent heat retention and even heat distribution, making it ideal for cooking

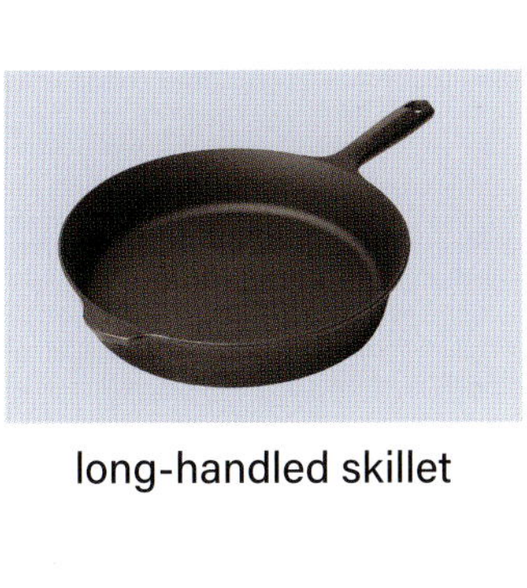
long-handled skillet

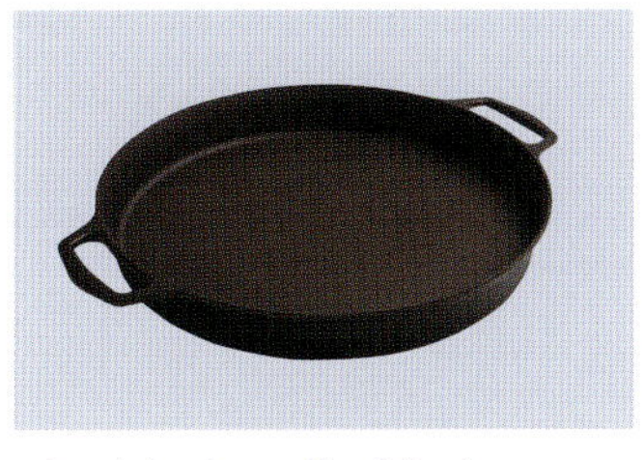
double-handled frying pan
or baker's skillet

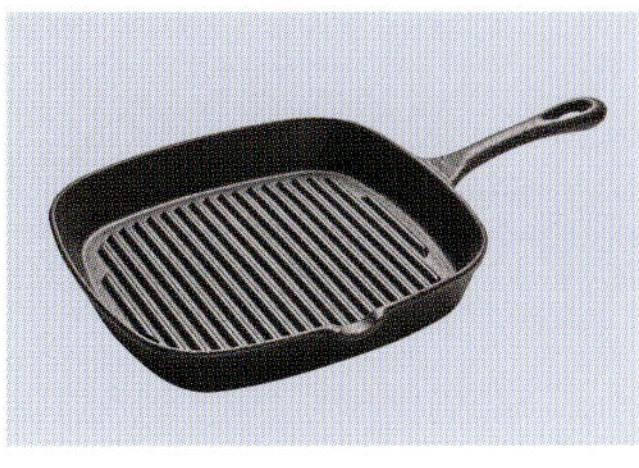
grill pan

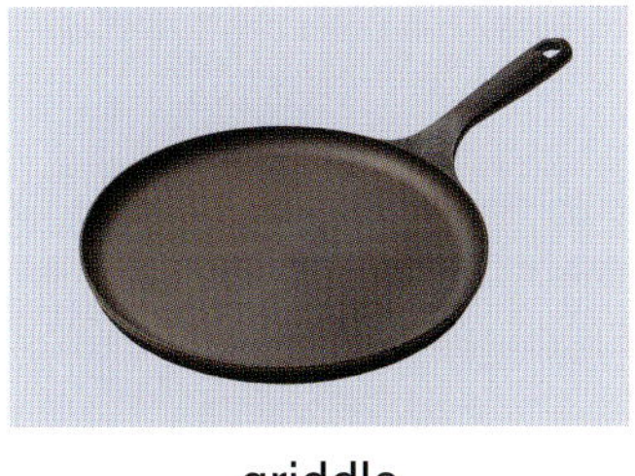
griddle

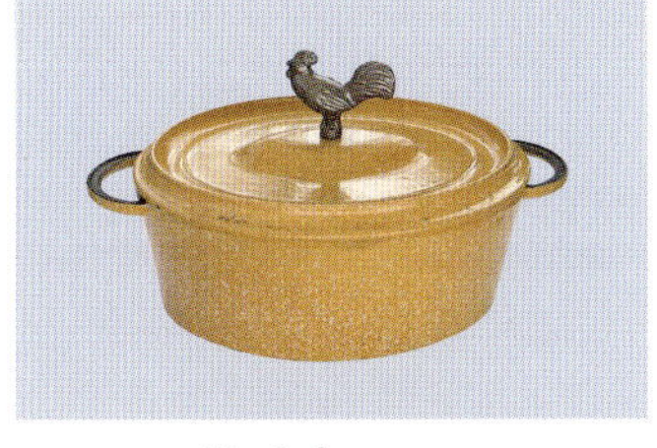
Dutch oven

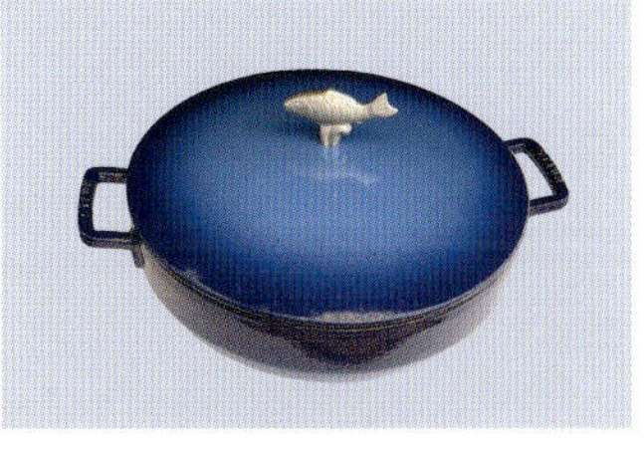
brasier

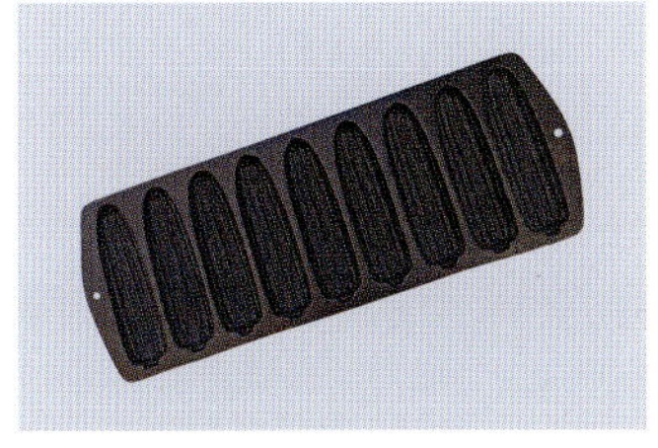
cornstick pan

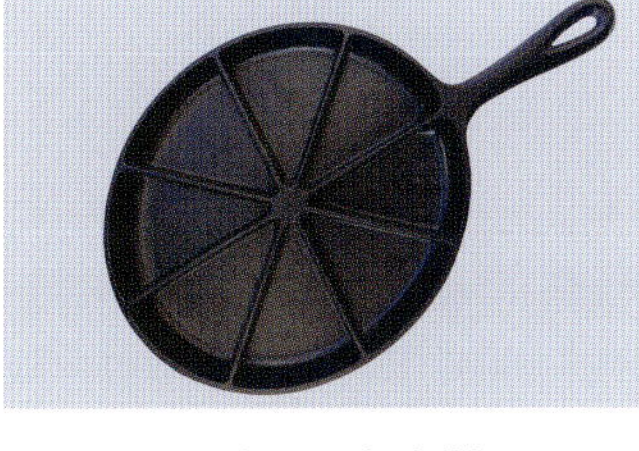
cornbread skillet

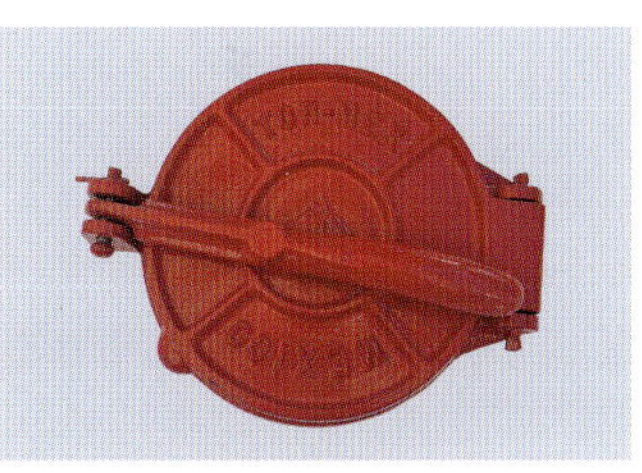
tortilla press

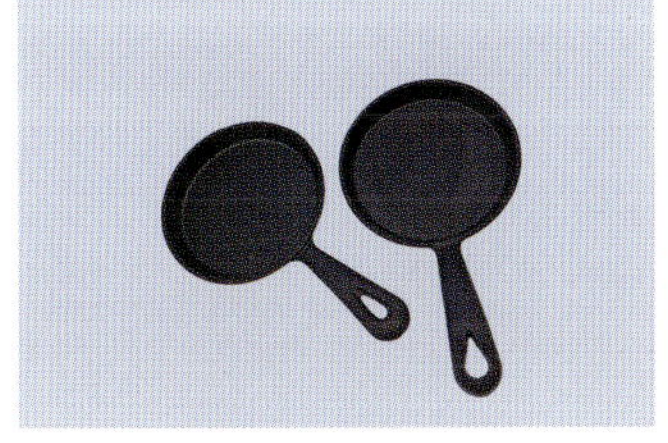
cookie skillets

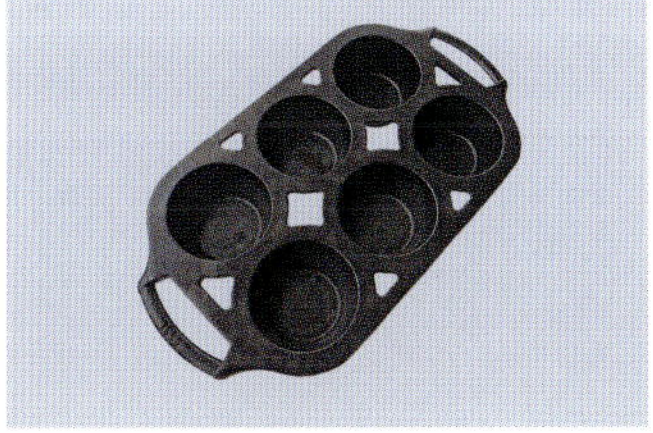
muffin pan

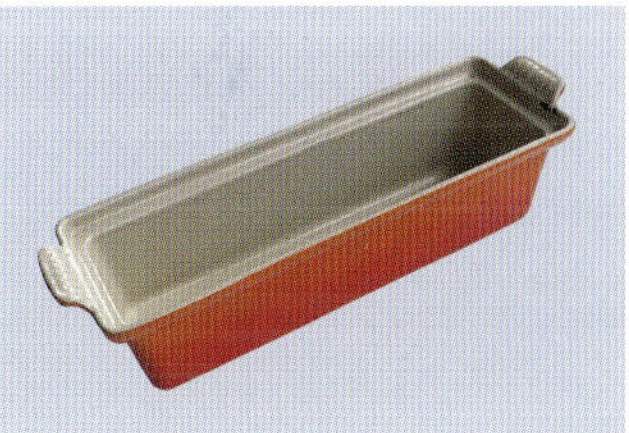
terrine

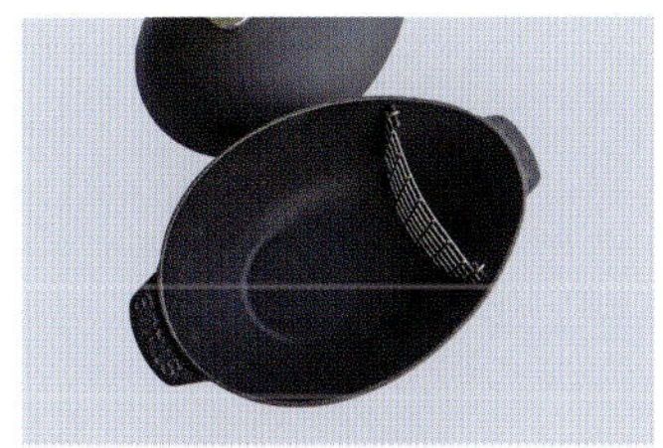
mussels pan

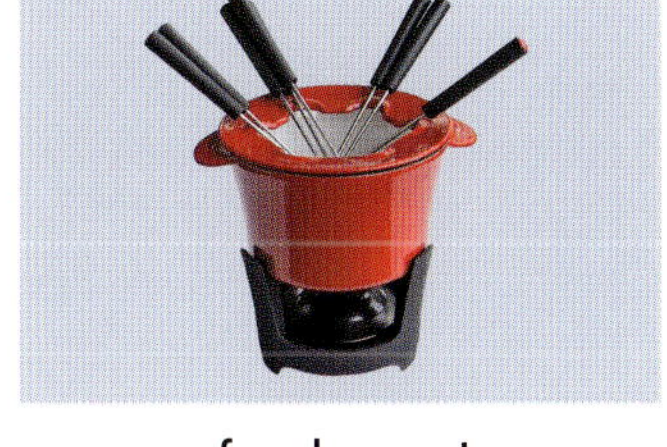
fondue pot

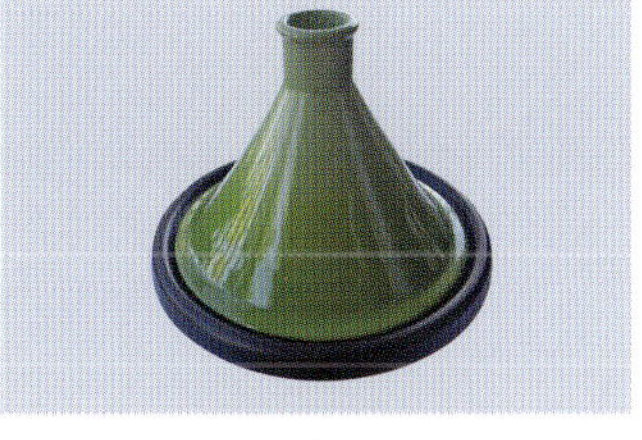
tagine

at consistent temperatures over extended periods. Dutch ovens can be used on stovetops, in ovens, or over open flames (except enamel-coated versions), making them suitable for both indoor and outdoor cooking. They are often used to make soups, stews, casseroles, breads, and other hearty dishes.

Brasier: Designed for braising, a cooking method that involves browning food at high temperatures and then slow-cooking it in liquid at a lower temperature, a brasier typically has a wide, shallow base and slightly sloped sides, which allow for good browning and even heat distribution. It comes with a tight-fitting lid to help retain moisture and flavors during cooking. Brasiers are versa-tile and can be used on the stovetop, in the oven, or even on the grill, making them suitable for a variety of dishes, such as roasts, stews, casseroles, and one-pot meals.

Specialty pans have limited or specialized uses; however, they maintain all the benefits of cast-iron construction. Here are some of my favorite examples.

Cornstick pan: This pan is designed specifically for baking cornsticks, which are a type of cornbread shaped like small ears of corn. The pan features multiple mold forms, each shaped like a miniature ear of corn, allowing the batter to bake into individual cornsticks. The cast-iron construction ensures even heat distribution and excellent heat retention, resulting in uniformly baked cornsticks with a crisp, golden crust. They are ideal for making traditional Southern-style cornbread sticks. You can also find novelty-shaped cornstick pans with regional, seasonal, or holiday designs.

Cornbread skillet: Designed with triangular segments to bake cornbread or other batter-based recipes, this pan is divided into individual portions.

Tortilla press: This kitchen tool isn't used for cooking tortillas. Instead, it is designed to flatten balls of dough into thin, round tortillas. It consists of two flat, circular plates hinged together, with a handle used to apply pressure. The cast-iron construction provides the weight and durability needed to press the dough evenly and efficiently, creating consistent tortillas every time. It can also be used for flattening empanadas or dumplings.

Cookie skillet: This mini-skillet with shallow sides is about 3½ inches wide and is used to bake individual cookies, brownies, or other single-serving desserts.

Muffin pan: Significantly heavier than common muffin pans, cast-iron muffin pans can not only be used in the oven but also over a campfire. This can be an advantage for stability, but the pan may require more effort to handle.

Terrine: Specifically designed for making terrines, pâtés, meat loaf, and other molded dishes and desserts, this pan is typically rectangular or oval and comes with a tight-fitting lid. The cast-iron construction ensures even heat distribution and excellent heat retention, which is crucial for the slow, even cooking required for these types of dishes.

Mussels pan: The deep, lidded pot is designed for cooking mussels or other shellfish. It features wire mesh on one side, allowing access to the cooking liquid that is delicious when dipped with pieces of French baguette.

Fondue pot: This small pot has excellent heat retention and even heat distribution, making it ideal for melting cheese, heating broth, or keeping chocolate at the perfect consistency for dipping.

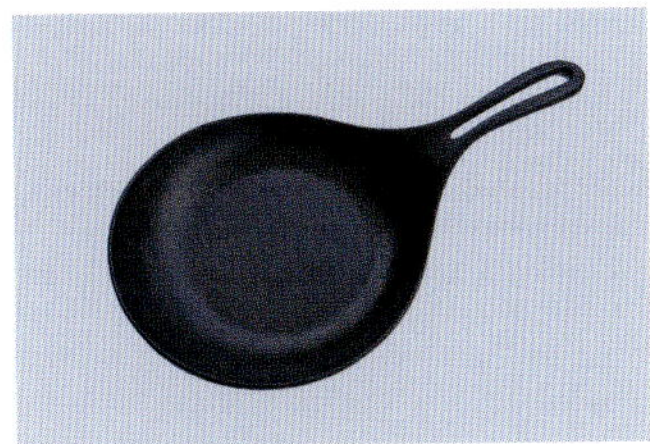
Japanese omelet pan

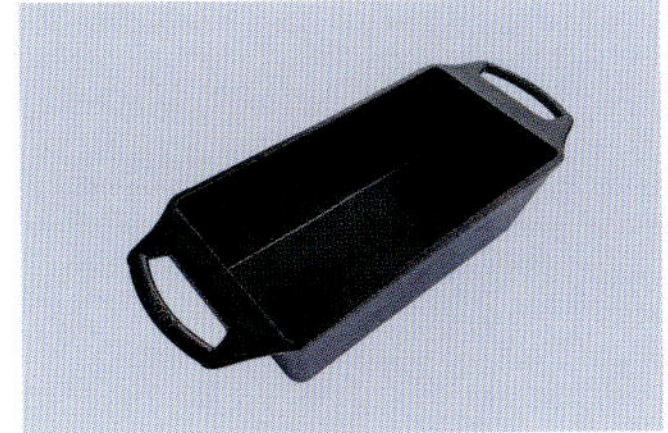
bread pan

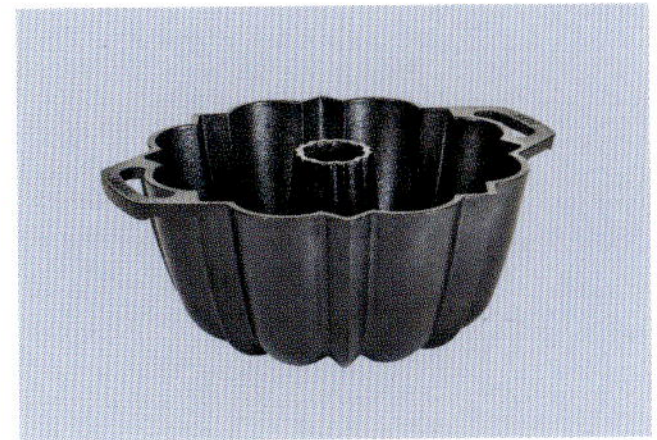
fluted cake pan

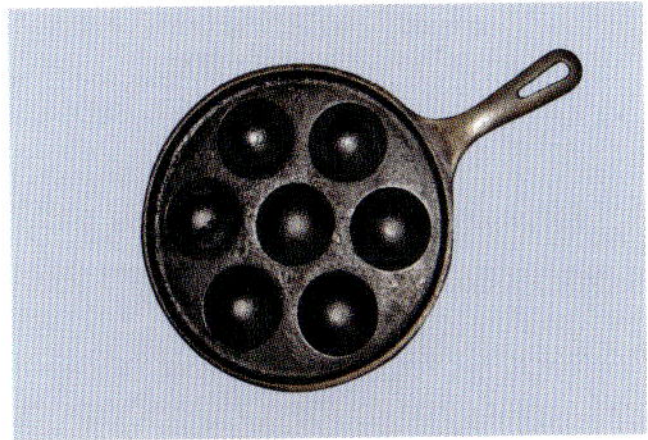
aebleskiver pan

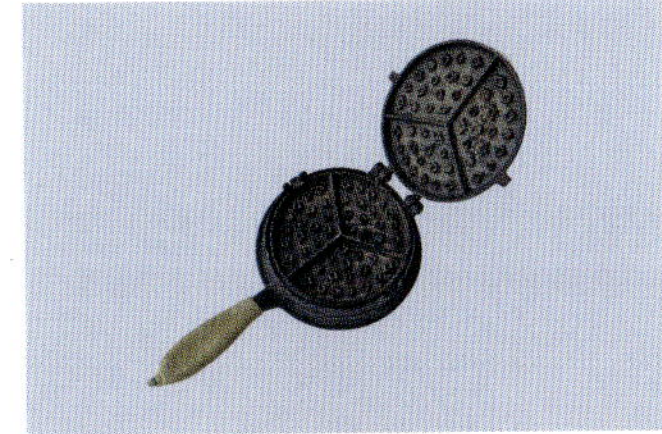
waffle iron

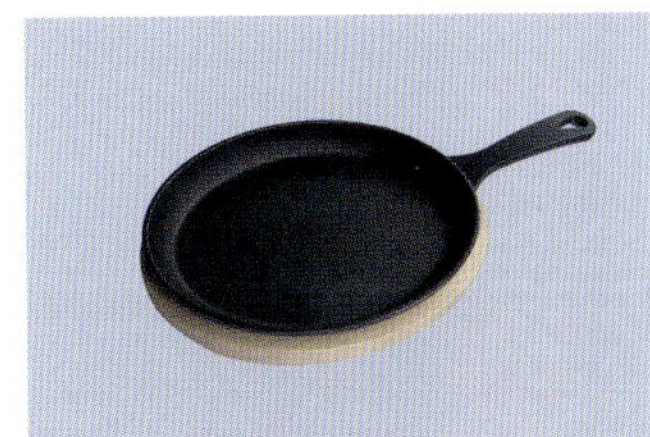
fajita pan

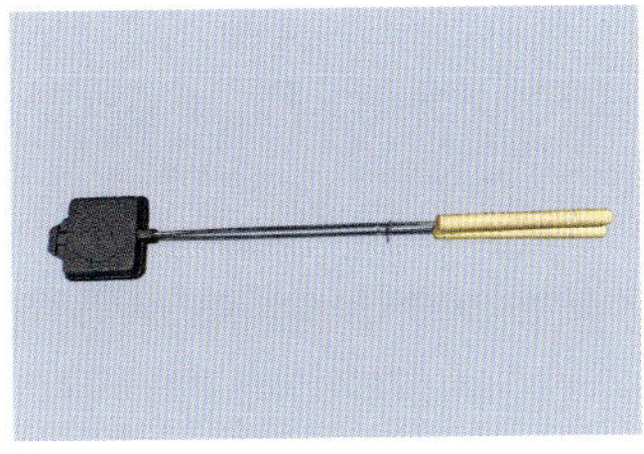
pie iron

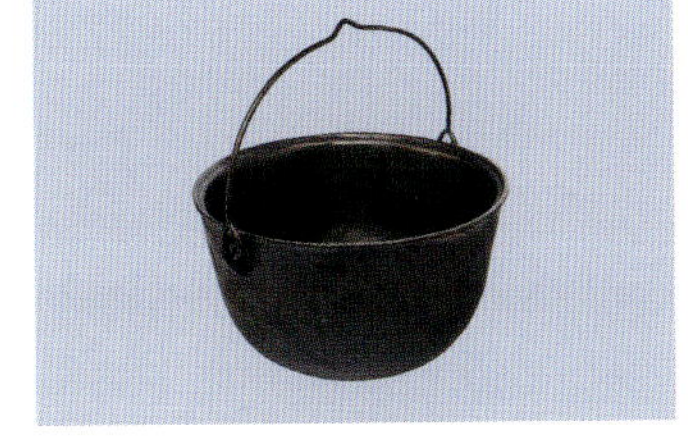
cauldron

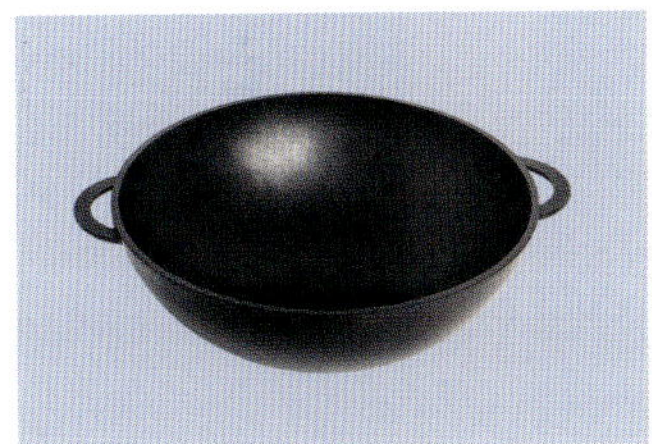
wok

Tagine: This type of cookware is designed for making tagine, a traditional North African stew. It features a wide, shallow base and a conical lid, which helps circulate steam and moisture for slow cooking, resulting in tender, flavorful dishes. A cast-iron version can be used on the stovetop, followed by oven baking.

Japanese omelet pan: This pan features an ergonomic design with gently curved edges and high sides that deepen toward the front, making flipping effortless. Its compact, lightweight build is ideal for cooking omelets or scrambling or frying eggs. The handle is designed to stay cooler on the stove, allowing for safe handling.

Bread pan: This can be used in the oven or over an open flame, offering versatility in bread baking.

Fluted cake pan: This heavy-duty cake pan is beautifully shaped to create a cake with a crisp exterior and tender interior.

Aebleskiver pan: This pan has multiple round indentations for making Danish pancake balls.

HOW TO SEASON CAST-IRON COOKWARE

The process involves a few steps, but each one is easy. Repeat the process below two or three times to build up a strong, even seasoning layer, especially if the cookware is new or has been stripped of seasoning. Re-season the skillet if food starts sticking or the surface appears dull; this will restore its nonstick properties and prolong its life.

Clean cast-iron cookware thoroughly with hot water and a stiff brush or sponge to remove any food residue or rust. For particularly resistant (stuck-on) food, use a chain mail metal scrubber designed to clean cast iron.

Dry the cookware completely with a towel. You can also place it on a stovetop burner over low heat for a few minutes to ensure all moisture is evaporated.

Preheat oven to 450–500°.

Apply a thin, even layer of vegetable oil to the entire surface of the cookware, including the handle and exterior. I prefer avocado or grapeseed oil because they have very high smoke points.

Wipe off any excess oil with a clean paper towel or cloth, leaving only a very thin film on the surface. **Note:** It is important that there is no excess oil puddling in the pan. It will not completely harden and may cause additional sticking. (Occasionally, tiny fibers of paper towels catch on the surface, depending on the brand or texture of the pan. Ignore or use a lint-free kitchen towel.)

Place cookware upside down on the middle rack of your preheated oven.

Bake the cast iron for 1 hour to allow the oil to polymerize and form a durable, nonstick coating.

Turn off the oven and let the cookware cool inside the oven to room temperature.

Store seasoned cast iron in a dry place to prevent rust and maintain its nonstick properties.

Waffle irons: These two-part cast-iron molds create classic or Belgian-style waffles when heated on a stovetop or over an open flame.

Fajita pan: This oval griddle-like pan is used for searing, sautéing, or browning food. Its small size is best for one or two small servings. Commercially, the pan is used as a serving dish, as food is cooked on larger griddles back in a restaurant kitchen. The intensely preheated pan will keep the food hot longer for the customer, and a proprietary sauce is added right before serving to add steam and sizzle.

Pie irons: These clamshell-shaped molds on long handles are used for making toasted sandwiches and pies over a campfire.

Cauldron: This large, rounded pot has a handle and often comes with feet; it's traditionally used for soups, stews, and large batches of food cooked over an open fire.

Wok: A wok can reach and maintain high temperatures; its wide cooking surface enables foods to cook quickly.

PURCHASING TIPS

Buying cast-iron products in stores and online is hassle-free because the items are new and stores often have return policies if there is an issue. However, there is an enduring market for pre-owned cast iron, so use these tips for both new and used pieces.

- Check for a smooth cooking surface, as this will improve with seasoning and provide better nonstick properties.
- Inspect the cookware for any cracks, chips, or imperfections that could affect its performance and longevity. This is especially important for enamel-coated pieces.
- Consider the weight of the cast-iron cookware, ensuring you can comfortably lift and handle it.

Compare prices and features, but remember that a higher initial investment in high-quality cast iron can pay off in durability and performance.

- Look for a brand with a good reputation for quality and durability. Well-made cast iron can last a lifetime.
- Choose the right size and shape for your cooking needs, such as skillets, Dutch ovens, or griddles. While I tried to use a variety of pieces, most of my recipes are made in 12- and 10-inch skillets. These sizes are very readily available and often included in sales. I typically use either a 7- or 5-quart Dutch oven for most of my soups, stews, and braises.
- Consider pre-seasoned options if you want to start cooking right away, although seasoning your own can yield better long-term results. Most of the major brands pre-season their pieces, but the first few uses will require additional seasoning after washing.
- Compare prices and features, but remember that a higher initial investment in high-quality cast iron can pay off in durability and performance.
- If buying vintage cast-iron pieces, especially those of unknown origin, consider using a lead test kit prior to use. The skillet or pot itself wasn't made to include lead; however, very old cast-iron pans were often used to melt lead for toys and bullets (since lead melts at a lower temperature than cast iron).

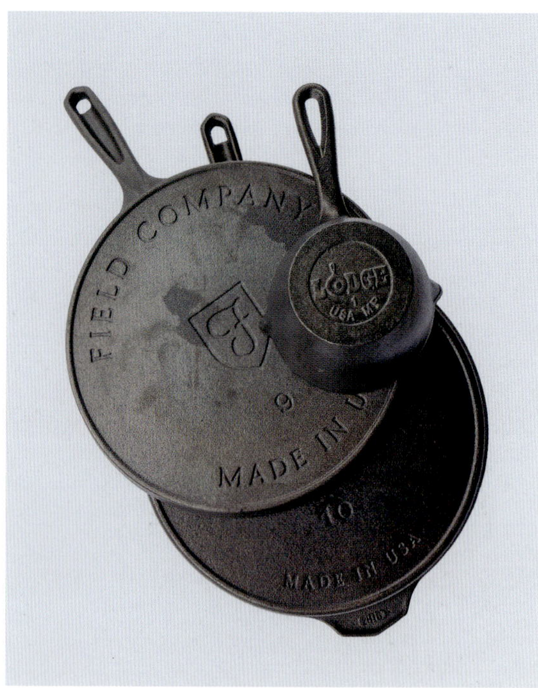

SKILLET NUMBERING

The number of a particular skillet doesn't always align with its diameter. Originally, the number on the skillet referred to the stove eye (burner) size that the skillet would fit, rather than the actual diameter of the pan itself. This number system was used to match skillets to the round openings of wood or coal stoves common at the time when skillets were first manufactured in the US.

Over the years, as stoves evolved, the number continued to be used more as a general size reference rather than an exact measurement. Additionally, different manufacturers might have slight variations in how they measured their skillets or what dimensions they emphasized. As a result, a number 8 skillet from one brand might have a slightly different diameter than a number 8 skillet from another brand. Many foreign manufacturers often use the metric system to label the diameter of the skillet. For example, a 26-centimeter skillet would measure 10.2 inches.

NOTE ABOUT ACIDIC FOODS

Cooking acidic food in cast-iron cookware can strip away the seasoning and impart a metallic taste to the dish. It is best to limit the cooking time of acidic ingredients, like tomatoes or citrus, to minimize these effects.

CLEANING TIPS

- Allow cast-iron cookware to cool slightly after use, but clean it while it's still warm to make residue easier to remove. To avoid thermal shock, do not run cold water over a hot pan.
- Scrape off any food particles with a spatula or brush. For stubborn bits, use coarse salt as a gentle abrasive.
- Rinse the skillet with hot water. If necessary, use a small amount of mild soap, and rinse thoroughly. I usually use a bit of soap when cooking meat, but I tend to use only very hot water after cooking vegetables and other mild-flavored foods.
- Scrub the surface with a nonabrasive scrubber or brush to remove any remaining food particles.
- Dry the cookware immediately and thoroughly with a towel to prevent rust. If necessary, heat the pan on the stove over low heat for a few minutes to ensure all moisture is evaporated. This is useful for cornstick pans or novelty pans with crevices that are difficult to dry with a towel.
- Apply a thin layer of oil (vegetable oil or flaxseed oil works well) to the entire surface of the skillet using a paper towel or cloth.
- Wipe off any excess oil, leaving a light, even coating.
- Store the cookware in a dry place, preferably with a paper towel between the skillet and its lid to absorb any moisture.

- **Handwash only!** Never place the cast iron in a dishwasher, including enamel-coated pieces. If you are exhausted after a party, don't be tempted to use the dishwasher or soak the pan in water. Instead, scrape out and dispose of all the food remnants and set the pan aside until morning when you can tend to the pan properly.

HOW TO FIX PROBLEMS

Rust: For small areas or just a film, scrub the spot with a coarse pad. Rub vegetable oil liberally into the area with a lint-free towel, and season the rest of the skillet as usual. For larger rust areas, scrub rust with steel wool or a stiff brush. Rinse in hot water and dry completely with a towel. Apply a thin layer of oil to the entire surface and bake upside down at 450° for an hour. Let cast iron cool in the oven. Very heavily rusted pieces need more dramatic measures that are best left to a professional.

Odors: Protein foods, especially fish, can leave odors in cast iron. Excessive oil used for seasoning that is not wiped off well can go rancid. To remedy the problem, bake empty cast iron at 350° for an hour. Cool; rinse with hot water to remove any carbon or burnt food bits, then re-season. If necessary, use a small amount of dish soap.

Stickiness: Too much oil during seasoning can leave small puddles of oil, and insufficient heating during seasoning can prevent oils from polymerizing; both mistakes will leave a sticky residue. To remedy the issue, scrub the sticky spot with coarse salt, and rinse. Apply a thin layer of oil to the entire surface, then bake upside down at 450° for an hour. Let cast iron cool in the oven.

Scratches: The smooth glass top on electric and induction cooktops can get scratched if the bottom of the cast iron is rough. Don't slide the skillet or Dutch oven around, but instead lift carefully and move it aside to prevent damage to the glass. Some enameled pieces will slide safely without scratching, but use discretion.

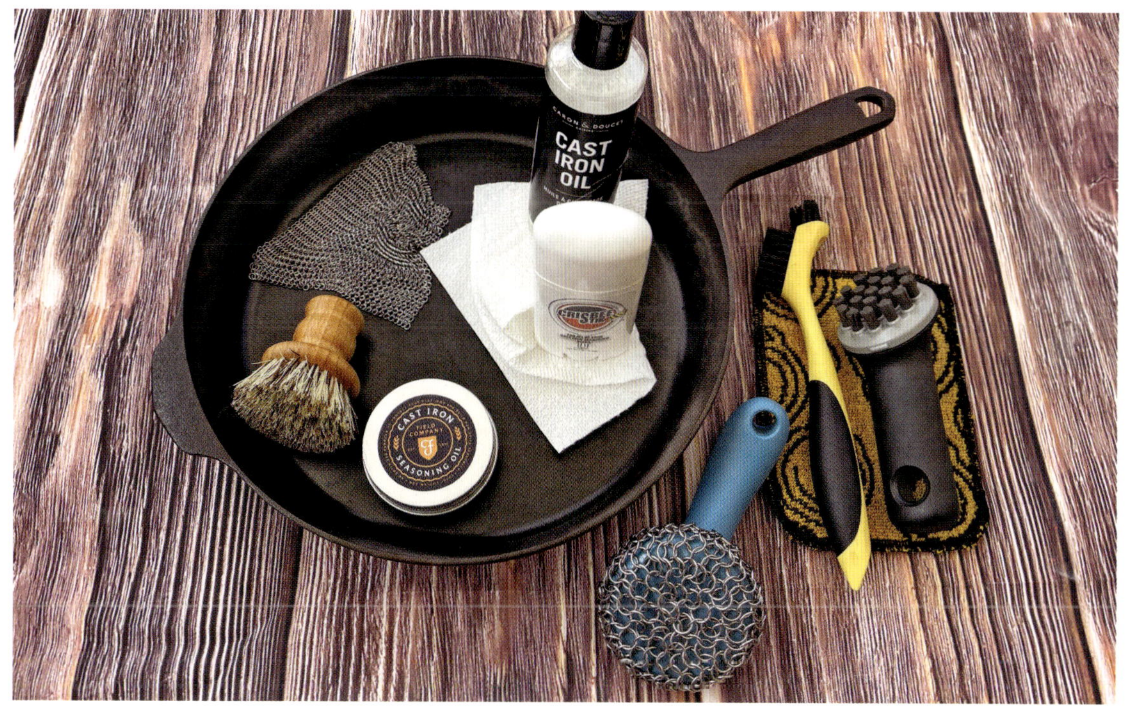

ENAMEL-COATED CAST IRON

Typically more expensive than bare or seasoned, enameled cast iron is a type of cookware that features a vitreous enamel glaze coating over a cast-iron core. This coating provides a nonreactive and somewhat nonstick surface, making it easier to clean and ideal for cooking acidic foods, which can otherwise react with bare cast iron. Enameled cast iron does not require seasoning and is resistant to rust, although it can chip if mishandled. Additionally, the enamel coating comes in various colors, enhancing the aesthetic appeal of the cookware.

There are some cast-iron enamel-coated pieces that have colorful exteriors while the interior is a dark gray or black enamel, giving it the appearance of traditional cast iron. This is a benefit because pale enamel can stain. Some manufacturers coat their pieces inside and out in a black or dark-charcoal enamel, giving the illusion that it is bare metal.

TIPS FOR USING ENAMEL-COATED COOKWARE

Use an eye or burner closest to the size of the skillet or pot. This ensures even heating and avoids hot spots.

Do not preheat enameled cast iron on a cooktop without oil, butter, or food. When preheating a Dutch oven for baking bread, place it in the oven first, and then let it slowly heat up.

Avoid high heat unless you're boiling water or bringing soups or other liquid foods up to a boil.

Use silicone or wood utensils to avoid scratch marks, and avoid metal scouring pads or abrasive cleaners.

Allow cookware to cool to room temperature before washing to prevent thermal shock. Thermal shock occurs when there is a rapid change in temperature, causing the material to expand or contract quickly. This sudden temperature shift can create stress within the cast iron, leading to cracking or warping. The colorful enamel coating is more susceptible to thermal shock than the core material itself. For example, placing a hot cast-iron skillet into cold water or moving it from a hot oven to a cold countertop can induce thermal shock; to avoid this, it is essential to allow cast-iron cookware to heat up or cool down gradually.

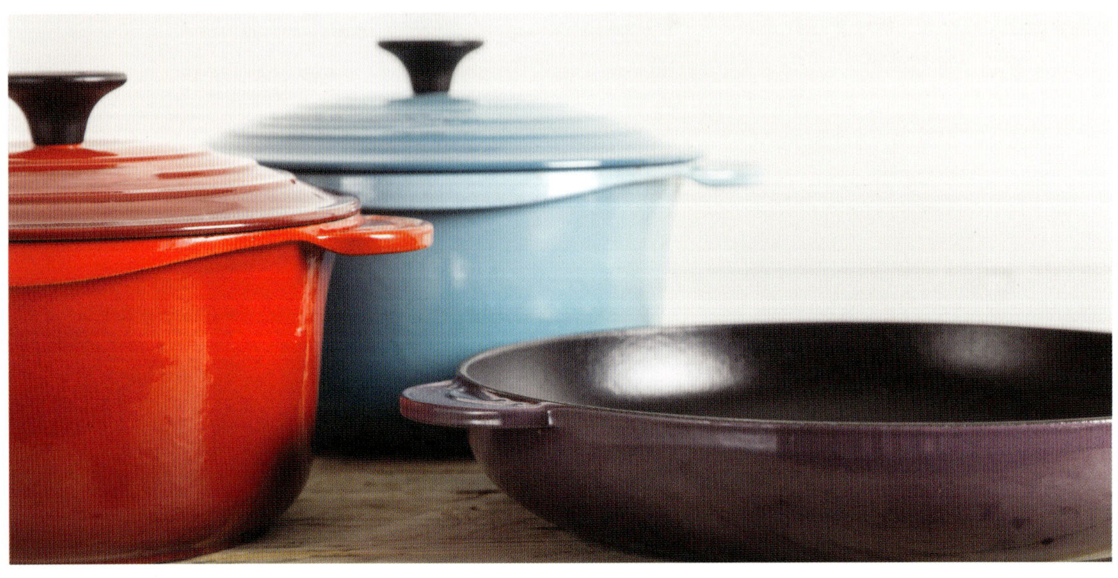

Soak stubborn food that is sticking with warm, soapy water for several minutes before gently scrubbing the cookware. If necessary, make a paste out of baking soda and water, then use it to scour gently to remove stains.

Dry cookware after washing to avoid water spots. If stacking enameled cookware, place a paper plate or towel in between to avoid scratches.

COOKING WITH CAST IRON

Season your cast-iron skillet regularly to maintain its nonstick surface. This involves coating it with a thin layer of vegetable oil and heating it until it polymerizes.

Preheat the cast-iron skillet before adding any ingredients. This ensures even cooking and helps prevent food from sticking. I admit to not being consistent with preheating. If the pan is not very well seasoned, I preheat dry to allow the pores on the surface to open, then I add oil.

Use the right amount of oil or fat when cooking to further enhance the nonstick properties and flavor of your food. Don't be stingy with oil, especially if the pan is newly purchased and not well seasoned.

Avoid cooking acidic foods for long periods, especially in an unseasoned skillet, as this can strip the seasoning.

Use wooden or silicone utensils to prevent scratching the seasoned surface.

Heat the skillet gradually to avoid thermal shock, which can cause cracking or warping.

Remove cast iron from heat as soon as the food tests done. Since cast iron retains heat, food will continue to cook or bake after removal from the cooktop or oven. For baked goods, check a few minutes before the suggested time to avoid overbaking.

Preheat the cast iron in the oven before adding batter for a crispy crust on items such as cornbread or pizza. For a soft, tender crust, pour batter or dough into a cold pan.

Avoid sliding cast-iron skillets across a glass cooktop to avoid scratching. There's a little more freedom with enamel-coated pieces because the bottoms are smooth.

Use the correct-size burner in proportion to the skillet. This applies to all types of skillets as well. Using a burner the same size as the skillet ensures an evenly heated surface. A burner too small leads to longer cooking times, while an oversize burner wastes energy and, if gas, may cause flames to lick up the sides of the skillet, thereby posing a fire hazard.

Avoid placing cast-iron pieces directly on countertops or tables immediately after cooking. Use a trivet, potholder, or folded towels underneath to avoid scorching, melting, or cracking surfaces.

STAY SAFE! Potholders are essential for comfortably handling cast-iron cookware. Cast iron holds heat exceptionally well, meaning the skillet, pan, or pot will remain very hot for a long time after it's removed from a heat source. Remember that there is an even heat distribution, so the handle will be as hot as the skillet. In the rare chance of a grease fire (this can happen no matter the type of skillet), immediately turn off the burner. Cover the flames with a metal lid or baking sheet. You can also douse the flames with salt, baking soda, or a fire extinguisher. Never use water on a grease fire, and don't attempt to move the pan. Both can cause flames to spread and spill.

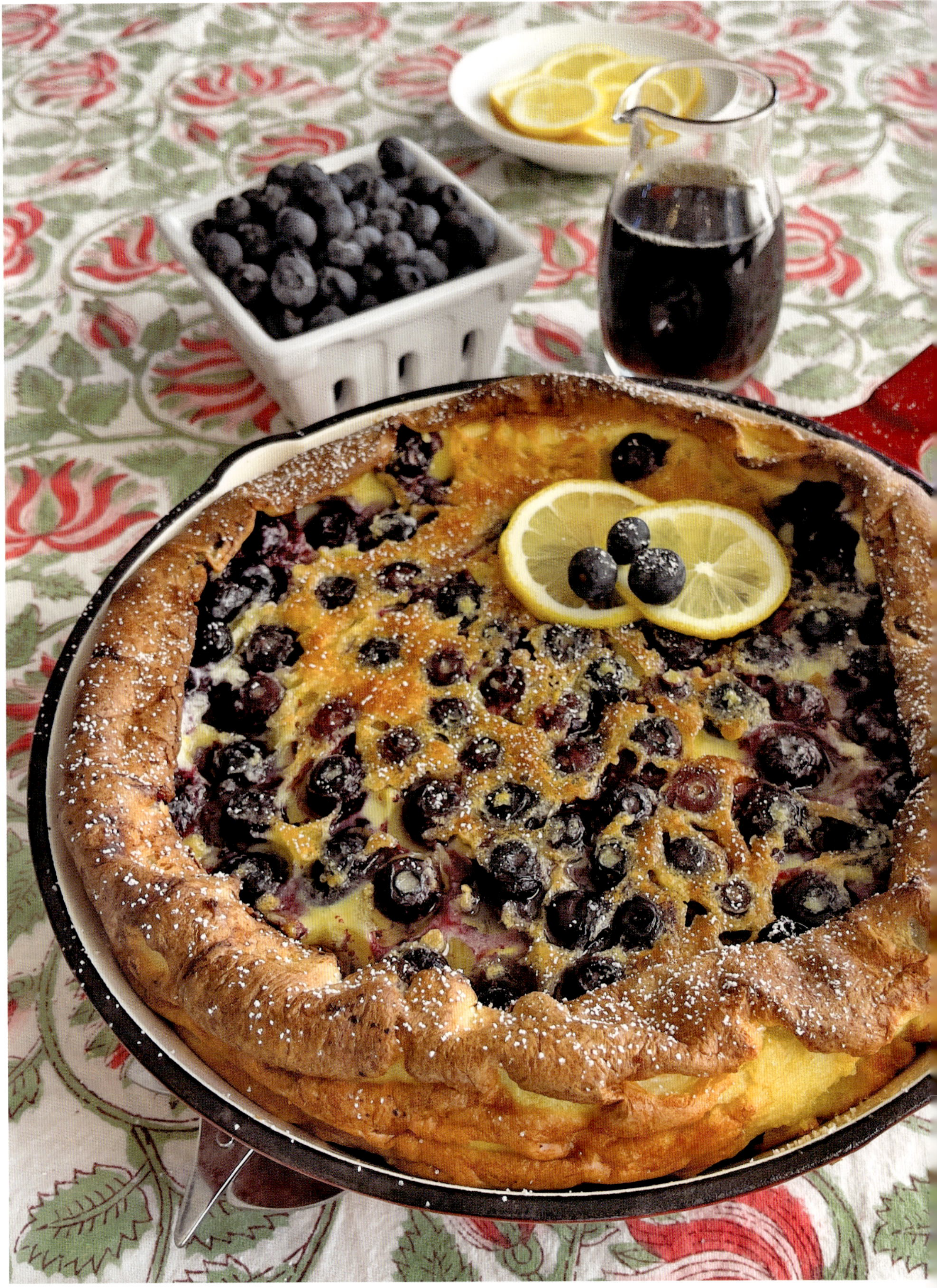

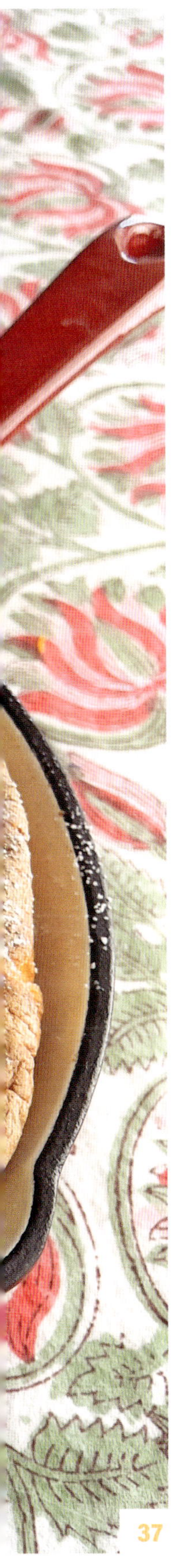
37

BREADS *and* BREAKFAST

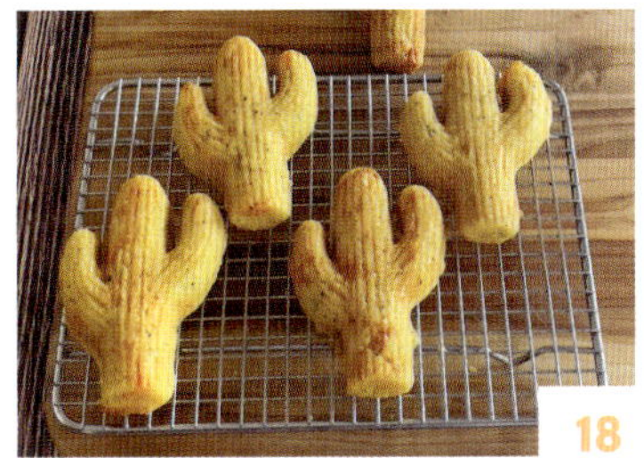
18

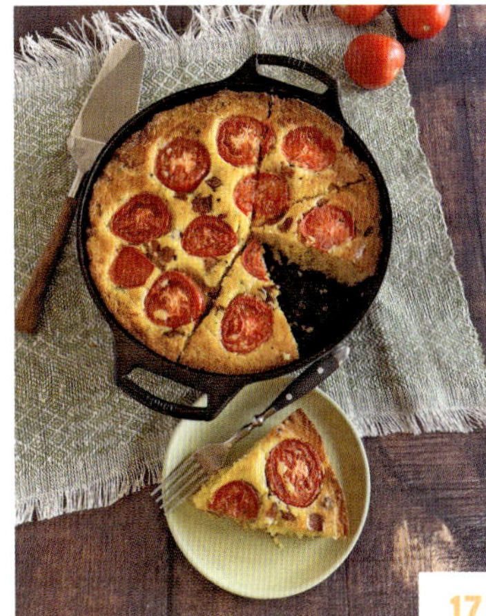
17

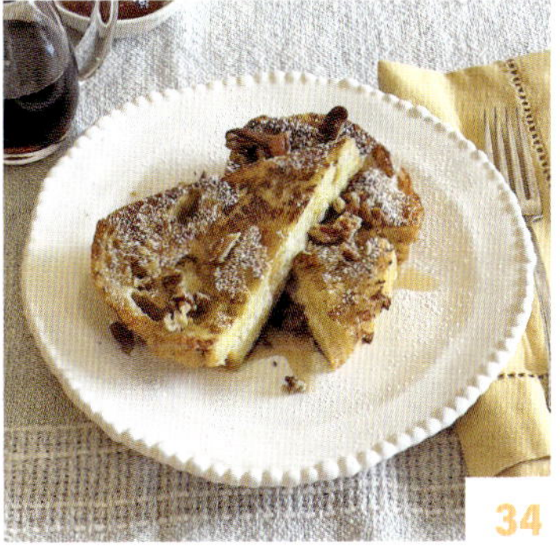
34

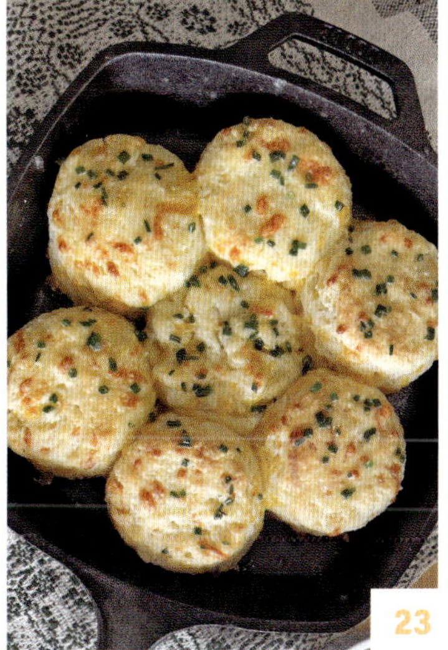
23

BASIC SKILLET CORNBREAD

MAKES 6 TO 8 SERVINGS

EQUIPMENT: *10-inch cast-iron skillet*

PAN SAVVY: *This will make multiple batches of cornsticks. Keep remaining batter away from the hot oven, and oil the cornstick pan in between batches, if necessary, to avoid sticking.*

1½ cups medium-grind cornmeal

1 cup all-purpose flour or 1:1 gluten-free baking mix

2 tablespoons granulated sugar (optional)

2 teaspoons baking powder

1½ teaspoons fine sea salt

1½ cups buttermilk, whole milk, or half-and-half

2 large eggs

6 tablespoons unsalted or salted butter, divided

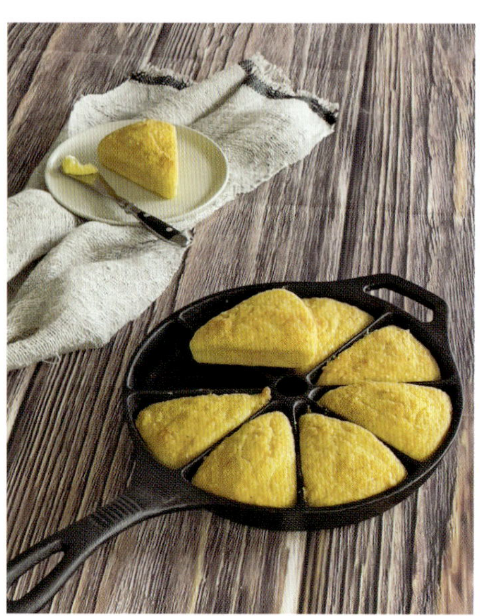

I will debate anyone on this: A cast-iron skillet is the best way to cook cornbread. It creates a deliciously crispy edge and tender interior. I like the rustic texture of stone-ground cornmeal mixed with regular flour or gluten-free baking mix. There is a larger debate about adding sugar to cornbread. Purists insist that it shouldn't be added, and I respect that position. But I like it, and I say that whoever is making the cornbread gets to decide. It's your call!

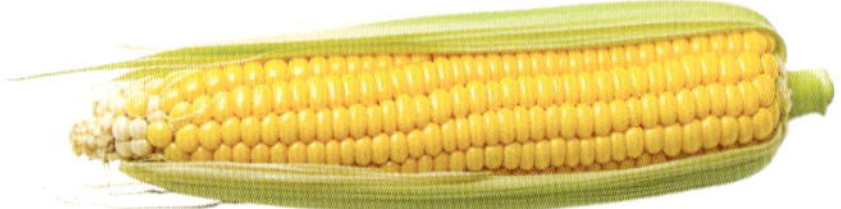

1. Preheat oven to 375°. Place a 10-inch cast-iron skillet in oven while it preheats.
2. Combine cornmeal; flour; sugar, if desired; baking powder; and salt in a large bowl. Combine buttermilk and eggs in another bowl, whisking until well blended.
3. Melt 4 tablespoons butter in a small bowl in the microwave.
4. Stir milk mixture into flour mixture. Stir in melted butter.
5. Place remaining 2 tablespoons butter in hot skillet, allowing to melt. Carefully tilt pan to coat. Carefully spoon batter into skillet, smoothing top.
6. Bake for 25 to 30 minutes or until golden brown on top.

Variation: Cornbread Wedges: Divide recipe ingredients in half (because the wedge-style pan holds less batter). Melt 3 tablespoons butter in a microwave-safe bowl; brush inside of pan evenly with 1 tablespoon melted butter. Stir remaining melted butter into batter. Pour batter into prepared cornbread wedge pan, filling ¾ full. Bake for 25 to 30 minutes or until golden brown. Makes 8 wedges.

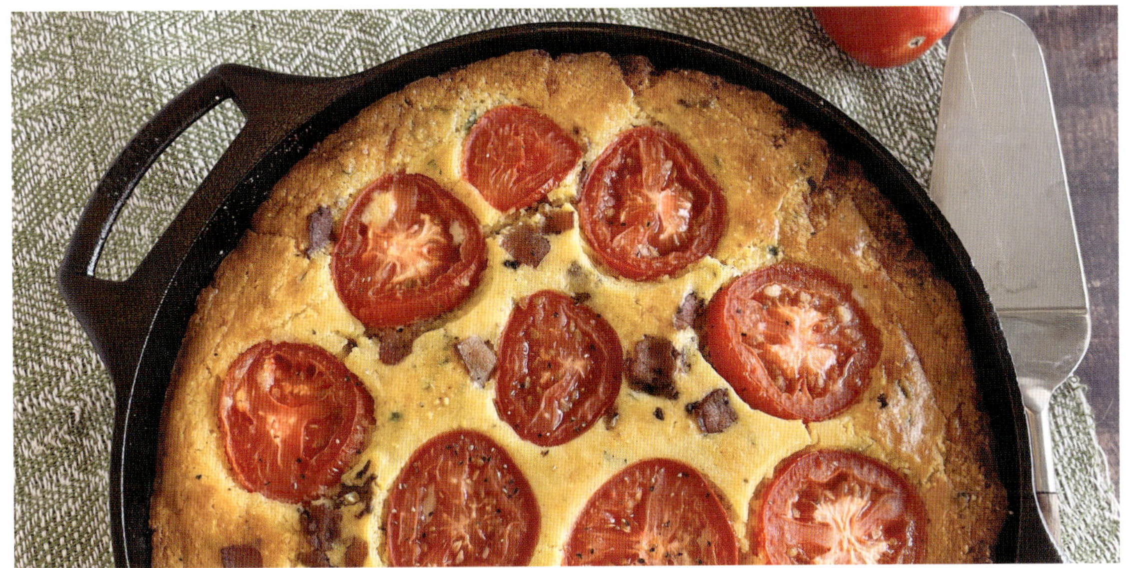

TOMATO-BASIL-BACON CORNBREAD

MAKES 6 SERVINGS

EQUIPMENT: *10-inch cast-iron skillet*

PAN SAVVY: *Use a 10-inch square skillet if you want to make portions with a slice of tomato in the center of each one.*

6 slices lean bacon, chopped
1¼ cups cornmeal
1 cup all-purpose flour
2 tablespoons granulated sugar
1 tablespoon baking powder
½ teaspoon salt
2 large eggs
1½ cups half-and-half or whole milk
6 tablespoons salted or unsalted butter, melted
1½ cups (6 ounces) shredded smoked cheddar or cheddar cheese
3 tablespoons chopped fresh basil
2 ripe Roma or other small tomatoes, sliced

This bread is so hearty, it's almost a meal. Use it as a side dish for grilled burgers or chicken, or serve it for breakfast as a filling start to the day.

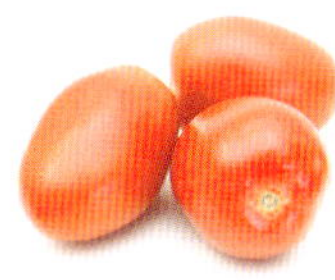

1. Preheat oven to 375°.
2. Cook bacon in a 10-inch cast-iron skillet over medium heat until crisp; remove from heat. Transfer bacon to paper towels using a slotted spoon, reserving 1 tablespoon drippings in pan.
3. Combine cornmeal, flour, sugar, baking powder, and salt in a large bowl. In a separate bowl, whisk together eggs, half-and-half, and melted butter. Stir egg mixture into cornmeal mixture. Fold in cheese, bacon, and basil. Pour batter into skillet. Arrange tomatoes on top.
4. Bake for 30 minutes or until golden brown and firm.

SOUTHWESTERN CORNSTICKS

MAKES ABOUT 8 CORNSTICKS

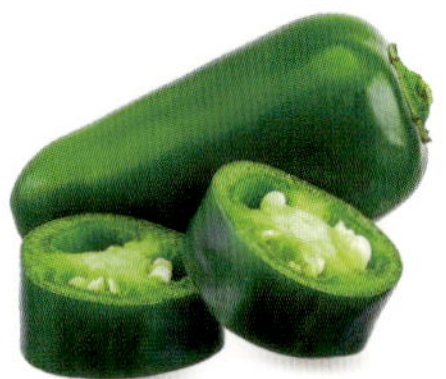

EQUIPMENT: *cornstick pan*

PAN SAVVY: *Cactus-shaped or other whimsical pans can be used, but make sure the pan is well greased so the cheese in the recipe doesn't stick. This recipe makes about half the amount of batter that you'd need to prepare cornbread in a skillet. Use a small (6- or 8-inch) skillet, or double the recipe and bake it in a 10-inch skillet for 25 minutes.*

½ teaspoon avocado or vegetable oil
⅔ cup cornmeal
¼ cup all-purpose flour
¾ teaspoon baking powder
1 teaspoon ground cumin
½ teaspoon salt
½ teaspoon garlic powder
¼ teaspoon coarsely ground black pepper
⅔ cup buttermilk
¼ cup extra-virgin olive or avocado oil
1 large egg
3 tablespoons chopped green chilies
½ cup (2 ounces) shredded cheddar cheese

Try these flavorful cornsticks with grilled steak or a Southwestern-style salad. If you make cornbread dressing, these will add a little something extra to your regular recipe.

1. Preheat oven to 425°. Brush wells of a cornstick pan with avocado oil; place in oven to preheat.
2. Combine cornmeal, flour, baking powder, cumin, salt, garlic powder, and pepper in a large bowl. Stir in buttermilk, olive oil, egg, chilies, and cheese.
3. Carefully remove hot cornstick pan from oven, and spoon batter into each well, filling ¾ full. Bake in batches if your cornstick pan doesn't have enough wells for the amount of batter.
4. Bake for 10 to 12 minutes or until golden brown. Turn out onto a plate or cutting board to serve.

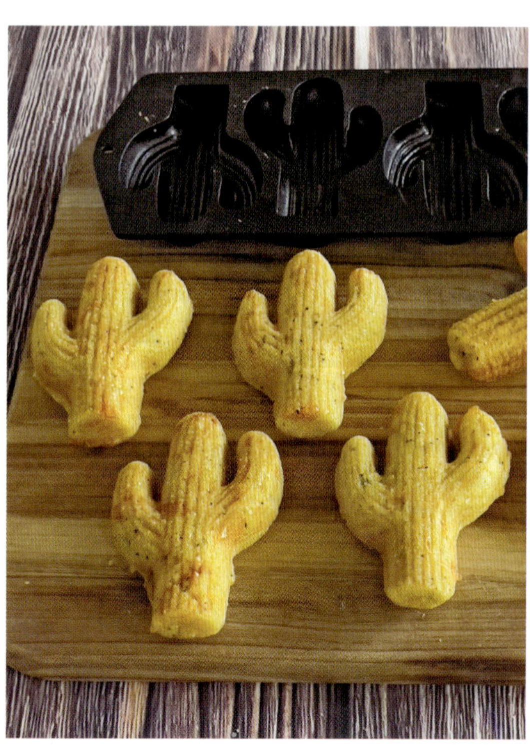

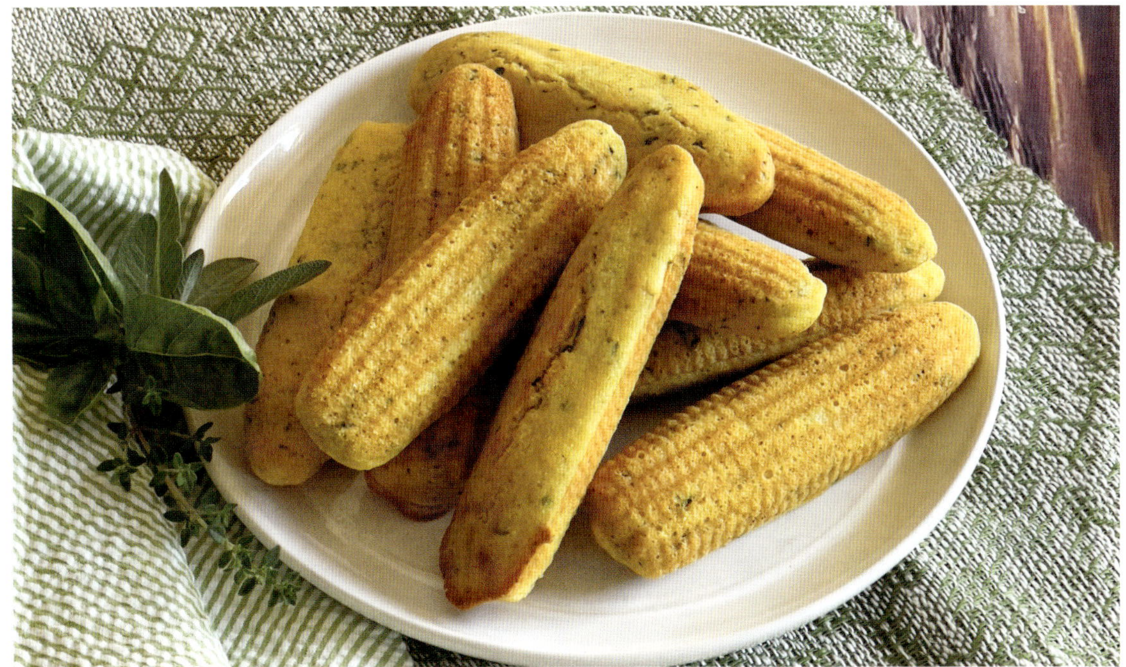

HERBED CORNSTICKS

MAKES ABOUT 9 CORNSTICKS

EQUIPMENT: *cast-iron cornstick pan*

½ teaspoon avocado or vegetable oil
⅔ cup cornmeal
¼ cup all-purpose flour
1 teaspoon granulated sugar
1 teaspoon baking powder
½ teaspoon salt
½ teaspoon garlic powder
¼ teaspoon coarsely ground black pepper
⅔ cup half-and-half or milk
¼ cup extra-virgin olive or avocado oil
1 whole egg
2 tablespoons chopped fresh herbs, such as oregano and basil

Fresh herbs and olive oil create a bread with Italian flavor—delicious alongside soups and salads. Use a mix of herbs, such as thyme, oregano, basil, and rosemary. The quantity of cornsticks depends on how many wells your pan has. If you have a smaller pan, bake in batches, but be sure to brush additional oil into the crevices before spooning in the remaining batter.

---

1. Preheat oven to 450°. Brush wells of a cornstick pan with avocado oil; place in oven to preheat.
2. Combine cornmeal, flour, sugar, baking powder, salt, garlic powder, and pepper in a large bowl. Stir in half-and-half, olive oil, egg, and herbs.
3. Carefully remove hot cornstick pan from oven, and spoon batter into each well, filling ¾ full.
4. Bake for 10 to 12 minutes or until golden brown. Turn out onto a plate or cutting board to serve.

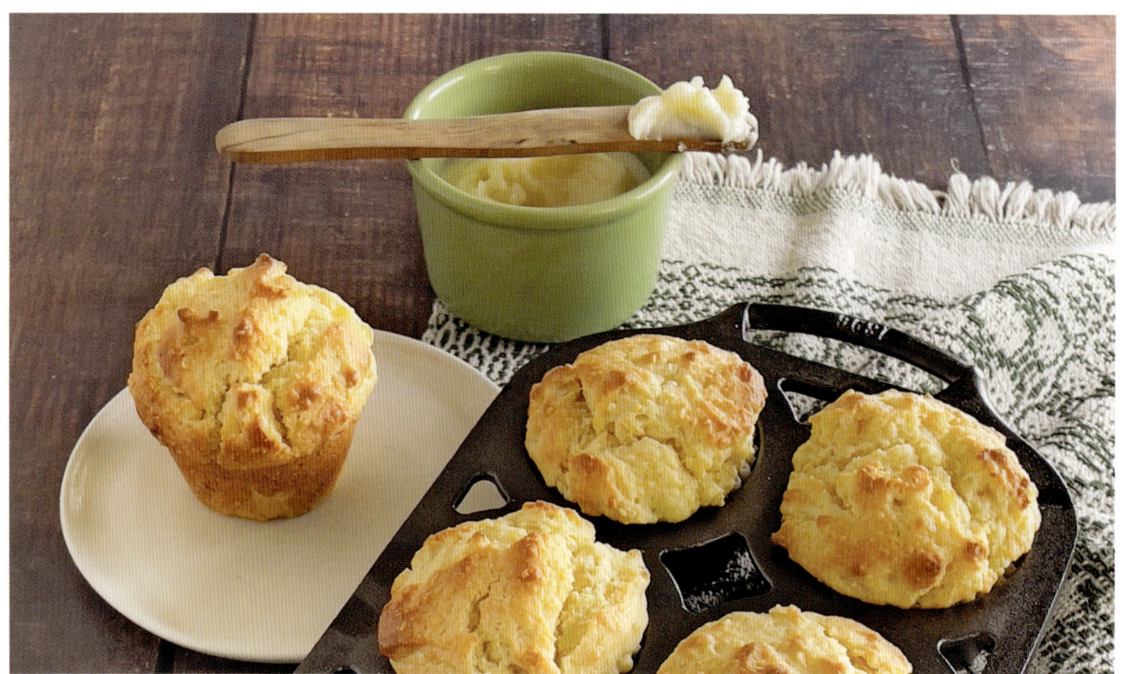

SWEET CORN MUFFINS

MAKES 6 MUFFINS

EQUIPMENT: *cast-iron muffin pan*

1 cup all-purpose flour
½ cup yellow cornmeal
¼ cup granulated sugar
2 tablespoons cornstarch
1½ teaspoons baking powder
½ teaspoon salt
⅓ cup olive, avocado, or vegetable oil
1 large egg, lightly beaten
½ cup whole milk
½ cup sour cream
¾ cup fresh, frozen, or canned corn kernels
Honey Butter (recipe at right)

Served with a naturally sweet butter, these muffins make a delicious breakfast bread. Or skip the sugar and butter, and serve them with chili or soup for a savory treat. Don't worry about mounding up the batter when evenly dividing among the muffin cups—the thick texture holds up while baking.

---

1 Preheat oven to 400°. Generously grease a 6-cup cast-iron muffin pan with olive oil (or line with paper liners).

2 Combine flour, cornmeal, sugar, cornstarch, baking powder, and salt in a large bowl. Add oil, egg, milk, sour cream, and corn, stirring just until blended. Spoon batter into prepared muffin cups, filling ¾ full.

3 Bake for 18 to 22 minutes or until golden brown and cooked through. Let cool in pan for 5 minutes, then turn out onto a wire rack. Serve warm or at room temperature with Honey Butter.

Honey Butter: Combine **½ cup softened salted butter** and **2 tablespoons honey** in a small bowl. Cover and refrigerate until ready to use. Let stand at room temperature for 30 minutes to soften. Makes ½ cup.

CUSTARD-FILLED CORNBREAD

MAKES 8 TO 9 SERVINGS

EQUIPMENT: *10-inch square or round cast-iron skillet*

PAN SAVVY: *The custard layer in this recipe is tender. I find it easier to cut 9 square portions from a square-shaped pan than 8 wedges from a round pan. Also, wedges from a round pan tend to fall apart, while squares hold together.*

- 1 cup all-purpose flour
- ¾ cup stone-ground yellow cornmeal
- 3 tablespoons granulated sugar
- 1 teaspoon fine sea salt
- 1 teaspoon baking powder
- ½ teaspoon baking soda
- ¼ cup plus 1 tablespoon salted or unsalted butter, divided
- 2 large eggs
- 2 cups whole milk
- 1½ tablespoons white vinegar
- 1 cup heavy whipping cream

This unique variation on cornbread includes a creamy layer just below the surface. There isn't a lot of sugar in this recipe, but the creaminess makes the bread seem slightly sweet. This bread is delicious with richly smoked pastrami or beef brisket.

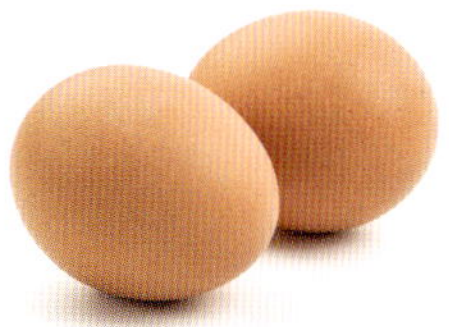

1. Preheat oven to 350°. Place skillet in oven to preheat.
2. Combine flour, cornmeal, sugar, salt, baking powder, and baking soda in a large bowl.
3. Melt ¼ cup butter in a medium-size bowl. Whisk in eggs, milk, and vinegar. Stir egg mixture into flour mixture.
4. Place remaining 1 tablespoon butter in hot skillet and allow to melt, swirling pan to coat bottom.
5. Pour batter into pan. Pour cream into center of batter, about ½ to 1 inch from edges of skillet. Do not stir.
6. Bake for 35 minutes or until lightly golden brown. Transfer to a wire rack to cool.

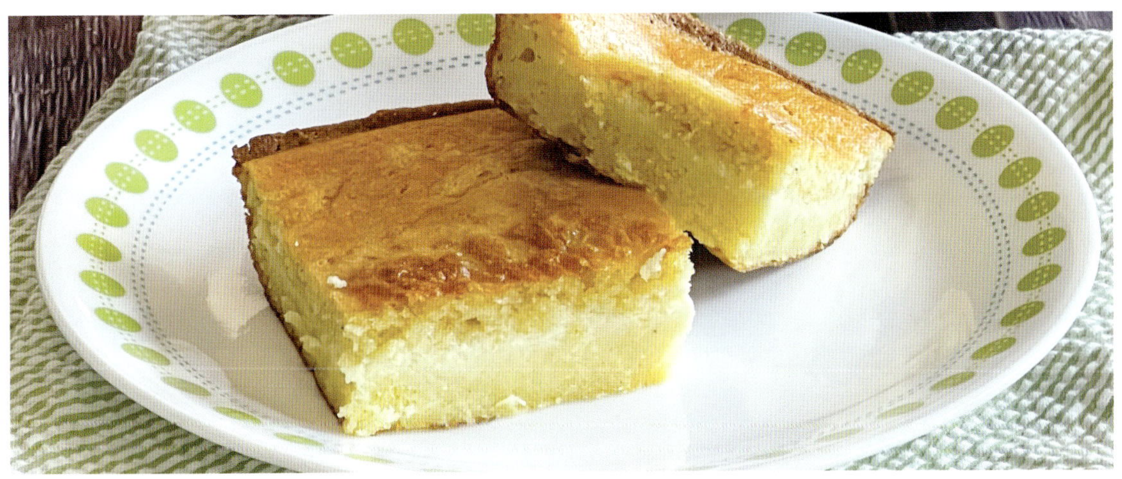

SWEET ONION HUSH PUPPIES

MAKES ABOUT 1½ DOZEN

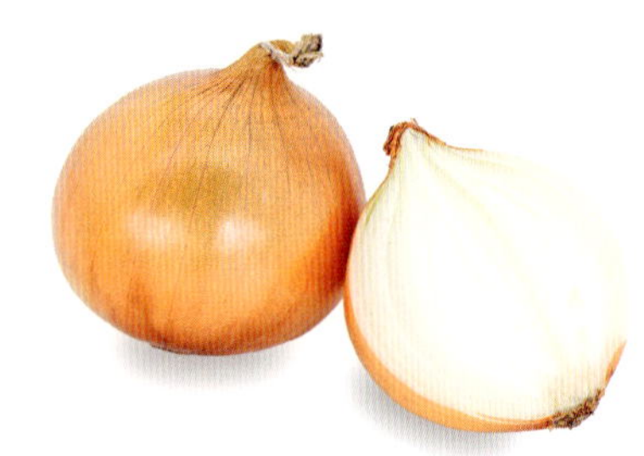

EQUIPMENT: *Dutch oven*

PAN SAVVY: *I always prefer Dutch oven pans for frying because the high sides keep oil splatters to a minimum. My smallest one is my favorite for this recipe, as it requires less oil to get to the 2- to 3-inch depth. If the oil is shallow and the hush puppies touch the bottom, you may get a scorch mark. If that happens, turn the hush puppies frequently once the batter is cooked enough to be firm.*

1½ cups cornmeal
½ cup all-purpose flour
1 tablespoon granulated sugar
1 teaspoon baking powder
½ teaspoon baking soda
½ teaspoon fine sea salt
1 cup buttermilk
1 large egg
¼ cup coarsely grated sweet onion
1 green onion, finely chopped
Vegetable oil (about 2½ to 3 cups)

The loose batter with freshly grated onion creates very tender hush puppies, though sometimes they're a bit wonky-shaped instead of perfectly round. These pair well with Southern favorites, such as catfish, ribs, shrimp and grits, and side dishes like greens and coleslaw.

1. Whisk together cornmeal, flour, sugar, baking powder, baking soda, and salt in a large bowl.
2. Stir together buttermilk, egg, grated onion, and green onion in a medium-size bowl. Stir buttermilk mixture into cornmeal mixture.
3. Pour vegetable oil into a Dutch oven or skillet to a depth of 2 inches; heat to 350°.
4. Scoop batter into 1-inch balls and carefully place in oil. Fry for 2 to 3 minutes, turning occasionally, until golden brown. Remove with a slotted spoon and place on a paper towel-lined plate to drain.

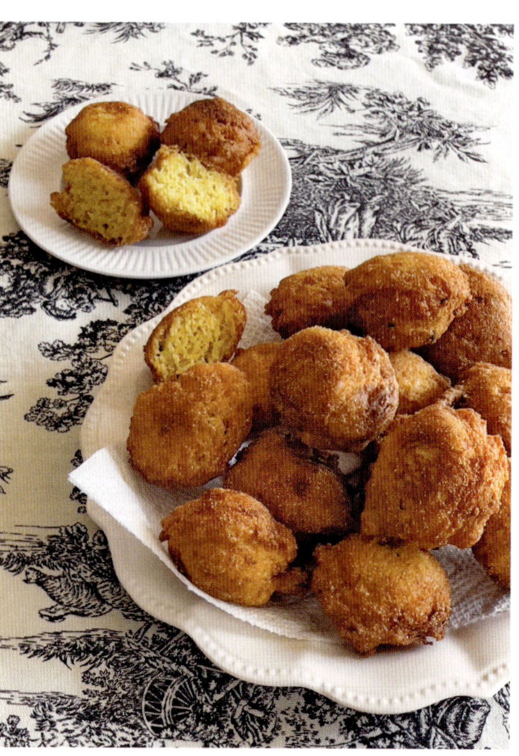

BUTTERMILK-CHEDDAR BISCUITS

MAKES 7 TO 9 BISCUITS

EQUIPMENT: *10- or 12-inch cast-iron skillet*

2 cups all-purpose flour
1 tablespoon granulated sugar
1 tablespoon baking powder
¾ teaspoon fine sea salt
½ cup (1 stick) salted butter, chilled
1 cup (4 ounces) shredded cheddar cheese
1 cup buttermilk
Garlic-and-Herb Butter (recipe at right)

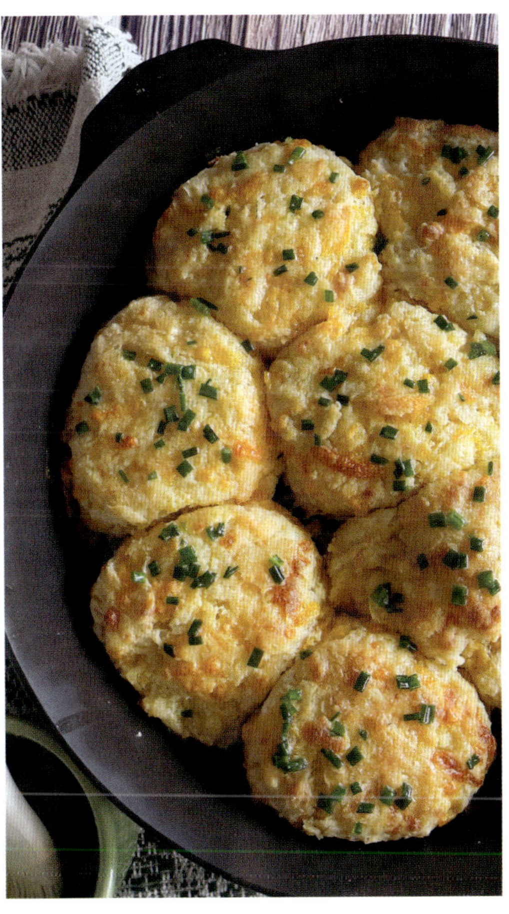

Folding the dough onto itself a few times is something professional bakers call "laminating." This technique creates tender layers. It's also how a puff pastry is made. Some people find grating chilled or frozen butter with a box grater is easier than cutting it in with a pastry blender. The key is to use very cold butter. Another tip for creating tall biscuits is to cut the dough straight down—without twisting the cutter—to ensure the dough isn't sealed on the sides.

---

1. Preheat oven to 400°.
2. Combine flour, sugar, baking powder, and salt in a large bowl. Grate butter with a box grater to create small, shaved pieces; stir into flour mixture. (You can also cut butter into flour mixture with a pastry blender or fork.) Stir in cheese.
3. Add buttermilk, stirring just until combined. Transfer to a well-floured surface and gently work dough into a large disk. Fold dough in half (over itself) and gently flatten. Rotate dough 90 degrees and repeat. Repeat 4 or 5 times, taking care not to overwork dough.
4. Pat dough into a 1-inch-thick circle. Cut straight down into dough (don't twist) with a biscuit cutter or 3-inch round cutter. Roll scraps of remaining dough and cut. Arrange in skillet.
5. Bake for 20 minutes or until golden brown. Remove from oven and brush with Garlic-and-Herb Butter.

Garlic-and-Herb Butter: Combine **2 tablespoons melted salted butter, 1 tablespoon finely chopped chives,** and **¼ teaspoon garlic powder** in a small bowl. Makes about ⅓ cup.

BUTTER SWIM BISCUITS

MAKES 8 SERVINGS

3 cups all-purpose flour
1 tablespoon granulated sugar
1½ tablespoons baking powder
1½ teaspoons salt
2 cups buttermilk
½ cup unsalted or salted butter, cut into pieces

These biscuits are known for their rich, buttery flavor and soft, tender texture. They're unique because they are baked in a cast-iron skillet that is "swimming" in butter before the batter is poured in. The edges get crisp and are arguably the best part. Make sure the sides of the skillet are at least 2 inches tall. If the skillet has short sides, the butter will puddle over the edges into the oven.

EQUIPMENT: *10-inch cast-iron skillet*

PAN SAVVY: *Place a short-sided skillet on a baking sheet to catch any butter drips, or use a 12-inch skillet for thinner biscuits. It's easier to cut portions from a square skillet; substitute, if available.*

1. Place a 10-inch skillet in oven. Preheat oven to 425°.
2. Combine flour, sugar, baking powder, and salt in a large bowl. Add buttermilk, stirring just until combined (mixture will be loose).
3. Remove hot skillet from oven. Add butter and allow to melt. (It's okay if it browns a bit, but watch for burning.)
4. Tilt skillet to coat bottom and sides with melted butter. Scoop batter by ½ cupfuls into skillet (batter will tend to spread out).
5. Bake for 25 minutes or until golden brown.

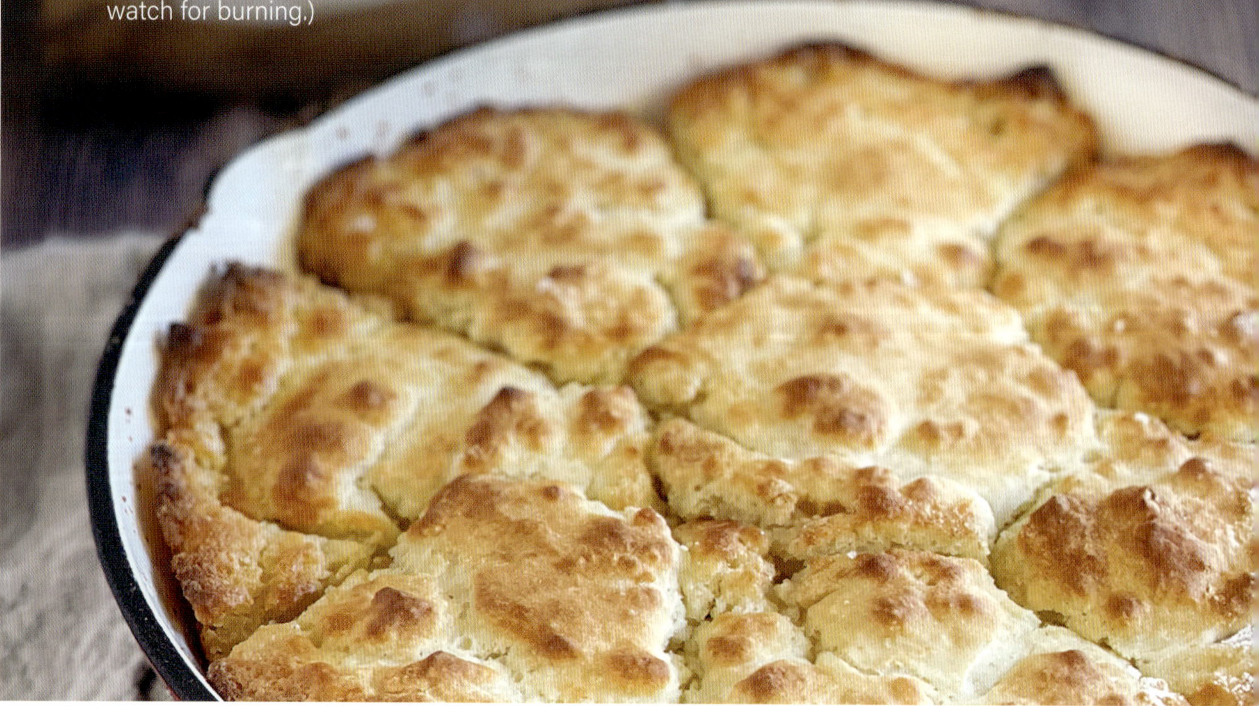

BLUEBERRY BUTTER SWIM BISCUITS

MAKES 8 SERVINGS

EQUIPMENT: *10-inch cast-iron skillet*

PAN SAVVY: *It's easier to cut portions from a square skillet, if available.*

2½ cups all-purpose flour
¼ cup granulated sugar
1 tablespoon baking powder
1 teaspoon salt
2 cups half-and-half
1½ cups fresh (or frozen and thawed) blueberries
½ cup unsalted butter
½ cup powdered sugar
1 tablespoon lemon or orange juice

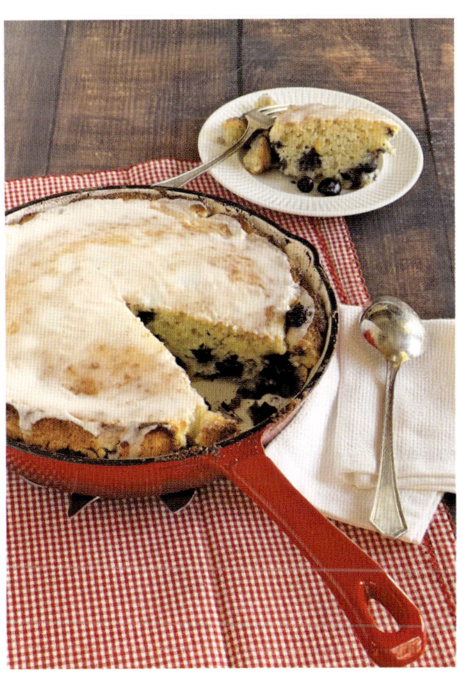

Using the same technique as in regular Butter Swim Biscuits (page 24), this version includes blueberries and a little more sweetness. If you're using frozen blueberries, allow them to thaw, then drain on paper towels to remove excess water. The mixture will rise in the pan, taking the delicious melted butter along with it. Use a 10-inch or larger skillet to avoid spills.

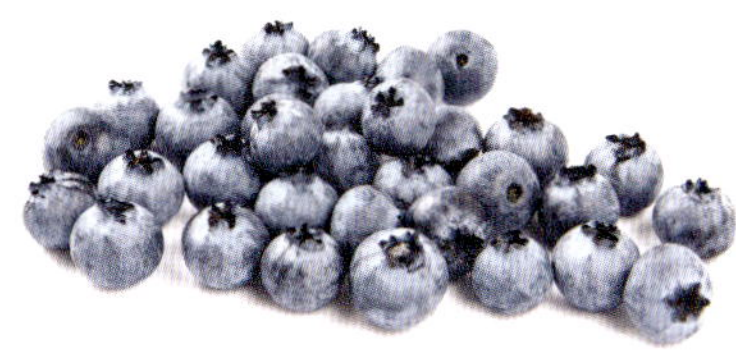

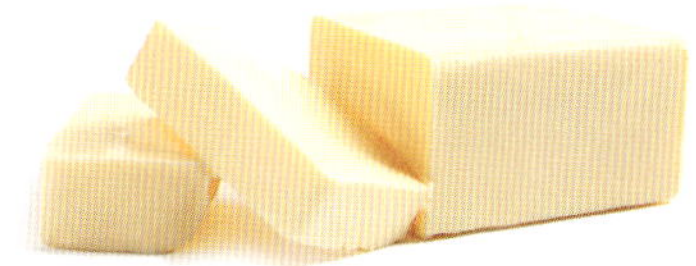

1. Place a 10-inch skillet in oven. Preheat oven to 375°.
2. Combine flour, granulated sugar, baking powder, and salt in a large bowl. Add half-and-half, stirring just until combined (mixture will be sticky). Stir in blueberries.
3. Remove hot skillet from oven. Add butter and allow to melt. (It's okay if it browns a bit, but watch for burning.) Tilt skillet to coat bottom and sides with melted butter. Carefully spoon in batter, spreading evenly. Bake for 25 minutes or until golden brown. (You may see some liquid along the edges; that isn't raw batter but butter that creates a delicious crunchy edge.)
4. Whisk together powdered sugar and juice until smooth. Drizzle over biscuits. Cut into wedges to serve.

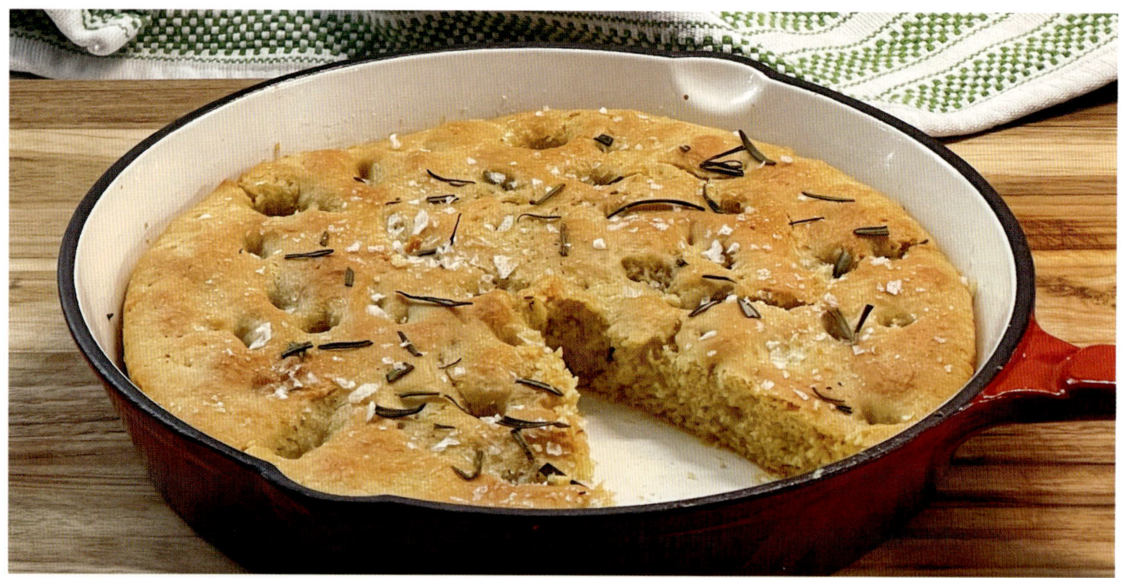

ROSEMARY FOCACCIA

MAKES 6 SERVINGS

EQUIPMENT: *10-inch cast-iron skillet*

PAN SAVVY: *9- or 12-inch skillets can be used for bread that's thicker or thinner; adjust baking time accordingly by 3 to 5 minutes.*

¾ cup warm (105° to 115°) water
½ teaspoon granulated sugar
1½ teaspoons active dry yeast
3 tablespoons extra-virgin olive oil, divided
2 cups all-purpose flour
½ teaspoon salt
1 tablespoon fresh rosemary
½ teaspoon flaky sea salt

This super-easy, no-knead bread gets more flavorful by resting in the refrigerator for several hours or overnight. You can add a few pieces of ultra-thinly sliced red onion and/or halved Kalamata olives for a delightful snack.

1. Combine ¾ cup water, sugar, and yeast in the bowl of an electric mixer. Let stand for 5 minutes or until foamy. Stir in 1 tablespoon olive oil.
2. With mixer on low speed, gradually add flour and salt, mixing until dough pulls away from sides of bowl. Grease a bowl with olive oil. Transfer dough to bowl, turning to coat. Cover with a damp kitchen towel or plastic wrap. Refrigerate for 8 hours or overnight.
3. Drizzle 1 tablespoon olive oil into a 9- or 10-inch cast-iron skillet, spreading to coat bottom and sides. Transfer dough to skillet and spread out to edges. With fingers, make indentations throughout dough. Cover and let rise at room temperature for 2 hours.
4. Preheat oven to 425°. Drizzle dough with remaining 1 tablespoon olive oil. Sprinkle with rosemary and sea salt.
5. Bake for 20 minutes or until golden brown. Serve with additional olive oil, if desired.

CHEDDAR-JALAPEÑO BREAD

MAKES 1 LOAF

EQUIPMENT: *cast-iron Dutch oven*

PAN SAVVY: *Cast-iron baking cloches are ideal for this bread because they are perfectly shaped and you don't have to lift the loaf out of the pan with parchment paper. If you bake bread often, the spendy pieces are a worthy investment. Otherwise, a Dutch oven works well too. Make sure the handle on your Dutch oven lid is metal or ovenproof.*

1 (¼-ounce) package or 2¼ teaspoons active dry yeast

1 tablespoon granulated sugar

1½ cups warm water (105° to 110°)

3 cups bread or all-purpose flour

1 teaspoon salt

½ teaspoon garlic powder

1½ cups (6 ounces) shredded cheddar cheese, divided

¼ cup sliced pickled jalapeño peppers, chopped

Extra-virgin olive oil

¼ cup fine cornmeal, divided

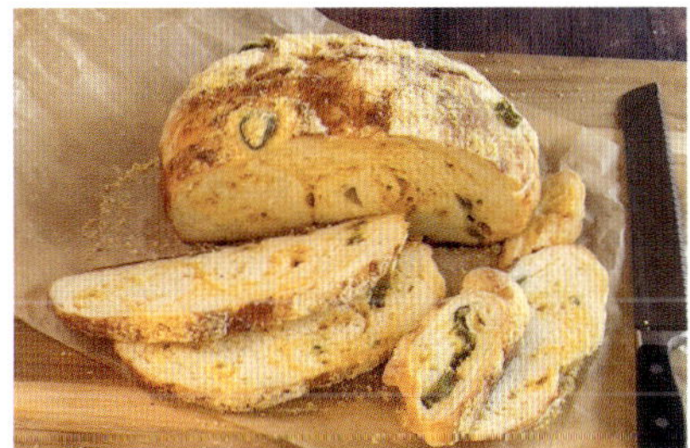

Delicious with soup or chili, this bread takes a traditional grilled cheese to the next level. For a bit of flair, you can arrange a few slices of jalapeño on top of the loaf before it bakes. **Tip:** If your parchment rolls up and won't stay flat, crumple it into a ball first, then press flat.

---

1. Combine yeast, sugar, and 1½ cups water in bowl of a stand-up electric mixer; let stand for 5 minutes. Combine flour, salt, and garlic powder in another large bowl.
2. Add flour mixture to yeast mixture, stirring with a dough hook to form a soft, shaggy dough. Add cheese and jalapeños, mixing until well blended. (Some cheese and peppers may not blend into dough.) Turn dough out onto a floured surface and knead in any remaining cheese and peppers.
3. Lightly grease a bowl with olive oil. Transfer dough to bowl, turning to coat. Cover and let rise in a warm place (85°), free from drafts, for 2 hours or until doubled in size.
4. Sprinkle 2 tablespoons cornmeal onto a large sheet of parchment paper (parchment should be large enough to fit inside Dutch oven and extend up sides).
5. Turn dough out and place on parchment paper. Sprinkle with remaining 2 tablespoons cornmeal. Create 4 to 6 (½-inch-deep) slashes, if desired. Let rise in a warm place while oven preheats.
6. Place a Dutch oven with lid in oven, and preheat to 450°. (See note below.)
7. Using parchment as handles, carefully place dough into hot Dutch oven. Cover with lid. Bake for 25 minutes. Uncover and bake for 15 more minutes. Remove from pan and cool on a wire rack.

Note: Some manufacturers recommend not preheating enamel-coated cast iron without food in it. I have not had any problems preheating enamel-coated cookware in the oven. Some online sources suggest placing some ice cubes in the Dutch oven with the bread to create steam. This is dangerous, as the thermal shock of the differing temperatures can shatter the enamel from the pan or crack the cast iron. Covering the bread during baking will provide adequate moisture.

SKILLET FLATBREAD

MAKES 16 PIECES

EQUIPMENT: *10-inch or larger cast-iron griddle or skillet*

PAN SAVVY: *Unless you use a very large rectangular griddle, it's easier, although slower, to cook pieces one at a time.*

1 (¼-ounce) package or 2¼ teaspoons active dry yeast

1 tablespoon granulated sugar

1½ cups warm water (105° to 110°)

2 tablespoons extra-virgin olive oil

3½ cups bread or all-purpose flour

2 teaspoons salt

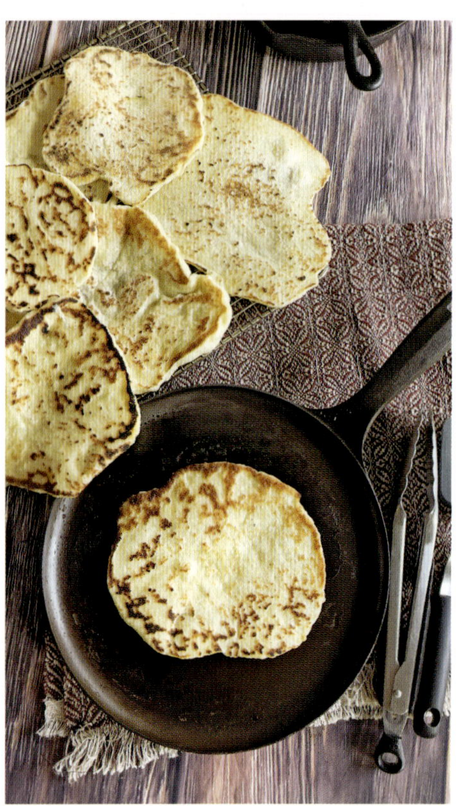

Cooking flatbread on a cast-iron griddle or large skillet yields delicious results. The griddle's consistent heat creates a crispy exterior and fluffy interior while imparting a subtle smoky flavor. Use this recipe as a replacement for pita or naan, or as a base for individual pizzas.

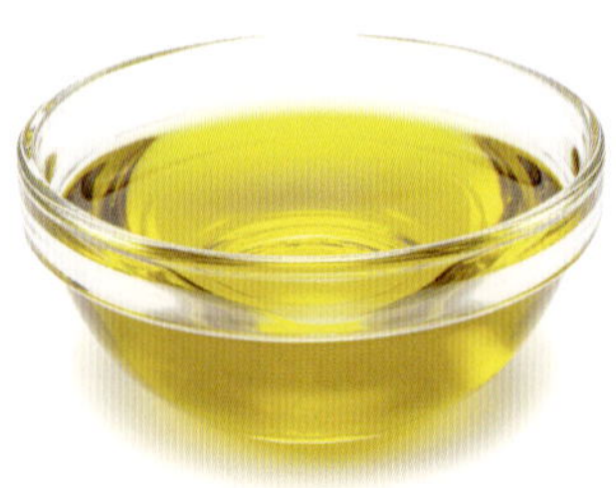

1. Dissolve yeast and sugar in 1½ cups water in bowl of a stand-up electric mixer; let stand for 5 minutes. Stir in olive oil.
2. Combine flour and salt in another large bowl. Add flour mixture to yeast mixture, stirring with a dough hook or paddle attachment at low speed until combined to make a soft, slightly sticky dough. Knead at low speed for 1 minute.
3. Lightly grease a bowl with olive oil. Transfer dough to bowl, turning to coat. Cover and let rise in a warm place (85°), free from drafts, for 1 to 1½ hours or until doubled in size.
4. Divide dough into 16 pieces. Form each into a ball and let rest for 5 minutes. Roll dough balls out on a floured surface into ⅛-inch-thick circles, about 5 to 6 inches in diameter.
5. Preheat a cast-iron griddle or skillet over medium-high heat. Brush lightly with olive oil and place a piece of flatbread dough on hot surface. Cook for 30 seconds or until bubbles form. Flip over and cook for 30 seconds. Brush griddle periodically with oil, adjusting heat up or down to avoid scorching.

HOMEMADE CORN TORTILLAS

MAKES 12 TO 15 TORTILLAS

Get the flavor of authentic corn tortillas at home with this easy recipe. The key to making soft tortillas that don't crack is to allow the dough to rest, giving the corn flour time to absorb the liquid.

EQUIPMENT: *Cast-iron tortilla press, griddle*

PAN SAVVY: *Heavy cast-iron tortilla presses are ideal for creating round, even tortillas. If a press is unavailable, use a rolling pin. It's easiest to flip a tortilla that's cooked on a griddle or in an extra-large cast-iron skillet, but an 8-inch or larger skillet will work.*

2 cups corn flour (masa harina)
½ teaspoon fine sea salt
1½ cups hot water

1 Combine corn flour and salt in a large bowl. Add 1½ cups water (adding more, if necessary); stir to create a firm, springy dough. Turn dough out onto a lightly floured surface, and knead for 2 to 3 minutes or until smooth.

2 Cover dough and let rest for 30 to 45 minutes. Separate dough into 1½- to 2-inch balls.

3 Preheat a well-seasoned cast-iron skillet over medium to medium-high heat.

4 To keep dough from sticking, place dough balls, 1 at a time, in a zip-top plastic storage bag; flatten each dough ball, using a cast-iron tortilla press or rolling pin.

5 Place flattened dough on hot griddle or skillet, and cook for about 45 seconds or until edges start to lift up and bottom is cooked. Flip over and cook for about 30 seconds. Tortillas will puff up slightly and have some dark spots. Adjust heat as necessary.

6 Place in a tortilla warmer or bowl covered with a cloth. Repeat with remaining dough.

7 Store leftover tortillas in an airtight container in the refrigerator up to 3 days. Heat them in a dry skillet over medium heat.

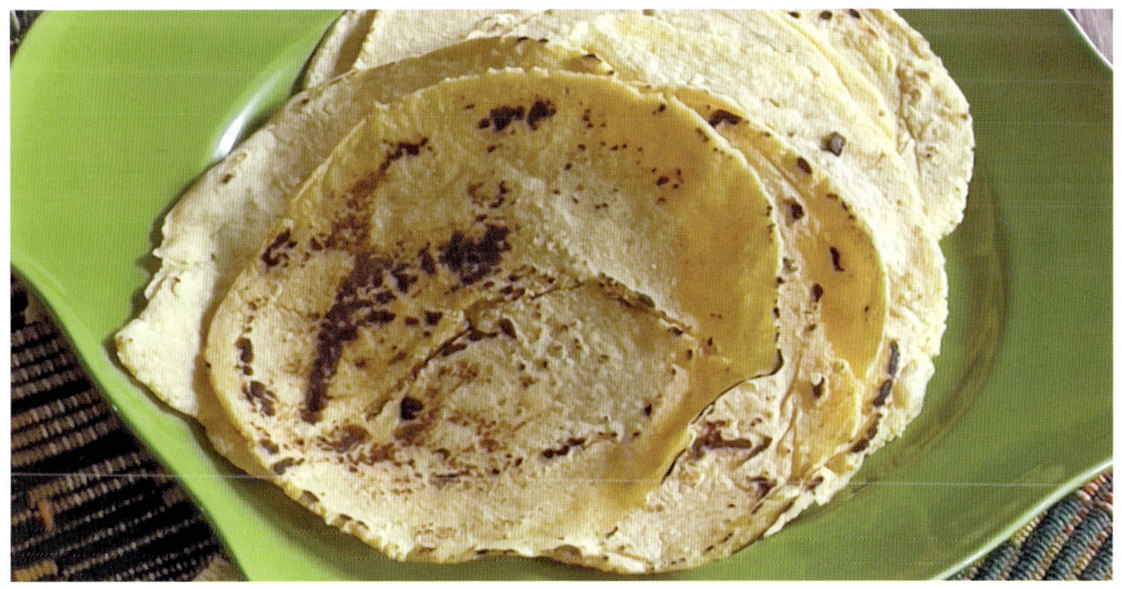

CINNAMON ROLL COFFEE CAKE

MAKES 6 TO 8 SERVINGS

EQUIPMENT: *10-inch cast-iron skillet*

PAN SAVVY: *Either round or square cast-iron skillets will work. Square or rectangle servings are typical, but the sweet bread will taste just as delicious when cut into wedges from a round pan.*

1½ cups all-purpose flour
½ cup granulated sugar
2 teaspoons baking powder
⅛ teaspoon fine sea salt
¾ cup whole milk
¼ cup melted salted or unsalted butter
2 large eggs
1 teaspoon vanilla extract
Brown Sugar-Cinnamon Topping (recipe at right)
½ cup chopped pecans
Glaze (recipe at right)

Start the day on a sweet note when you make this scrumptious coffee cake topped with the flavors of the beloved handheld breakfast treat. Or serve it in the late afternoon with tea and good conversation.

I initially placed this recipe in the dessert chapter before deciding to add it to the breads-and-breakfast section because it's essentially a sweet quick bread. Quick breads use baking powder and/or baking soda instead of yeast and are considered "quick" because there is no lengthy rising time involved.

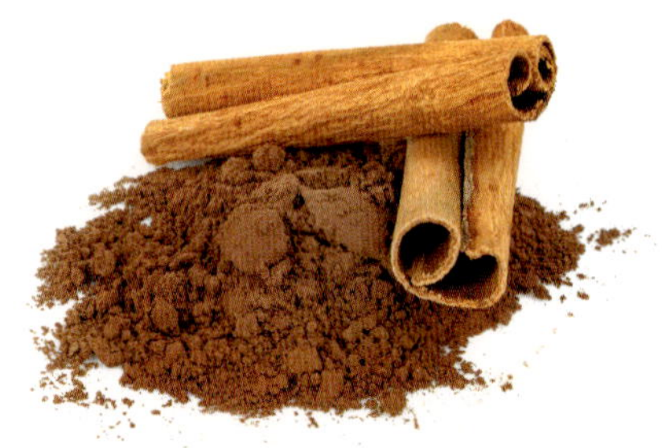

1 Preheat oven to 350°. Butter a 10-inch cast-iron skillet.

2 Combine flour, granulated sugar, baking powder, and salt in a large bowl. Combine milk, butter, eggs, and vanilla in another bowl. Add milk mixture to flour mixture, stirring just until blended (do not overmix).

3 Spoon batter into prepared skillet. Drizzle Brown Sugar-Cinnamon Topping over batter, sprinkle with pecans, and swirl with a knife.

4 Bake for 30 minutes or until golden brown and firm in center. Drizzle with Glaze.

Brown Sugar-Cinnamon Topping: Combine **½ cup melted salted or unsalted butter, ½ cup firmly packed light brown sugar, 2 tablespoons all-purpose flour,** and **1½ teaspoons ground cinnamon** in a medium bowl. Makes about ⅔ cup.

Glaze: Combine **½ cup powdered sugar, 1 tablespoon whole milk,** and **¼ teaspoon vanilla extract** in a small bowl. Makes ¼ cup.

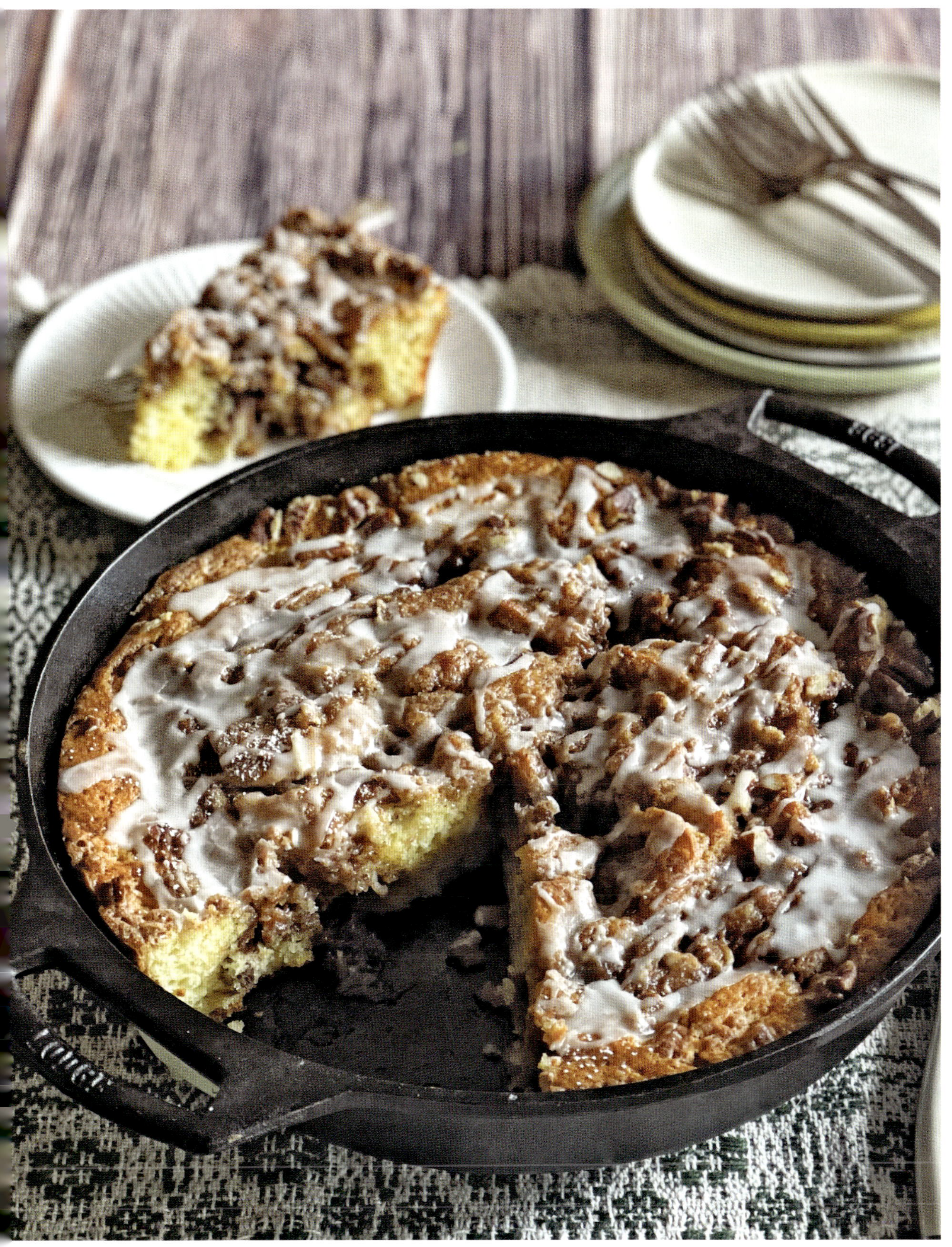
LODGE

ALMOND SWEET ROLLS

MAKES 1 DOZEN

EQUIPMENT: *10-inch cast-iron skillet*

PAN SAVVY: *Use a 10-inch baker's skillet or square skillet.*

2¾ to 3 cups all-purpose flour, divided
¼ cup granulated sugar
1 (¼-ounce) package or 2¼ teaspoons active dry yeast
½ teaspoon fine sea salt
¾ cup whole milk, divided
¼ cup water
7 tablespoons unsalted butter, softened and divided
1 large egg
1 (7- or 8-ounce) package almond paste
¼ cup firmly packed light brown sugar
1 teaspoon almond extract
½ cup sliced almonds
1 cup powdered sugar
½ teaspoon almond or vanilla extract

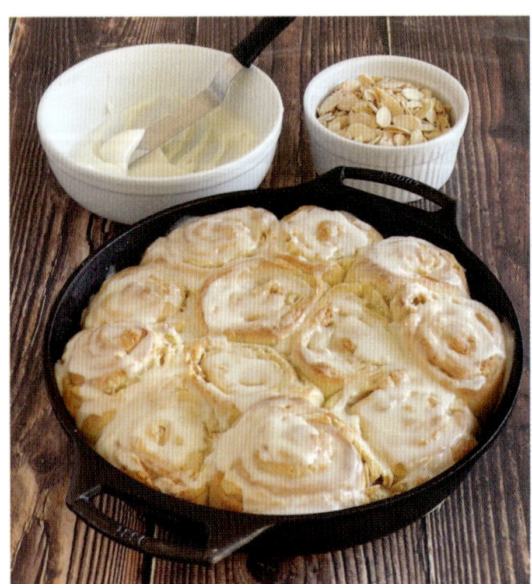

Almond paste is a sweet ground-almond concoction used in croissants, tarts, and cookies. Look for it in small cans or tubes in the baking section of markets. I like using a baking skillet for this recipe. It's essentially the same as a traditional skillet, except that it has short handles on either side, making it easier to transport to and from the oven.

---

1 To make dough, combine 2¼ cups flour, granulated sugar, yeast, and salt in a large mixing bowl.

2 Combine ½ cup milk, ¼ cup water, and 2 tablespoons butter in a small saucepan over medium-low heat. Heat until milk mixture reaches 120° to 130°.

3 Stir milk mixture into flour mixture. Beat in egg. Gradually add remaining ½ cup flour until a soft dough forms.

4 Lightly grease a bowl with butter. Transfer dough to bowl, turning to coat. Cover and let rise in a warm place (85°), free from drafts, for 1½ hours or until doubled in size.

5 Meanwhile, to make filling, combine almond paste, brown sugar, 4 tablespoons butter, and almond extract in a bowl. With remaining 1 tablespoon butter, grease bottom and sides of a 10-inch cast-iron skillet.

6 Punch dough down and turn out onto a lightly floured surface. Roll into a 12x15-inch rectangle. Spread filling over dough (it's easier if you crumble it over the surface first). Sprinkle with almonds. Roll up dough, starting with shorter side. Cut into 12 slices.

7 Arrange rolls, cut side up, in prepared skillet. Let rise for 30 minutes.

8 Preheat oven to 350°. Bake for 20 to 25 minutes or until golden brown. Cool on a wire rack.

9 Stir together powdered sugar, remaining ¼ cup milk, and extract. Spread over rolls.

MAPLE-WALNUT STICKY BUNS

MAKES 1 DOZEN

An easygoing weekend morning is the perfect time to bake these deliciously sweet breakfast rolls. The soft, fluffy dough is rolled with a cinnamon filling and baked with a sticky glaze with crunchy walnuts. Maple extract isn't always easy to find, so you may substitute vanilla extract.

EQUIPMENT: *12-inch cast-iron skillet*

1 (¼-ounce) package active dry yeast (about 1 packet)
1 cup warm milk (100° to 110°)
¼ cup granulated sugar
2 large eggs
3¾ cups all-purpose flour
1 teaspoon salt
¾ cup unsalted butter, softened and divided
Cinnamon Filling (recipe at right)
½ cup firmly packed dark brown sugar
¼ cup maple syrup
½ teaspoon maple or vanilla extract
1½ cups chopped walnuts or pecans

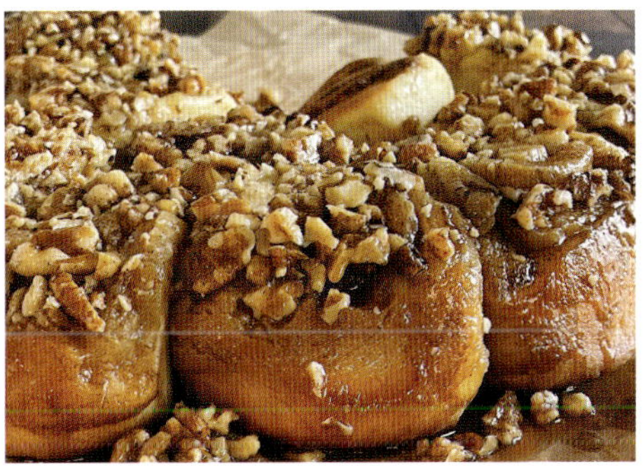

1. To make dough, combine yeast and warm milk in a large mixing bowl. Let stand for 5 minutes or until bubbly. Add granulated sugar and eggs, mixing well. Gradually add flour and salt to yeast mixture, beating at low speed with an electric mixture until a soft dough forms. Beat in ¼ cup softened butter.
2. Lightly grease a bowl with butter. Transfer dough to bowl, turning to coat. Cover and let rise in a warm place (85°), free from drafts, for 1 hour or or until doubled in size (or refrigerate overnight).
3. Prepare Cinnamon Filling; cover and refrigerate until ready to use. About 1 hour before using, let filling soften at room temperature.
4. Meanwhile, melt remaining ½ cup butter in a 12-inch cast-iron skillet over medium-low heat. Stir in brown sugar, maple syrup, and extract. Cook, stirring constantly, for 2 to 3 minutes or until mixture is smooth. Stir in walnuts. Remove from heat.
5. Punch dough down and turn out onto a lightly floured surface. Roll into a 12x15-inch rectangle. Spread filling over dough (it's easier if you crumble it over the surface first). Roll up dough, starting with shorter side. Cut into 12 slices.
6. Arrange rolls, cut side up, over walnut mixture in skillet. Let rise for 30 minutes. Preheat oven to 350°. Bake for 20 to 25 minutes or until golden brown. Let cool for 5 minutes on a wire rack. Place a platter or cutting board on top of skillet and carefully invert. Scrape any remaining walnut mixture out of pan and spoon onto rolls.

Cinnamon Filling: Combine **¾ cup firmly packed light or dark brown sugar, 1 tablespoon ground cinnamon,** and **½ cup softened unsalted butter** in a bowl, stirring until smooth. Makes about 1 cup.

STUFFED FRENCH TOAST

MAKES 6 SERVINGS

EQUIPMENT: *cast-iron griddle or 10- or 12-inch skillet*

1 (8-ounce) container mascarpone cheese or cream cheese

2 tablespoons powdered sugar

Pinch of salt

1 teaspoon vanilla extract

4 large eggs

1 cup milk

½ teaspoon ground cinnamon

6 (1½-inch-thick) slices soft bread

2 tablespoons salted or unsalted butter, melted

Toppings: maple syrup, powdered sugar, fruit jam

Toasted nuts (optional)

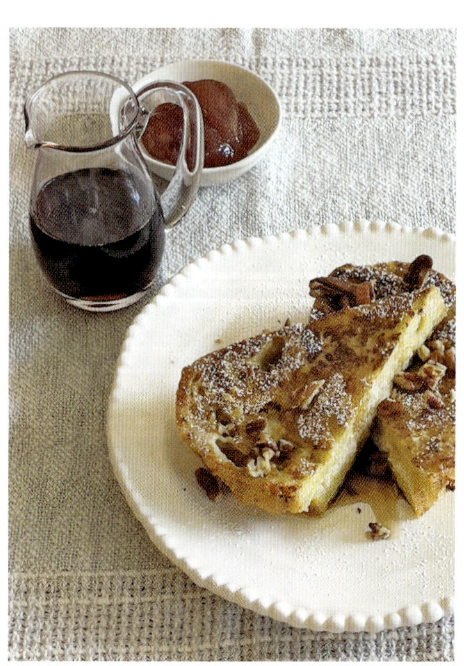

You don't have to grease the entire griddle with butter before cooking—just the area you use. I like to alternate areas, but you can also cook 2 or 3 at a time if your pan is large enough. Mascarpone is a rich, creamy cheese product that has a smooth, buttery flavor. For a substitute, looked for whipped cream cheese, or beat a block of cream cheese until it's soft and spreadable.

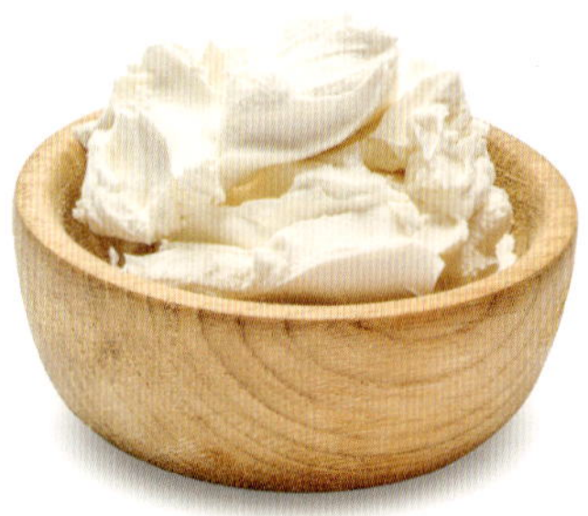

1. Combine mascarpone, powdered sugar, salt, and vanilla in a small bowl. Transfer cheese mixture to a large zip-top plastic storage bag; set cheese mixture aside.
2. Whisk together eggs, milk, and cinnamon in a wide, shallow bowl; set egg mixture aside.
3. Cut a pocket in the side of each slice of bread (do not cut all the way through). Snip one corner of plastic bag and pipe reserved cheese mixture into each pocket.
4. Preheat cast-iron griddle or large skillet over medium heat.
5. Dip each stuffed bread slice into reserved egg mixture, turning to coat both sides. Let bread soak until completely saturated with egg mixture. Drain, letting excess drip off.
6. Brush griddle with melted butter. Cook for about 2 minutes on each side or until golden brown. Repeat with remaining butter and stuffed bread.
7. Serve with desired toppings. Sprinkle with toasted nuts, if desired.

BACON-AND-BROWN SUGAR PANCAKES

MAKES 4 SERVINGS

EQUIPMENT: *griddle or cast-iron skillet*

PAN SAVVY: *It may seem excessive to use two pans, but I like cooking bacon in a skillet (in case there is a lot of grease), while pancakes are easier to flip when cooked on a flat or shallow-sided griddle. I continue to cook pancakes in both pans simultaneously, getting breakfast on the table in half the time.*

4 slices bacon, chopped

1½ cups all-purpose flour

3 tablespoons light or dark brown sugar

1 tablespoon baking powder

½ teaspoon fine sea salt

1 large egg

1¼ cups buttermilk or whole milk

3 tablespoons salted or unsalted butter, melted

1 teaspoon vanilla extract

Maple syrup

Try these salty-and-sweet pancakes as an indulgent breakfast. If you use maple-flavored bacon, it may stick a bit in the skillet because it often contains added sugar. It'll come off, but you may get harmless little dark specks of caramelized (or burnt!) sugar on the pancakes.

1. Cook bacon in a large skillet or griddle until crispy. Transfer to paper towels to drain, reserving excess drippings in a small bowl; set bacon aside. Do not wipe skillet clean.
2. Combine flour, brown sugar, baking powder, and salt in a large bowl. Combine egg, buttermilk, butter, and vanilla in another bowl.
3. Add egg mixture to flour mixture, stirring just until combined (do not overmix).
4. Heat griddle or skillet over medium heat. Brush lightly with reserved bacon drippings.
5. Pour about ¼ cup batter for each pancake onto hot skillet. Sprinkle with reserved bacon. Cook for 2 minutes or until bubbles form; turn over and cook for 1 minute or until golden brown. Transfer to a platter; cover with aluminum foil to keep warm. Serve with maple syrup.

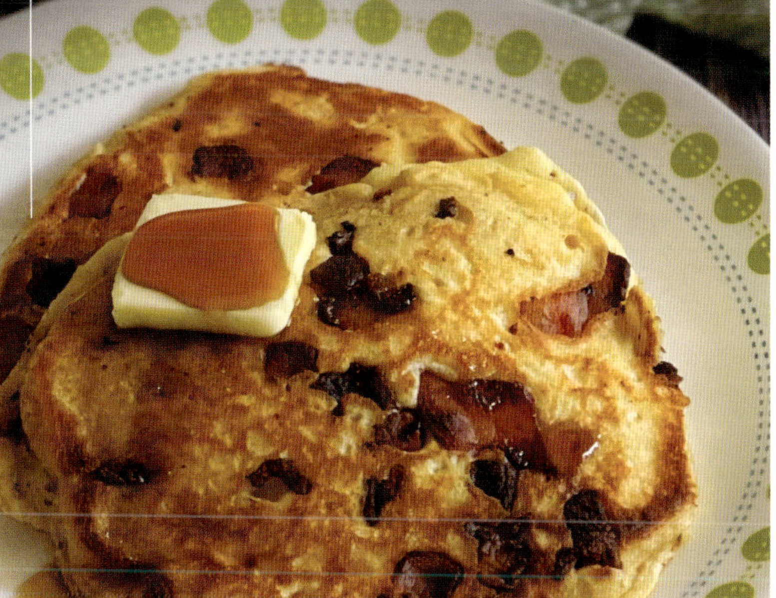

ORANGE-RICOTTA PANCAKES

MAKES 1 DOZEN

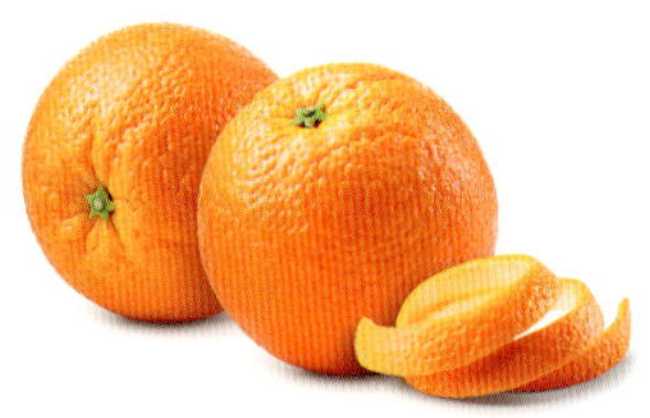

EQUIPMENT: *griddle or large skillet*

PAN SAVVY: *Griddles tend to be easier to use because there are no sides to get in the way of a spatula, allowing space to cook more than one pancake at a time. I like a round griddle that fits perfectly on the eye of my cooktop. Extra-long rectangular griddles are particularly good on a grill (adding yummy outdoorsy flavor!), but take care to keep the griddle on the element when using a cooktop.*

1½ cups all-purpose flour
¼ cup granulated sugar
1½ teaspoons baking powder
½ teaspoon baking soda
¼ teaspoon salt
2 large eggs
1 cup ricotta
1 tablespoon grated orange zest
⅔ cup fresh orange juice
½ teaspoon vanilla extract
2 to 3 tablespoons melted salted or unsalted butter
Maple-Orange Butter (recipe at right)
Garnish: orange slices

Adding ricotta cheese to pancake batter creates a rich, moist pancake with a little protein boost. Adding a bit of baking soda along with the baking powder increases the lift, while orange zest bumps up the flavor. Plain maple syrup is just fine on top, but adding orange zest is delightful.

1. Combine flour, sugar, baking powder, baking soda, and salt in a large bowl. Combine eggs, ricotta, zest, juice, and vanilla in another bowl.
2. Add egg mixture to flour mixture, stirring just until combined (do not overmix).
3. Heat a large skillet or griddle over medium heat. Brush lightly with melted butter.
4. Pour about ⅓ cup batter for each pancake onto hot skillet. Cook for 2 to 3 minutes or until bubbles form; turn over and cook for 1 minute or until golden brown. Transfer to a platter; cover with aluminum foil to keep warm.
5. Serve pancakes with Maple-Orange Butter. Garnish, if desired.

Maple-Orange Butter: Combine **⅓ cup maple syrup, ⅓ cup salted or unsalted butter, ½ teaspoon zest,** and **¼ teaspoon salt** in a small saucepan over medium heat, stirring until butter melts. Makes 1 cup.

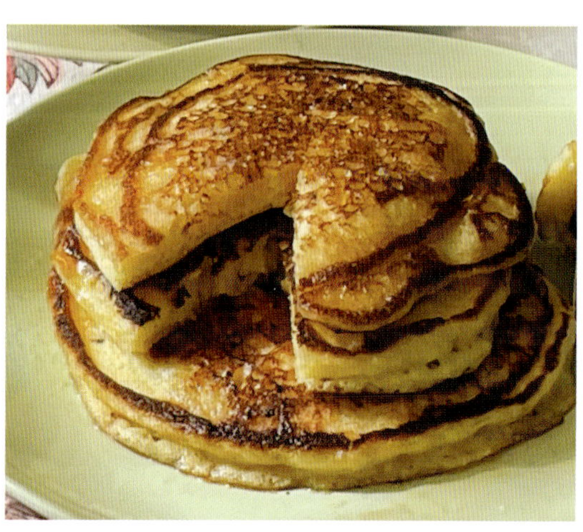

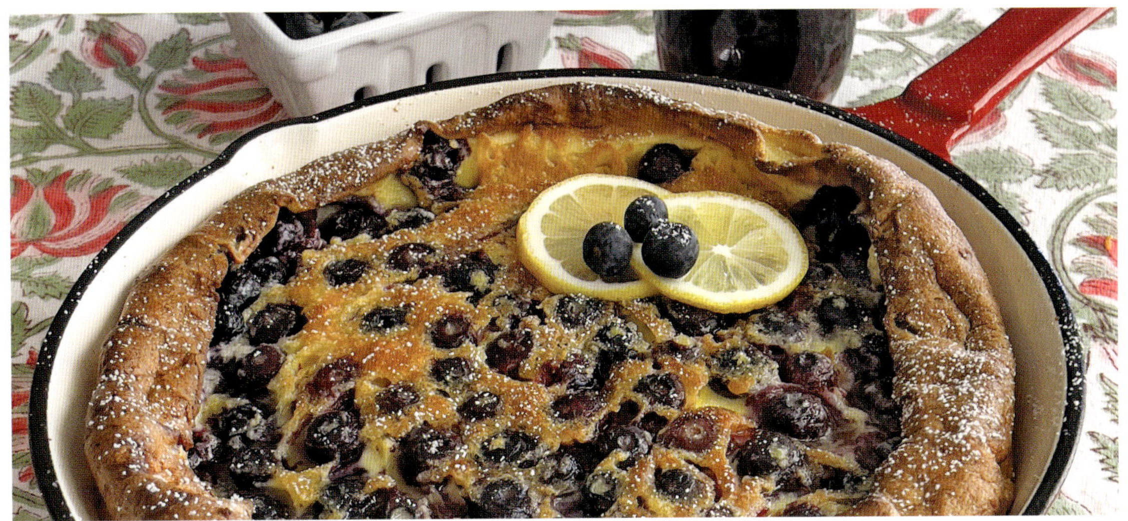

BLUEBERRY-LEMON DUTCH BABY PANCAKE

MAKES 6 SERVINGS

EQUIPMENT: *10-inch cast-iron skillet*

PAN SAVVY: *Substitute a 10-inch baker's skillet. Two short handles on either side make it easier to lift and move in and out of the oven.*

4 large eggs
¾ cup whole milk
¾ cup all-purpose flour
3 tablespoons granulated sugar
½ teaspoon lemon zest
⅛ teaspoon fine sea salt
1 teaspoon vanilla extract
4 tablespoons unsalted butter
1 cup fresh blueberries
Powdered sugar
Blueberry or maple syrup
Garnish: lemon slices

Delicious, easy, and fun to watch while it's baking in the oven, this breakfast dish should be on permanent rotation. Feel free to substitute other quick-cooking fruit like chopped strawberries. The Dutch baby will collapse as it cools. Call everyone to the kitchen as it's removed from the oven to get the full effect of the puffy dish.

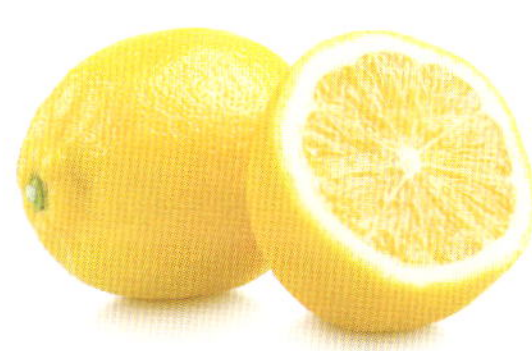

1. Combine eggs, milk, flour, granulated sugar, zest, salt, and vanilla in a blender. Blend until smooth. Let batter rest for 20 minutes.
2. Preheat oven to 450°.
3. Place a 10-inch skillet in hot oven for 10 minutes or until hot. Add butter to skillet and let melt. Tilt pan to coat bottom and sides. Add blueberries, stirring to coat. Pour in batter.
4. Bake for 15 to 20 minutes or until puffed and golden brown. Sprinkle with powdered sugar, and serve warm with blueberry or maple syrup. Garnish, if desired.

SAVORY DUTCH BABY PANCAKE

MAKES 4 TO 6 SERVINGS

EQUIPMENT: *10-inch cast-iron skillet*

PAN SAVVY: *Substitute a 10-inch baker's skillet for easier handling.*

- 4 large eggs
- ¾ cup whole milk
- ¾ cup all-purpose flour
- ¾ teaspoon fine sea salt
- ¼ teaspoon coarsely ground black pepper
- 2 tablespoons chopped fresh chives
- 4 tablespoons unsalted butter
- Toppings: smoked salmon, crème fraîche, red onion slices, fresh dill, and capers

Try this herb-filled puffed pancake with a variety of toppings. Some of my favorites include smoked salmon with crème fraîche, red onion, and dill. You can also layer chopped cooked bacon with a sprinkling of shredded cheddar cheese. Or try thinly shaved ham and thinly sliced Gruyère cheese. Have all the toppings ready before baking because the egg mixture deflates quickly after it comes out of the oven.

---

1. Combine eggs, milk, flour, salt, and pepper in a blender. Blend until smooth. Stir in chives. Let batter rest for 20 minutes.
2. Preheat oven to 450°.
3. Place a 10-inch skillet in hot oven for 10 minutes or until hot. Add butter to skillet and let melt. Tilt pan to coat bottom and sides. Pour in batter.
4. Bake for 15 to 20 minutes or until puffed and golden brown. Remove from oven and serve immediately with desired toppings.

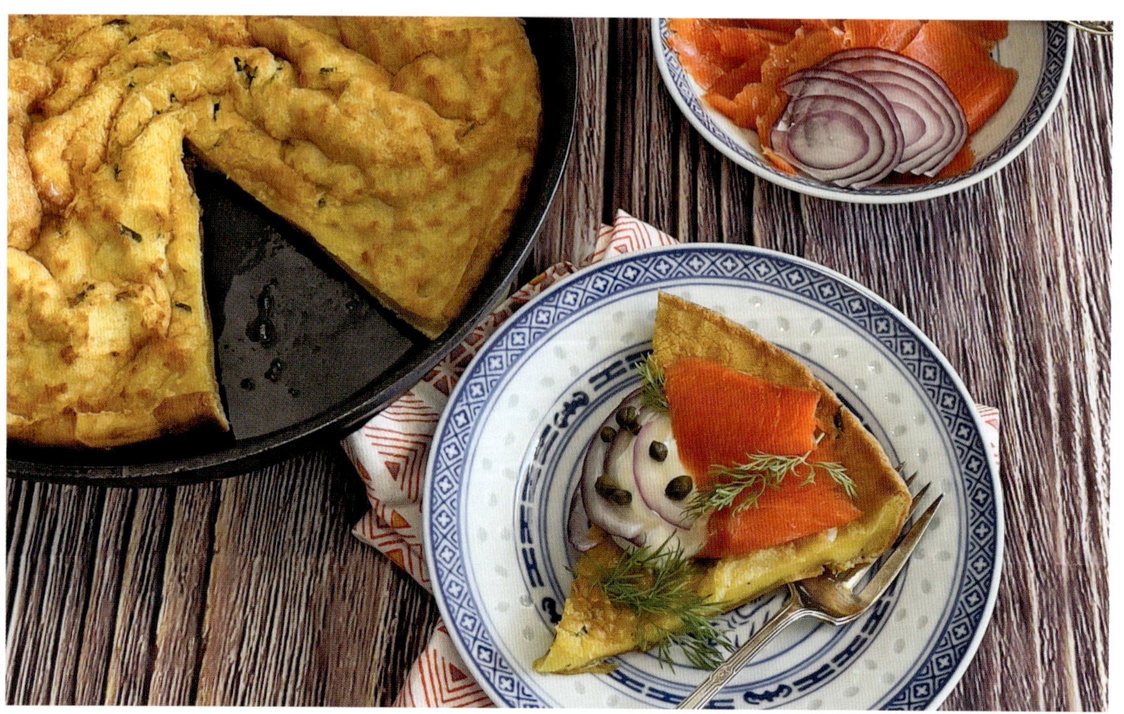

SPINACH-TOMATO FRITTATA

MAKES 6 SERVINGS

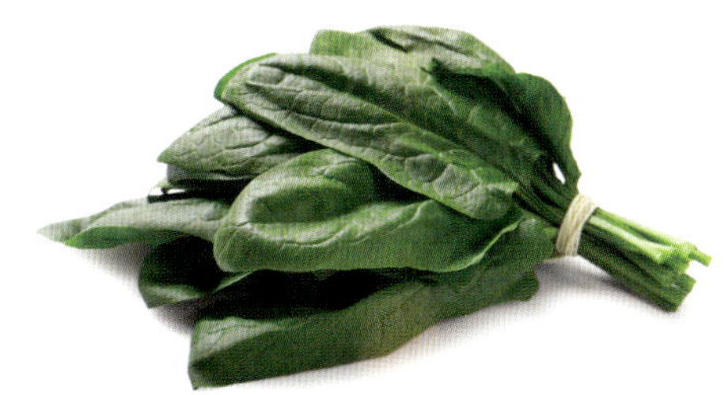

EQUIPMENT: *10-inch cast-iron skillet*

PAN SAVVY: *While eggs are often tricky to make in cast iron, especially in pans that are not well seasoned, this recipe releases quite easily from the skillet. Cast iron holds heat. While it's fine to use moderate-to-high heat to cook the onions and spinach, the heat should be low when the eggs are stirred in. If the heat is too high, the bottom will overbrown. Substitute a 10-inch baker's skillet for easier handling.*

8 large eggs
½ cup half-and-half or whole milk
1 teaspoon hot sauce
1¼ teaspoons salt
¼ teaspoon coarsely ground black pepper
1 tablespoon extra-virgin olive oil
½ small onion, chopped
1 (5-ounce) container baby spinach or arugula
½ cup (2 ounces) crumbled feta cheese
4 Roma or very small tomatoes, sliced and seeded

While delicious for breakfast or brunch, this is one of my favorite recipes to make for an easy dinner. In the summer, I'll use whatever tomatoes happen to be ripe in the garden and the arugula I can't seem to stop growing. I love the saltiness feta provides, but you can substitute any type of cheese you prefer. Add a few slices of chopped cooked bacon for a meaty BLT variation.

1. Whisk together eggs, half-and-half, hot sauce, salt, and pepper in a large bowl.
2. Heat oil in a 10-inch skillet over medium heat. Add onion and cook, stirring occasionally, for 5 to 7 minutes or until tender. Add spinach and cook, turning with tongs, for 2 minutes or until spinach wilts. Reduce heat to low. Stir in egg mixture. Sprinkle with cheese. Top evenly with tomato slices. Cook, without stirring, for 2 to 3 minutes or until mixture begins to set on bottom and edges.
3. Transfer to oven and bake for 20 minutes or until set. Let stand for 5 minutes before slicing.

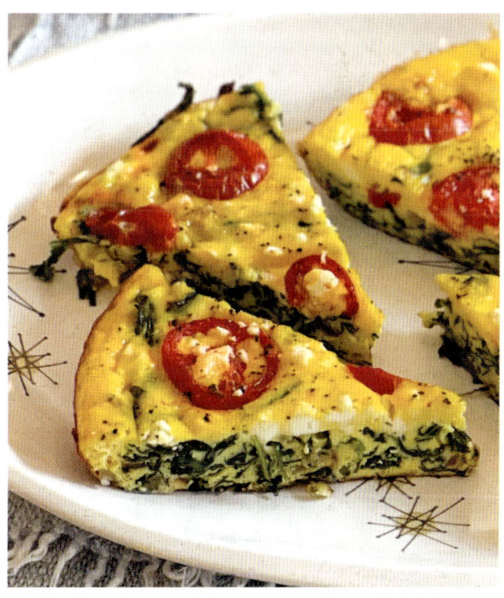

SPAGHETTI FRITTATA

MAKES 6 SERVINGS

EQUIPMENT: *10-inch cast-iron skillet*

PAN SAVVY: *Substitute a 10-inch baker's skillet for easier handling.*

What started as a way to use leftover spaghetti has turned into a delightful meal with fresh-cooked pasta. Adding cooked bacon makes it reminiscent of spaghetti carbonara (made with pancetta and egg yolks). The tomatoes add a bit of acidity to cut some of the heaviness while adding nutrients and a pop of color.

2 cups cooked spaghetti (about 4 ounces uncooked)

8 large eggs

½ cup half-and-half or whole milk

¾ teaspoon salt

½ teaspoon coarsely ground black pepper

1 tablespoon chopped fresh basil

½ cup (1 ounce) shredded Italian-blend cheese or half mozzarella and half Parmesan, divided

1 tablespoon extra-virgin olive oil

1 shallot, minced

2 garlic cloves, minced

⅛ teaspoon crushed red pepper

1 cup cherry tomatoes, halved

5 to 6 slices fresh mozzarella (optional)

Garnish: chopped fresh basil

1. Prepare spaghetti according to package directions (or use leftovers); drain and set pasta aside.
2. Preheat oven to 375°.
3. Whisk eggs, half-and-half, salt, and pepper in a bowl. Stir in basil and ¼ cup cheese. Heat oil in a 10-inch cast-iron skillet over medium heat. Add shallot, garlic, and crushed red pepper. Cook, stirring frequently, for 2 to 3 minutes or until shallot is translucent. Add tomatoes. Cook for 2 minutes. Stir in reserved pasta.
4. Pour egg mixture into skillet, gently moving pasta mixture around until combined. Sprinkle with remaining ¼ cup cheese.
5. Transfer frittata to oven; bake for 18 to 20 minutes or until center is set. If desired, arrange mozzarella on top of frittata. Broil for 2 to 3 minutes or until mozzarella is melted. Garnish, if desired.

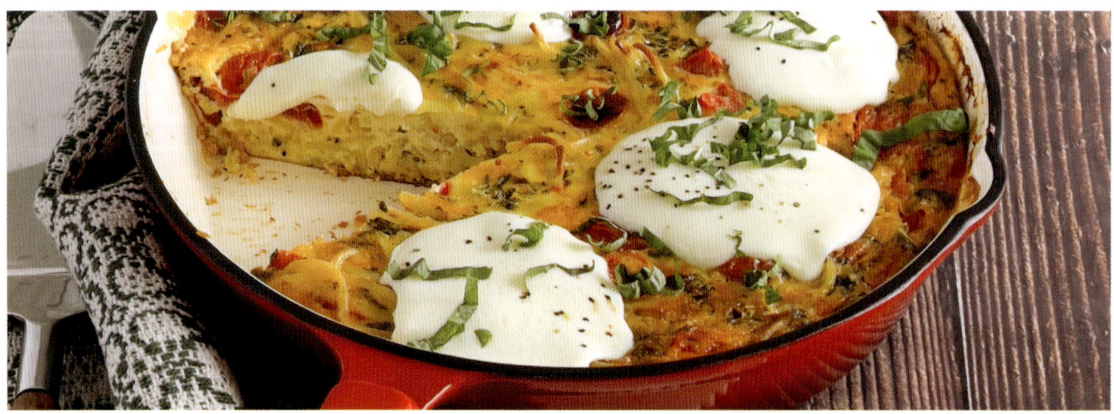

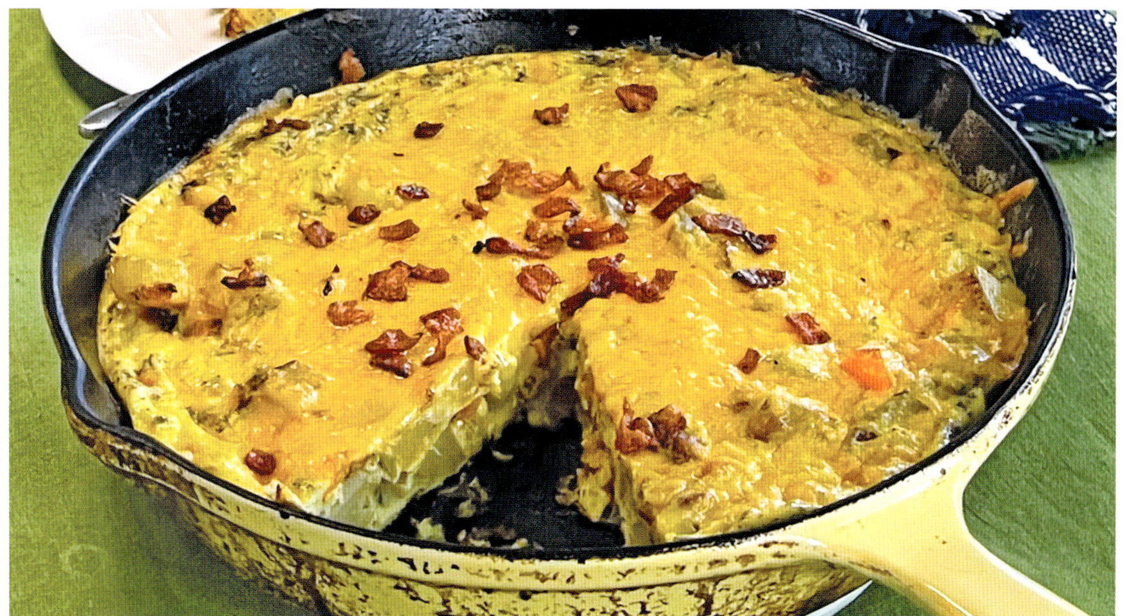

POTATO-AND-BACON BREAKFAST SKILLET

All the early-morning favorites are in this one-dish meal! For a spicier dish, use 4 to 6 ounces of soft Mexican or soy-based chorizo sausage.

MAKES 4 TO 6 SERVINGS

EQUIPMENT: *10-inch cast-iron skillet*

PAN SAVVY: *Substitute a 10-inch baker's skillet for easier handling.*

4 slices bacon, chopped
1 pound baby red or gold potatoes, cubed
½ onion, finely chopped
1 bell pepper (any color), chopped
6 large eggs
¼ cup milk
1 teaspoon salt
½ teaspoon dried Italian seasoning
½ teaspoon coarsely ground black pepper
1 cup (4 ounces) shredded cheddar or other cheese

1. Cook bacon in a 10-inch skillet over medium heat until crisp. Transfer bacon to a plate, reserving 1 to 2 tablespoons drippings in skillet.
2. Add potatoes, onion, and bell pepper to skillet. Cover and cook over medium-low heat, stirring occasionally, for 12 to 15 minutes or until potatoes are just cooked. Stir in bacon, reserving some to sprinkle on top, if desired.
3. Preheat oven to 350°.
4. Whisk together eggs, milk, salt, seasoning, and black pepper in a bowl. Pour over potato mixture, stirring gently. Sprinkle with cheese and, if desired, reserved bacon.
5. Bake, uncovered, for 15 minutes or until golden brown and set.

BREAKFAST SPUDS WITH PEPPERS AND ONIONS

MAKES 4 SERVINGS

EQUIPMENT: *12-inch cast-iron skillet*

PAN SAVVY: *The ingredients will fit in a 10-inch skillet; however, the thicker layer will prevent potatoes from getting crispy browned edges.*

2 tablespoons avocado oil, extra-virgin olive oil, or bacon drippings
2 tablespoons salted or unsalted butter
1½ pounds large red, gold, or russet potatoes, cubed
1 teaspoon fine sea salt
½ teaspoon coarsely ground black pepper
1 small bell pepper (any color), chopped
½ onion, chopped
½ teaspoon paprika
½ teaspoon garlic powder
Garnish: chopped fresh chives

For easiest prep, buy large potatoes and skip peeling them. It's important to use a large skillet so the potatoes are cooked in an even layer with maximum crispness. Feel free to fry up some bacon and use the drippings to cook this dish rather than oil. Use your favorite potatoes—russets will have a crispier crust, while waxier gold or red potatoes will hold their shape best. Just make sure to cut potatoes to the same size so they cook evenly.

1. Heat oil and butter in a 12-inch cast-iron skillet over medium heat. Stir in potatoes, salt, and black pepper, spreading out into an even layer. Cover and cook, without stirring, for 10 minutes.
2. Stir in bell pepper, onion, paprika, and garlic powder. Cover and cook for 10 minutes, without stirring. Uncover and turn potatoes over or stir. Cook for 5 minutes or until potatoes are golden brown and vegetables are tender. Garnish, if desired.

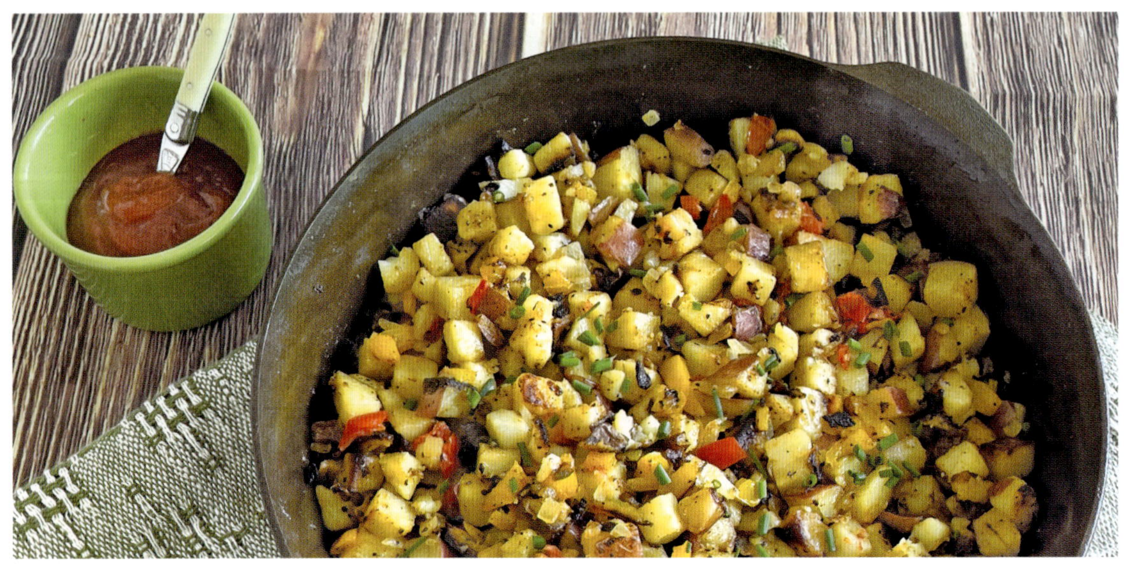

CORNED BEEF HASH

MAKES 6 TO 8 SERVINGS

EQUIPMENT: *12-inch cast-iron skillet*

4 large Yukon Gold potatoes, peeled and cubed

3 tablespoons avocado or extra-virgin olive oil, divided

1 onion, chopped

2 garlic cloves, minced

½ teaspoon salt

½ teaspoon coarsely ground black pepper

½ teaspoon paprika

2 to 3 cups cooked corned beef, diced or shredded

2 green onions, chopped

Hollandaise Sauce (optional; recipe at right)

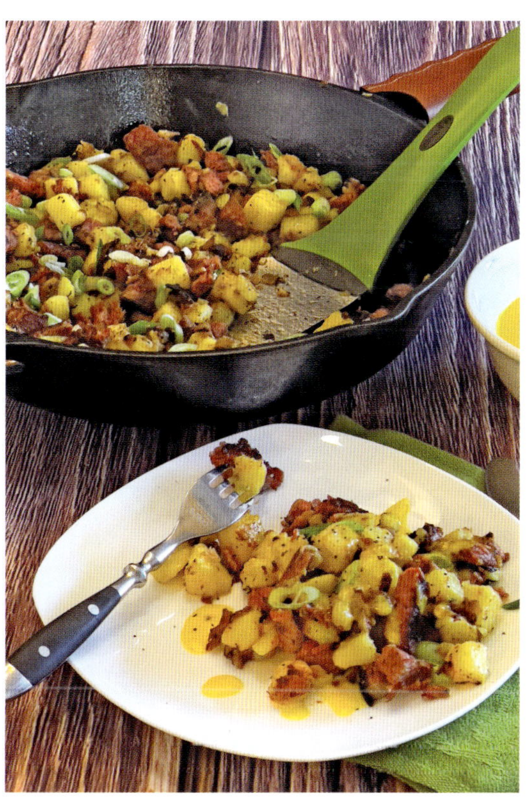

Use this hearty recipe anytime you have leftover corned beef. You can also buy thickly sliced corned beef from the deli. To take this dish to a decadent level, top each serving with a fried egg.

---

1. Cook potatoes in boiling salted water to cover for 5 to 6 minutes or until just tender (do not overcook; potatoes should be slightly firm in the center). Drain well, and set potatoes aside.
2. Heat 1 tablespoon oil in a large (12-inch) cast-iron skillet over medium heat. Add onion and cook, stirring frequently, for 3 to 5 minutes. Add garlic, salt, pepper, and paprika; cook, stirring constantly, for 1 minute.
3. Add corned beef and reserved potatoes; lightly press down into an even layer. Drizzle with remaining 2 tablespoons oil. Cook, without stirring, for 5 to 7 minutes or until bottom of potato mixture is browned and crispy.
4. Stir and press down again. Cook for 5 minutes or until mixture begins to brown on bottom. Continue cooking and turning for 5 minutes or until potatoes are crisp on all sides and golden brown. Sprinkle with chopped green onions. Serve with Hollandaise Sauce, if desired.

Hollandaise Sauce: Whisk together **4 egg yolks, 1 tablespoon lemon juice, and ⅛ teaspoon cayenne pepper** in the top of a double boiler. Place over barely simmering water. Add **½ cup unsalted butter,** cut into pieces, a few pieces at a time. Cook over hot water, whisking constantly, for 3 minutes or until thickened. Makes ⅔ cup.

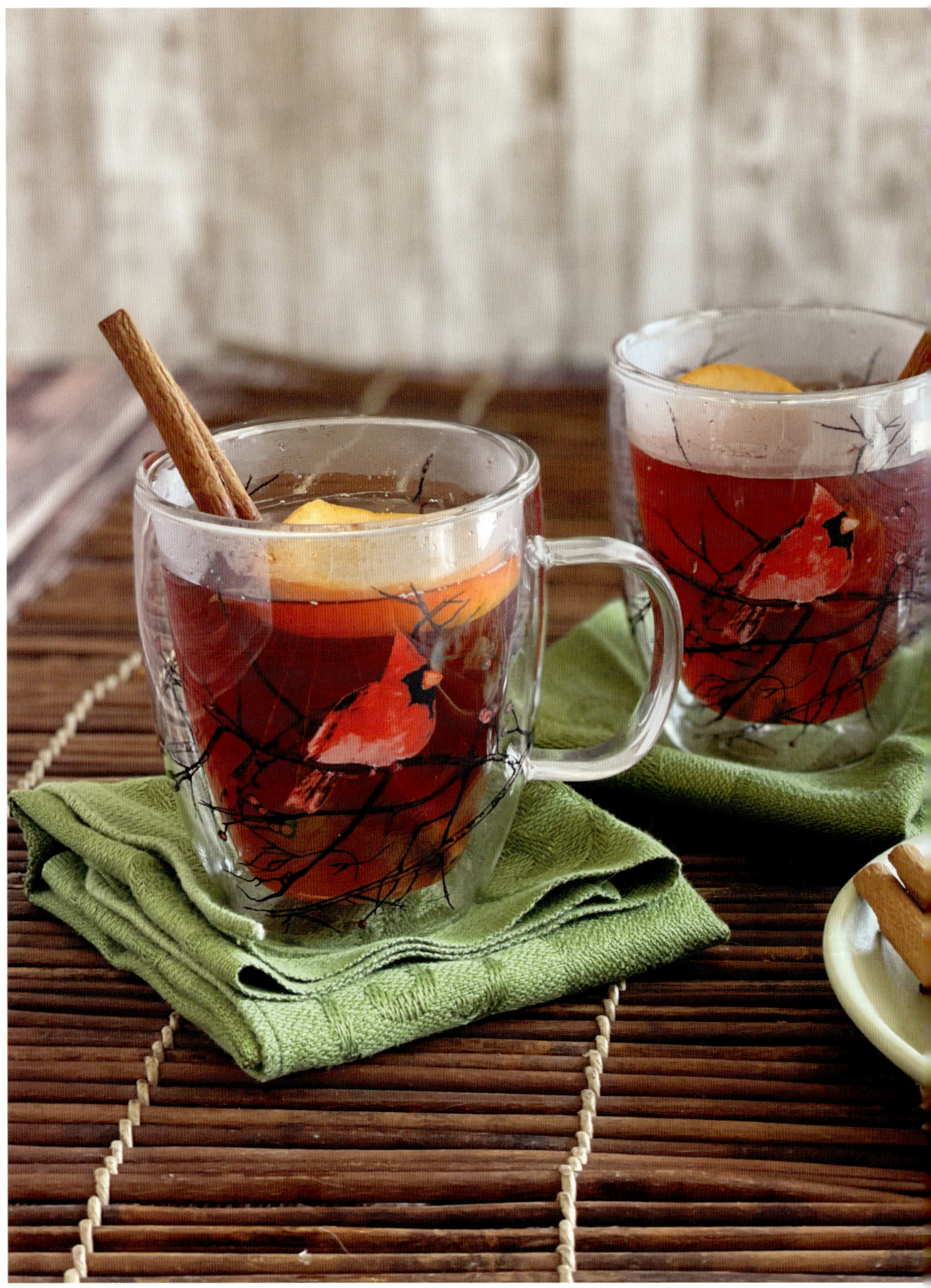

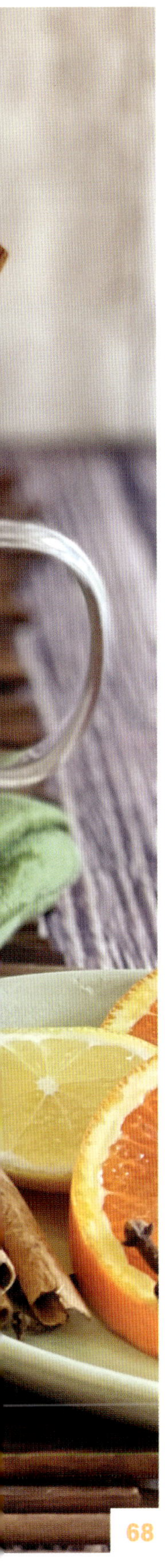
68

APPETIZERS *and* BEVERAGES

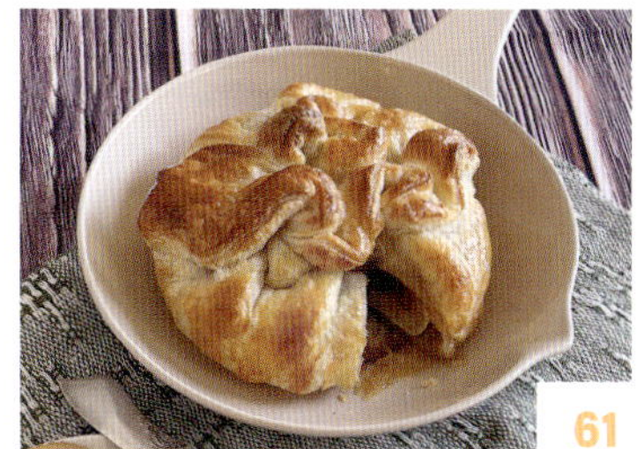
61

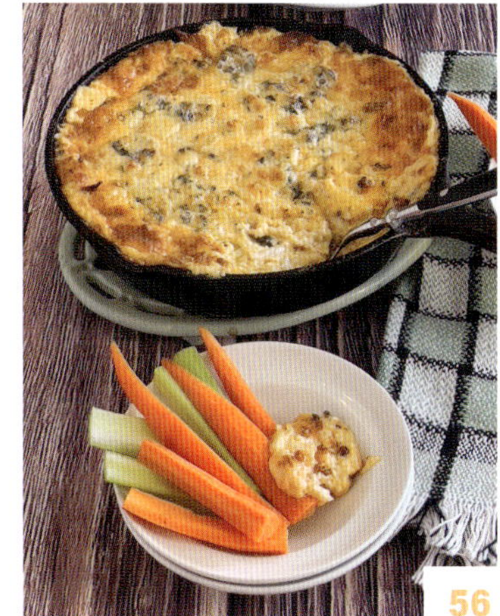
56

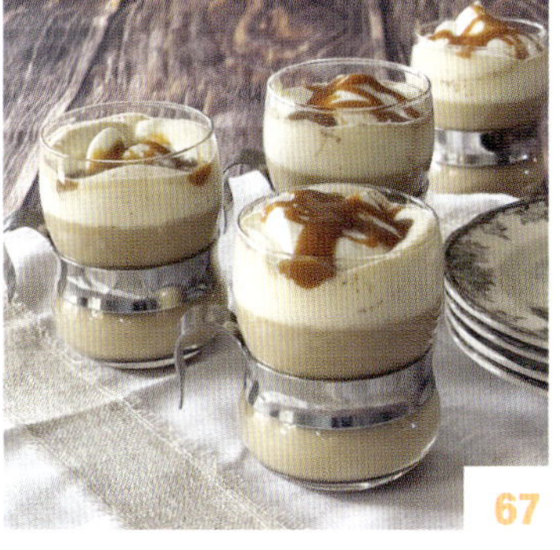
67

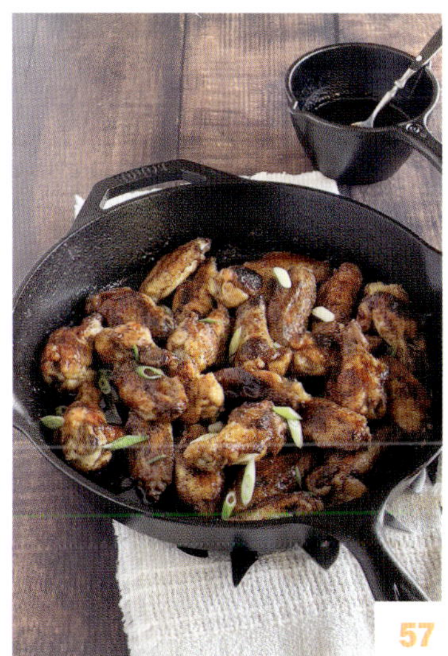
57

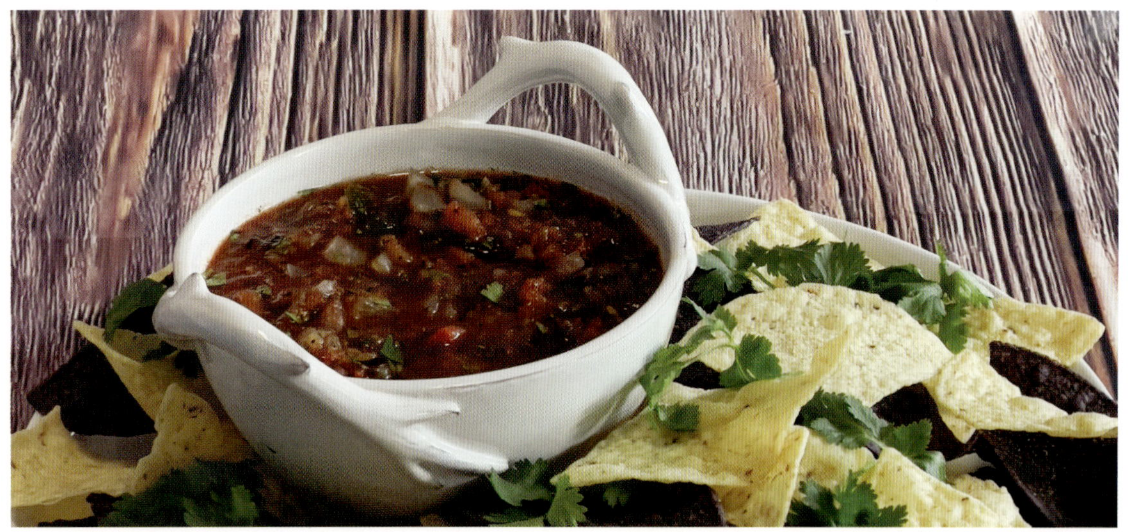

CHARRED TOMATO SALSA

MAKES 2½ CUPS

This is the type of recipe where cast iron is required—the material can reach the high heat that blisters and chars fresh tomatoes and jalapeño peppers, creating an earthy, smoky flavor.

EQUIPMENT: *10- or 12-inch cast-iron skillet, griddle*

PAN SAVVY: *The high heat necessary to char the tomatoes and vegetables may discolor enamel-coated pans. Use a bare-but-seasoned cast-iron pan. Wash and re-season the pan as soon as it's cool enough to safely handle.*

1½ pounds Roma or plum tomatoes, halved
½ white onion, thickly sliced
1 jalapeño pepper, stems sliced off*
1 large garlic clove, unpeeled
½ teaspoon grated lime zest
2 tablespoons fresh lime juice
¼ cup lightly packed chopped fresh cilantro
½ teaspoon fine sea salt
¼ teaspoon coarsely ground black pepper

1. Heat a large cast-iron skillet over high heat. (Turn on the exhaust fan—this is going to smoke!) Working in batches, sear tomatoes, onion, jalapeño pepper, and garlic, turning occasionally, for 5 to 8 minutes or until all sides are charred.
2. Transfer vegetables to bowl of a food processor (remove peel from garlic first). Pulse several times until evenly chopped.
3. Add zest, juice, cilantro, salt, and black pepper. Pulse until well blended.

*The heat in jalapeño peppers resides in the seeds and pithy insides. For a milder salsa, cut jalapeño peppers in half, and remove seeds and ribs along the inside. In general, a smooth jalapeño without the white striations or "stretch marks" is milder.

CAST-IRON QUESO

MAKES 4 CUPS

EQUIPMENT: *5-cup cast-iron fondue pot or small Dutch oven*

PAN SAVVY: *Use a small Dutch oven or saucepan if you don't own a fondue pot.*

1½ cups half-and-half

½ teaspoon ground cumin

1 (4.5-ounce) can chopped Hatch or other green chili peppers

1 pound yellow or white American cheese, cubed

Tortilla chips

The creamy, irresistible cheese dip at Mexican restaurants relies on one thing—American cheese. You can find it at the deli counter instead of the aisle with the other packaged cheeses. Heat it low and slow to avoid scorching. Serve it with a side of Charred Tomato Salsa (page 46) or pico de gallo, so you can dip into both!

1 Combine half-and-half, cumin, and chilies in a fondue pot, saucepan, or small Dutch oven over medium-low heat. Cook until mixture is hot but not boiling.

2 Add cheese, stirring constantly, until mixture is smooth and creamy. Serve with chips.

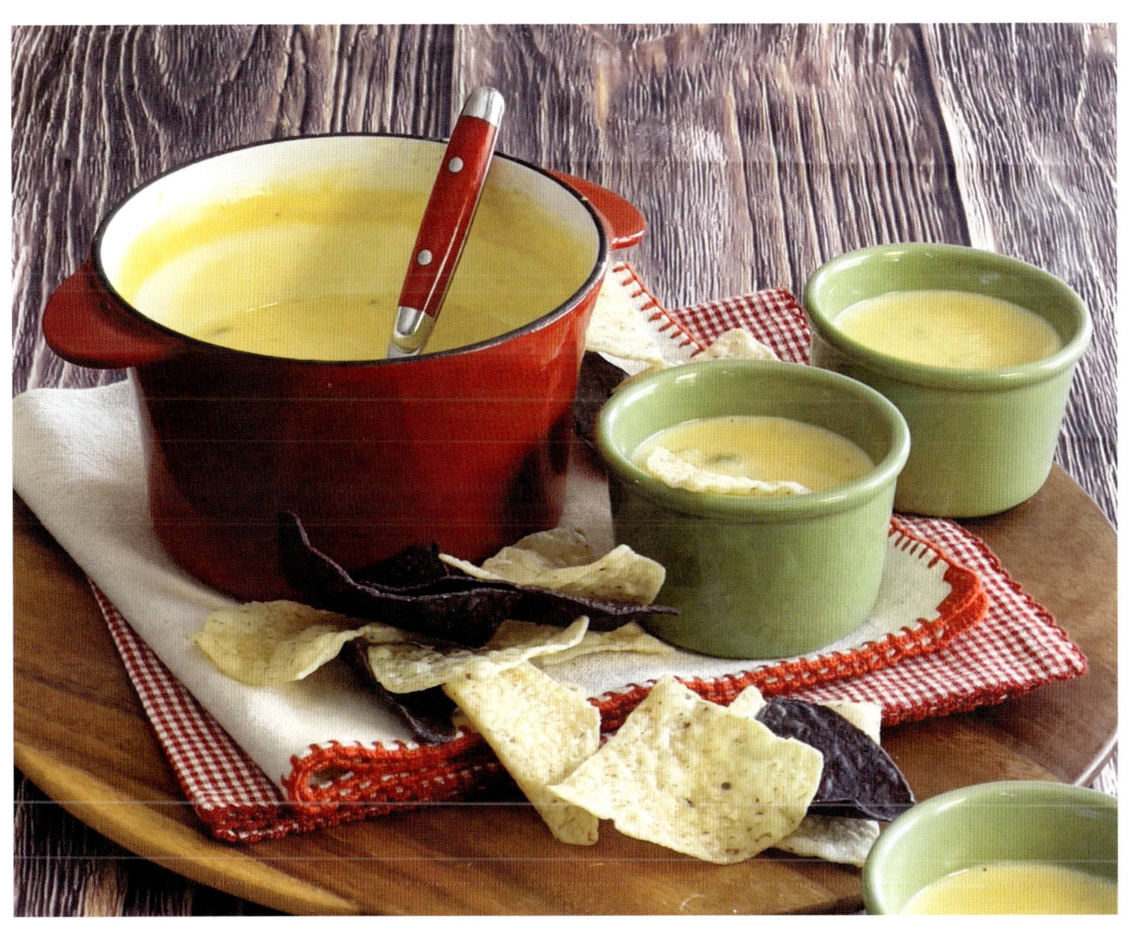

BAKED SPINACH DIP

MAKES 10 TO 12 SERVINGS

EQUIPMENT: *10-inch cast-iron skillet*

PAN SAVVY: *Substitute a 10-inch baker's skillet. It has two short handles on either side, rather than one short and one long. It's often easier to transfer into an oven than a traditional skillet. Baker's skillets are also easier to arrange on a serving table.*

1 (8-ounce) package cream cheese, softened
1 cup sour cream
¼ cup mayonnaise
1 teaspoon hot sauce
½ teaspoon fine sea salt
¼ teaspoon coarsely ground black pepper
1 garlic clove, minced
1 (9- or 10-ounce) package frozen chopped spinach, thawed and squeezed dry
1 (4-ounce) can diced mild or hot chilies (optional)
1 (14-ounce) can hearts of palm, drained and chopped
1 cup (4 ounces) shredded Parmesan cheese
1 cup (4 ounces) shredded mozzarella cheese
1 tablespoon butter
Crackers, bruschetta, chips

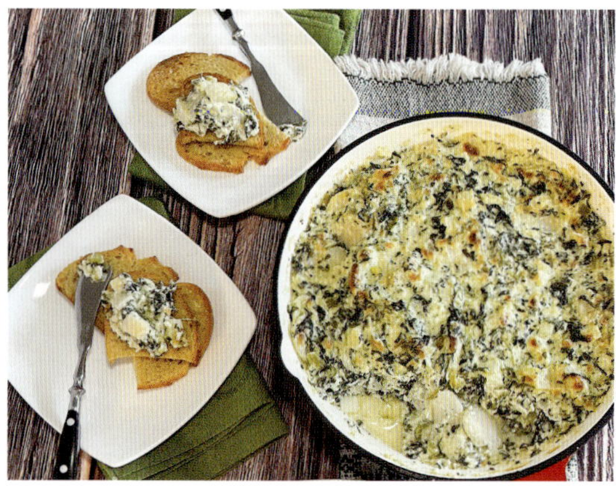

This popular dip is a riff on the hot spinach-artichoke dips that have graced party tables for decades. Artichokes are one of my favorite foods, but canned versions can be tough and prickly. Hearts of palm have a similar flavor with a tender texture. Keep all of these ingredients in your pantry and fridge (they stay fresh for weeks to months) from October until January, and you'll have a quick-and-easy appetizer for any spontaneous holiday visitors.

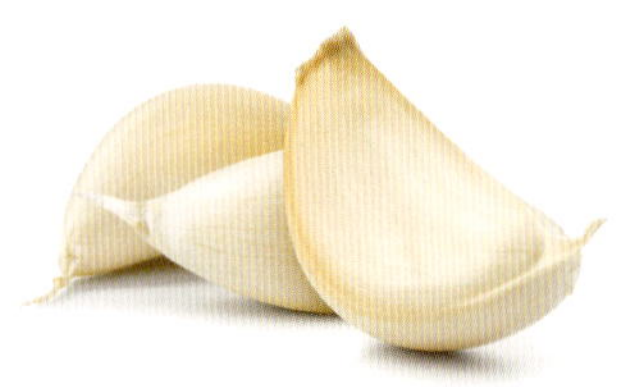

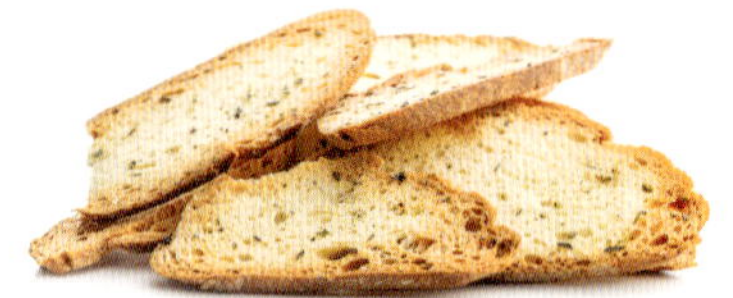

1. Preheat oven to 375°.
2. Beat together cream cheese, sour cream, mayonnaise, hot sauce, salt, pepper, and garlic in a large bowl. Stir in spinach; chilies, if desired; hearts of palm; Parmesan; and mozzarella.
3. Grease a 10-inch cast-iron skillet with butter; transfer mixture to prepared pan. Bake, uncovered, for 30 minutes or until hot and bubbly. For a golden-brown top, broil for 2 to 3 minutes before serving. Serve with crackers, bruschetta, or chips.

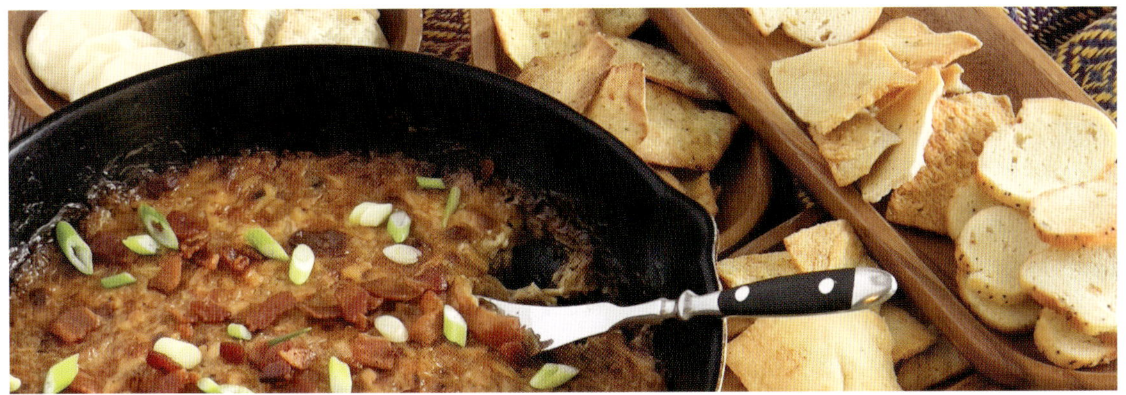

SMOKY CARAMELIZED ONION DIP

MAKES 8 TO 10 SERVINGS

EQUIPMENT: *10-inch cast-iron skillet*

PAN SAVVY: *Use a 10-inch baker's skillet, if available, for easier handling.*

4 strips bacon, chopped
1 tablespoon salted butter
3 yellow or sweet onions, chopped
½ teaspoon granulated sugar
½ teaspoon fine sea salt
1 tablespoon sherry vinegar
1 teaspoon fresh thyme leaves
1 cup (4 ounces) smoked Gouda cheese
¾ cup (3 ounces) shredded Gruyère or Swiss cheese
½ cup sour cream
½ cup mayonnaise
¼ teaspoon coarsely ground black pepper
Garnish: sliced green onions
Pita chips, crackers, toasted baguette slices

Serve this rich-and-hearty dip on game day or at other casual get-togethers. You can make it ahead, but let the dip and skillet come to room temperature before placing in a hot oven.

1. Cook bacon in a skillet over medium heat until crisp. Drain on paper towels; set bacon aside. Discard excess oil in skillet, but don't wipe clean.
2. Add butter to skillet and let melt over medium heat. Add onions and cook, covered, for 10 minutes or until softened. Uncover; stir in sugar and salt. Cook, stirring occasionally, for 30 minutes or until onions are deep golden brown. Stir in vinegar and thyme. Cook, stirring constantly, until liquid evaporates.
3. Preheat oven to 400°.
4. Combine cheeses, sour cream, mayonnaise, and pepper in a large bowl. Stir in most of reserved bacon, saving some for garnishing after baking. Stir cheese mixture into onions.
5. Bake for 20 minutes or until golden brown and bubbly. Garnish, if desired. Serve dip with pita chips, crackers, or toasted baguette slices.

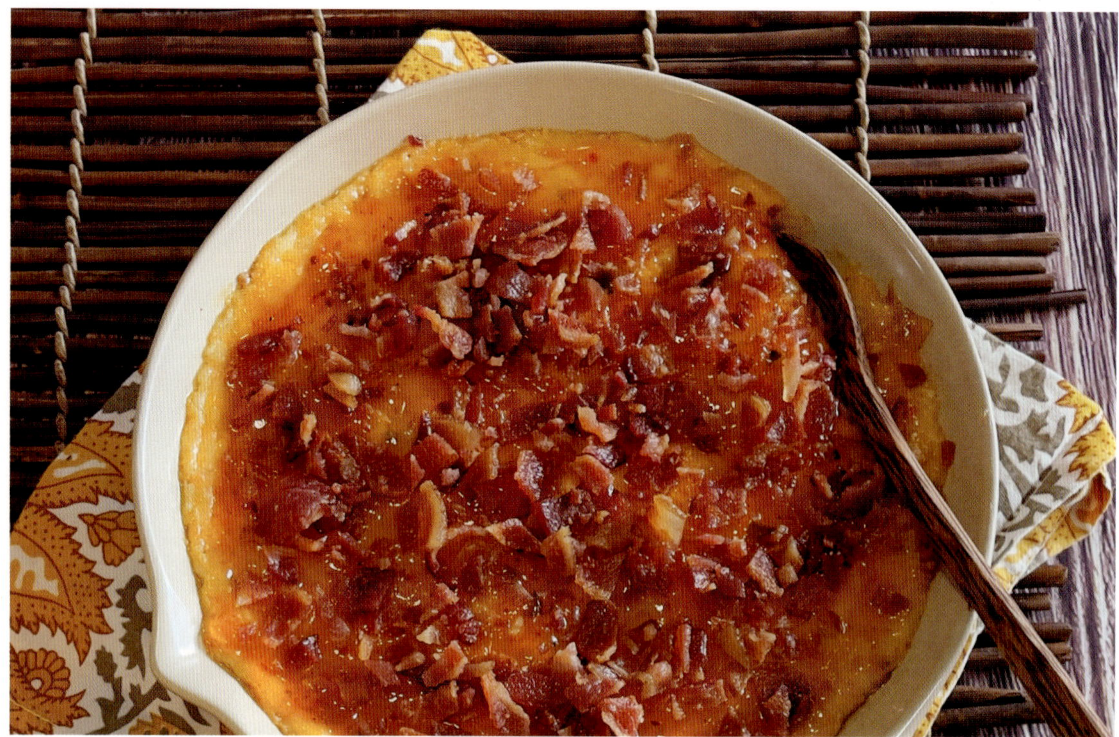

TRIPLE PEPPER–HOT CHEESE DIP

MAKES 2 CUPS (6 SERVINGS)

EQUIPMENT: *6-inch cast-iron skillet*

Vegetable oil
1 (8-ounce) package cream cheese, very softened
1 cup (4 ounces) shredded cheddar cheese
1 cup (4 ounces) shredded pepper-Jack cheese
1 tablespoon chopped pickled jalapeño peppers
⅔ cup pepper jelly, divided
6 slices crisp cooked bacon, chopped
Toasted baguette slices, crackers, tortilla chips

I first concocted this recipe about 15 years ago, inspired by melted pimiento cheese. It still delivers. Since then, I've tweaked it to add even more flavors—sweet, salty, and spicy!

---

1. Preheat oven to 375°. Grease bottom and inside of a 6-inch cast-iron skillet with vegetable oil.
2. Combine cream cheese, cheddar, pepper-Jack, jalapeños, and ⅓ cup pepper jelly in a bowl, stirring until well blended. Spoon into prepared skillet.
3. Bake for 15 minutes or until hot and bubbly. Spread remaining ⅓ cup pepper jelly on top of cheese mixture and sprinkle with bacon. Serve with toasted baguette slices, crackers, or tortilla chips.

HOT BACON–CORN DIP

MAKES 15 TO 25 SERVINGS

EQUIPMENT: *10-inch cast-iron skillet*

PAN SAVVY: *Use a 10-inch baker's skillet, if available, for easier handling.*

6 slices bacon, chopped
3 cups fresh (or frozen and thawed) corn kernels
1 small red or orange bell pepper, chopped
½ onion, chopped
2 garlic cloves, minced
1 (8-ounce) package cream cheese, softened
½ cup sour cream
½ cup mayonnaise or sour cream
½ teaspoon coarsely ground black pepper
1 (8-ounce) package Colby-Jack cheese, shredded and divided
½ teaspoon chili powder

Perfect for parties or tailgating, this dip is a creamy, savory delight. It's easy to downsize by half for smaller gatherings, and it can even be made ahead and baked later—just cook it a little longer, until the center is hot.

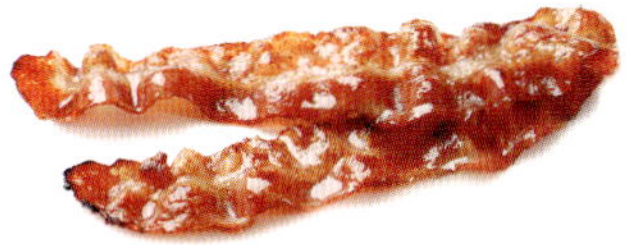

1. Heat a 10-inch skillet over medium heat. Add bacon and cook, stirring frequently, for 7 to 10 minutes or until crispy. Drain excess drippings, reserving 1 tablespoon in skillet.
2. Preheat oven to 350°.
3. Add corn, bell pepper, onion, and garlic to bacon. Cook over medium heat, stirring frequently, for 5 minutes or until vegetables are tender.
4. Stir in cream cheese, sour cream, mayonnaise, black pepper, and half of shredded cheese. Sprinkle with remaining half of shredded cheese and chili powder.
5. Bake for 30 minutes or until golden brown and bubbly.

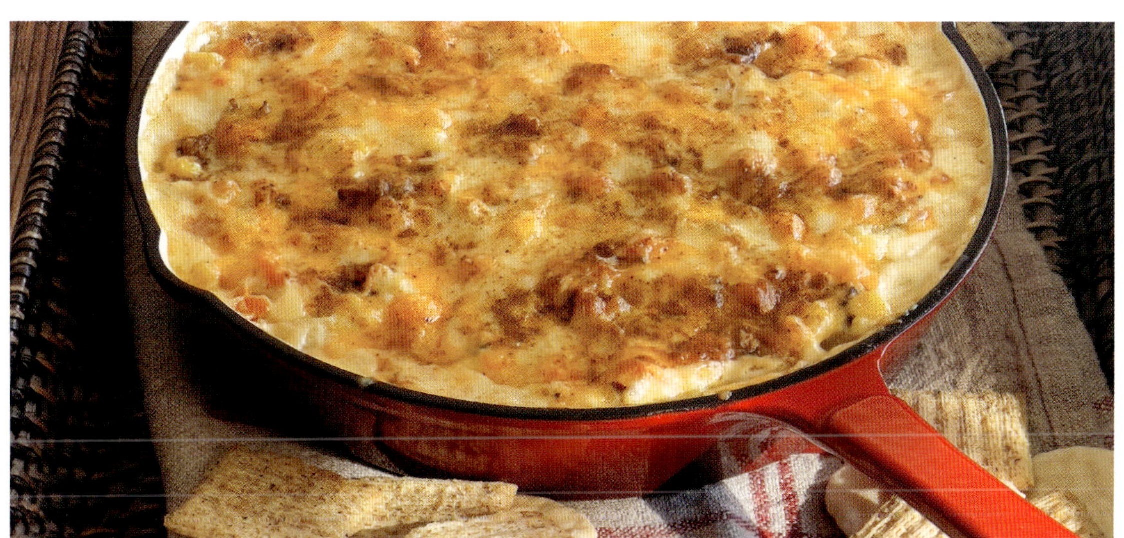

ITALIAN SAUSAGE-AND-SPINACH DIP

MAKES 8 SERVINGS

EQUIPMENT: *10-inch cast-iron skillet*

PAN SAVVY: *Use a 10-inch baker's skillet, if available, for easier handling.*

12 to 14 ounces bulk or plant-based sausage
¼ cup dry white wine
1 (8-ounce) package cream cheese, softened
1 (9-ounce) package frozen chopped spinach, thawed and squeezed dry
1 (15-ounce) can fire-roasted or seasoned diced tomatoes, drained
1 cup (4 ounces) shredded mozzarella cheese
¾ cup (3 ounces) shredded Parmesan cheese
Baguette slices, pita chips, crackers

Serve this hearty appetizer at a potluck party. It's easy to make, and the ingredients can be kept on hand for a long time in the pantry, fridge, or freezer. I use plant-based sausage if I don't know all the guests. Even with a vegetarian note, people still question, "Are you sure this doesn't have meat?"

1. Preheat oven to 375°.
2. Heat a skillet over medium heat. (If using plant-based sausage, add 1 tablespoon olive oil to skillet.) Add sausage and cook, stirring frequently, for 7 minutes or until browned and crumbly. Drain any excess oil.
3. Add wine and cream cheese, stirring until well blended. Stir in spinach and tomatoes.
4. Combine shredded cheeses, and stir in half. Smooth top of dip, and sprinkle with remaining half of shredded cheese mixture.
5. Bake for 20 minutes or until golden brown and bubbly. Serve with baguette slices, pita chips, or crackers.

PAN-ROASTED BABA GHANOUSH

MAKES 2 CUPS

EQUIPMENT: *12-inch cast-iron pan*

PAN SAVVY: *Use the largest skillet you own—ideally all the pieces will fit in a single layer. Fewer-but-thicker pieces work better than many thin slices. If you don't have a lid, use a sheet pan to cover. If you're using a smaller skillet, rotate the pieces so they cook evenly.*

1 (1¼- to 1½-pound) eggplant
2 tablespoons avocado oil, divided
2 tablespoons Greek yogurt
2 tablespoons tahini
½ teaspoon lemon zest
1½ tablespoons fresh lemon juice
¾ teaspoon fine sea salt
½ teaspoon ground cumin
1 garlic clove, pressed
Garnishes: extra-virgin olive oil, chopped fresh parsley, diced pimiento
Skillet Flatbread (page 28) or pita, warmed

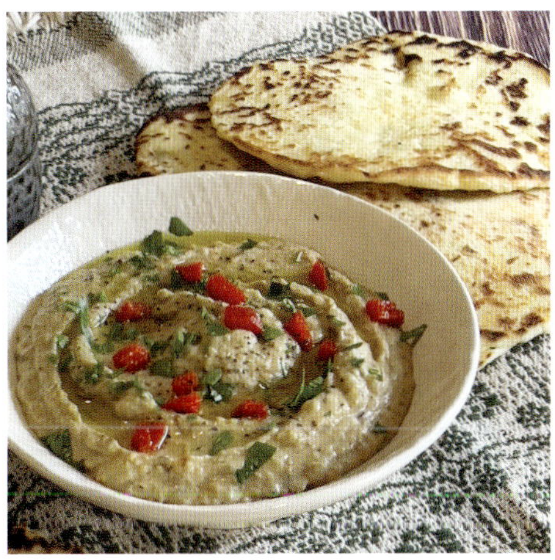

This Middle Eastern dip is typically made from eggplant that is charred over an open flame, lending its naturally smoky flavor. There's no need to set up a grill, though—very hot cast iron will cook and slightly char the eggplant for an authentic flavor. Check the eggplant slices as they cook. You want them deep brown with a few flecks of char—not pitch-black. Reduce the heat, if necessary.

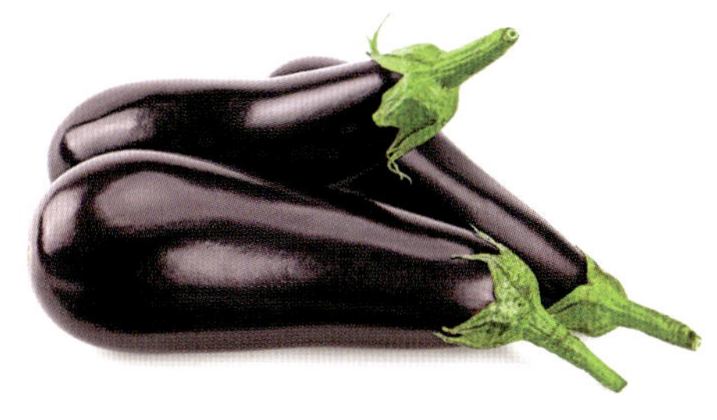

1. Heat a 12-inch cast-iron skillet over medium-high heat.
2. Slice eggplant into 1-inch-thick pieces. Brush skillet with 1 tablespoon oil and arrange eggplant slices in a single layer (cut pieces to fit). Sear for 4 minutes or until eggplant is deep brown to slightly charred.
3. Turn eggplant slices over, drizzle with remaining 1 tablespoon oil, and sear for 4 minutes. Reduce heat to medium-low. Cover and cook for 5 to 7 minutes or until eggplant is very tender. Allow to sit until cool enough to handle.
4. Pull skin off of eggplant and put flesh into a food processer. Add yogurt, tahini, zest, juice, salt, cumin, and garlic. Process until smooth and well blended. Transfer to a serving bowl. Garnish, if desired. Serve at room temperature or chilled with Skillet Flatbread.

CLASSIC SWISS FONDUE

MAKES 2½ CUPS

Cheese fondue heats evenly and stays warm in cast iron. Be sure to buy blocks of good-quality cheese, and gradually add it to the hot wine mixture. Tradition says that if someone drops their piece of bread in the dip, they have to perform a task or dare—good luck!

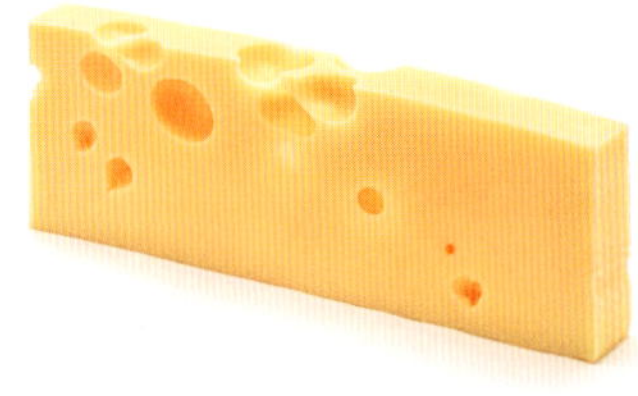

EQUIPMENT: *4- to 5-cup cast-iron fondue pot. Use canned fuel as recommended by the manufacturer of the fondue pot to keep the dip warm and spreadable.*

PAN SAVVY: *Fondue pots are narrow and deep, ideal for evenly melting cheese or submersing foods in broth or oil. You can substitute a saucepan, but watch carefully to avoid scorching on the bottom.*

1 garlic clove, halved

2 cups (8 ounces) grated Emmentaler cheese

2 cups (8 ounces) shredded Gruyère cheese

1½ tablespoons cornstarch

1 cup white wine

1 tablespoon lemon juice

1½ tablespoons kirsch or cherry brandy

Pinch of ground nutmeg

French bread cubes, apple wedges, cocktail sausages

1. Rub the inside of a cast-iron fondue pot with garlic; discard clove.
2. Combine cheeses and cornstarch in a large bowl.
3. Combine wine and lemon juice in fondue pot over medium heat. Bring to a gentle simmer, decreasing heat to low, if necessary. Add cheese mixture gradually, stirring until cheese melts and mixture is smooth. Stir in kirsch and nutmeg.
4. Spear bread, apples, and sausages onto long fondue forks and dip into cheese mixture. Stir fondue occasionally.

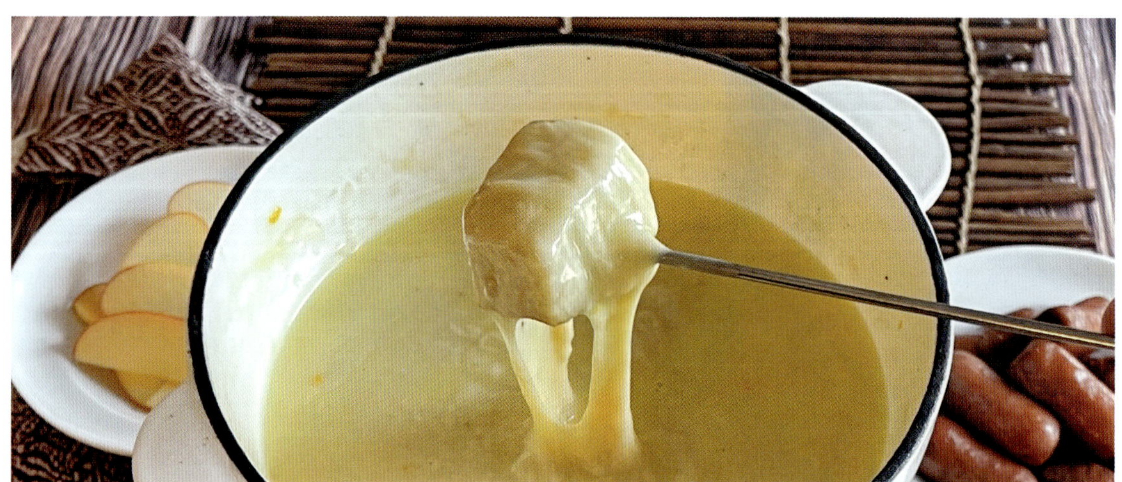

BEER CHEESE FONDUE

MAKES ABOUT 3 CUPS

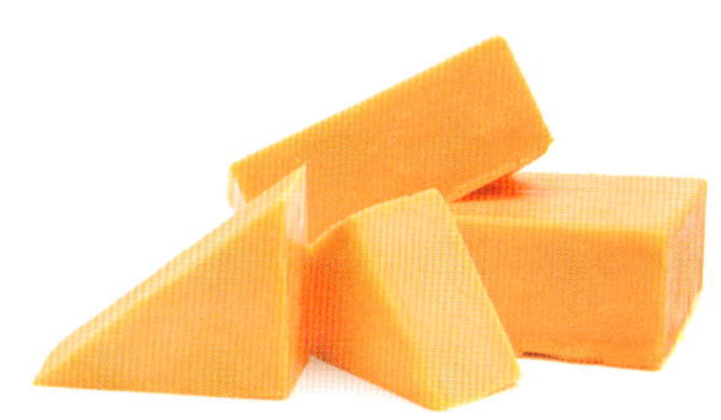

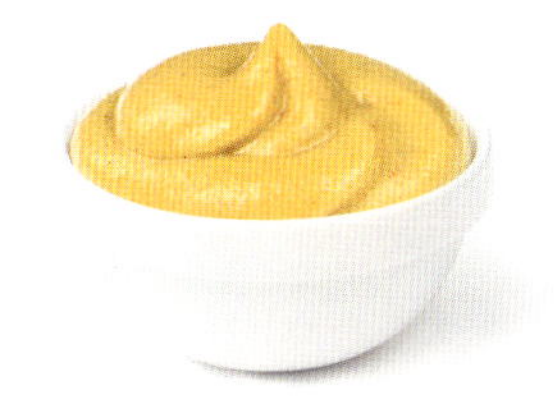

EQUIPMENT: *5½-cup cast-iron fondue pot or skillet*

PAN-SAVVY: *For easiest cleanup, use an enamel-coated pot or pan because the cheese tends to stick.*

2 cups (8 ounces) sharp cheddar cheese, coarsely grated

2 cups (8 ounces) Gruyère cheese, coarsely grated

2 tablespoons cornstarch

¼ teaspoon garlic powder

¼ teaspoon cayenne pepper

1 cup lager or pilsner beer

½ teaspoon Dijon mustard

½ teaspoon Worcestershire sauce

Soft pretzels, roasted baby potatoes, grilled sausage slices

Use freshly grated cheese because packaged cheese contains ingredients to keep it from clumping that can prevent smooth melting. I opt for a heavy cast-iron fondue pot that can be used on a cooktop, but you can also melt the ingredients in a well-seasoned skillet.

1 Combine cheeses, cornstarch, garlic powder, and cayenne pepper in a large bowl. Allow to reach room temperature.

2 Pour beer into fondue pot over medium heat. Bring beer to a simmer; add cheese and cook, stirring constantly, until melted and smooth. Stir in mustard and Worcestershire sauce.

3 Remove from cooktop and set fondue pot over low flame or a tea light. Serve with soft pretzels, roasted potatoes, and grilled sausage slices.

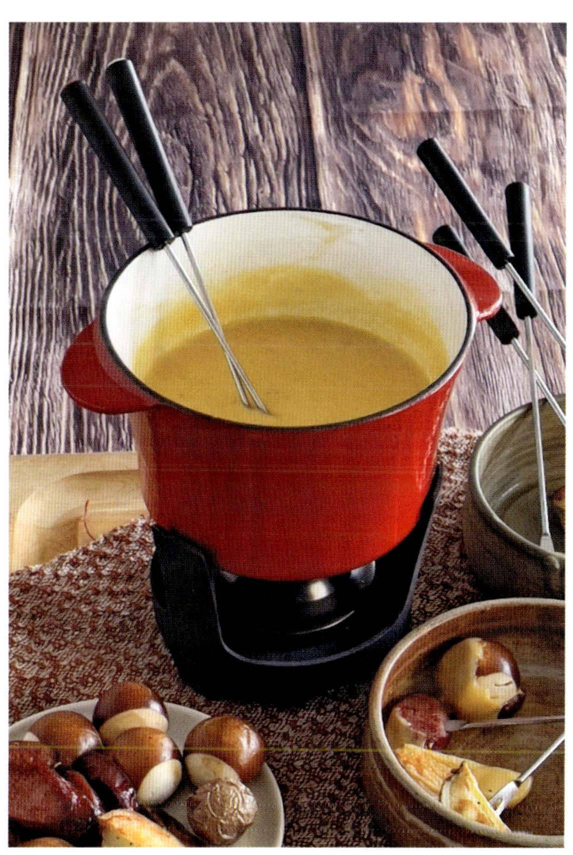

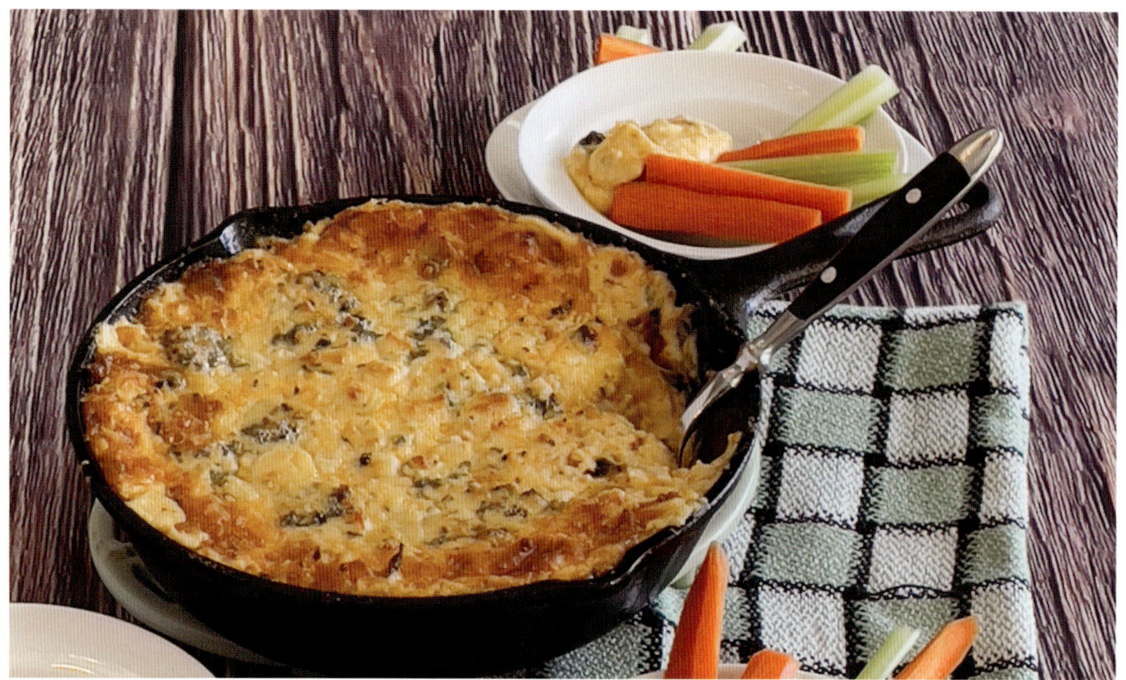

BUFFALO CHICKEN DIP

MAKES 4 CUPS (8 TO 10 SERVINGS)

EQUIPMENT: *12-inch cast-iron skillet*

PAN SAVVY: *This recipe just fits in a 10-inch skillet but may bubble over. If a 12-inch skillet is unavailable, go ahead and use a 10-inch, but place it on a baking sheet to catch spills.*

1 (8-ounce) package cream cheese, cubed

1 cup (4 ounces) shredded mozzarella cheese

½ (8-ounce) package sharp cheddar cheese, shredded

2 cups shredded rotisserie or roasted chicken

⅔ cup Homemade Buffalo Sauce (recipe at right) or store-bought buffalo sauce

⅓ cup store-bought ranch dressing

¼ cup crumbled blue cheese (optional)

Carrot and celery sticks

This high-flavor dish is very rich. Reduce the hot sauce by half if you prefer a milder dish (it's OK to taste before cooking because the chicken is already cooked).

1 Preheat oven to 375°.

2 Combine cream cheese, mozzarella, cheddar, chicken, Homemade Buffalo Sauce, and ranch dressing in a large bowl, stirring until well blended.

3 Spoon into a 12-inch cast-iron skillet. Sprinkle with blue cheese crumbles, if desired. Bake for 20 minutes or until hot and bubbly.

4 Serve with carrot and celery sticks.

Homemade Buffalo Sauce: Combine **⅓ cup hot sauce, ⅓ cup melted butter,** and **2 tablespoons light brown sugar** in a bowl, stirring until well blended. Makes ⅔ cup.

MAPLE-RYE STICKY WINGS

MAKES 4 SERVINGS

EQUIPMENT: *12-inch cast-iron skillet*

2½ pounds chicken wings
½ teaspoon salt
¼ teaspoon coarsely ground black pepper
2 tablespoons avocado oil, divided
⅓ cup thick tomato sauce or ketchup
¼ cup maple-flavored rye whiskey or other whiskey
¼ cup maple syrup
¼ cup apple cider vinegar
2 tablespoons low-sodium soy sauce
¼ cup firmly packed light brown sugar
1 teaspoon chili powder
½ teaspoon smoked paprika (optional)
1 chopped green onion

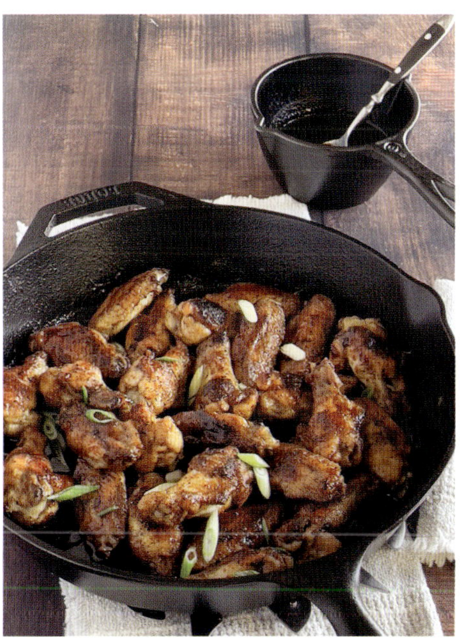

Maple-rye whiskey adds amazing flavor to this sticky sauce that you can also use over grilled chicken quarters or baby back ribs. My local distiller, Catoctin Creek, finished some of their product in maple syrup barrels, inspiring this sauce recipe. If you can't find it, check your area for local distillers with craft spirits. Be sure to cook the wings until they are almost done before adding the sauce—lengthy cooking will cause the sauce to burn. If you want to make these without alcohol, substitute an equal amount of broth plus a drop or two of maple extract.

---

1. Preheat oven to 400°.
2. If wings are not separated into drumettes and flats, remove wing tips on chicken and cut in half at joint. Sprinkle wings with salt and pepper.
3. Heat 1 tablespoon oil in a 12-inch cast-iron skillet over medium-high heat. Add half of wings and cook for 2 minutes on each side or until browned. (Cook in batches so outside browns. Wings will steam if crowded.) Repeat with remaining 1 tablespoon oil and remaining half of wings. Place all wings in skillet.
4. Transfer skillet to oven and bake, turning occasionally, for 30 minutes or until wings are cooked through.
5. Meanwhile, to make sauce, combine tomato sauce, rye whiskey, maple syrup, vinegar, soy sauce, brown sugar, chili powder, and, if desired, paprika in a saucepan over medium-high heat. Bring to a boil, reduce heat, and simmer for 5 to 7 minutes or until mixture is reduced and slightly thickened.
6. Spoon half of sauce carefully over wings, tossing to coat. Bake for 5 minutes or until golden brown. Sprinkle with green onion and serve with remaining sauce.

SKILLET NACHOS

MAKES 6 SERVINGS

EQUIPMENT: *12-inch cast-iron skillet*

PAN SAVVY: *A large skillet works well, so the ingredients are well distributed, but you can snuggle the nachos into a smaller 10-inch skillet by pressing down and gently crushing the chips a little bit. You can also arrange the nachos on a cast-iron pizza plate, keeping the ingredients in the center.*

1 tablespoon avocado or extra-virgin olive oil

8 ounces meatless crumbles or lean ground beef

6 ounces soy chorizo or other chorizo

10 cups white, yellow, or blue tortilla chips

1 cup canned black beans, rinsed and drained

2 cups (8 ounces) shredded cheddar cheese

1 cup (4 ounces) shredded pepper-Jack or Monterey Jack cheese

¼ cup sliced pickled jalapeño peppers

⅓ cup sliced black olives

Charred Tomato Salsa (page 46) or store-bought salsa

Sour cream

Prepared guacamole (optional)

Chopped fresh cilantro

Layering the ingredients in the skillet helps ensure the best bite every time! Enjoy this flavorful, fun appetizer when you're cheering on your team.

Get deliciously crispy nachos by baking them in your cast-iron skillet. I prefer soy-based chorizo and meatless crumbles. They are just as flavorful, and my vegetarian friends can dive right in. If you're using ground beef and pork chorizo, skip the oil and drain any excess fat after browning. There is a lot of wiggle room in this recipe. You can add other ingredients like shredded chicken or grilled veggies, as long as they fit in the skillet!

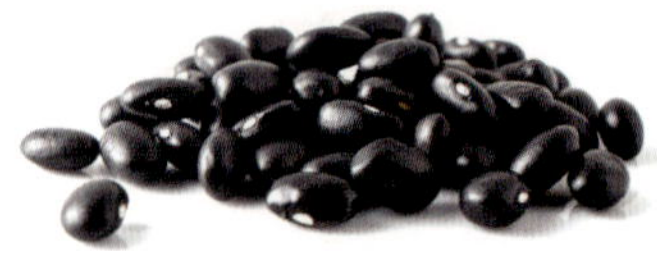

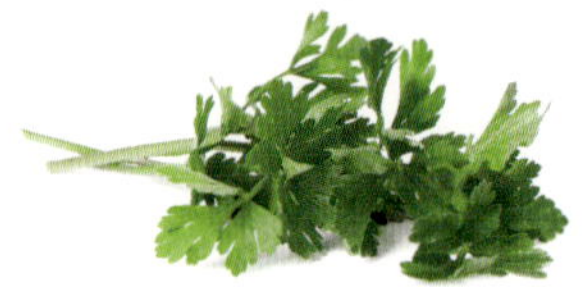

1. Preheat oven to 350°.
2. Heat oil in a 12-inch cast-iron skillet over medium heat. Add beef and chorizo, and cook, stirring frequently, until browned and crumbly. Transfer meat mixture to a large bowl.
3. Arrange half of tortilla chips in bottom of skillet (no need to wipe skillet clean first). Sprinkle half of meat mixture, half of black beans, half of cheeses, half of jalapeños, and half of olives over chips. Repeat with remaining half of chips, meat, beans, cheeses, jalapeños, and olives.
4. Bake for 10 to 12 minutes or until cheeses melt and mixture is hot. Serve with salsa, sour cream, and guacamole, if desired. Sprinkle with chopped fresh cilantro.

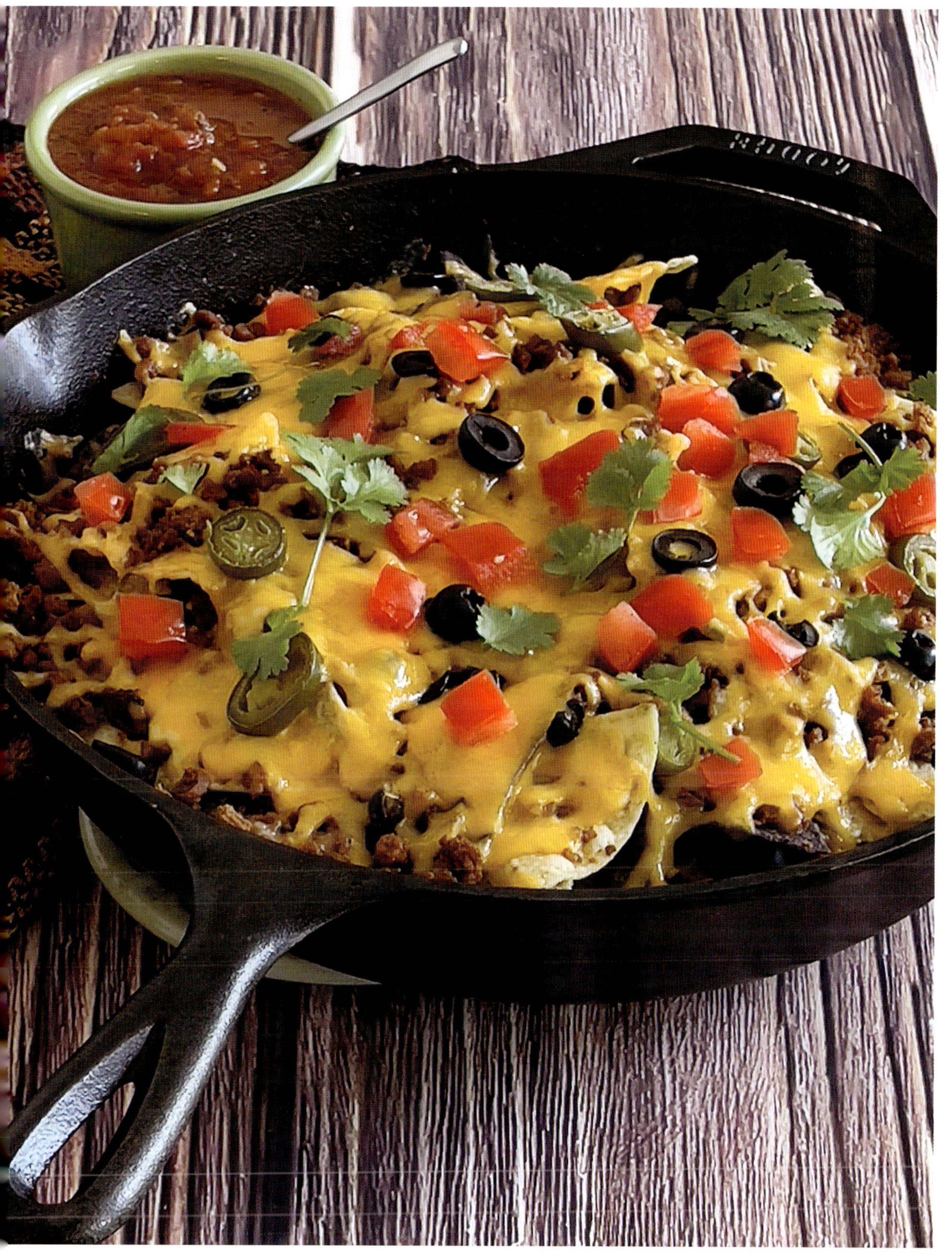
LODGE

CHEESE-STUFFED ARANCINI

MAKES 2 DOZEN

EQUIPMENT: *Small Dutch oven for cooking arborio rice; Dutch oven for frying*

PAN SAVVY: *Because the arancini are round and almost 2 inches in diameter, I prefer a Dutch oven for frying. It holds the oil with sides high enough to reduce splattering on my cooktop. If you use a skillet, make sure it's at least 2½ inches deep. Only fry a couple of arancini at a time, so the oil doesn't spill over the side of the skillet.*

1 cup uncooked arborio rice
3½ cups vegetable or chicken broth
1 tablespoon salted butter
½ cup shredded Parmesan cheese
4 ounces provolone or Manchego cheese
⅓ cup all-purpose flour
2 large eggs
1 tablespoon water
1 cup seasoned panko breadcrumbs
½ teaspoon fine sea salt
Vegetable oil
Pizza Sauce (page 109) or store-bought marinara, warmed
Garnishes: freshly grated or shredded Parmesan cheese, chopped fresh parsley

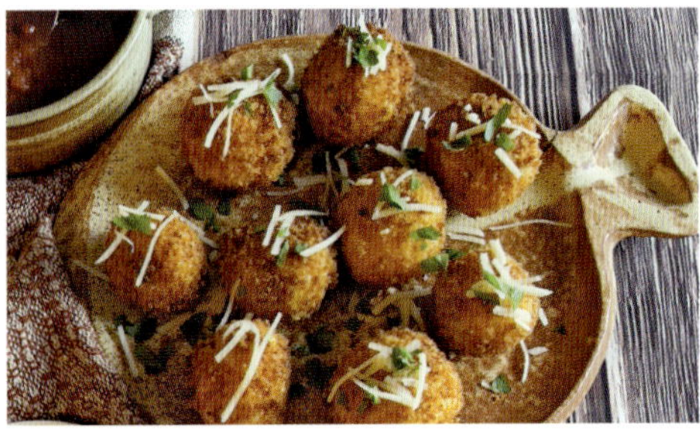

These can't-stop-at-one appetizers begin with a recipe for risotto. While you can simply use plain cooked risotto as the base, the recipe tastes better if the risotto has a bit of flavor from broth. Substitute any firm cheese you wish. The breading technique is easy but tedious. The uncooked arancini freeze beautifully, so make and freeze ahead—they're not only ideal for parties but also when you just want to enjoy a couple at a time.

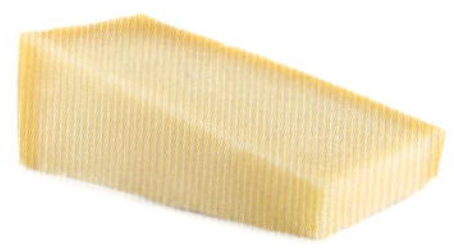

1. Cook rice according to package directions using vegetable broth. After rice is cooked, add butter and Parmesan cheese, stirring until well blended. Transfer to a rimmed baking sheet, spreading out to a thin layer. Cover and refrigerate for 1 hour or until completely chilled (or overnight).
2. Cut provolone cheese evenly into 24 cubes. Divide chilled risotto into 24 portions. Wrap each portion around 1 cube of cheese to form a small ball.
3. Place flour in a shallow bowl. Combine eggs and 1 tablespoon water in a second shallow bowl. Combine breadcrumbs and salt in a third shallow bowl. Roll balls in flour to coat, then coat with egg mixture, then roll evenly in breadcrumb mixture. (Arancini may be frozen up to a month at this point. Thaw completely before frying.)
4. Pour oil in a Dutch oven to a depth of 2½ to 3 inches. Heat to 350°.
5. Fry arancini, in batches, turning occasionally, for 3 to 5 minutes or until golden brown. Remove with a slotted spoon and let drain. Serve warm with Pizza Sauce. Garnish, if desired.

BAKED BRIE WITH CHUTNEY

MAKES 6 SERVINGS

EQUIPMENT: *8-inch cast-iron skillet*

PAN SAVVY: *Use a 10- or 12-inch skillet if doubling recipe.*

1 (8-ounce) round or piece of Brie cheese

1 sheet refrigerated (or frozen and thawed) puff pastry

¼ cup prepared mango chutney or raspberry jam

2 to 3 tablespoons Caramelized Onions (page 115)

2 tablespoons chopped pecans

2 tablespoons cooked and crumbled bacon

1 large egg, lightly beaten

2 teaspoons water

Gingersnaps, baguette slices, crackers

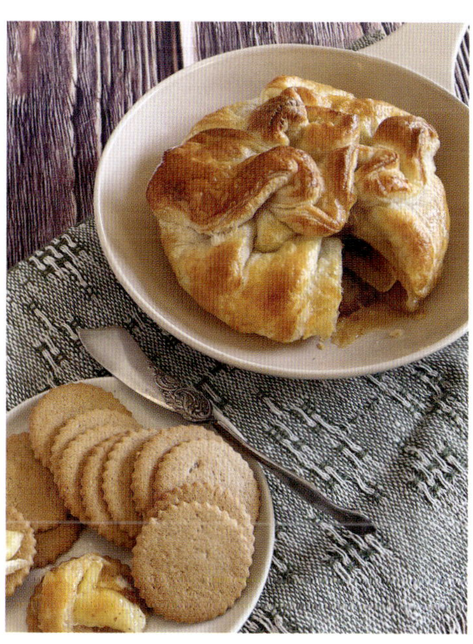

This recipe is best with young, firm Brie that is usually some of the least expensive in the market. For a semi-savory dessert, serve with thin gingerbread cookies—an amazing combination even with bacon. For parties, you can double the chutney and use larger (18-ounce) wheels of Brie found at big-box member stores (like Costco), but the puff pastry will not wrap completely around unless you patch some of the pieces.

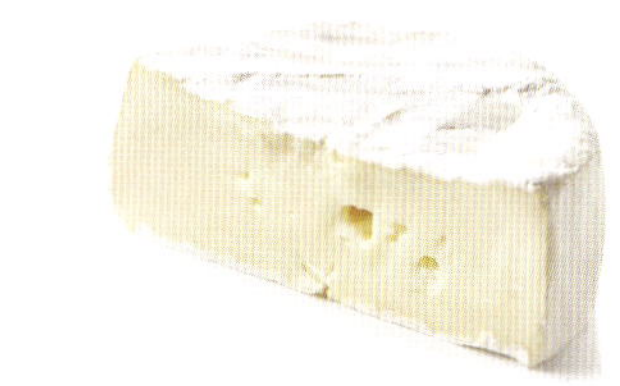

1 Preheat oven to 400°.

2 For whole-rind Brie: Place Brie on a cutting board. Cut a circle on top of cheese, about ¼ inch from edge. Cut away inner circle of rind, leaving a rim of rind around top edge of cheese. Set cheese aside.

3 Place pastry on a lightly floured surface. If you want to add decorations to top of pastry, cut a few shapes of small leaves or strips near a corner, making sure pastry is still large enough to fit around cheese.

4 Place reserved cheese in center of pastry. Spoon chutney in center and top with Caramelized Onions, pecans, and bacon. Wrap pastry around Brie, pressing seams of pastry to seal.

5 Whisk together egg and 2 teaspoons water. Brush pastry with egg mixture; add any scrap pastry pieces for decoration.

6 Carefully place wrapped cheese in skillet. Bake for 25 minutes or until puffed and golden brown. Serve with toasted gingersnaps, baguette slices, or crackers.

COUNTRY PÂTÉ

MAKES 15 TO 20 SERVINGS

EQUIPMENT: *enamel-coated cast-iron terrine*

PAN SAVVY: *Because the appetizer cooks in a water bath, use an enamel-coated terrine dish. Bare cast iron shouldn't soak in hot water.*

- 2 tablespoons salted or unsalted butter
- 1 large onion, chopped
- ¼ teaspoon crushed red pepper flakes
- 3 garlic cloves, minced
- 2 teaspoons fine sea salt
- 1½ teaspoons dried thyme
- 1 teaspoon coarsely ground black pepper
- ½ teaspoon ground allspice
- ½ teaspoon dried sage leaves or ¼ teaspoon ground sage
- 3 tablespoons Cognac or brandy
- 2 large eggs, lightly beaten
- 1 pound ground pork or pork sausage, removed from casing
- ½ pound ground beef
- 1 pound boneless, skinless chicken thighs, finely chopped or coarsely ground
- 3 ounces (¼- to ½-inch-thick) ham steak
- 4 ounces thinly sliced prosciutto
- ½ cup pistachios
- French bread, coarse-grain mustard, cornichons (tiny pickles)

This rustic, coarse-textured spread is cooked in a pan called a terrine. Country Pâté features robust flavors with visible pieces of meat that contrast with the consistency of traditional spreads. Terrines are served in slices.

---

1. Melt butter in a skillet over medium heat. Add onion and pepper flakes. Cook, stirring occasionally, for 7 to 10 minutes or until very tender. Add garlic, salt, thyme, black pepper, allspice, and sage; cook for 3 minutes. Stir in Cognac; cook until almost evaporated. Cool slightly.
2. Whisk eggs in a large bowl. Add pork, beef, and chicken, stirring (with hands, if necessary) until well blended. Fold in onion mixture.
3. Cut ham steak into long, ¼-inch-wide strips.
4. Preheat oven to 350°. Grease a 1½-quart (about 13x4-inch) enamel-coated cast-iron terrine with butter.
5. Line inside of terrine with slices of prosciutto, letting ends hang over edges if long enough.
6. Spoon in half of meat mixture, pressing down. Add ham in rows; top with pistachios. Spoon in remaining meat mixture. Cover with any remaining prosciutto slices, tucking in edges.
7. Cover terrine with a heavy ovenproof lid or wrap top tightly with aluminum foil. Place terrine inside a large roasting pan. Add boiling water to pan until it reaches halfway up the side of the terrine.
8. Bake for 1½ to 2 hours or until a meat thermometer reads 155°. Carefully remove terrine from water and transfer to a rimmed baking sheet. Remove lid; drain excess oil. Fold a large piece of foil several times until it just fits on top of pâté mixture inside terrine. Place 2 or 3 cans of food on top of pâté to weigh it down. Refrigerate for several hours until completely chilled.
9. Remove cans and foil. Run a knife around edges. Invert onto a platter. Use a spatula to softly scrape away any congealed fat or oil around top and sides. To serve, cut into slices and place on a charcuterie board with crusty bread, coarse mustard, and cornichons. Cover and refrigerate leftovers up to a week.

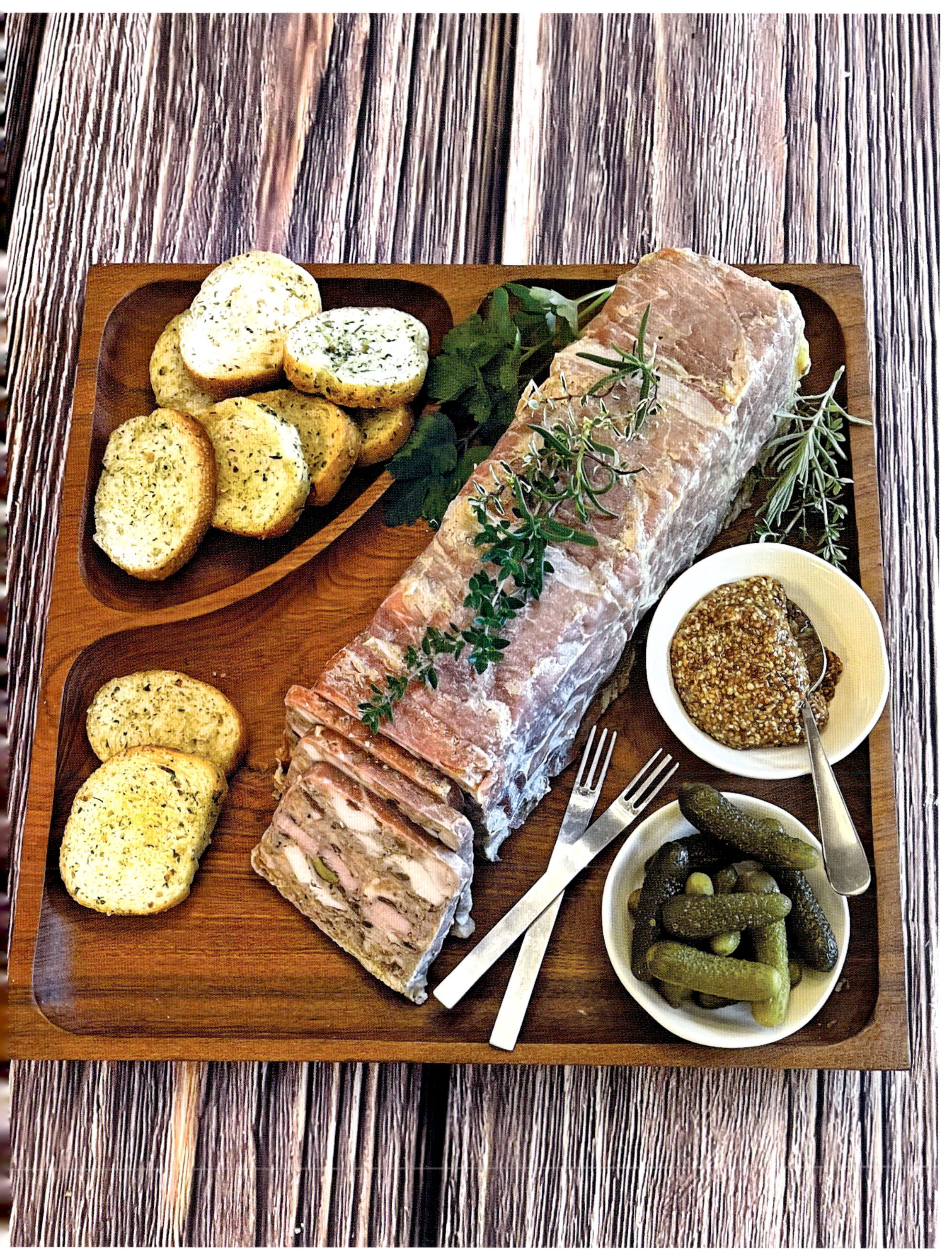

INDIVIDUAL SEAFOOD AU GRATINS

MAKES 4 SERVINGS

EQUIPMENT: *4 (1-cup) au gratin pans*

PAN SAVVY: *You can use a variety of options if you don't have au gratin pans, including a 6- (shown in photo) or 8-inch skillet, fajita pan, or 5-inch cookie skillet (shown in photo).*

3 tablespoons salted butter, divided

2 shallots, minced

½ cup white wine

1 pound medium-size peeled and deveined shrimp

1 pound bay scallops

2 tablespoons all-purpose flour

⅓ cup whole milk

Pinch of cayenne pepper

1 cup (4 ounces) shredded Gruyère, mild cheddar, or Swiss cheese, divided

2 teaspoons chopped fresh herbs, such as chives, thyme, or parsley

Toasted baguette slices

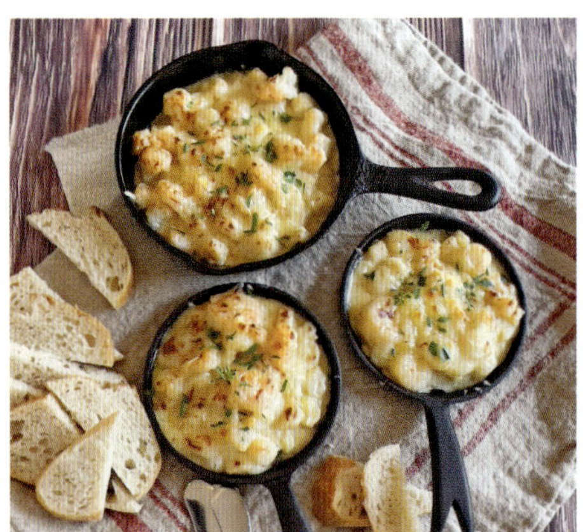

This appetizer feels fancy, but it's quite easy to prepare—especially on the spur of the moment—because you can use frozen-and-thawed seafood. Arrange the shrimp and scallops in a single layer on a wire rack set within a sheet pan. As the seafood thaws, excess liquid drains away. Small or medium-size shrimp and bay scallops are less expensive. If you're using large shrimp, slice it in half lengthwise; for large sea scallops, quarter them after removing the tough "foot" on the side.

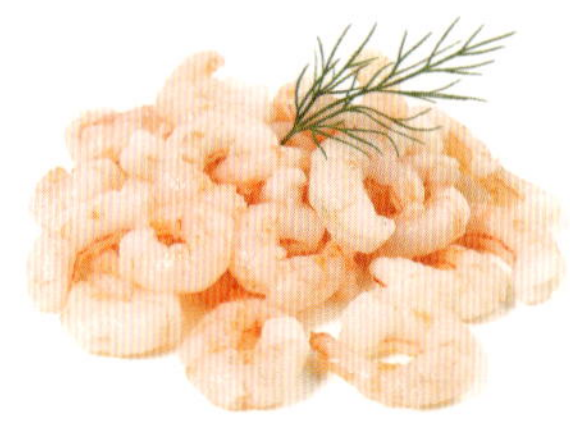

1. Melt 1 tablespoon butter in a large cast-iron skillet over medium heat. Add shallots and cook, stirring frequently, for 3 minutes. Add wine, shrimp, and scallops. Cook for 3 to 5 minutes or until seafood is done. Drain, reserving ⅔ cup cooking liquid in a bowl. Transfer seafood to a plate.
2. Heat remaining 2 tablespoons butter in same skillet. Add flour and cook, stirring constantly, for 1 minute. Whisk in reserved ⅔ cup cooking liquid, milk, and cayenne pepper. Cook, stirring constantly, for 2 minutes or until smooth and thickened. Stir in half of cheese. Cook, stirring constantly, until cheese melts. Fold in seafood.
3. Spoon seafood mixture into 4 lightly buttered (1-cup) cast-iron gratin pans (each serving is about ¾ cup), if available; otherwise, spoon into an 8-inch cast-iron skillet. Sprinkle evenly with remaining half of cheese.
4. Broil for 3 minutes or until golden brown and bubbly. Sprinkle with herbs, and serve with baguette slices.

HOT CRANBERRY-APPLE CIDER

MAKES 12 CUPS

Enjoy a hot cider drink on a chilly evening. The longer it simmers, the more flavorful the spices become. Adults can add a tablespoon or two of orange liqueur or spiced rum to each serving.

EQUIPMENT: *5- to 7-quart enamel-coated Dutch oven*

PAN SAVVY: *Use an enamel-coated Dutch oven because acidic liquids may leach metallic flavors from an uncoated cast-iron pot. In addition, the brightly colored enamel sets a more festive table.*

- 1 (64-ounce) bottle apple cider
- 1 (32-ounce) bottle unsweetened cranberry juice
- ¾ cup lightly packed brown sugar
- 6 cinnamon sticks
- 4 whole star anise (optional)
- ½ teaspoon whole cloves
- ¼ teaspoon ground nutmeg
- 1 orange, sliced
- 1 apple, sliced
- 1 cup fresh (or frozen and thawed) cranberries

1. Combine cider; cranberry juice; brown sugar; cinnamon sticks; anise, if desired; cloves; and nutmeg in an enamel-coated Dutch oven, stirring until well blended. Add orange slices, apple slices, and cranberries.
2. Cook over medium-low heat for at least 1 hour, stirring occasionally.

DUTCH OVEN HOT CHOCOLATE

MAKES 5½ CUPS

EQUIPMENT: *3- to 5-quart Dutch oven*

3 cups whole milk

1 cup half-and-half

⅓ cup granulated sugar

¼ cup firmly packed light brown sugar

⅓ cup unsweetened cocoa powder

8 ounces semisweet chocolate, chopped

2 teaspoons vanilla extract

Mini-marshmallows (optional)

Perfect for a party, this rich-and-satisfying hot beverage is ideally made in an enamel-coated Dutch oven, especially if you're keeping it warm for a few hours. The heavy cast iron will hold its heat for a long while, so keep it on low to ensure the mixture doesn't boil. You can double the recipe for larger crowds—just cook the mixture low and slow.

1. Combine milk and half-and-half in a Dutch oven over medium-low to medium heat. Cook until hot and steamy but not boiling.
2. Whisk together granulated sugar, brown sugar, and cocoa powder in a small bowl. Whisk sugar mixture into milk mixture. Cook, stirring frequently, for 3 minutes or until sugar dissolves.
3. Stir in chopped chocolate and vanilla. Cook, stirring frequently, for 5 minutes or until chocolate melts and mixture is smooth and creamy. Cover to retain heat, or keep on very low heat, stirring occasionally. Top servings with mini-marshmallows, if desired.

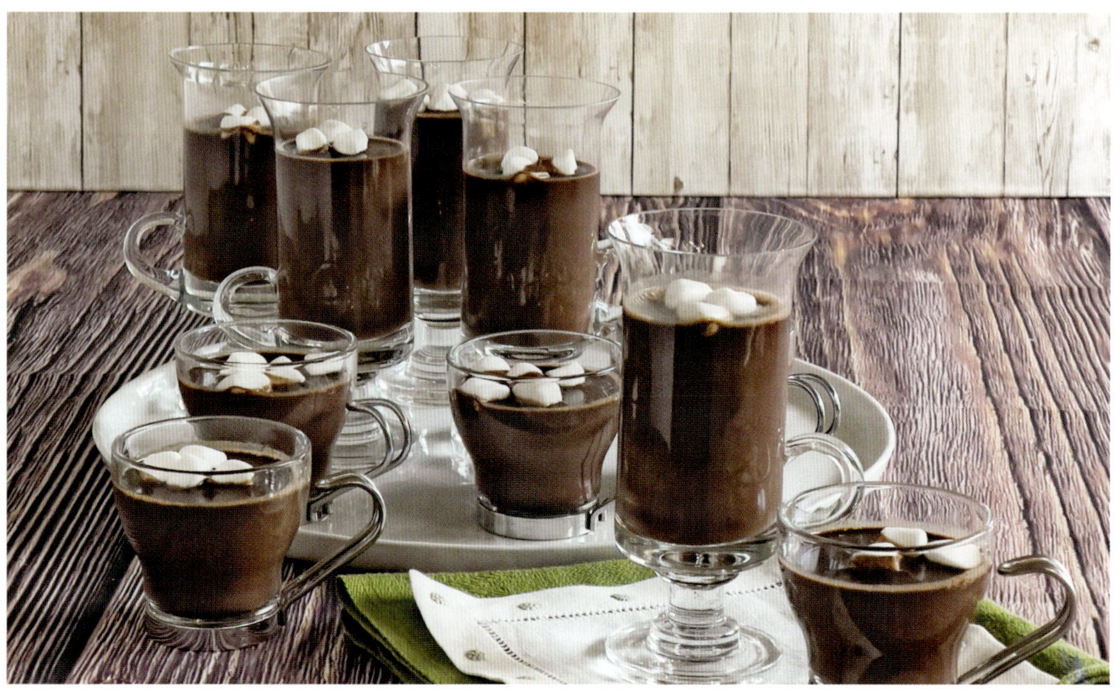

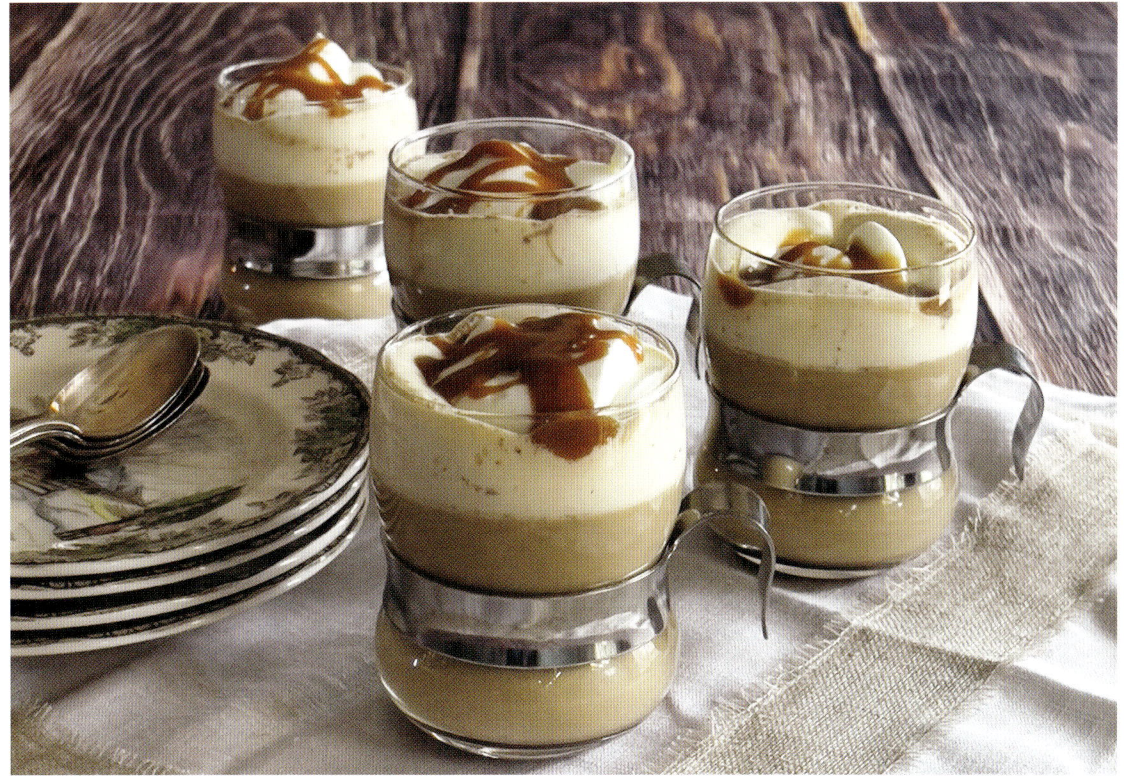

GINGERBREAD LATTE

MAKES 8 CUPS

This warm, spicy, and comforting hot drink starts with espresso, making it delightful on fall mornings. You can also use very strong coffee or even instant espresso powder in hot water. Topped with whipped cream and caramel sauce, it makes an uplifting dessert on winter evenings.

EQUIPMENT: *5-quart Dutch oven*

6 cups whole milk
2 cups espresso or strong brewed coffee
⅓ cup molasses
½ split vanilla bean or 1 teaspoon vanilla extract
½ cup firmly packed light brown sugar
2 teaspoons ground ginger
1 teaspoon ground cinnamon
¼ teaspoon ground nutmeg
⅛ teaspoon ground cloves
Toppings: whipped cream, caramel syrup

1. Combine milk, coffee, molasses, and vanilla bean in a Dutch oven over medium-low heat.
2. Whisk in brown sugar, ginger, cinnamon, nutmeg, and cloves. Cook, stirring frequently, until sugar dissolves.
3. Reduce heat to low. Cook for 45 minutes to allow flavors to infuse thoroughly (do not boil).
4. Pour into mugs and serve with desired toppings.

HOT RUM TEA PUNCH

MAKES 7 CUPS, STRAINED

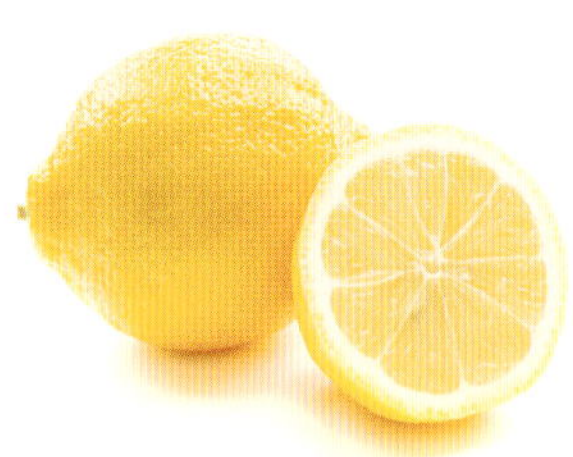

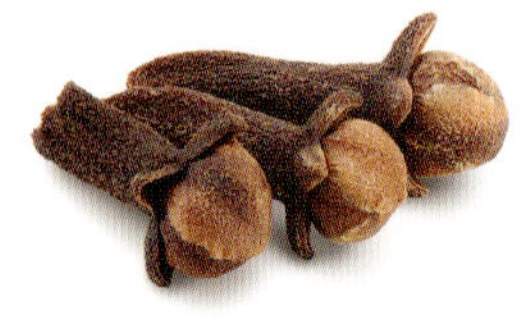

EQUIPMENT: *5- to 7-quart enamel-coated Dutch oven*

PAN SAVVY: *Because the citrus can react with iron, use an enamel-coated Dutch oven for best results.*

6 cups water
4 Earl Grey or black tea bags
3 hibiscus tea bags
2 oranges, sliced
1 lemon, sliced
1 inch fresh peeled gingerroot, sliced
3 cinnamon sticks
½ teaspoon whole cloves
½ cup rum, dark rum, or spiced rum
½ cup orange-flavored liqueur
¼ cup fresh lemon juice
½ cup granulated sugar
Garnishes: cinnamon sticks, orange or lemon slices

Scent your house with this tempting tea-based hot punch infused with ginger, cinnamon, and cloves. I like the citrusy bergamot flavor of Earl Grey tea, but black works too. Hibiscus tea is beautifully pink and tart. Add more sugar if you like a sweeter beverage.

1 Heat 6 cups water in a large enamel-coated Dutch oven over medium-high heat until water just begins to simmer. Add tea bags, orange and lemon slices, ginger, cinnamon, and cloves. Reduce heat to low and steep for 5 minutes. Remove and discard tea bags.

2 Stir in rum, liqueur, lemon juice, and sugar. Cook over low heat until hot and steaming. Garnish each serving, if desired.

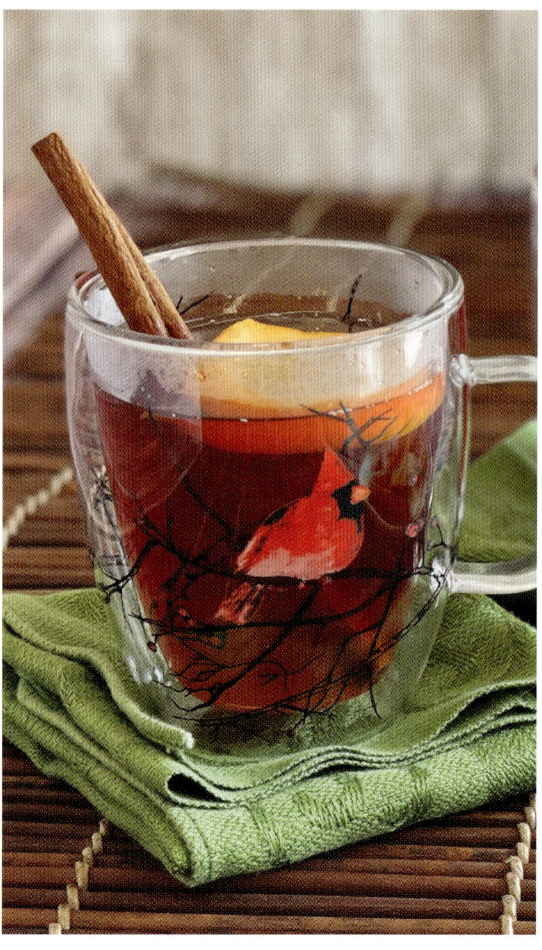

WASSAIL

MAKES ABOUT 13 CUPS

EQUIPMENT: *7-quart enamel-coated Dutch oven*

PAN SAVVY: *While adding delicious tartness to the beverage, the citrus can react with iron. Use an enamel-coated Dutch oven for best results.*

Wassail has a lot of similarities to mulled wine—cinnamon and cloves are usually both added. Wassail uses cider as a base, while mulled wine starts with red wine. Both are served warm and typically enjoyed during the winter when days are short and cold. Make this beverage an hour or more before guests arrive to fill your house with a spicy, tempting aroma. I use an enamel-coated cast-iron pot to avoid any reactions between the acidic apple cider and the metal.

1 (64-ounce) container apple cider
1 (750-ml) bottle white wine
1 (12-ounce) can frozen lemonade concentrate, thawed
1 orange, thickly sliced
½ cup firmly packed light brown sugar
4 (3-inch) cinnamon sticks
12 whole cloves
Garnishes: cinnamon sticks, halved apple slices, halved orange slices

1. Combine apple cider, wine, lemonade, orange slices, brown sugar, cinnamon, and cloves in a Dutch oven or soup pot over medium heat.
2. Bring mixture just to a boil. Immediately reduce heat and simmer over low heat for 30 to 60 minutes. Garnish each serving, if desired.

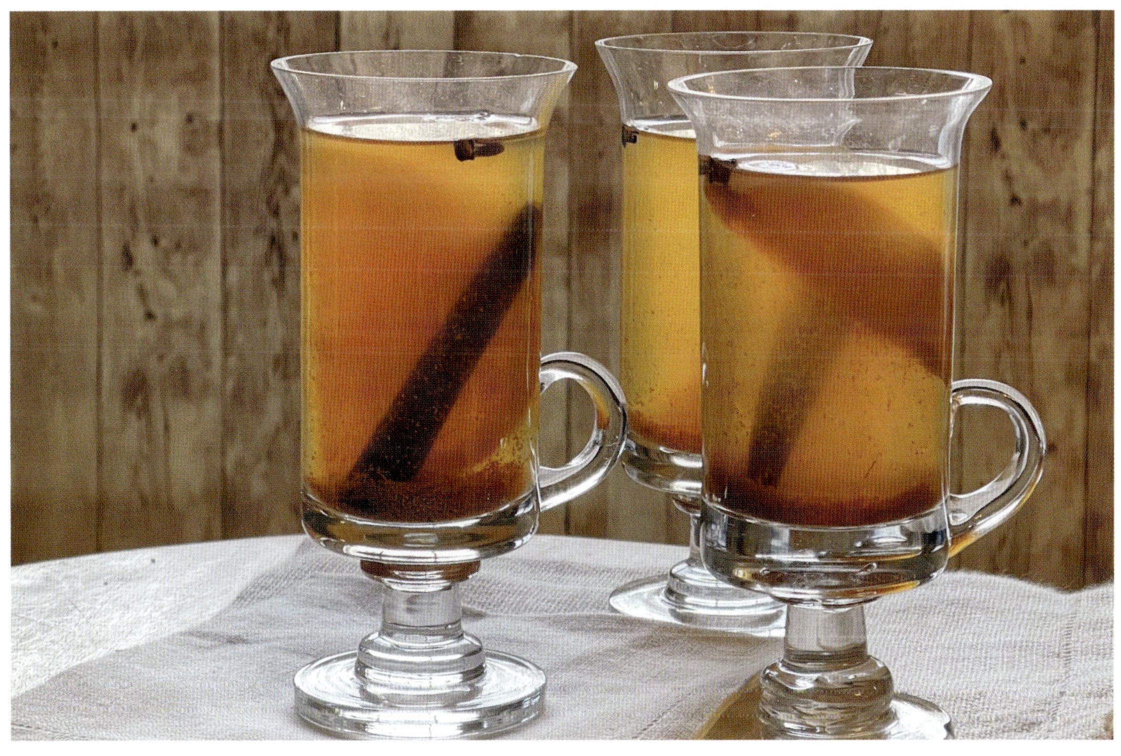

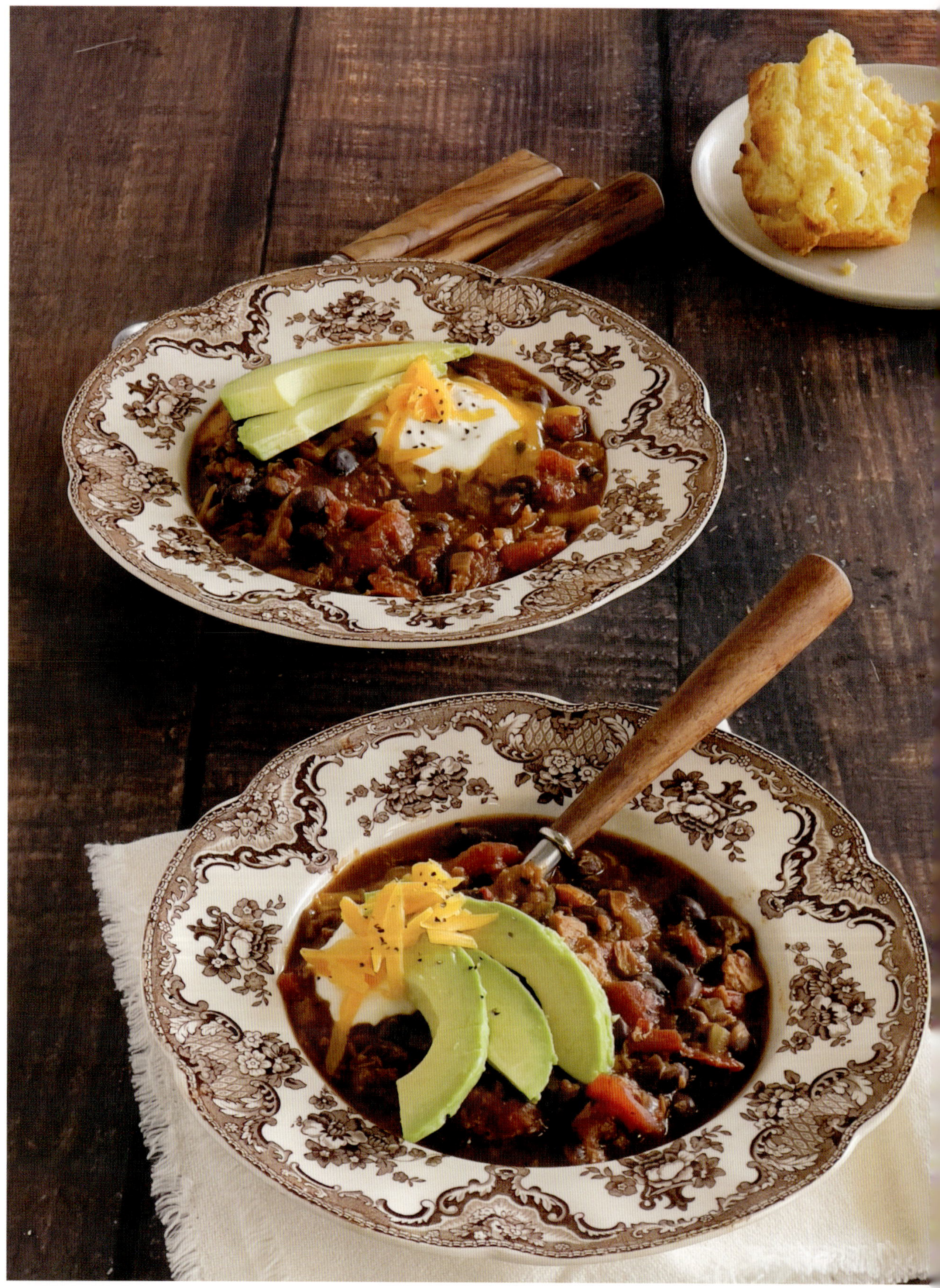

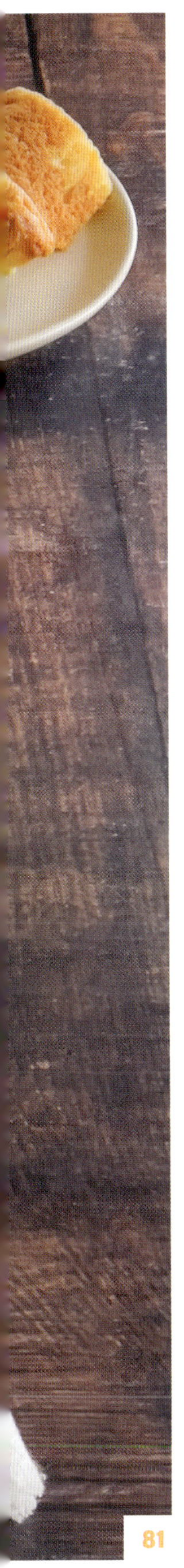
81

SOUPS and STEWS

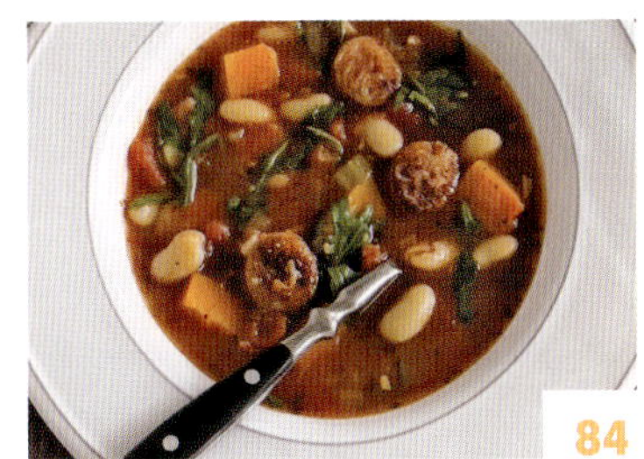
84

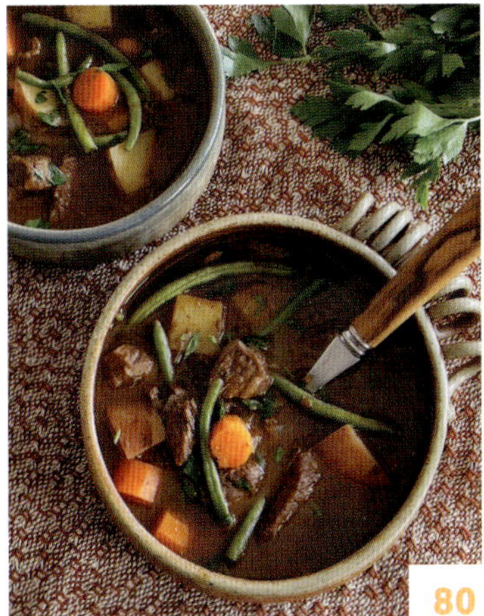
80

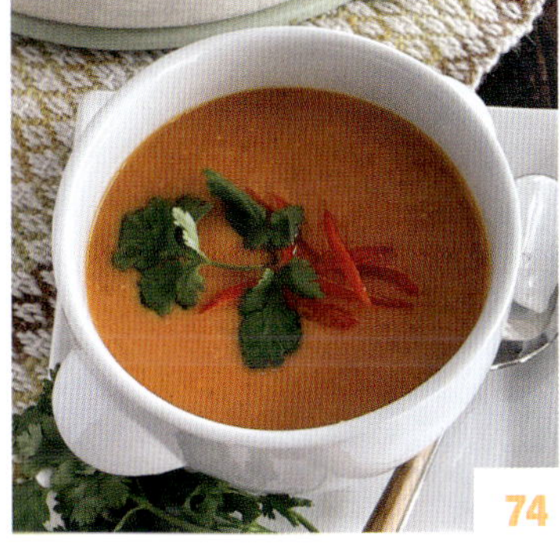
74

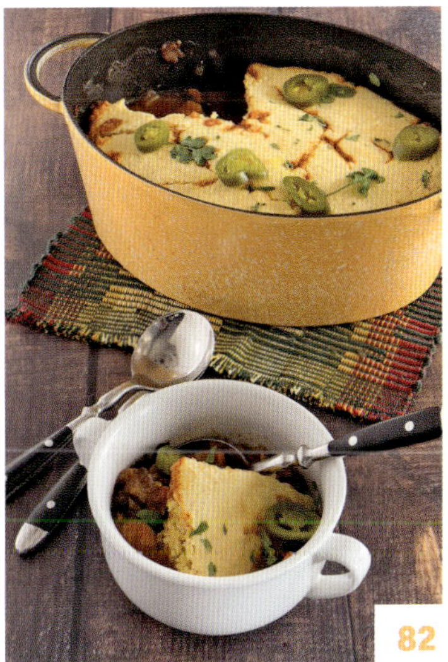
82

NEW YEAR'S DAY BLACK-EYED PEA-AND-GREENS SOUP

MAKES 10 CUPS

EQUIPMENT: *3- to 5- quart Dutch oven (cocotte)*

PAN SAVVY: *Many cast-iron Dutch ovens are enamel coated. This is a benefit because a lot of soups and stews are tomato based and require lengthy cooking times. The other reason I prefer them is that their cheery enamel colors make them pretty enough for buffet serving.*

2 tablespoons extra-virgin olive oil
12 ounces smoked sausage, sliced
1 onion, chopped
1 bell pepper (any color), chopped
1 celery rib, finely chopped
4 garlic cloves, minced
4 cups chicken broth
2 (15-ounce) cans black-eyed peas, rinsed and drained
1 (15-ounce) can fire-roasted tomatoes, undrained
2 teaspoons dried Italian seasoning
¼ to ½ teaspoon crushed red pepper flakes
1 (10- to 12-ounce) bunch Swiss chard or kale, chopped (about 4 lightly packed cups)
1 tablespoon apple cider vinegar
Basic Skillet Cornbread (page 16)

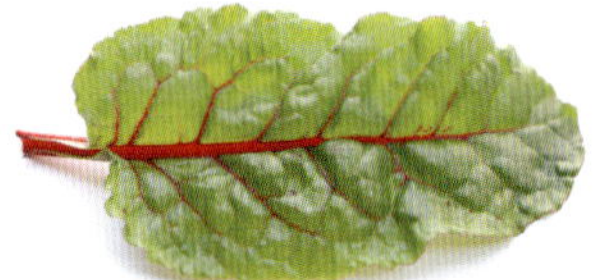

Popular in the South, black-eyed peas, pork, and collard greens are traditional New Year's Day foods that symbolize good luck, prosperity, and wealth. It's a happy, delicious superstition that I indulge in every year. In this recipe, I've taken liberties with shortcuts using canned beans and Swiss chard because dried beans and the traditional greens are time-consuming to cook.

1 Heat oil in a Dutch oven over medium heat. Add sausage and cook, stirring frequently, for 5 to 7 minutes or until browned. Transfer to a plate and set sausage aside.

2 Add onion, bell pepper, celery, and garlic to pan. Cook, stirring frequently, for 5 to 7 minutes or until vegetables are almost tender.

3 Stir in broth, black-eyed peas, tomatoes, seasoning, and pepper flakes. Return reserved sausage to pot.

4 Bring broth mixture to a boil. Reduce heat and simmer for 10 minutes. Add chard and vinegar. Simmer for 7 minutes or until wilted. Serve with cornbread.

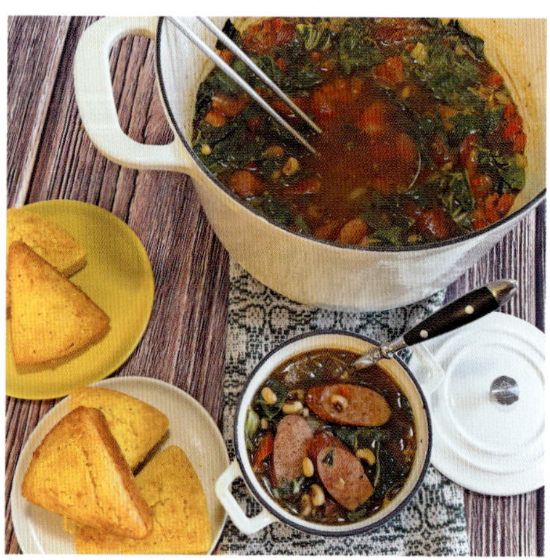

KITCHEN SINK VEGETABLE SOUP

MAKES 9 CUPS

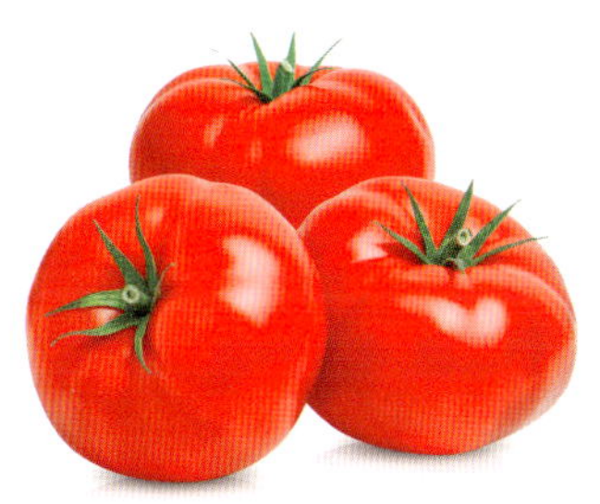

EQUIPMENT: *5- to 7-quart Dutch oven*

2 tablespoons olive oil
1 large onion, chopped
3 garlic cloves, minced
2 carrots, chopped
2 celery ribs, chopped
1 red, yellow, or orange bell pepper, chopped
5 ripe medium-size tomatoes, seeded and chopped
¼ cup tomato paste
4 cups vegetable broth
2 teaspoons dried Italian seasoning
1 teaspoon salt
½ teaspoon coarsely ground black pepper
1½ cups baby green beans, halved
1 small zucchini, chopped
2 cups fresh baby spinach
1 to 2 tablespoons chopped fresh basil, parsley, or cilantro (optional)
Southwestern Cornsticks (page 18)

I first started thinking of the ingredients in this soup as "everything but the kitchen sink" because of the wide variety of vegetables in it—really what's randomly growing in the garden. I like making this when there are a few things here and there that I can harvest. Feel free to skip or substitute any of the veggies. Before serving, I'll stir in a tablespoon or so of whatever fresh herb is growing well in my container garden. It's optional, but it adds a lovely fresh lift to the soup.

1. Heat oil in a Dutch oven over medium heat. Add onion and cook, stirring frequently, for 5 minutes. Add garlic and cook, stirring frequently, for 1 minute.
2. Add carrots, celery, and bell pepper. Cook, stirring frequently, for 7 to 10 minutes or until vegetables begin to soften.
3. Stir in tomatoes, tomato paste, broth, seasoning, salt, black pepper, green beans, and zucchini. Bring soup to a boil, reduce heat, and simmer for 15 to 20 minutes. Stir in spinach. Cook for 5 minutes. Stir in fresh basil, if desired. Serve with Southwestern Cornsticks.

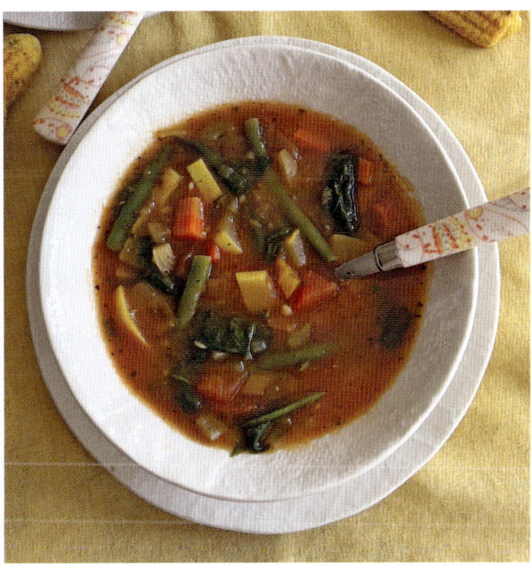

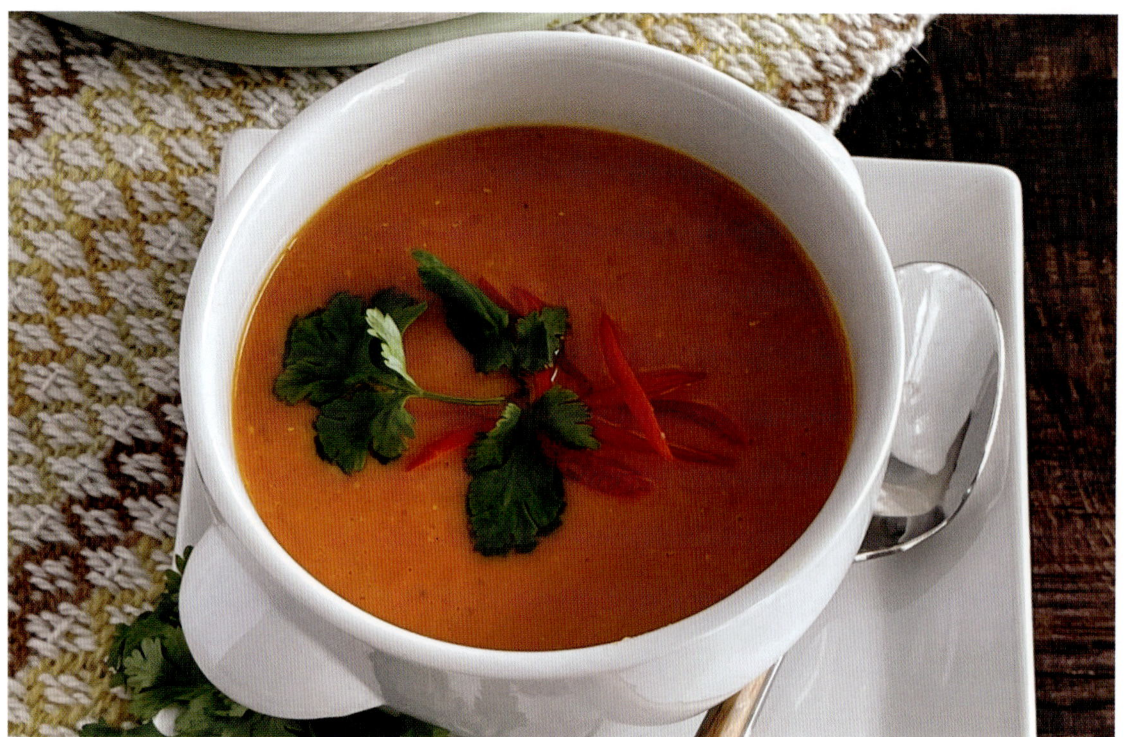

THAI PUMPKIN-AND-LENTIL SOUP

MAKES 8 CUPS

EQUIPMENT: *5-quart Dutch oven (cocotte)*

1 tablespoon extra-virgin olive oil
½ small onion, finely chopped
2 teaspoons freshly grated ginger
2 garlic cloves, minced
4 cups vegetable or chicken broth
1 (15-ounce) can pumpkin
1 (13.66-ounce) can coconut milk
1 cup uncooked split red lentils, rinsed
2 tablespoons red curry paste
2 teaspoons lime juice
1½ teaspoons fine sea salt
Garnishes: fresh cilantro, sliced red pepper

Red curry paste is a spicy, aromatic blend of chilies, garlic, lemongrass, lime, and a variety of other spices. It can be very spicy, but the pumpkin and coconut milk help diffuse the flavor, making the soup warm and comforting.

1. Heat oil in a Dutch oven over medium heat. Add onion and cook, stirring frequently, for 3 minutes or until tender. Add ginger and garlic; cook for 1 minute.
2. Stir in broth, pumpkin, coconut milk, lentils, curry paste, lime juice, and salt.
3. Bring mixture to a boil, reduce heat, and simmer for 25 minutes or until lentils are tender but still hold their shape. For a smooth soup, puree with an immersion blender. Garnish, if desired.

COCK-A-LEEKIE SOUP

MAKES 10 CUPS

EQUIPMENT: *5-quart Dutch oven (cocotte)*

2 tablespoons extra-virgin olive oil
2 large leeks, cleaned and thinly sliced
2 carrots, diced
2 celery ribs, sliced
2 garlic cloves, minced
6 cups chicken broth
1 bay leaf
½ teaspoon dried thyme
½ teaspoon fine sea salt
⅓ teaspoon coarsely ground black pepper
½ cup pearl barley
3 cups shredded rotisserie or cooked chicken
⅓ cup pitted prunes, chopped

Cock-a-leekie is a traditional Scottish soup that combines leeks, chicken, and prunes. It is usually served as a starter but can easily be a main dish alongside crusty bread and a side salad. Prunes are an interesting addition to this whimsically named soup. You can skip them, but they add a rustic sweetness that marries well with the broth and vegetables. Rotisserie chicken is a shortcut here. Use mostly dark meat for rich flavor.

---

1. Heat oil in a Dutch oven over medium heat. Add leeks, carrots, and celery. Cook, stirring frequently, for 10 minutes. Add garlic and cook, stirring constantly, for 1 minute.
2. Stir in broth, bay leaf, thyme, salt, and pepper. Add barley. Bring to a boil and reduce heat. Cover and simmer for 30 minutes. Add chicken and prunes. Simmer for 10 to 15 minutes. Remove and discard bay leaf before serving.

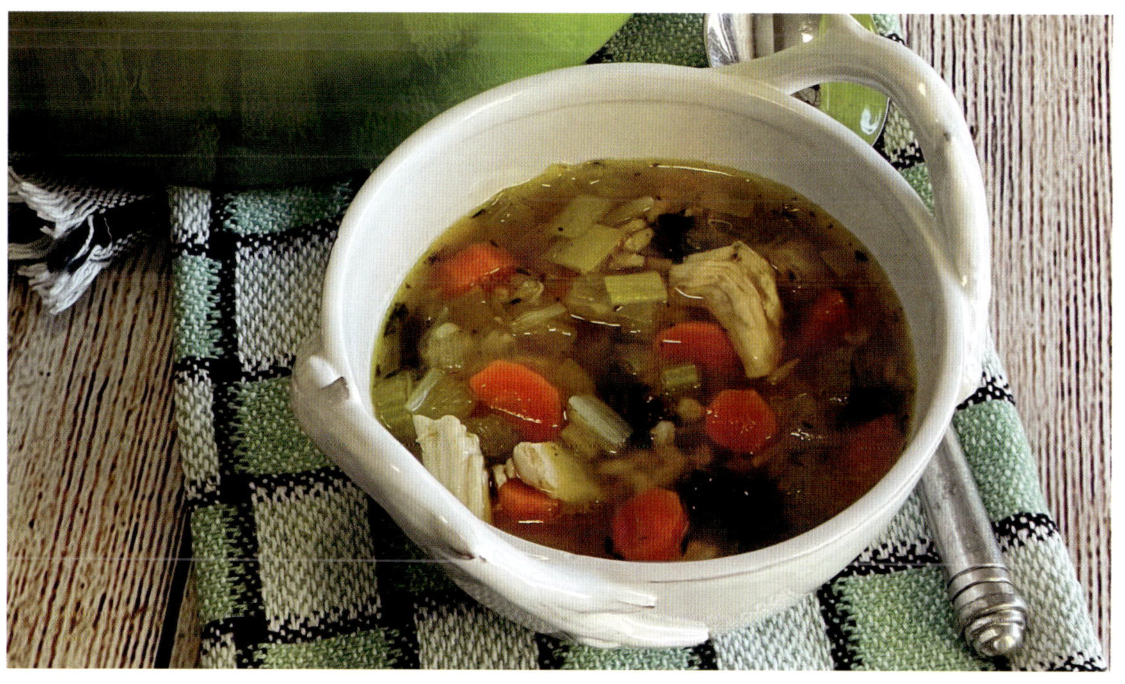

CHICKEN-TORTILLA SOUP

MAKES 10 CUPS

EQUIPMENT: *5- to 7-quart Dutch oven*

½ cup vegetable oil
6 to 8 corn tortillas, cut into strips
¼ teaspoon garlic salt (optional)
½ teaspoon paprika (optional)
1 onion, chopped
2 poblano peppers or 1 green bell pepper, chopped
3 garlic cloves, minced
2 teaspoons fine sea salt
1 teaspoon ground cumin
½ teaspoon chili powder
½ teaspoon coarsely ground black pepper
3 boneless, skinless chicken breasts or 6 thighs, cubed
4 cups chicken broth
1 (14.5-ounce) can fire-roasted tomatoes, undrained
1 (15.25-ounce) can fire-roasted corn, rinsed and drained, or 1 cup (frozen and thawed) fire-roasted corn kernels
1 (15.5-ounce) can black beans, rinsed and drained
3 tablespoons lime juice
¼ cup chopped fresh cilantro
1 avocado, thinly sliced (optional)

Gather a crowd to warm up on a chilly night with these hearty bowls of goodness.

This vibrant, hearty dish features a rich, tomato-based broth infused with garlic, onions, and Mexican spices. The crispy tortilla strips add delightful crunch and flavor. You can buy them, but consider making them fresh. I like to add a bit of garlic salt and paprika for next-level taste.

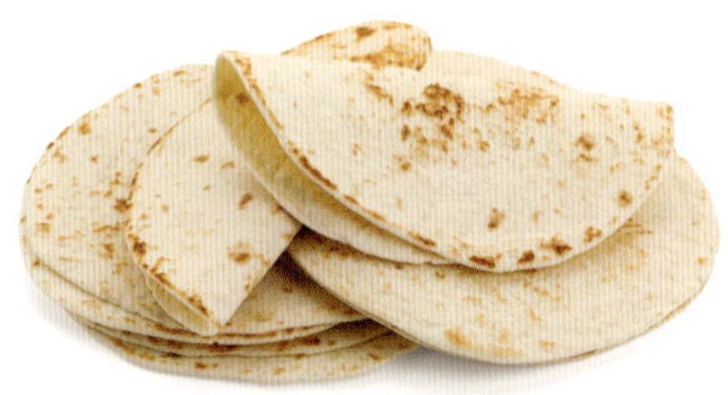

1. Heat oil in a Dutch oven over medium-high heat. Add tortilla strips, in batches, and fry until golden brown and crisp. Drain on paper towels, reserving 1 tablespoon oil in Dutch oven. Sprinkle evenly with garlic salt and paprika, if desired, and set fried tortilla strips aside.
2. Heat reserved oil in Dutch oven over medium heat. Add onion, poblano peppers, garlic, sea salt, cumin, chili powder, and black pepper. Cook, stirring frequently, for 5 minutes or until vegetables are tender. Add chicken breasts, stirring until well coated.
3. Stir in broth, tomatoes, corn, and black beans. Bring to a boil, reduce heat, and simmer for 20 minutes or until chicken is cooked. Stir in lime juice and cilantro.
4. Serve soup with reserved fried tortilla strips and, if desired, avocado slices.

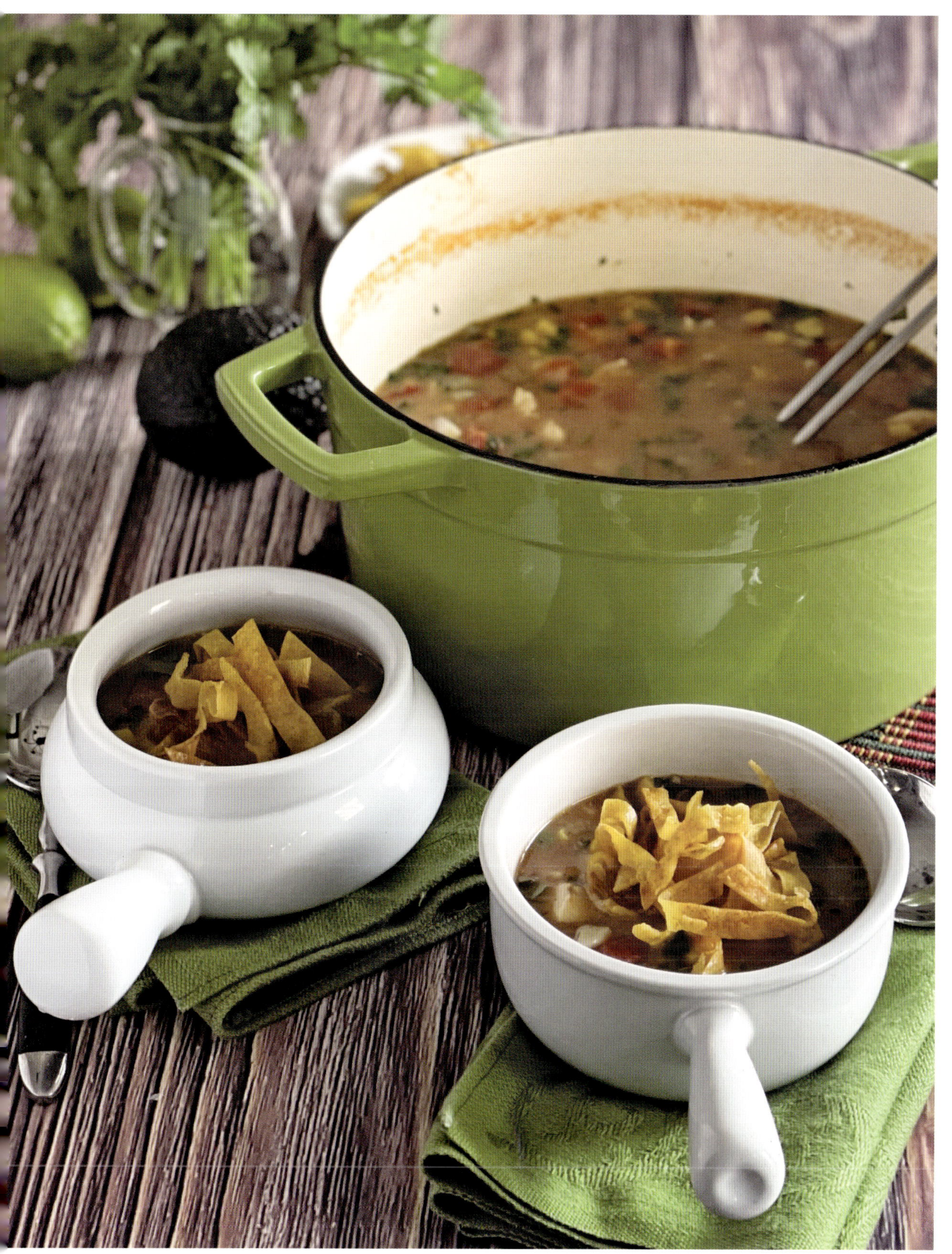

CHICKEN WITH CORNMEAL-HERB DUMPLINGS

MAKES 4 TO 6 SERVINGS

EQUIPMENT: *5- to 7-quart Dutch oven (cocotte)*

2 tablespoons extra-virgin olive oil
1 small onion, chopped
2 celery ribs, chopped
2 carrots, chopped
1 teaspoon Italian seasoning, herbes de Provence, or poultry seasoning
4 cups chicken broth
½ teaspoon fine sea salt
½ teaspoon coarsely ground black pepper
3 cups chopped or shredded rotisserie or grilled chicken
Cornmeal-Herb Dumplings (recipe at right)
Chopped fresh herbs (optional)

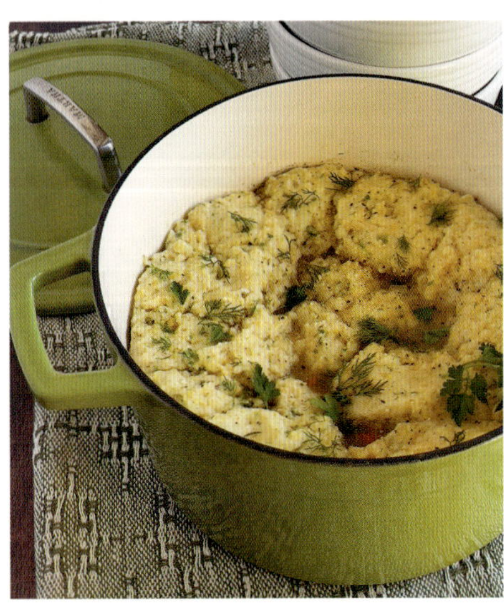

This recipe takes the shortcut of using rotisserie chicken to reduce prep and cooking time by more than half. It's a cozy recipe that's easy enough for a busy weeknight. The sauce is thin but thickens when mixed with the dumplings.

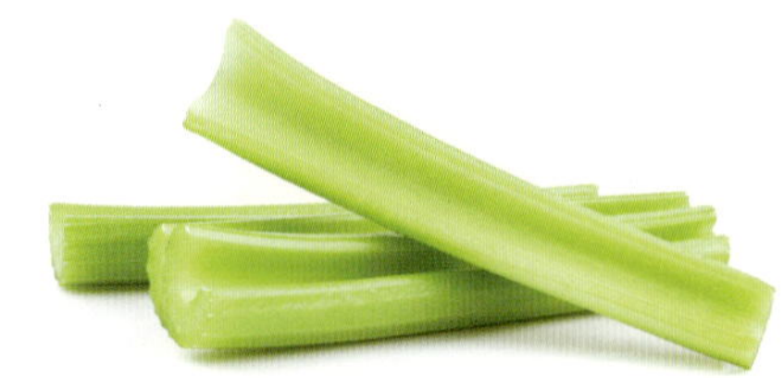

1. Heat oil in a large Dutch oven over medium to medium-high heat. Add onion, celery, carrots, and Italian seasoning; cook vegetables for 10 minutes, stirring constantly.
2. Stir in broth, salt, and pepper. Bring to a boil, reduce heat, and simmer for 10 minutes or until vegetables are tender. Stir in chicken; cook for 3 to 5 minutes or until heated through.
3. Drop tablespoonfuls of Cornmeal-Herb Dumplings into hot broth. Cover almost all the way. Reduce heat to medium-low and simmer for 15 to 20 minutes or until dumplings are cooked. Sprinkle with chopped fresh herbs, if desired.

Cornmeal-Herb Dumplings: Combine **1½ cups all-purpose flour, ½ cup medium-grind cornmeal, 1 tablespoon baking powder, 1 tablespoon granulated sugar,** and **½ teaspoon salt** in a food processor. Add **4 tablespoons salted or unsalted butter;** pulse until mixture resembles coarse meal. Transfer to a bowl, and stir in **1 cup half-and-half or whole milk.** Stir in **2 tablespoons chopped fresh parsley, chopped dill, or other fresh herbs.** Makes 2 cups.

ITALIAN WEDDING SOUP

MAKES ABOUT 10 CUPS

EQUIPMENT: *5- to 7-quart Dutch oven*

8 ounces lean ground beef or ground turkey

¼ cup seasoned breadcrumbs

¼ cup grated Parmesan or Romano cheese

1 garlic clove, minced

1 large egg, lightly beaten

1 tablespoon chopped fresh parsley

½ teaspoon salt

¼ teaspoon coarsely ground black pepper

2 tablespoons extra-virgin olive oil

1 onion, chopped

2 carrots, diced

2 celery ribs, chopped

½ cup white wine

6 cups chicken stock or broth

½ cup acini di pepe or orzo (or ¾ cup other small pasta, such as ditalini)

3 cups lightly packed escarole, kale, or Swiss chard, coarsely chopped

Shaved Parmesan or Romano cheese

Hearty bread

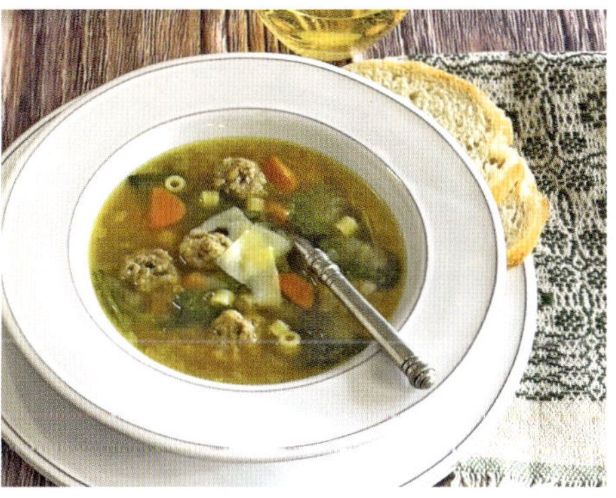

This meatball-and-pasta soup is a comforting dish that's more delicious the next day. Acini di pepe is a tiny pasta, and orzo is a fine substitute. If you want to use a pasta that is a bit larger, such as ditalini, increase the amount to ¾ cup. You may be tempted to add more pasta. Be patient—it will swell, especially if some is saved for leftovers. Escarole is the traditional green, but I often use mixed "power" greens or arugula because they're always available. Rolling meatballs by hand is tedious but quick work if you use a small scoop. I also find "scooped" meatballs more tender than hand rolled, but they may fall apart if the soup is boiled. To keep them intact, gently simmer until they're cooked through. If you want browned meatballs, place them on a rimmed baking sheet and bake at 375° for 7 minutes before adding to the soup.

---

1. Combine beef, breadcrumbs, cheese, garlic, egg, parsley, salt, and pepper in a large bowl, mixing well. Scoop or form mixture into small (½-inch) meatballs. Set meatballs aside.
2. Heat oil in a Dutch oven over medium heat. Add onion, carrots, and celery. Cook, stirring frequently, for 5 minutes or until tender. Add wine and cook for 2 minutes or until almost evaporated. Stir in broth.
3. Bring mixture to a boil; reduce heat to simmer. Add reserved meatballs and pasta. Simmer gently for 10 to 12 minutes or until meatballs are cooked through and pasta is tender.
4. Add escarole and cook for 2 minutes or until wilted. Sprinkle servings with Parmesan cheese. Serve with bread.

DUTCH OVEN BEEF STEW

MAKES ABOUT 10 CUPS

EQUIPMENT: *5- to 7-quart Dutch oven (cocotte)*

2 pounds beef chuck or other stew meat

¼ cup all-purpose flour

2½ teaspoons fine sea salt, divided

1 teaspoon coarsely ground black pepper

2 tablespoons avocado or extra-virgin olive oil, divided

1 cup red wine

3 tablespoons tomato paste

4 cups beef stock or broth

1 tablespoon Worcestershire sauce

1 teaspoon chopped fresh rosemary

2 bay leaves

4 medium-size carrots, thickly sliced

3 large red or gold potatoes (about 1 pound), cubed

1 large onion, chopped

2 cups fresh (or frozen and thawed) green beans, cut into 2-inch pieces

¼ cup lightly packed chopped fresh parsley

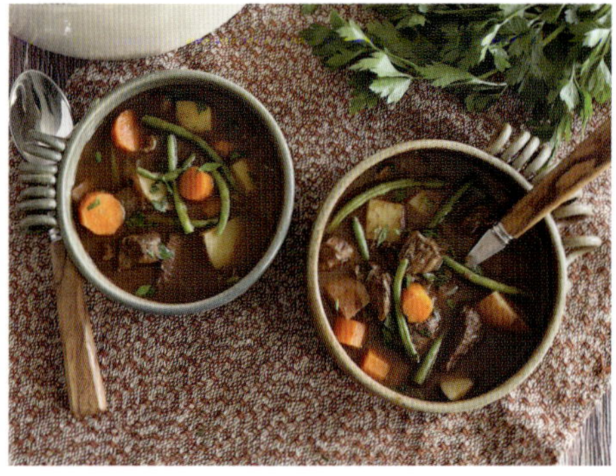

Beef chuck is generally pretty tough, but the lengthy cooking time will transform it into tender bites. You may also see packages of cubed stew meat at markets. These are probably cut from chuck or top and bottom round. If your store has butchers on-site, they might also include trimmings of nicer quality steaks like sirloin or flank. Green beans are not often seen in stew, but I included them here for extra nutrition and because they are sturdy enough to be cooked with the other ingredients.

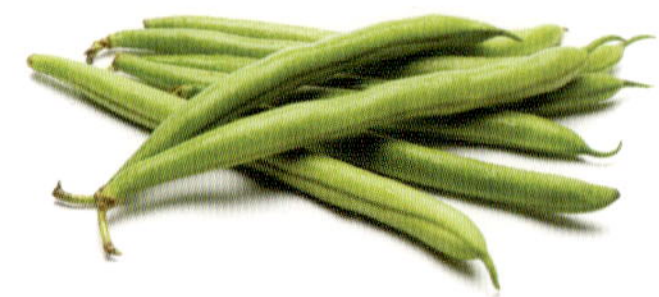

1. Cut beef into 1-inch cubes or pieces, removing any silverskin or particularly dense pieces of fat. Combine flour, 1½ teaspoons salt, and pepper in a bowl. Add beef, tossing to coat.
2. Heat 1 tablespoon oil in a large Dutch oven over medium to medium-high heat. Add half of beef and cook, turning occasionally, for 5 minutes or until browned on all sides. Repeat with remaining beef, adding remaining 1 tablespoon oil, if necessary. Transfer beef to a plate.
3. Add wine to pot. Cook over medium to medium-high heat, scraping browned bits from bottom of pot with a wooden spoon. Stir in tomato paste. Stir in broth, Worcestershire, rosemary, and bay leaves. Return beef to pot. Bring to a boil, reduce heat to low, and simmer, partially covered, for 1½ hours.
4. Add carrots, potatoes, onion, and remaining 1 teaspoon salt to stew. Cover and simmer for 30 minutes or until vegetables are almost tender. Add green beans and cook for 15 minutes or until tender. Remove and discard bay leaves. Stir in parsley.

VEGETARIAN BLACK BEAN CHILI

MAKES ABOUT 8 CUPS

EQUIPMENT: *5-quart Dutch oven (cocotte)*

2 tablespoons olive oil
1 large onion, chopped
1 (12-ounce) package meatless crumbles or ¾ pound lean ground beef
2 poblano peppers, chopped
1 orange, yellow, or red bell pepper, chopped
2 garlic cloves, minced
2 cups vegetable broth
2 (15-ounce) cans black beans, rinsed and drained
1 (28-ounce) can diced fire-roasted or chili-seasoned tomatoes, undrained
3 tablespoons tomato paste
2 tablespoons chili powder
1 tablespoon ground cumin
2 teaspoons chipotle peppers, minced
½ teaspoon fine sea salt
½ teaspoon coarsely ground black pepper
Toppings: sliced avocado, sour cream, shredded cheddar cheese
Sweet Corn Muffins (page 20)

Vegetarian or meaty—it's your choice! If you like a spicier chili, stir in another teaspoon or more of the liquid from the canned chipotle peppers. For a milder version, use green bell peppers instead of poblanos and skip the chipotle peppers.

1 Heat oil in a large Dutch oven over medium heat. Add onion and cook, stirring frequently, for 5 minutes or until tender. Add meat and cook for 3 to 5 minutes or until browned and crumbly. Add poblano peppers, bell pepper, and garlic. Cook for 5 minutes, stirring constantly.

2 Stir in broth, beans, tomatoes, tomato paste, chili powder, cumin, chipotle peppers with liquid, salt, and black pepper. Bring to a boil, reduce heat, and simmer for 15 minutes. Serve with desired toppings and Sweet Corn Muffins.

VEGAN CHILI WITH CORNBREAD TOPPING

MAKES 6 SERVINGS

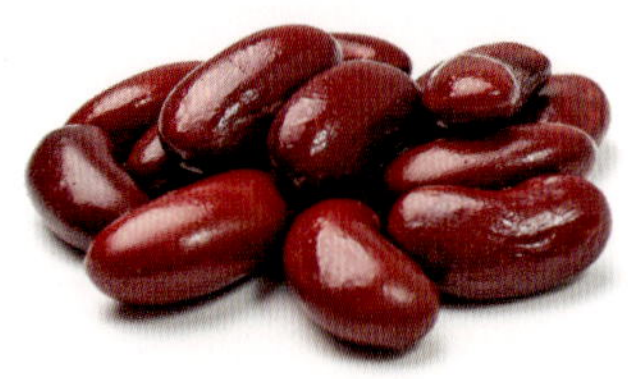

EQUIPMENT: *5-quart Dutch oven (cocotte)*

2 tablespoons extra-virgin olive oil
1 large onion, chopped
4 garlic cloves, finely chopped
1 bell pepper (any color), chopped
2 carrots, diced
2 cups vegetable broth
2 tablespoons tomato paste
1 (14.5-ounce) can fire-roasted diced tomatoes, undrained
1 (15.5-ounce) can black beans, rinsed and drained
1 (15.5-ounce) can kidney beans, rinsed and drained
1 tablespoon chili powder
1 teaspoon ground cumin
1 to 2 teaspoons minced chipotle peppers in adobo sauce
½ teaspoon fine sea salt
½ teaspoon coarsely ground black pepper
Cornbread Topping (recipe at right)
Toppings: chopped pickled jalapeños, fresh jalapeños, fresh cilantro

This vegan dish might be missing meat and dairy, but it's full of vibrant flavor. If you like spicy dishes, taste the chili before adding the cornbread topping, and increase chipotle peppers or salt and black pepper, if you like.

1. Heat oil in a Dutch oven over medium heat. Add onion, garlic, bell pepper, and carrots. Cook, stirring frequently, for 5 to 7 minutes or until vegetables are tender.
2. Stir in broth, tomato paste, tomatoes, black beans, kidney beans, chili powder, cumin, chipotle peppers, salt, and black pepper. Bring mixture to a boil, reduce heat, and simmer for 20 to 25 minutes.
3. Preheat oven to 350°. Prepare Cornbread Topping and dollop on top of chili.
4. Transfer Dutch oven to oven and bake, uncovered, for 25 minutes or until cornbread is golden brown and cooked through. Sprinkle with desired toppings.

Cornbread Topping: Combine **1 cup yellow cornmeal, 1 cup all-purpose flour, 1 tablespoon granulated sugar, 2 teaspoons baking powder**, and **½ teaspoon salt** in a bowl. Stir in **1 cup oat, almond, or whole milk** and **2 tablespoons extra-virgin olive oil.** Makes 2 cups.

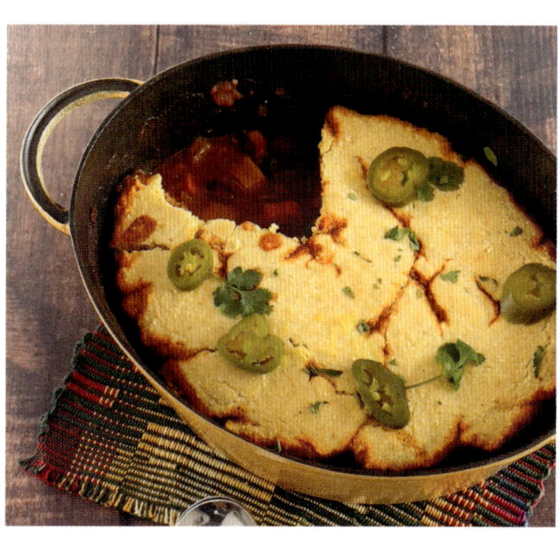

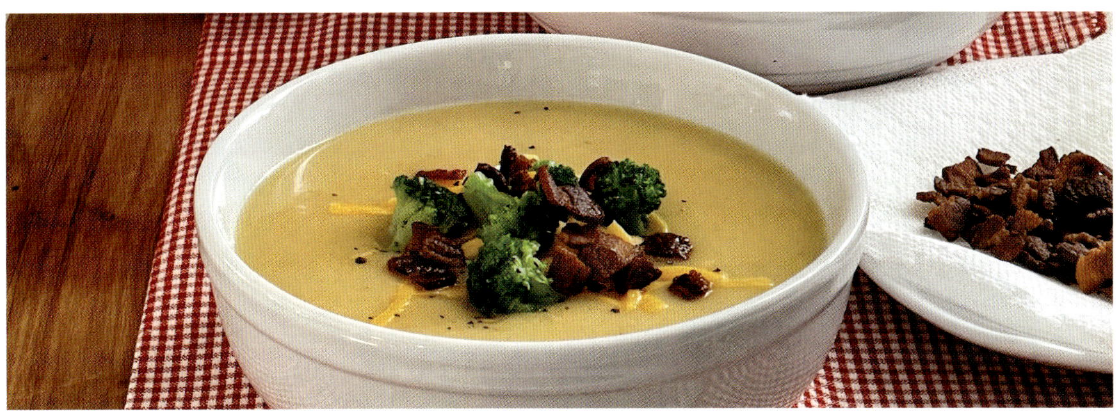

FULLY LOADED POTATO SOUP

MAKES 8 CUPS

Craving potato soup but not having as many potatoes as I wanted, I learned that supplementing with cauliflower is a great option. It adds the extra nutrition of a cruciferous vegetable and creates a lighter-textured soup. I often use frozen cauliflower and broccoli because I can stock up on the shelf-stable ingredients for a spontaneous meal.

EQUIPMENT: *5- to 7-quart Dutch oven (cocotte)*

4 slices lean center-cut bacon, chopped

1 small onion, chopped

4 cups chicken broth

1 pound gold or red potatoes (3 large), diced

1 pound fresh (or frozen and thawed) cauliflower florets

¼ to ½ teaspoon ground cayenne pepper

½ cup very small broccoli florets

1½ cups (6 ounces) shredded cheddar cheese, divided

½ teaspoon salt (optional)

⅓ cup sour cream

1. Cook bacon in a Dutch oven over medium heat, stirring occasionally, for 5 minutes or until crisp. Remove with a slotted spoon and drain on paper towels; reserving 1 tablespoon drippings in Dutch oven. Set bacon aside.
2. Heat drippings over medium heat. Add onion and cook, stirring frequently, for 5 minutes. Stir in broth, potatoes, cauliflower, and cayenne pepper. Bring to a boil, reduce heat, and simmer for 15 to 20 minutes or until vegetables are tender.
3. Meanwhile, steam or microwave broccoli for 2 minutes or until crisp-tender. Set broccoli aside.
4. Blend soup with an immersion blender until smooth. (If using a standard blender, fill blender no more than half full, and remove center cap from lid. Cover hole with a towel while blending, in batches, until smooth.) Add half of cheese to blended soup, stirring until smooth. Taste and add salt, if desired.
5. To serve, ladle soup into bowls, and top evenly with sour cream, remaining half of cheese, reserved broccoli, and reserved bacon.

BUTTERNUT, SAUSAGE, AND WHITE BEAN SOUP

MAKES 12 CUPS

EQUIPMENT: *7-quart Dutch oven (cocotte)*

1 tablespoon olive oil

12 ounces sweet Italian, smoked kielbasa, or other link sausage, sliced

1 onion, chopped

1 celery rib, chopped

4 garlic cloves, minced

1 tablespoon Italian seasoning

1 teaspoon salt

½ teaspoon coarsely ground black pepper

4 cups chicken broth

4½ cups peeled-and-diced butternut squash (about 1¾ pounds)

1 (28-ounce) can plain or seasoned diced tomatoes, undrained

¼ cup tomato paste

1 (15.5-ounce) can cannellini beans, rinsed and drained

2 cups lightly packed arugula

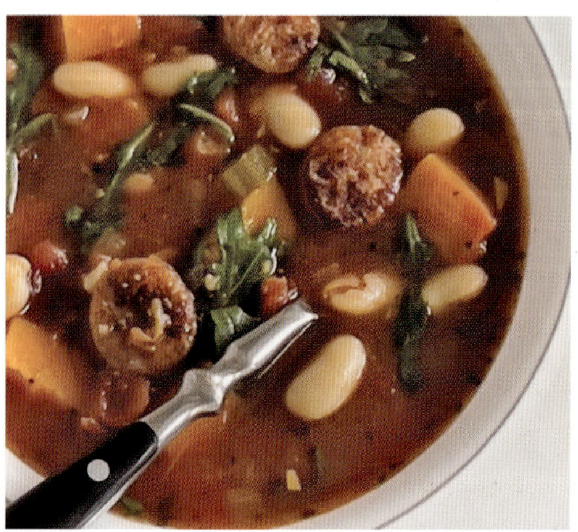

Sweet-and-nutty butternut squash pairs nicely with smoky sausage and creamy beans. Substitute any winter squash for the butternut—acorn, kabocha, or carnival, for example. Sweet potatoes will also work. There is a sweet Italian chicken sausage I like to use for this recipe, but any kind will do. I like link sausage because it holds its shape, but if you don't mind crumbles, you can use bulk sausage as well. Be sure to drain any excess oil.

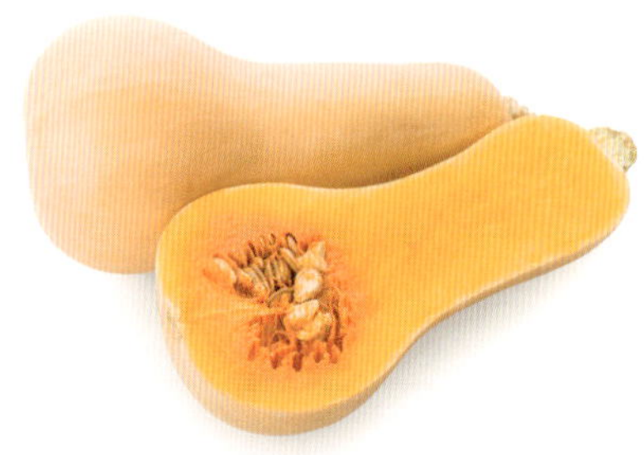

1. Heat oil in a Dutch oven or soup pot over medium to medium-high heat. Add sausage and cook, turning occasionally, for 5 minutes or until browned on all sides. Transfer to a plate, reserving 1 tablespoon oil in Dutch oven. Set sausage aside.
2. Heat reserved oil in Dutch oven. Add onion, celery, garlic, seasoning, salt, and pepper. Cook, stirring often, for 5 minutes or until vegetables are slightly softened.
3. Stir in broth, squash, tomatoes, and tomato paste. Stir in reserved sausage. Bring to a boil, reduce heat, and simmer, covered, for 20 minutes or until vegetables are tender. Stir in beans and arugula. Cook, stirring occasionally, for 5 minutes or until arugula wilts and beans are heated through.

SALMON-AND-POTATO CHOWDER

MAKES 8 CUPS

EQUIPMENT: *5-quart Dutch oven (cocotte)*

4 tablespoons butter
1 small onion, diced
2 celery ribs, diced
2 garlic cloves, minced
2 tablespoons all-purpose flour
½ teaspoon salt
¾ teaspoon paprika
4 cups chicken stock or broth
3 cups peeled-and-diced yellow potatoes (about 2 large)
1 tablespoon hot sauce
1 cup heavy cream
¾ to 1 pound skinless sockeye salmon, cut into pieces
3 teaspoons chopped fresh dill
Garnish: fresh dill sprigs

This comforting soup is hearty and simple, yet elegant enough for a company chowder-and-salad dinner. If you are a fan of fennel, you can substitute half a bulb, chopped, for the celery—along with fresh fennel fronds instead of chopped dill. You can use hot smoked salmon for a delicious variation that adds a rich earthiness to this hearty soup; however, it has a strong flavor, so reduce the amount to 8 ounces.

---

1. Melt butter in a Dutch oven over medium-high heat. Add onion, celery, and garlic; cook for 5 minutes or until translucent.
2. Add flour, salt, and paprika. Cook, stirring constantly, for 2 minutes.
3. Stir in chicken stock, potatoes, and hot sauce. Simmer, stirring occasionally, for 20 minutes or until potatoes are cooked through.
4. Add cream, salmon, and dill; cook for 1 minute or just until salmon is done. Garnish, if desired.

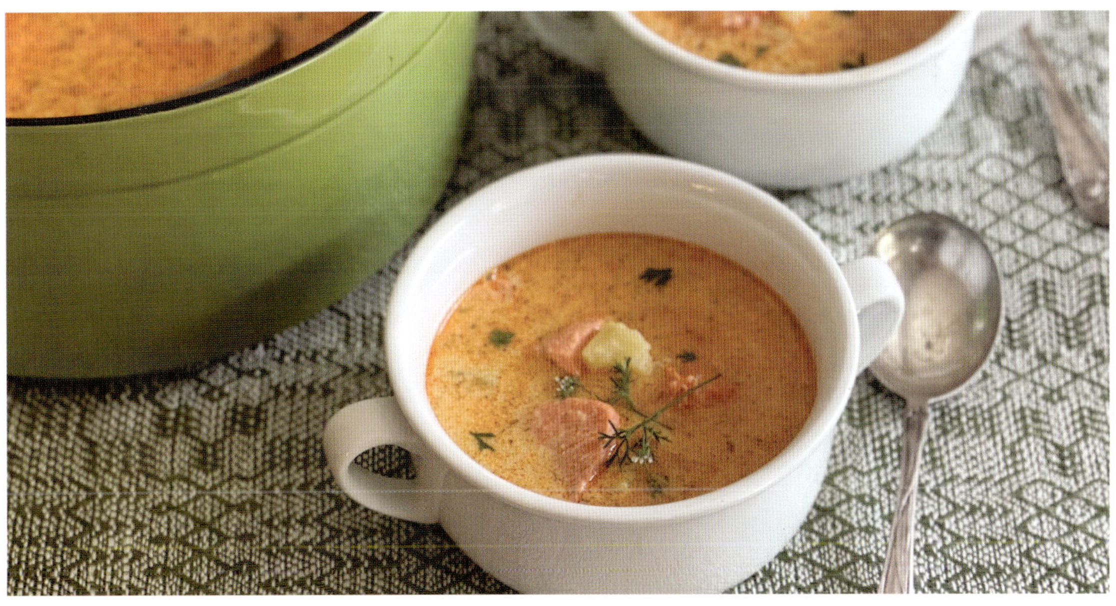

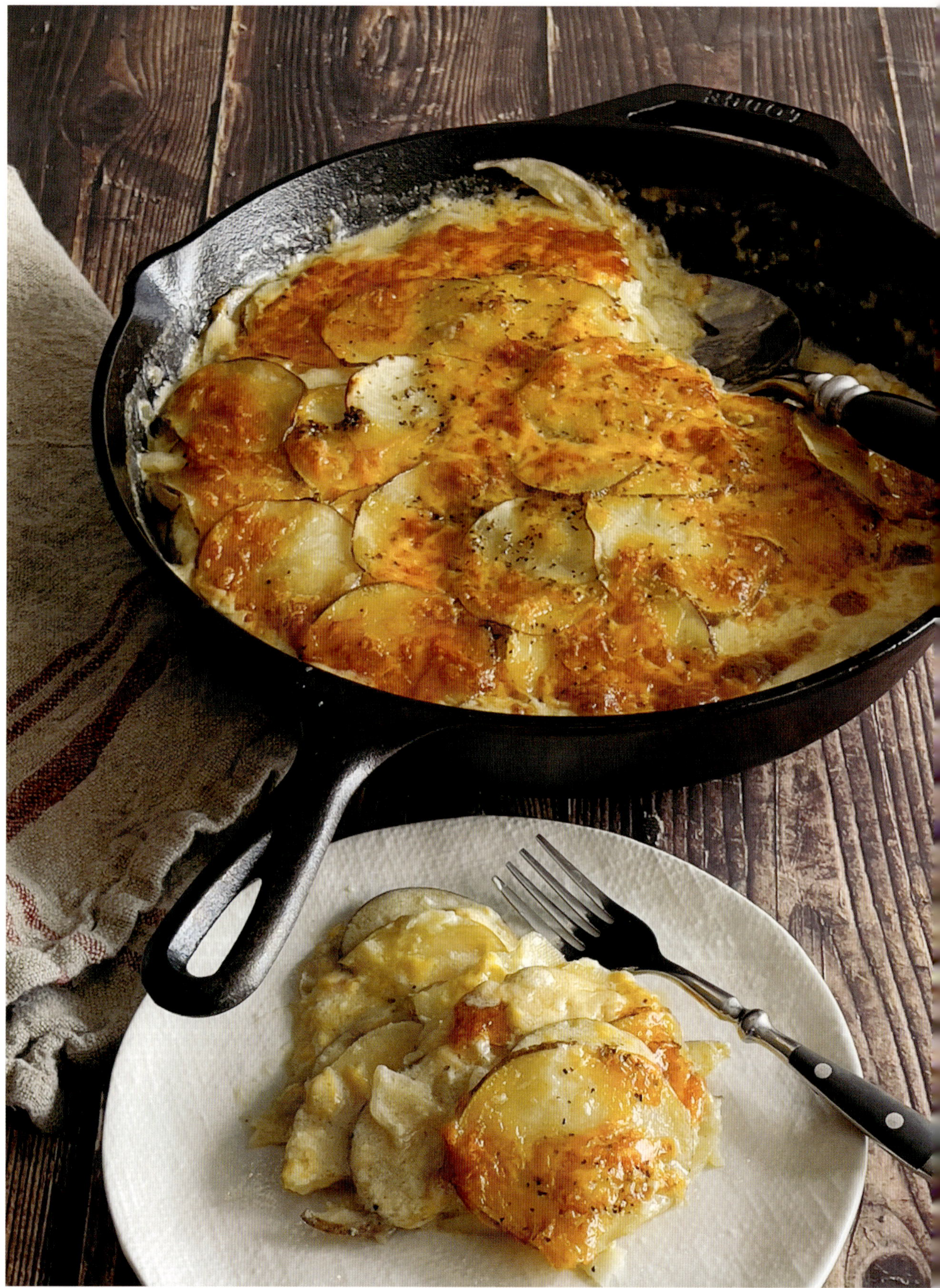

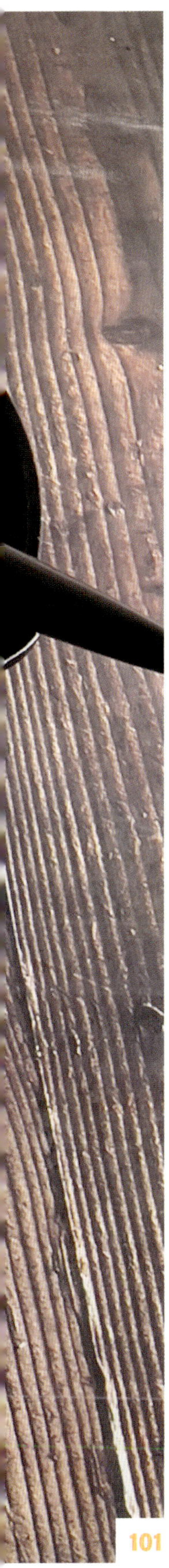

SIDES

101

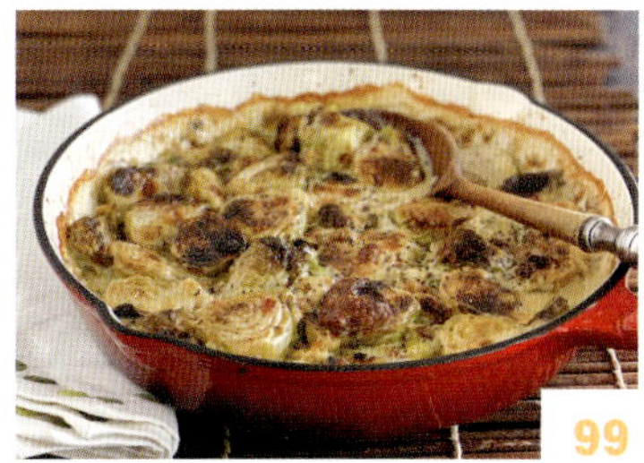

99

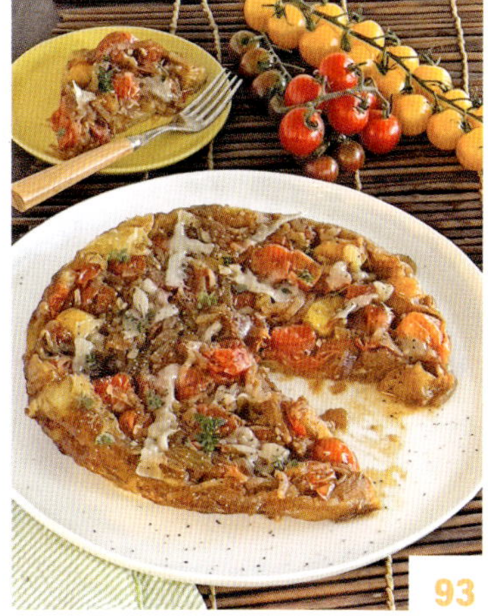

93

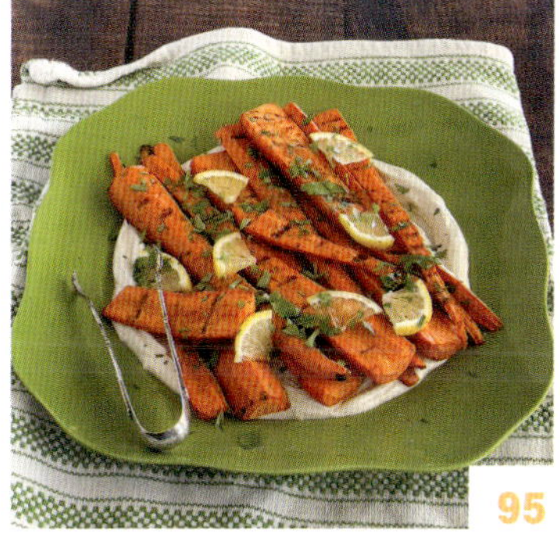

95

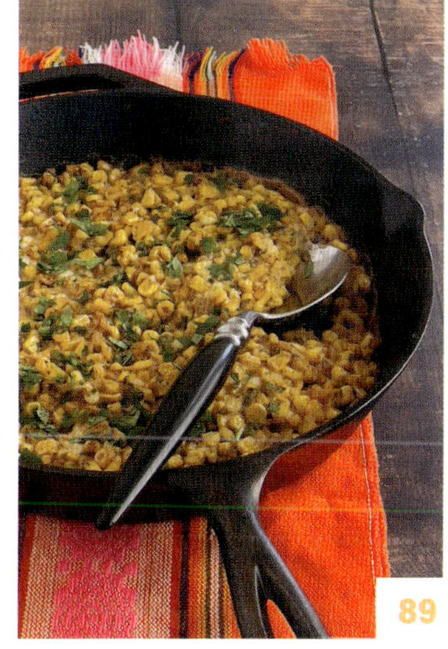

89

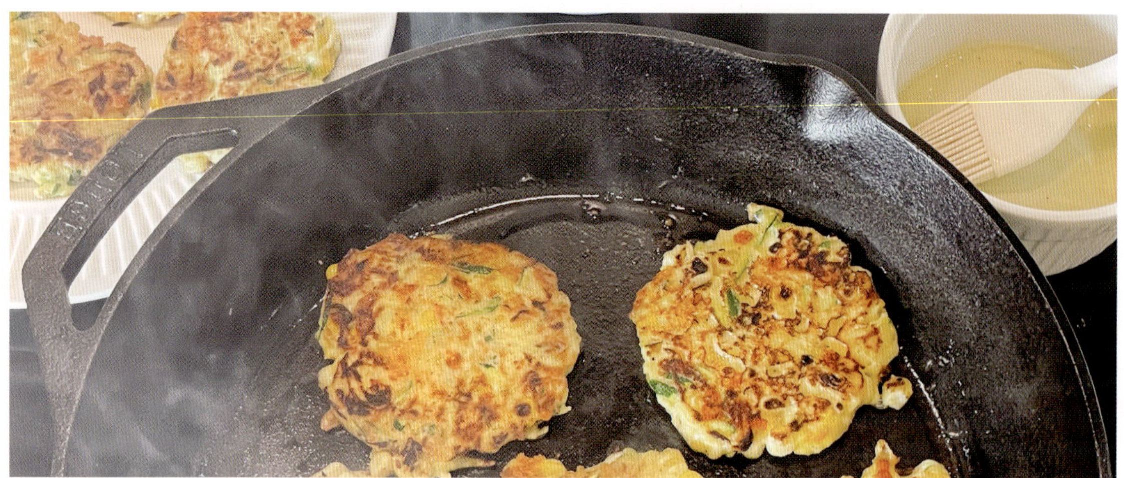

ZUCCHINI-AND-CORN FRITTERS

MAKES 1½ DOZEN

EQUIPMENT: *griddle or large cast-iron skillet*

PAN SAVVY: *Because these are cooked in batches, use whatever size griddle or skillet you prefer. Keep plenty of space around fritters to allow a spatula to get underneath for flipping.*

1 large zucchini, coarsely grated

1 teaspoon fine sea salt

2 large eggs

1 cup fresh (or frozen and thawed, well-drained) corn kernels

½ cup all-purpose flour

½ cup (2 ounces) shredded cheddar cheese

2 green onions, finely chopped

¼ teaspoon coarsely ground black pepper

½ teaspoon garlic powder

2 to 3 tablespoons avocado or vegetable oil

These crispy fritters make good use of summer vegetables. Eat them as a side dish with grilled chicken or on their own as a tasty snack.

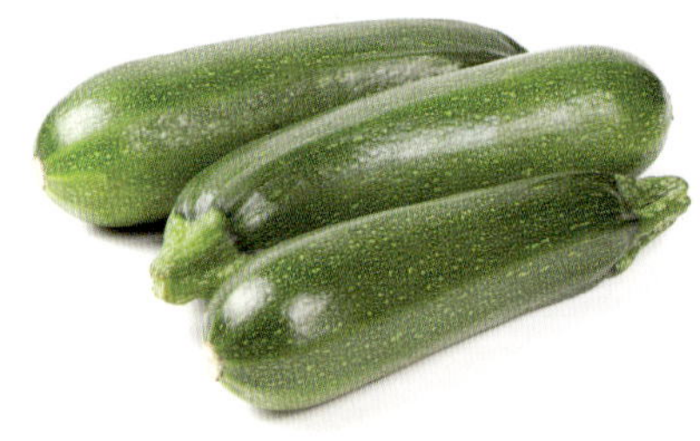

1. Place grated zucchini in a colander and sprinkle with salt. Let stand for 10 minutes. Squeeze out as much liquid as possible.
2. Beat eggs in a large bowl. Stir in zucchini, corn, flour, cheese, onions, pepper, and garlic powder.
3. Heat 1 to 2 tablespoons oil in a large skillet or griddle over medium to medium-high heat. Drop heaping tablespoonfuls of fritter batter into pan and flatten with a spatula. Cook, in batches, for 2 to 3 minutes on each side or until browned and crispy. Repeat with remaining batter, adding extra oil, if necessary.

MEXICAN STREET CORN SKILLET

MAKES 4 SERVINGS

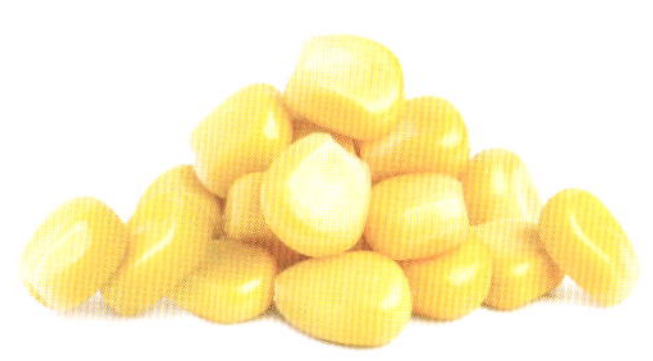

EQUIPMENT: *12-inch cast-iron skillet*

PAN SAVVY: *I recommend a 12-inch skillet so there's more room for the vegetables to get charred—crowded veggies steam instead. A 10-inch skillet can work, but the corn won't have the same texture or color.*

2 tablespoons avocado oil

4 cups fresh (or frozen and thawed) corn kernels

½ onion, finely chopped

1 jalapeño pepper, seeded and finely chopped

⅓ cup mayonnaise

1/3 cup sour cream

1 cup crumbled queso fresco or cotija cheese

1 teaspoon chili powder

½ teaspoon fine sea salt

½ teaspoon coarsely ground black pepper

¼ teaspoon grated lime zest

1 tablespoon fresh lime juice

¼ cup chopped fresh cilantro, divided

Mexican street corn, also known as "elote," is a popular dish often sold by vendors at roadside stands. Whole corn on the cob is roasted to bring out its sweetness and add a bit of smoky flavor; then it's topped with garlic, chili powder, mayo, and cotija cheese. This recipe is reminiscent but in an easy-to-serve hot casserole. If you're using frozen corn, drain it well on paper towels to remove excess liquid. If queso fresco cheese is unavailable, try cotija or crumbled feta and reduce the salt.

1. Preheat oven to 375°.
2. Heat oil in a 12-inch cast-iron skillet over medium-high heat. Add corn, onion, and jalapeño pepper. Cook, stirring occasionally, for 5 to 7 minutes or until vegetables are slightly charred and tender. Remove from heat.
3. Combine mayonnaise, sour cream, cheese, chili powder, salt, black pepper, zest, and juice in a large bowl. Stir mayonnaise mixture into corn mixture. Stir in 2 tablespoons cilantro.
4. Bake for 15 minutes or until hot and bubbly. Remove from oven. Sprinkle with remaining 2 tablespoons cilantro.

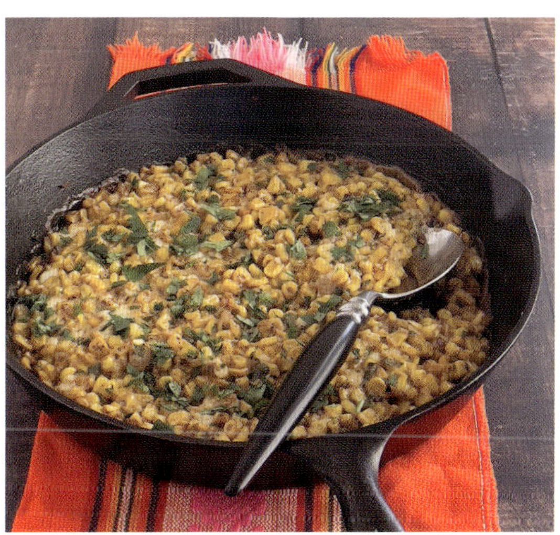

STOVETOP RATATOUILLE

MAKES 4 SERVINGS

EQUIPMENT: *12-inch brasier or skillet*

PAN SAVVY: *I use my brasier for this dish because it has a heavy lid that fits precisely. A large skillet works well, but most do not come with lids, so cover it with aluminum foil or a sheet pan, if necessary.*

1 small eggplant (skin on), diced
1 tablespoon kosher salt
1 tablespoon extra-virgin olive oil
1 onion, chopped
1 red bell pepper, chopped
2 garlic cloves, minced
¼ teaspoon red chili flakes
1 zucchini, diced
1 yellow squash, diced
2 (14.5-ounce) cans fire-roasted diced tomatoes, undrained
1 tablespoon capers, rinsed and drained
1 teaspoon Italian seasoning
½ teaspoon fine sea salt
½ teaspoon coarsely ground black pepper
2 tablespoons chopped fresh basil
Sliced fresh mozzarella or freshly grated Parmesan cheese
Garnish: chopped fresh basil
French bread

Call the vegetable lovers to the table! They'll adore this vibrant, healthy dish.

Ratatouille is a traditional French dish served as a side dish, but it's substantial enough to be a vegetarian main dish, especially when served with pasta or rice. Salting the eggplant pulls the excess moisture and some bitterness from the vegetable and creates a dish that's less watery and more flavorful, but the step isn't critical. Because there are other ingredients to prep, I salt the eggplant first; by the time all the prep is done, the eggplant is ready to use. I tend to use kosher salt on eggplant because the larger flakes are easier to distribute and don't dissolve as quickly, but you can use half the amount of fine sea salt.

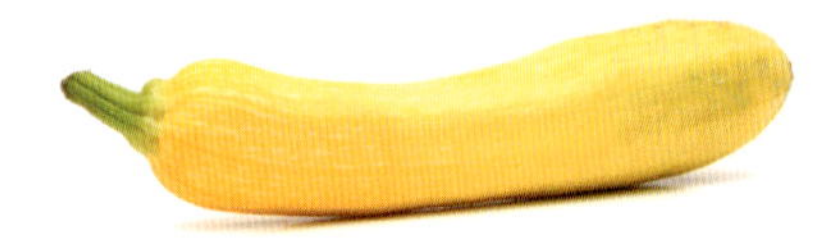

1. Place eggplant in a single layer on a baking sheet or in a colander. Sprinkle with kosher salt, tossing to coat. Let stand for 30 minutes to an hour. Rinse under cool running water and pat dry with a paper towel.
2. Heat oil in a large skillet, Dutch oven, or brasier over medium heat. Add onion, bell pepper, garlic, and chili flakes. Cook, stirring frequently, for 5 to 7 minutes or until tender. Add eggplant, zucchini, yellow squash, tomatoes, capers, seasoning, salt, and pepper. Cover and cook, stirring occasionally, for 15 minutes. Uncover and cook, stirring occasionally, for 10 to 15 minutes or until vegetables are tender. Stir in basil.
3. Top with slices of fresh mozzarella and garnish, if desired. Serve with French bread.

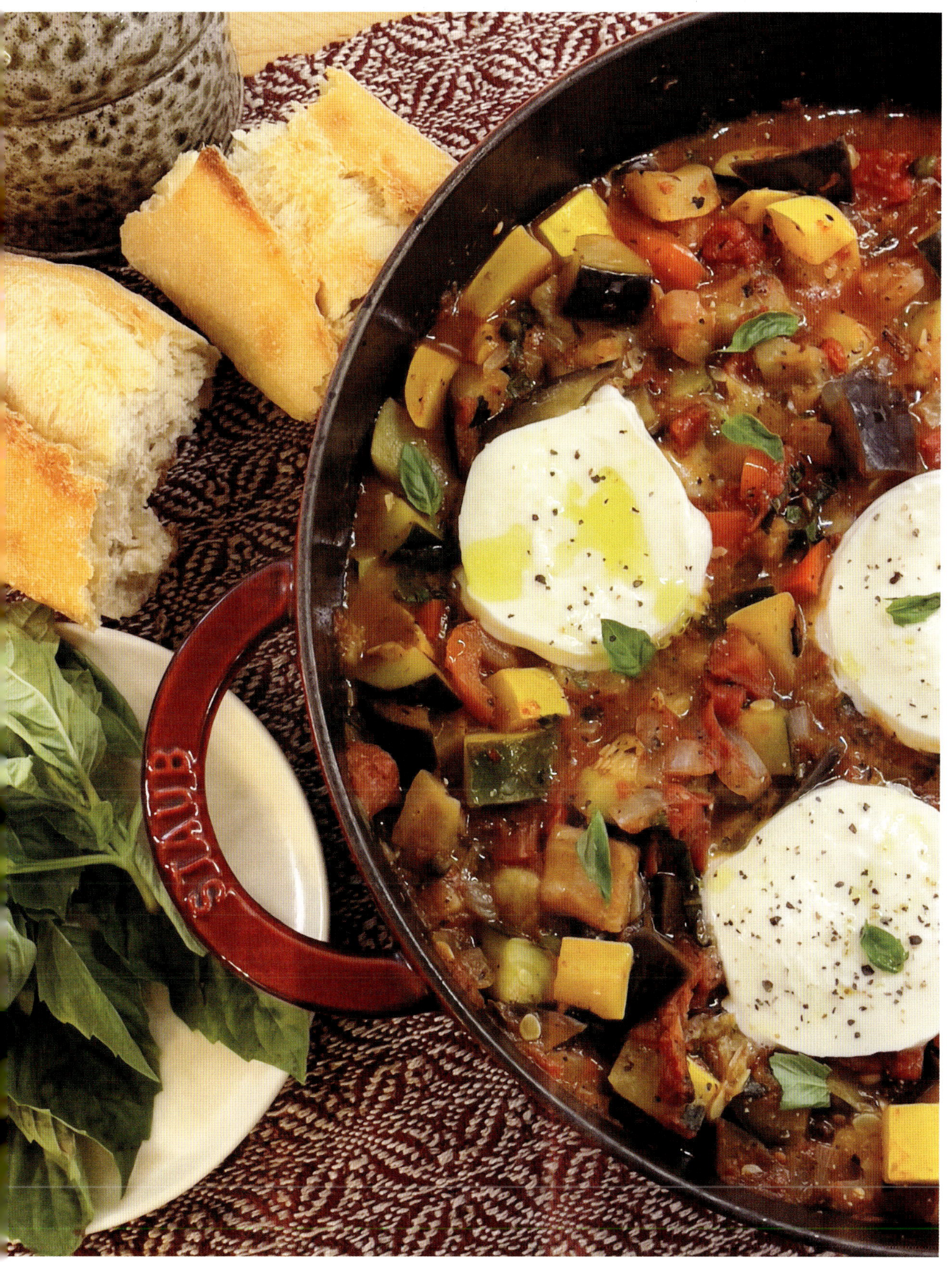
STAUB

FRIED GREEN TOMATOES WITH ROMESCO SAUCE

MAKES ABOUT 2 DOZEN

EQUIPMENT: *8- to 12-inch cast-iron skillet*

PAN SAVVY: *Less oil is needed for a smaller skillet, but it will require more batches and time to cook the tomatoes. Leave enough space around each one so they are easier to turn over.*

6 small- to medium-size green or pink tomatoes (2 pounds)
1 tablespoon seasoned salt
1 cup all-purpose flour
1½ teaspoons garlic powder
2 large eggs
½ cup buttermilk or milk
¾ cup cornmeal
¾ cup seasoned panko or dry breadcrumbs
Vegetable oil
Parmesan cheese (optional)
Pinch of salt (optional)
Romesco Sauce (optional; recipe at right)

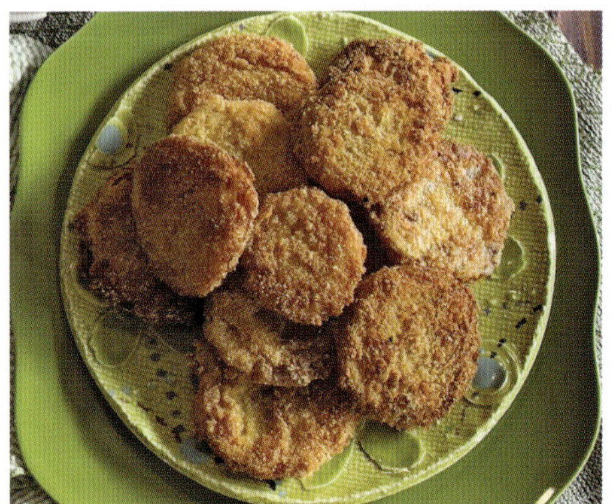

Next to cornbread, fried green tomatoes are the second-most-iconic food that's best cooked in a cast-iron skillet. If green tomatoes are unavailable, you can use very pink-but-underripe tomatoes. I've included a tangy roasted red bell pepper sauce, but these are delicious with just a sprinkling of grated Parmesan cheese or salt. Also try these on BLTs!

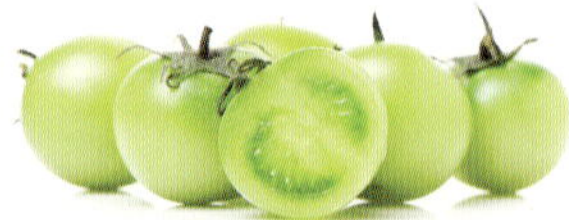

1. Remove cores from tomatoes, and cut into ¼-inch-thick slices. Sprinkle both sides evenly with seasoned salt (or sprinkle evenly with 1 teaspoon each of salt and pepper); set tomato slices aside.
2. Stir together flour and garlic powder in a shallow bowl. Whisk together eggs and buttermilk in a second shallow bowl. Stir together cornmeal and panko in a third shallow bowl.
3. Dredge reserved tomato slices in flour mixture. Dip in egg mixture, then dredge in cornmeal mixture.
4. Pour oil in skillet to a depth of ¼ to ½ inch. Preheat to 350° to 375°.
5. Fry tomatoes in hot oil, in batches, for 2 minutes on each side or until golden brown. Cool slightly on paper towels to drain excess oil. If desired, sprinkle with grated Parmesan cheese and salt. Serve with Romesco Sauce, if desired.

Romesco Sauce: Combine **2 roasted red bell peppers, jarred or homemade; 1 large ripe tomato, halved and seeded; 3 tablespoons slivered toasted almonds; 2 minced garlic cloves; 1 tablespoon sherry vinegar; 1 tablespoon extra-virgin olive oil; ¼ teaspoon salt;** and **⅛ teaspoon smoked paprika (optional)** in a blender or food processor. Blend until smooth. Makes 1¾ cups.

SAVORY CHERRY TOMATO TARTE TATIN

MAKES 6 SERVINGS

EQUIPMENT: *10-inch cast-iron baker's skillet*

PAN SAVVY: *I prefer a 10-inch baker's skillet (no larger) to make it easier to flip the tart onto a serving plate. A traditional 10-inch skillet with a long handle will work, but take care when transferring the tart onto the plate.*

2 tablespoons extra-virgin olive oil
½ small red onion, sliced
2 (10-ounce) containers mixed cherry tomatoes (about 3½ cups)
2 garlic cloves, minced
¾ teaspoon fine sea salt
¼ teaspoon coarsely ground black pepper
2 tablespoons white balsamic vinegar
1 tablespoon brown sugar
1 teaspoon chopped fresh thyme
1 sheet frozen puff pastry, thawed
Garnishes: freshly shaved Parmesan cheese, chopped fresh thyme

This recipe is ideal for summer when the cherry tomato plants offer a bounty of fruit. If you find yourself losing patience waiting for the cherry tomatoes to pop and release their liquid, you can speed things along by piercing the stragglers with the tip of a paring knife.

1 Heat oil in a 10-inch cast-iron skillet over medium heat. Add onion and cook for 5 minutes or until tender. Add tomatoes, garlic, salt, and pepper. Cook, stirring occasionally, for 7 to 10 minutes or until tomatoes start to wilt and release liquid (to speed this process, pierce each tomato with tip of a paring knife).

2 Stir in vinegar and brown sugar. Cook, stirring constantly, for 2 minutes or until brown sugar dissolves and mixture thickens. Stir in thyme and remove from heat.

3 Preheat oven to 400°.

4 Unfold puff pastry and carefully fit over tomato mixture, tucking in edges to fit inside hot skillet. Bake for 25 minutes or until golden brown and puffed. Let stand for 10 minutes (do not allow tart to completely cool). Protecting your hands, invert a large plate over top of hot skillet, then carefully flip over. Scrape any sauce mixture left in pan onto tomatoes. Garnish, if desired.

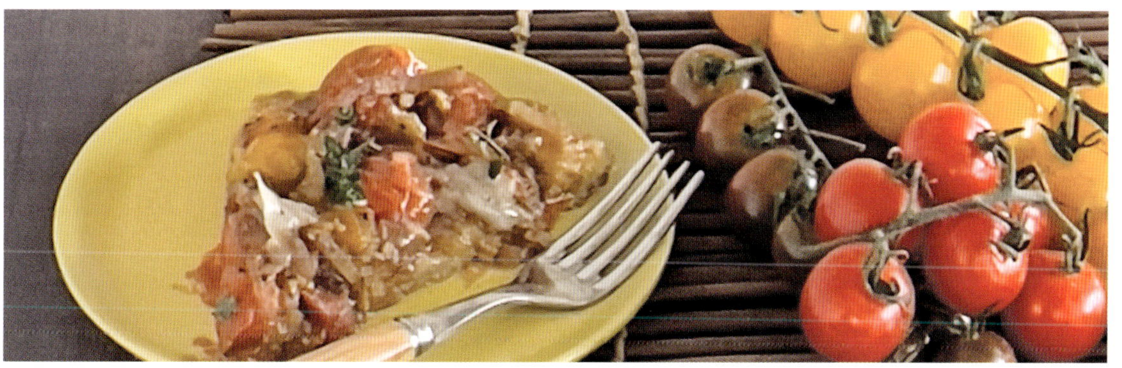

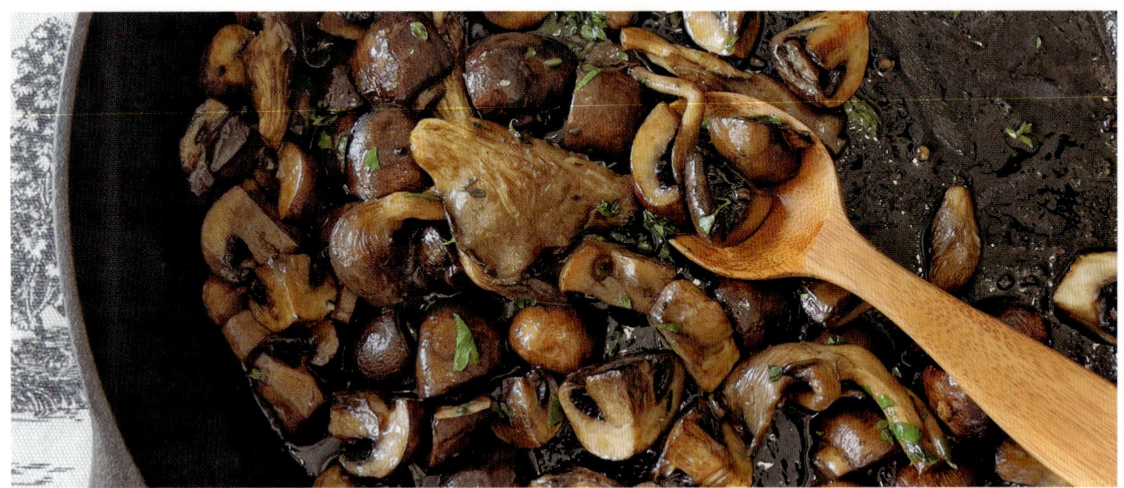

PAN-ROASTED MUSHROOMS

MAKES 6 SERVINGS

EQUIPMENT: *12-inch cast-iron skillet*

PAN SAVVY: *Use the largest skillet you have, leaving plenty of room around the mushrooms. If packed together, the mushrooms will steam rather than roast, and the pan will have excess liquid.*

- 2 tablespoons avocado oil
- ¼ teaspoon crushed red pepper flakes
- ¼ teaspoon fine sea salt
- 2 (8-ounce) containers cremini or button mushrooms, halved or quartered
- 1 (4-ounce) container shiitake or oyster mushrooms, sliced
- 3 tablespoons salted butter, cut into pieces
- 1½ tablespoons tamari or soy sauce
- 1 tablespoon chopped fresh herbs (parsley, thyme, and rosemary)

Wash mushrooms if you must, but keep them exposed to water as little as possible. Mushrooms are quite absorbent, and too much liquid will dilute the delicious umami flavor of this dish. Keep in mind that some mushrooms release more liquid than others. Open the oven door wide when stopping to stir the mushrooms, in order to let excess steam escape.

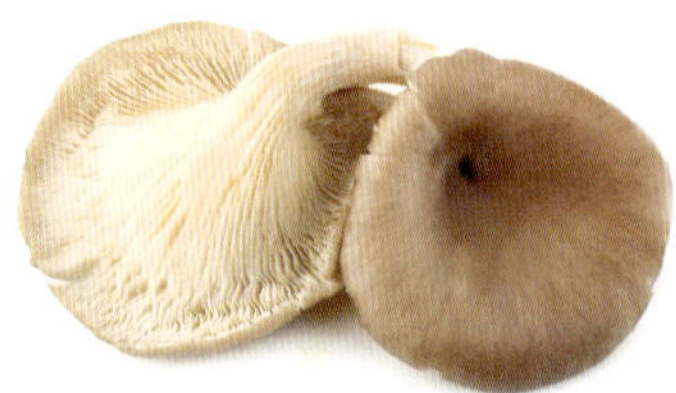

1. Preheat oven to 450°. Place skillet in oven to preheat.
2. Remove skillet from oven; add oil, red pepper flakes, and salt to hot skillet. Add mushrooms, stirring until coated with oil mixture.
3. Bake for 20 minutes, opening the oven door (to release steam) and stirring occasionally. Add butter and tamari to skillet, stirring until mushrooms are coated. Bake for 5 more minutes. Remove from oven and sprinkle with fresh herbs.

SPICY GRILL-PAN CARROTS WITH TAHINI-YOGURT SAUCE

MAKES 6 SERVINGS

EQUIPMENT: *Cast-iron grill pan*

PAN SAVVY: *A 10- or 12-inch cast-iron skillet can be substituted, but reduce heat to 400° and check for doneness a few minutes earlier. The raised grill pieces on a grill pan lift the vegetables from the bottom of the pan. A solid pan surface may char the carrots too much.*

2 tablespoons avocado or extra-virgin olive oil

2 teaspoons harissa paste, chili-garlic sauce, or sriracha

½ teaspoon fine sea salt

1 pound carrots, sliced in half lengthwise

⅓ cup Greek yogurt

¼ cup tahini sauce

1 tablespoon fresh lemon juice

½ teaspoon ground cumin

2 tablespoons water (optional)

2 tablespoons chopped fresh cilantro

Garnishes: lemon slices, quartered or slivered Preserved Lemons (page 134)

Capsaicin is the compound that gives chili peppers their heat; it is fat soluble, so water, beer, or soda can't wash away the burning sensation like high-fat dairy. For this reason, yogurt, sour cream, and milk are often paired with spicy foods to tame the heat.

---

1. Preheat oven to 450°. Place a large cast-iron grill pan in oven until very hot.
2. Combine oil, harissa paste, and salt in a small bowl. Brush oil mixture over carrots.
3. Carefully remove hot grill pan from oven, and arrange carrots in pan. Return to oven and bake, turning occasionally, for 12 to 15 minutes or until carrots are tender and slightly charred on edges.
4. Stir together yogurt, tahini, lemon juice, and cumin in a small bowl. Add 2 tablespoons water, if necessary, to make a spreadable sauce. Spread sauce on bottom of a serving plate.
5. Arrange carrots on top of sauce, and sprinkle with cilantro. Garnish, if desired.

RED LENTILS, RICE, AND SPINACH

MAKES 4 SERVINGS

EQUIPMENT: *3- to 5-quart Dutch oven*

PAN SAVVY: *A 3- to 5-quart saucepan with lid may be substituted.*

2 tablespoons ghee or unsalted butter
1 onion, chopped
2 garlic cloves, minced
1 teaspoon chopped gingerroot
1 teaspoon mustard seeds
1 teaspoon ground cumin
½ teaspoon turmeric
½ teaspoon fine sea salt
¾ cup basmati rice
4½ cups vegetable broth
¾ cup split red lentils
3 cups lightly packed fresh baby spinach or arugula

This vegetarian dish can also be called a variation on "Kitchari," an Indian comfort food eaten in times of fasting or digestive rest. I was introduced to this when I participated in an Ayurvedic detox, and it's now on regular rotation in my kitchen. Ghee is clarified butter, but you can use regular butter as a shortcut. Traditional Kitchari doesn't usually include greens, but I really enjoy adding baby spinach or arugula to make it more of a meal than a side dish.

---

1. Heat ghee in a Dutch oven over medium heat. Add onion, garlic, and ginger. Cook, stirring frequently, for 3 to 5 minutes or until onion is tender.
2. Stir in mustard seeds, cumin, turmeric, and salt. Stir in rice; cook, stirring constantly, for 1 minute or until rice is coated.
3. Stir in broth and lentils. Bring mixture to a boil, reduce heat, and cook, partially covered, for 20 minutes or until lentils and rice are tender. Stir in spinach.

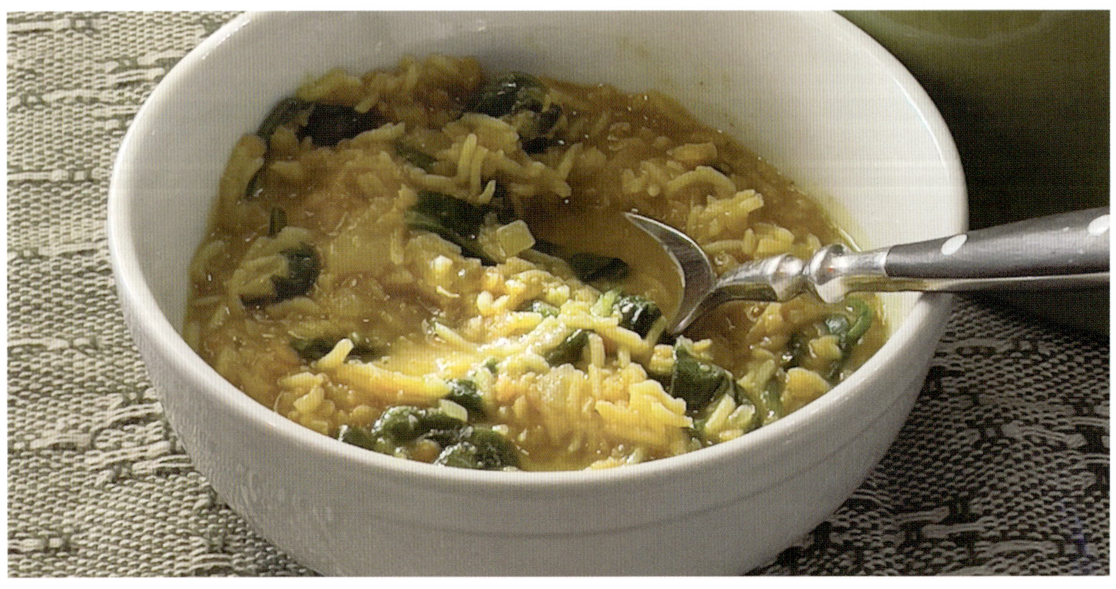

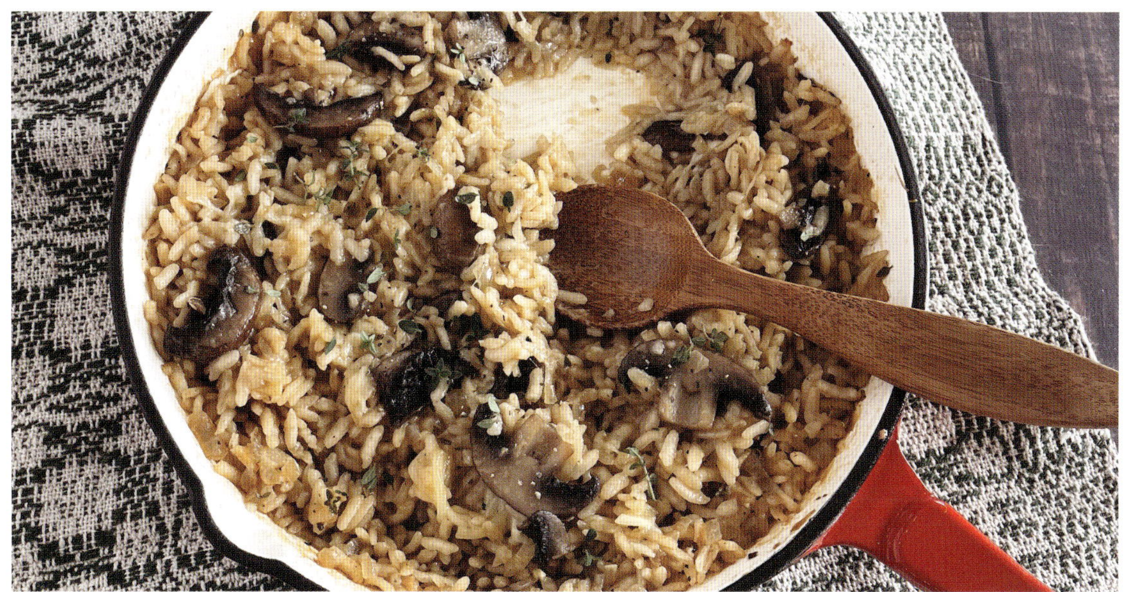

SKILLET BAKED RISOTTO WITH MUSHROOMS

MAKES 4 SERVINGS

Classic risotto is cooked slowly on the stovetop, requiring the gradual and constant stirring of small amounts of broth into a short-grain rice mixture. It's labor-intensive but yields a very creamy dish. This version eliminates much of the hands-on work and is almost as creamy as the real thing.

EQUIPMENT: *10-inch cast-iron skillet*

PAN SAVVY: *Substitute a 10-inch baker's skillet for easier handling.*

- 2 tablespoons salted butter
- ½ onion, finely chopped
- 2 garlic cloves, minced
- 1 cup Arborio rice
- ¼ cup white wine
- 2 cups vegetable or chicken broth
- 1 teaspoon fresh thyme leaves
- ½ teaspoon fine sea salt
- ¼ teaspoon coarsely ground black pepper
- ½ cup freshly grated Parmesan cheese

1. Melt butter in a 10-inch skillet over medium heat. Add onion and garlic; cook for 4 to 5 minutes or until tender.
2. Stir in rice. Cook, stirring frequently, for about 3 minutes or until edges of rice are translucent (do not brown).
3. Stir in wine. Cook, stirring constantly, for 3 minutes or until wine is absorbed.
4. Stir in broth, thyme, salt, and pepper. Cover with aluminum foil, and bake for 20 to 25 minutes or until liquid is absorbed and rice is tender.
5. Remove from oven and uncover. Stir in Parmesan cheese.

ROASTED CAULIFLOWER WITH LEMON, RAISINS, AND PINE NUTS

MAKES 4 SERVINGS

EQUIPMENT: *15.75-inch oval or 12-inch cast-iron skillet*

PAN SAVVY: *I use my largest skillet for this dish, which happens to be a shallow, oval-shaped one. The shallow sides enable the cauliflower to get a good crisp roast on the outside. You can substitute a 12-inch round skillet.*

¼ cup pine nuts

3 tablespoons avocado oil or extra-virgin olive oil

1 large head cauliflower, cut into florets

1 teaspoon salt

½ teaspoon coarsely ground black pepper

¼ teaspoon crushed red pepper flakes

½ cup golden or dark raisins

½ teaspoon ground cumin

½ teaspoon grated lemon zest

⅛ teaspoon garlic powder

1 tablespoon fresh lemon juice

1 teaspoon honey

1 tablespoon chopped fresh parsley or cilantro

Use the largest skillet or cast-iron roasting pan you have, so there is plenty of space around the cauliflower to ensure that it browns well.

---

1. Preheat oven to 425°.
2. Place a very large cast-iron skillet over medium-high heat. Add pine nuts and cook, shaking pan and stirring frequently, for 3 to 5 minutes or until golden brown. (Watch carefully; pine nuts burn quickly.) Transfer to a plate; set pine nuts aside.
3. Heat oil in skillet over medium-high heat. Add cauliflower and sprinkle with salt, pepper, and pepper flakes. Cook for 1 to 2 minutes, tossing gently to thoroughly coat cauliflower.
4. Transfer skillet to oven, and roast, stirring occasionally, for 20 to 25 minutes or until cauliflower is tender and edges are golden brown.
5. Combine raisins, cumin, lemon zest, and garlic powder in a small bowl. Stir in lemon juice and honey. Remove cauliflower from oven, and sprinkle with raisin mixture, tossing to coat. Return to oven for 3 to 5 minutes to heat raisin mixture. Transfer to a serving platter, if desired, and sprinkle with parsley and reserved pine nuts.

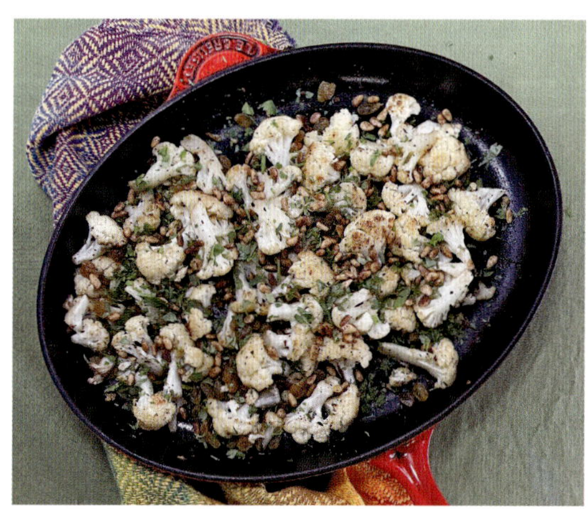

CREAMY GARLIC-PARMESAN BRUSSELS SPROUTS

MAKES 6 SERVINGS

These small, leafy green vegetables resemble miniature cabbages and are known for their nutty and occasionally bitter flavor. Although many recipes recommend roasting—and that's delicious too—this creamy dish is unique and hearty.

EQUIPMENT: *10-inch cast-iron skillet*

PAN SAVVY: *A 12-inch skillet works, but check for doneness 5 minutes earlier.*

2 thick slices bacon, chopped
1 tablespoon salted butter
1 pound fresh Brussels sprouts, trimmed and halved
½ teaspoon salt
¼ teaspoon coarsely ground black pepper
2 large garlic cloves, minced
1 cup heavy whipping cream
½ cup (2 ounces) shredded mozzarella or Gruyère cheese
¼ cup (1 ounce) shredded Parmesan cheese

1 Preheat oven to 400°.

2 Cook bacon in a 10-inch cast-iron skillet over medium heat, stirring occasionally, for 7 minutes or until crispy. Transfer to a plate, reserving 1 tablespoon drippings in pan; set bacon aside.

3 Add butter and let melt. Add Brussels sprouts, salt, and pepper to skillet; cook over medium-high heat for 3 to 5 minutes or until sprouts are just beginning to brown on the edges. Add garlic and cook, stirring constantly, for 30 seconds.

4 Add cream and cheeses, stirring until well blended. Transfer to oven, and bake for 25 minutes or until sprouts are tender and mixture is golden brown and bubbly. Sprinkle with reserved bacon.

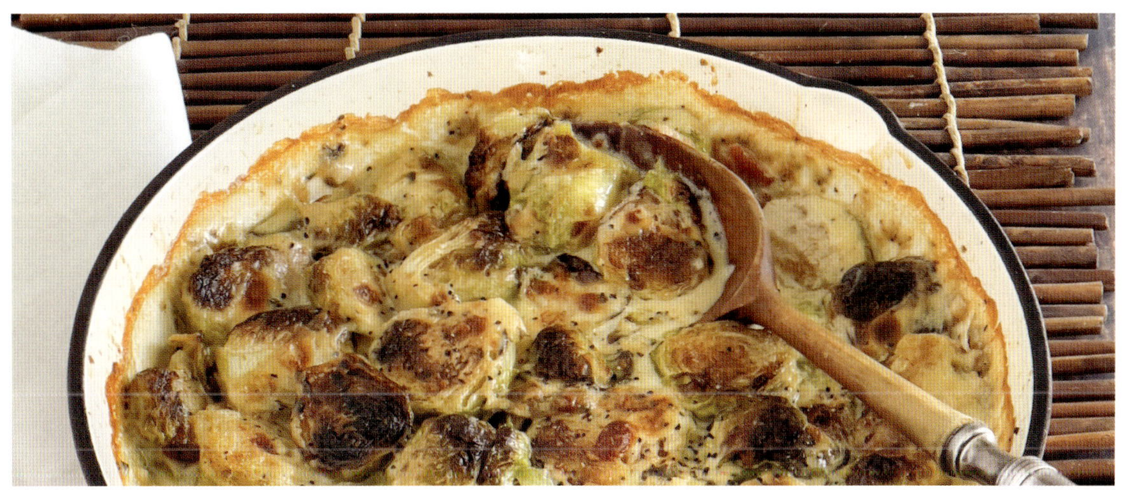

SKILLET SWEET POTATOES WITH ORANGE AND CRANBERRIES

MAKES 4 TO 6 SERVINGS

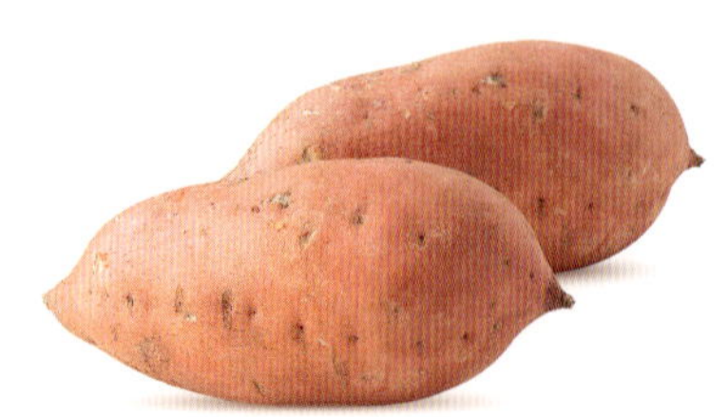

EQUIPMENT: *12-inch cast-iron skillet or brasier*

PAN SAVVY: *If a larger skillet is unavailable, the recipe will fit in a 10-inch skillet. Take care when stirring because the skillet will be full. Increase baking time by 10 to 15 minutes.*

1 tablespoon extra-virgin olive or avocado oil

¼ cup salted or unsalted butter

¼ cup packed light brown sugar

1 teaspoon grated orange zest

¼ cup fresh orange juice

½ teaspoon ground cinnamon

¼ teaspoon salt

2 large sweet potatoes (2 to 2¼ pounds), peeled and cubed

⅔ cup chopped pecans or walnuts

½ cup dried cranberries

1 tablespoon chopped fresh parsley

Naturally sweet potatoes pair well with tart cranberries. This dish makes a nice alternative to mashed sweet potatoes on the holiday table. Brown sugar and orange juice contribute to the sweetness but not as much as the marshmallow-topped dishes that are almost desserts.

1. Preheat oven to 350°.
2. Heat oil and butter in a large skillet over medium heat, stirring until butter melts. Add brown sugar, orange zest, juice, cinnamon, and salt, stirring until well blended.
3. Stir in sweet potatoes, pecans, and cranberries.
4. Bake for 40 to 45 minutes or until sweet potatoes are tender, stirring every 15 to 20 minutes. Remove from oven and sprinkle with parsley.

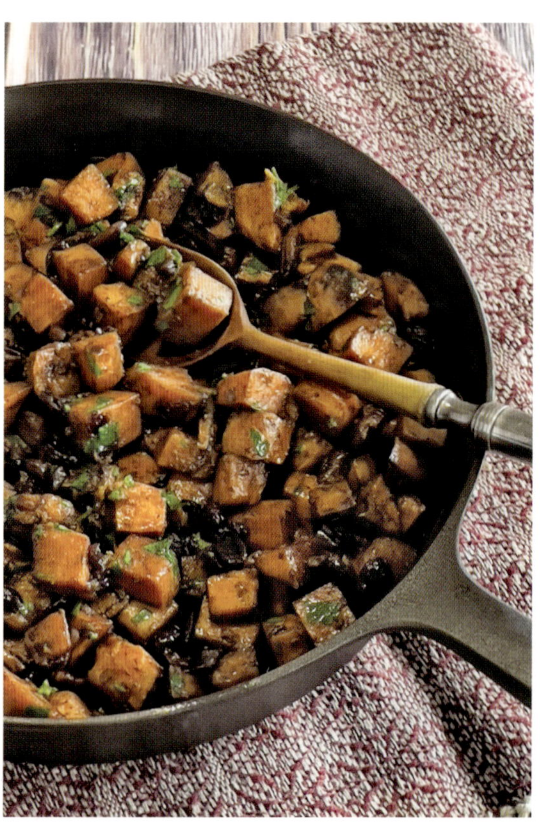

SKILLET POTATOES AU GRATIN

MAKES 4 TO 6 SERVINGS

EQUIPMENT: *12-inch cast-iron skillet*

PAN SAVVY: *The potatoes will fit in a 10-inch skillet if the sides are tall; otherwise, the mixture might bubble over into the oven. You can place the skillet on a sheet pan or a large piece of aluminum foil to catch any spills. Potatoes in a smaller-diameter skillet may take longer to cook, and less liquid will evaporate; add 10 to 15 minutes to the baking time.*

2 tablespoons salted butter
1 small onion, finely chopped
2 garlic cloves, minced
2 pounds russet or gold potatoes, thinly sliced (about 3 medium to large)
2 cups (8 ounces) shredded cheddar cheese
1 cup heavy whipping cream
1 cup vegetable or chicken broth
1 teaspoon fine sea salt
½ teaspoon coarsely ground black pepper
Garnish: chopped fresh parsley

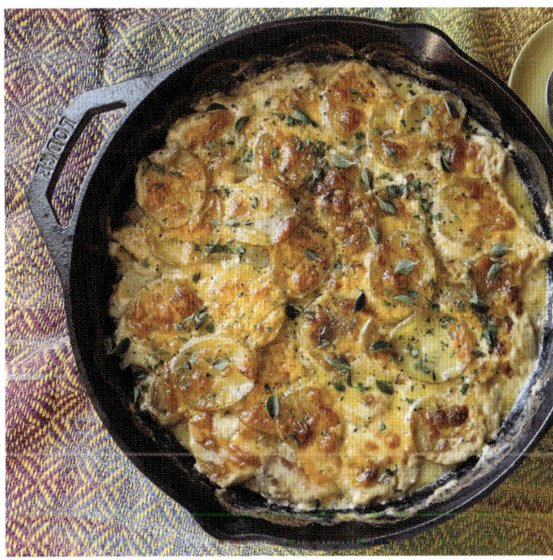

Enjoy this cheesy, easy-to-make side dish directly from the skillet. Serve with burgers, steaks, or grilled chicken. This version substitutes some broth for cream to lighten up the texture, making it less rich but equally delicious. Use almost any potato—they'll all taste good—but avoid waxy types like new or baby potatoes. Russets or Yukon Golds are ideal, whether peeled or rustic. Russet potatoes tend to have thicker skin, so I peel those but skip that step with gold potatoes.

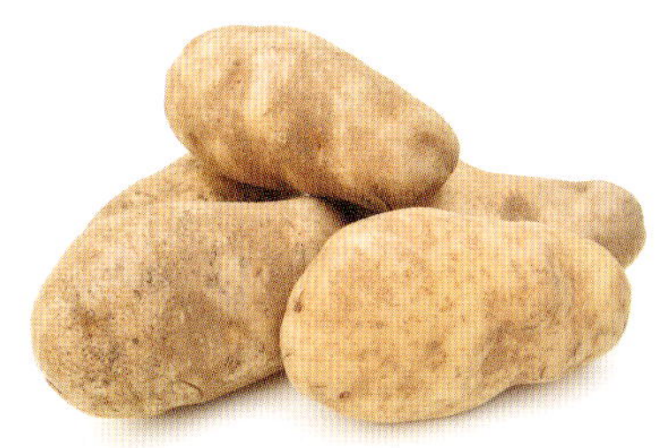

1. Preheat oven to 375°.
2. Melt butter in a 12-inch cast-iron skillet over medium heat. Add onion and garlic. Cook, stirring frequently, for 3 to 5 minutes or until onion is translucent. Remove from heat.
3. Layer one-third of potatoes in bottom of skillet, overlapping somewhat, and sprinkle with one-third of cheese. Repeat layers twice.
4. Combine cream, broth, salt, and pepper in a medium-size bowl, stirring until well blended. Pour over layered potatoes and cheese.
5. Cover skillet with lid or aluminum foil, and bake for 30 minutes. Remove foil and bake for 30 more minutes or until potatoes are tender and top is golden brown. Garnish, if desired.

HASSELBACK POTATOES

MAKES 6 SERVINGS

EQUIPMENT: *12- or 10-inch cast-iron skillet*

PAN SAVVY: *The same weight of small potatoes will take up more room in the skillet than fewer, larger potatoes. Adjust the size of the pan based on the size of the potatoes. You can test by placing them in the skillet before washing and prepping.*

1½ pounds small Yukon Gold or gold potatoes

¼ cup salted butter, melted

¼ teaspoon paprika

⅛ teaspoon fine sea salt

⅛ teaspoon coarsely ground black pepper

2 tablespoons grated Romano or Parmesan cheese

1 garlic clove, minced

1 tablespoon chopped fresh herbs (rosemary and/or parsley)

These interesting-looking potatoes are fun to eat! It's easy to adjust this recipe to suit the number of people you're serving.

This dish is distinctive with its accordion-like slices of potato cooked with butter, fresh herbs, and cheese. The edges become crispy in the oven, while the interior of the potato remains tender. Multiple slices mean the tempting flavors can seep into the potato, making every bite delicious. I prefer smaller Yukon Gold or gold potatoes, but you can use russet potatoes, if you like. Large potatoes will require more baking time to become tender.

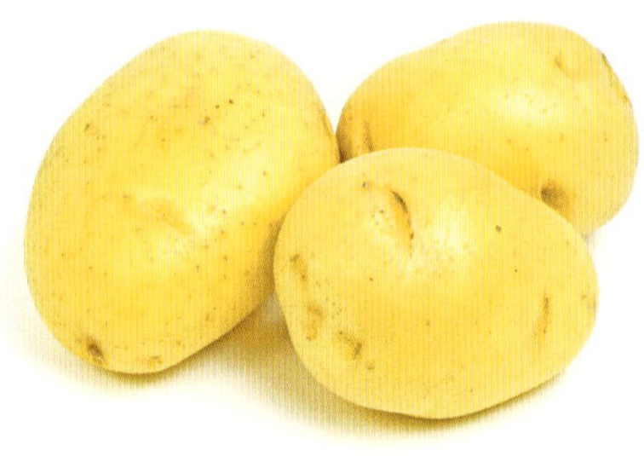

1. Preheat oven to 425°.
2. Slice a thin layer along each potato to create a flat base so potatoes don't roll. Place, flat side down, on a cutting board; cut ⅛-inch-thick slices into—but not completely through—each potato. (Place chopsticks or wooden spoons on either side as guides to stop you from cutting all the way through.)
3. Place potatoes in a large skillet. Combine butter, paprika, salt, pepper, cheese, and garlic in a bowl. Brush about half of butter mixture over potatoes, making sure butter mixture gets in between slices. Cover with aluminun foil, and bake for 45 minutes or until potatoes are almost tender.
4. Brush potatoes with remaining half of butter mixture. Bake, uncovered, for 15 to 20 more minutes or until crisp and golden on the outside and tender on the inside. Spoon melted butter from bottom of pan over potatoes. Sprinkle with fresh herbs.

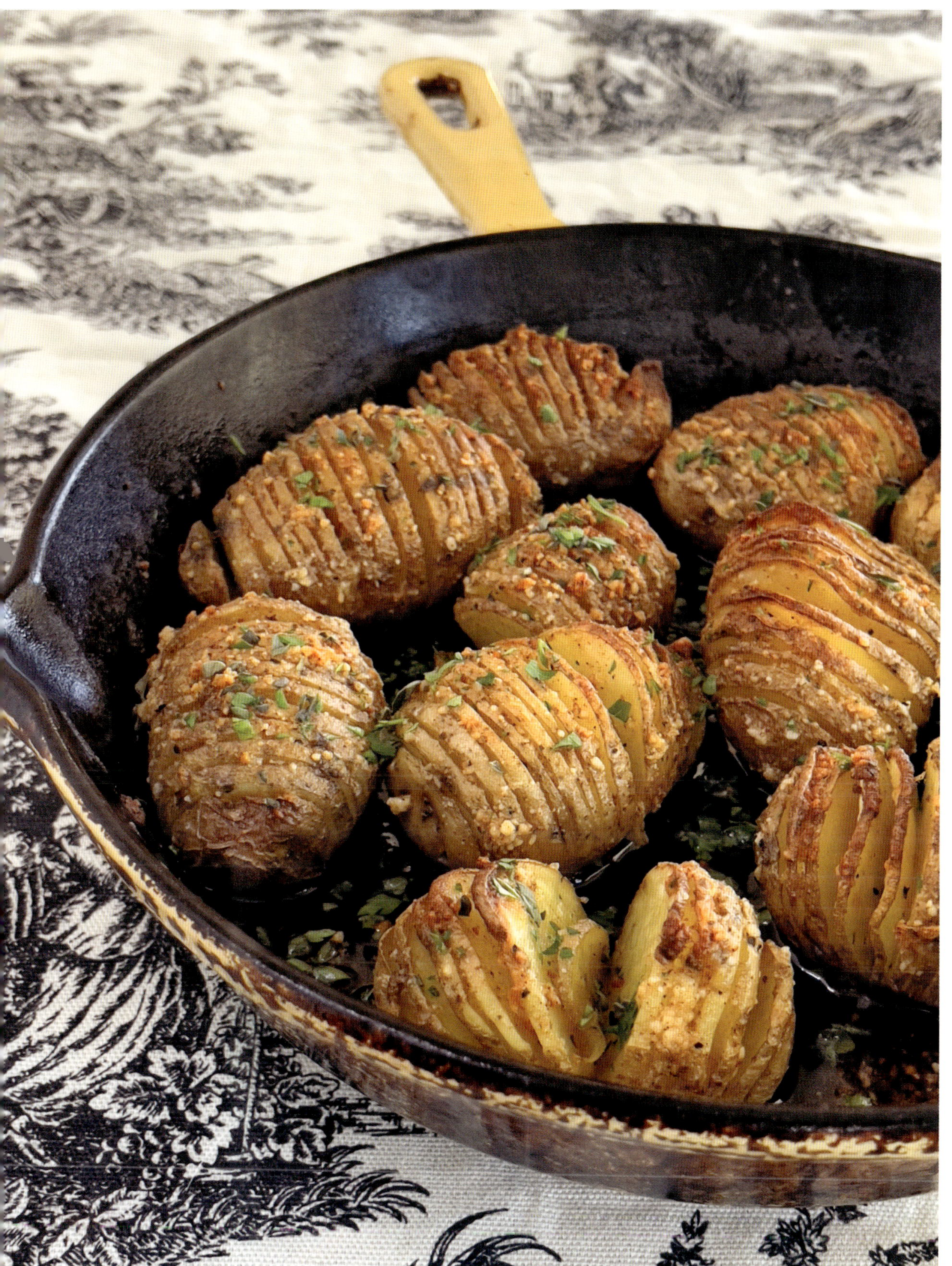

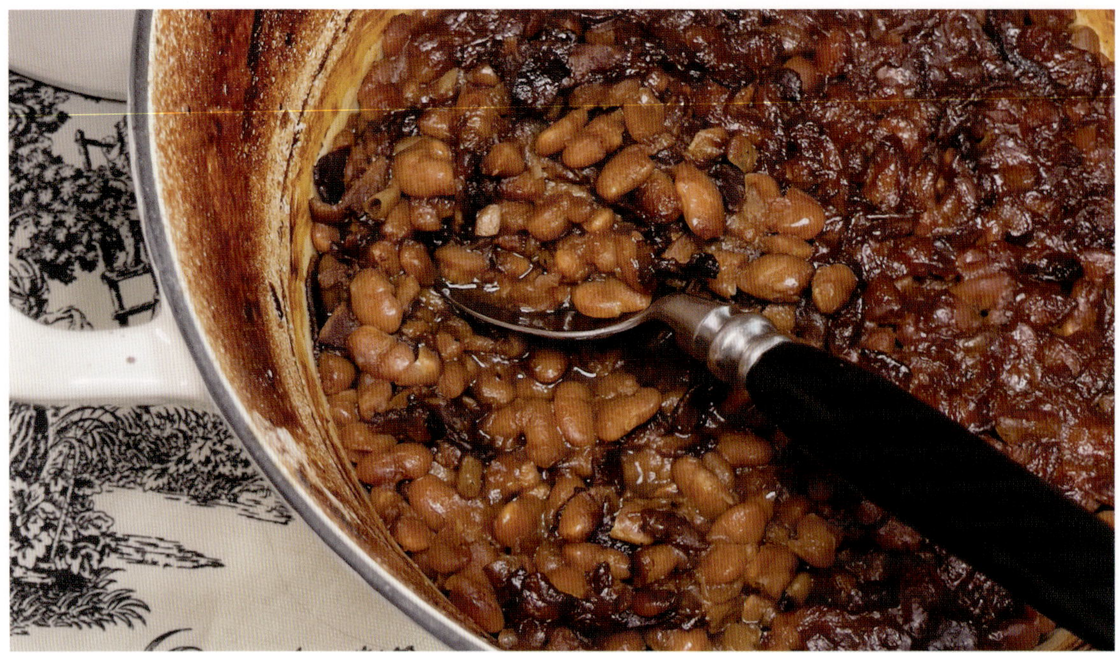

BOSTON BAKED BEANS

MAKES 6 SERVINGS

This old-school recipe requires the beans to be soaked overnight, followed by hours-long baking in the oven. The result is a richly flavored side dish. Cast iron is great for this recipe because it starts on the stovetop and ends in the oven.

EQUIPMENT: *5- to 7-quart Dutch oven*

1 pound (2½ cups) dried navy or small white beans, rinsed

6 slices thick-cut bacon, chopped

1 large yellow or white onion, chopped

4 garlic cloves, minced

8 cups water

⅓ cup firmly packed dark brown sugar

⅓ cup mild molasses

2 tablespoons brown or Dijon mustard

1 teaspoon salt

¾ teaspoon coarsely ground black pepper

1. Soak beans in a large bowl of water for 8 hours or overnight. Drain and set beans aside.
2. Cook bacon in a Dutch oven over medium heat, stirring occasionally, for 7 to 10 minutes or until lightly browned and most of fat is rendered. Add onion and cook, stirring occasionally, for 8 minutes or until tender. Add garlic, and cook for 1 minute.
3. Preheat oven to 325°.
4. Stir in 8 cups water, reserved beans, brown sugar, molasses, mustard, salt, and black pepper. Bring to a boil over medium-high heat. Cover and transfer to oven.
5. Bake for 4 hours, stirring every hour. Remove lid and bake for 1 to 1½ hours or until sauce has thickened and top is crusty.

ROASTED CABBAGE AND BACON

MAKES 6 SERVINGS

EQUIPMENT: *12-inch cast-iron skillet*

6 slices bacon, chopped
1 head green cabbage (about 2 to 2¼ pounds)
1 yellow onion, halved and thickly sliced
¾ cup chicken or vegetable broth
¼ cup apple cider vinegar
2 tablespoons tomato paste
2 garlic cloves, minced
½ teaspoon salt
½ teaspoon coarsely ground black pepper
Garnish: chopped fresh parsley

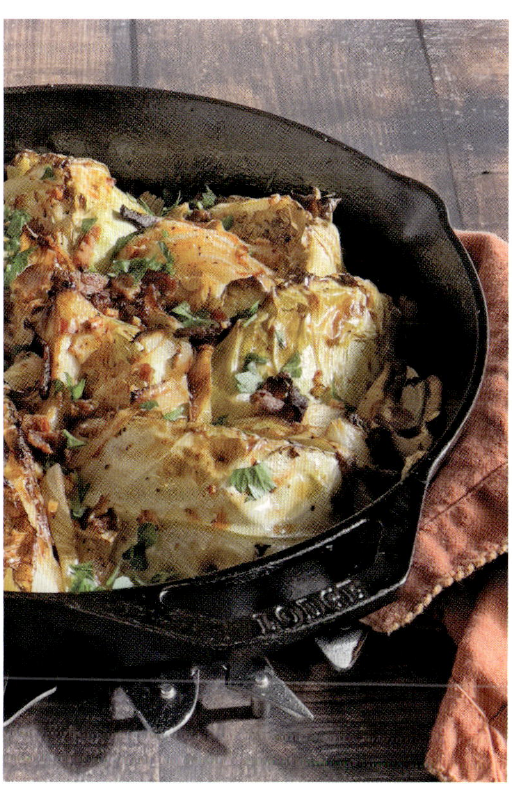

I use a large, wide skillet to prepare this recipe because the cabbage is cut into pieces that are small enough to cook well without covering. Medium-high to high heat is required to get a good char on the edges of the cabbage, so use an uncoated-but-seasoned (not enamel coated) cast-iron skillet.

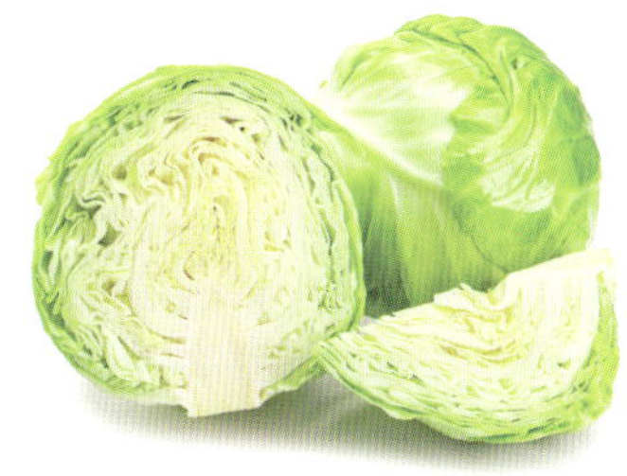

1 Preheat oven to 350°.
2 Cook bacon in a 12-inch cast-iron skillet over medium heat until crispy. Transfer to paper towels, reserving 2 tablespoons drippings in skillet; set bacon aside.
3 Cut cabbage into 8 wedges; remove most (but not all) of the core, keeping wedges intact.
4 Heat bacon drippings over medium-high to high heat. Cook cabbage wedges, in batches, for 2 to 3 minutes on each side or until lightly charred. Remove skillet from heat and arrange onion slices around cabbage.
5 Combine broth, vinegar, tomato paste, garlic, salt, and pepper in a small bowl. Stir in half of reserved bacon. Pour broth mixture gently over cabbage mixture.
6 Bake for 45 to 60 minutes or until vegetables are tender. Sprinkle with remaining half of reserved bacon. Garnish, if desired.

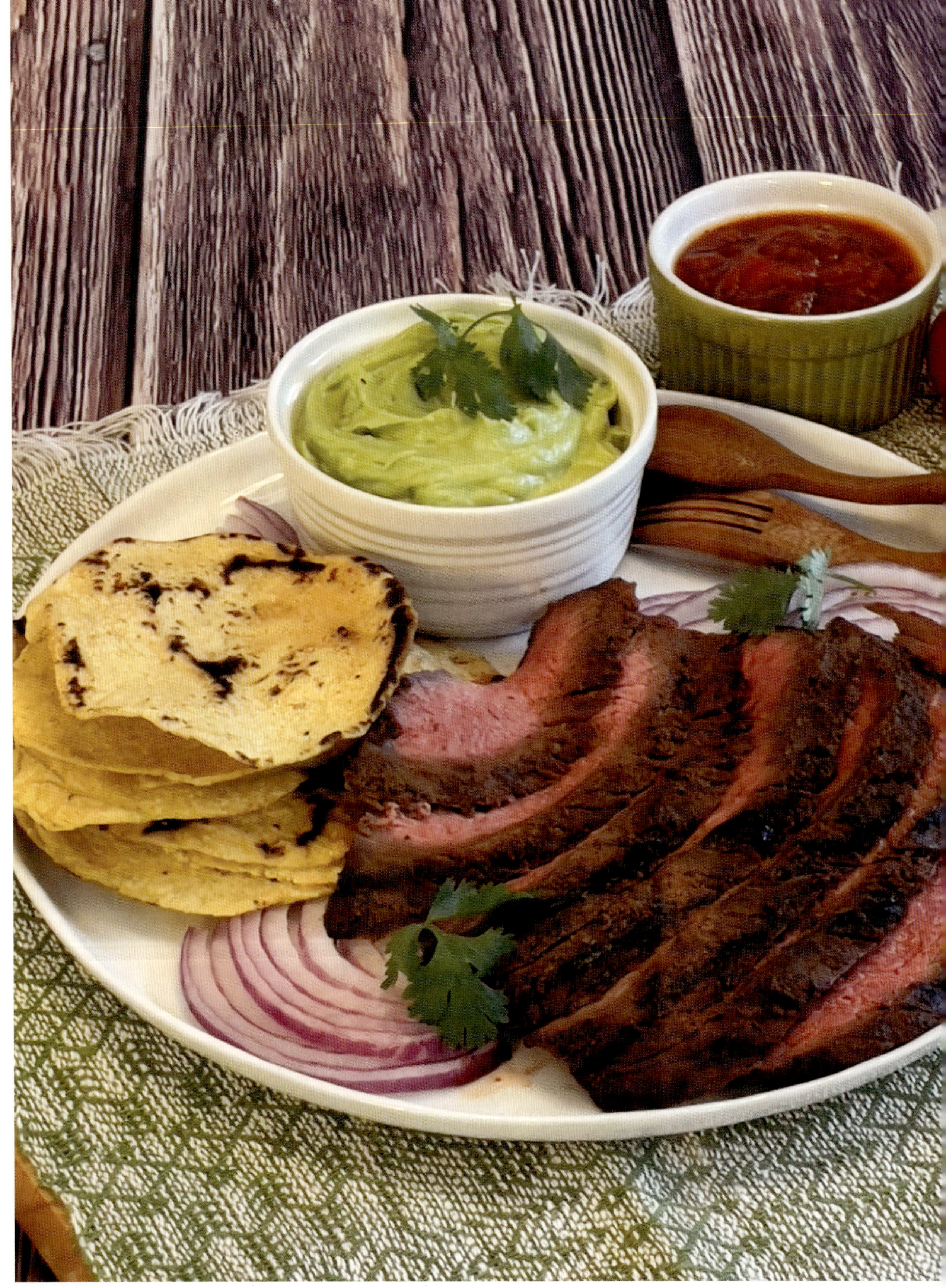

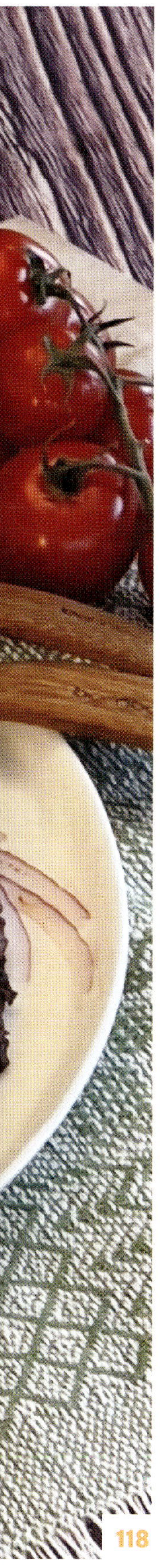

118

PIZZA, SANDWICHES, *and* TACOS

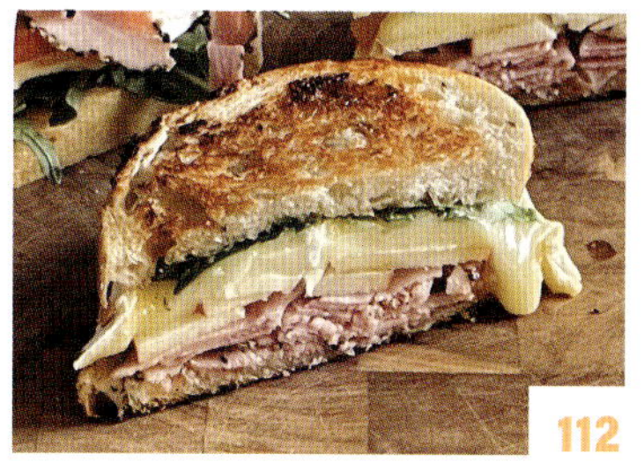

112

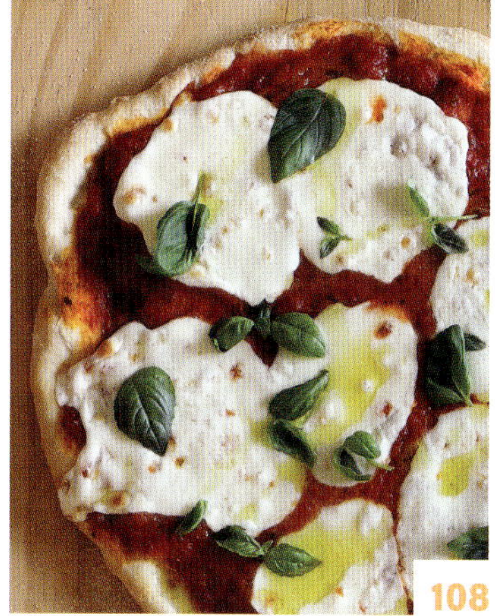

108

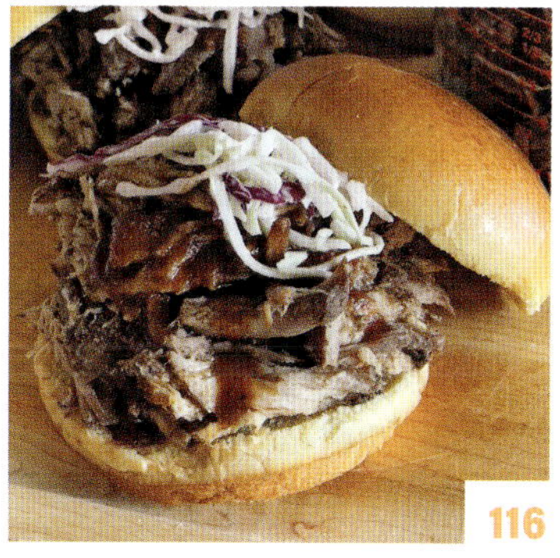

116

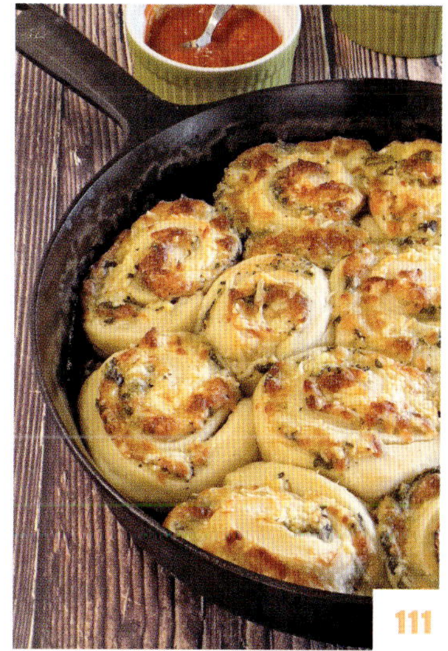

111

PIZZA STONE MARGHERITA PIZZA

MAKES 1 (12-INCH) PIZZA (4 TO 6 SERVINGS)

EQUIPMENT: *14-inch cast-iron pizza stone*

PAN SAVVY: *Keep the crust at least 1 inch from the perimeter. A large pizza stone will prevent errant melted cheese from dripping into the oven. You can also bake this in a 10- or 12-inch cast-iron skillet like the recipe on page 110.*

½ recipe Pizza Dough (page 109) or 12- to 14-ounce ball store-bought pizza dough

¼ cup semolina flour or cornmeal

½ to ¾ cup Pizza Sauce (page 109) or store-bought sauce

4 to 6 ounces fresh mozzarella, sliced

¼ cup lightly packed fresh basil, torn

1 tablespoon extra-virgin olive oil

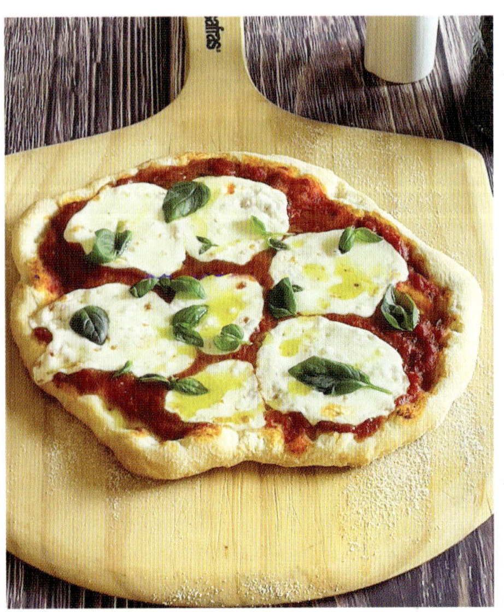

I've owned a terra-cotta pizza stone for almost 30 years, and its color has transformed from a pale beige to a slick-and-shiny chocolate brown, proving that you can season things besides cast iron! I used to always bake pizzas on the stone, but the one disadvantage is that mine can't be used on a grill. Outdoor grills can heat up well past temperatures an indoor oven can provide. Very high heat means a shorter baking time and a pizza with a crunchy crust and chewy toppings. Cast-iron pizza stones can handle the heat without cracking, they often have handles for easy carrying, and they either arrive pre-seasoned or become seasoned to a nonstick surface faster than stone. Cooking pizza straight on the grill grate works well for small, individual pizzettes, but it's very tricky with a full-size pie, heavy with fillings. So, load up the pizza crust and use a cast-iron pizza stone on the grill.

---

1. Allow Pizza Dough to reach room temperature (this could take 1 to 2 hours).
2. Place cast-iron pizza stone or pan on grill grates, and preheat grill to high heat (550° or higher). (Or preheat oven to 450°.)
3. Dust a pizza peel or rimless baking sheet with semolina or cornmeal. Place dough in center; flatten and stretch dough into a 12-inch circle.
4. Spread Pizza Sauce evenly over pizza, leaving a 1-inch border. (If adding additional toppings, arrange on top of sauce.) Arrange fresh mozzarella slices on top.
5. Carefully slide pizza off peel and onto hot pizza stone. Cover with grill lid and cook for 8 to 10 minutes or until crust is golden brown on bottom and cheese is melted. Using peel, transfer pizza to a cutting board.
6. Sprinkle with fresh basil and drizzle with olive oil.

PIZZA DOUGH

MAKES CRUSTS FOR 2 (10- TO 12-INCH) PIZZAS

Specially milled for pizza crusts, 00 pizza flour is lovely to use, but all-purpose flour is a great substitution. Letting the dough rest in the refrigerator for a day enhances its flavor.

1 (¼-ounce) envelope active dry yeast
2 teaspoons granulated sugar
1 cup warm water (100° to 110°)
2 tablespoons extra-virgin olive oil
2½ cups 00 pizza flour or all-purpose flour
½ cup semolina flour, plus more for rolling out
1 teaspoon salt

1. Combine yeast, sugar, and 1 cup warm water in a large bowl; let stand for 5 minutes. Stir in olive oil.
2. Combine pizza flour, semolina, and salt; beat with an electric mixer until a soft dough forms. Turn dough out onto a surface lightly sprinkled with semolina; knead for 2 minutes. (Or leave dough in mixing bowl and knead with a dough hook for 1 minute or until smooth and elastic.)
3. Lightly grease a bowl with olive oil. Shape dough into a ball, and transfer to bowl, turning to coat. Cover and let rise in a warm place (85°), free from drafts, for 1 hour or until doubled in size.
4. Punch dough down. Divide in half. Dough may be placed in a large zip-top plastic storage bag and refrigerated for up to 3 days or frozen up to 3 months.

PIZZA SAUCE

MAKES 3 CUPS

EQUIPMENT: *3- to 5-quart Dutch oven*

PAN SAVVY: *If cooking the sauce, I like a deep saucepan that keeps splatters inside. Unless your cast iron is not seasoned well, the quick cooking time shouldn't affect the seasoning, but transfer the sauce soon after cooking.*

1 (6-ounce) can tomato paste
1 tablespoon extra-virgin olive oil
1 tablespoon dried Italian seasoning
2 teaspoons dried oregano
1 teaspoon fine sea salt
¾ teaspoon garlic powder
¼ teaspoon crushed red pepper flakes
1 (28-ounce) can crushed tomatoes
1 teaspoon granulated sugar

Cooking and reducing the tomato mixture deepens the flavor and thickens the sauce a bit. However, it is perfectly delicious if you just stir the ingredients together in a bowl before using. You'll end up with more than you need for just one pizza. Serve the extra on pasta another day, or freeze it up to 3 months. I like to portion the sauce and freeze using a label on the freezer bag that reads: sauce for 1 pizza—no waste! Use ½ to 1 cup sauce per pizza.

1. Combine tomato paste, olive oil, seasoning, oregano, salt, garlic powder, and pepper flakes in a Dutch oven. Cook over medium heat, stirring constantly, for 1 minute.
2. Stir in crushed tomatoes and sugar. Cook over medium heat, stirring frequently, for 5 to 7 minutes or until slightly thickened.

SPINACH-AND-THREE-CHEESE SKILLET PIZZA

MAKES 3 TO 4 SERVINGS

EQUIPMENT: *12-inch cast-iron skillet*

PAN SAVVY: *For a deep-dish version with a thick crust, use a 10-inch skillet.*

½ recipe Pizza Dough (page 109) or 1 (14- to 16-ounce) ball store-bought pizza dough

3 tablespoons extra-virgin olive oil, divided

1 large shallot or ¼ onion, thinly sliced

2 garlic cloves, minced

⅛ to ¼ teaspoon crushed red pepper flakes

1 (5-ounce) package fresh baby spinach

½ teaspoon fine sea salt

1 cup ricotta cheese

1 large egg

½ cup crumbled feta cheese

1½ cups (6 ounces) shredded mozzarella or provolone cheese

Garnish: crushed red pepper flakes

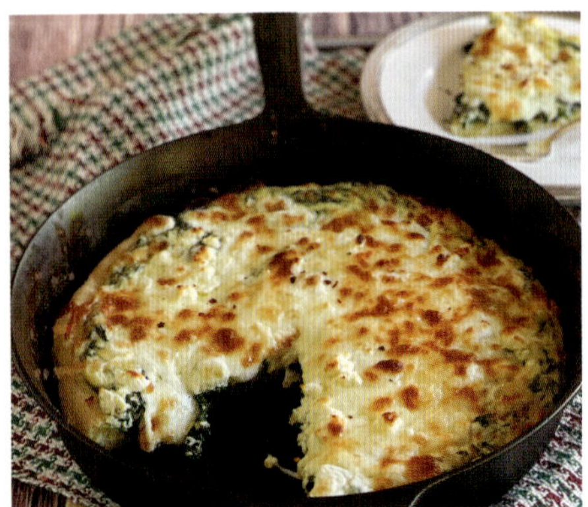

If you are a fan of lots of sauce, filling, and cheese, then this pizza delivers. The high rim of the cast-iron skillet will hold everything in, so go ahead and spread everything to the edges!

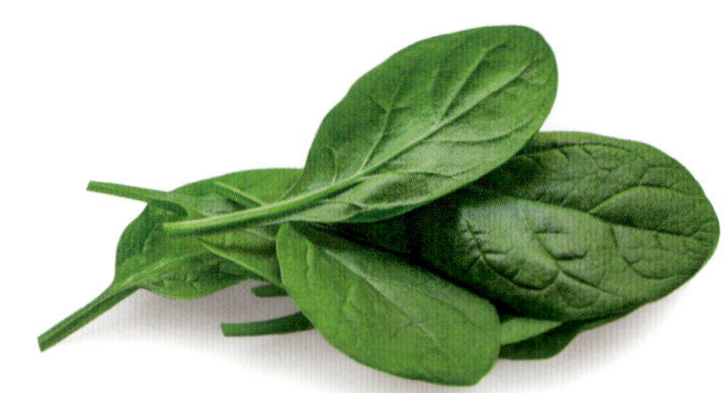

1. Allow Pizza Dough to reach room temperature (this could take 1 to 2 hours).
2. Heat 1 tablespoon oil in a 12-inch cast-iron skillet over medium heat. Add shallot, garlic, and crushed red pepper flakes. Cook for 3 minutes or until tender. Add spinach and salt. Cook, tossing frequently with tongs, for 2 to 3 minutes or until wilted. Transfer to a bowl and stir in ricotta cheese and egg; set spinach-ricotta mixture aside.
3. Drizzle remaining 2 tablespoons oil into skillet. Stretch dough by hands (or roll dough on a lightly floured surface into a circle). Add to skillet, pressing with fingers to edges of pan (be careful because skillet might still be hot). Allow dough to rest for 10 minutes in pan.
4. Place oven rack in the lower third of oven. Preheat oven to 450°.
5. Spread reserved spinach-ricotta mixture over dough, and sprinkle evenly with feta and mozzarella. Bake for 15 minutes or until golden brown and cheese is melted.
6. Remove from oven, and run a knife around edges of pizza to release any cheese stuck to the skillet. Let rest in skillet for 5 minutes. Garnish, if desired.

ROASTED GARLIC, HERB, AND CHEESE PIZZA ROLLS

MAKES ABOUT 1 DOZEN

EQUIPMENT: *12-inch cast-iron skillet*

PAN SAVVY: *The rolls will be snug, but they'll fit in a 10-inch skillet. Add 5 to 7 minutes baking time, if necessary.*

1 large or 2 small garlic bulbs
1 tablespoon extra-virgin olive oil
¼ cup unsalted or salted butter, softened
¼ cup chopped fresh parsley
¼ cup chopped fresh basil
½ teaspoon coarsely ground black pepper
¼ teaspoon fine sea salt
½ recipe Pizza Dough (page 109) or 1 (14- to 16-ounce) ball store-bought pizza dough, at room temperature
1 cup (4 ounces) shredded mozzarella cheese
1 cup (4 ounces) shredded Parmesan cheese
Pizza Sauce (page 109) or store-bought sauce, warmed

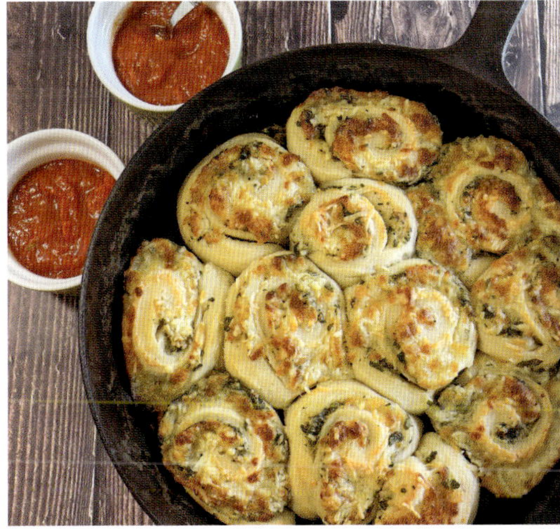

Roasted garlic is amazingly mellow and easy to make ahead. Whenever you have the oven going, make some roasted garlic on the side to store in the freezer. You may substitute 2 to 3 minced fresh garlic cloves, but expect the garlic flavor to be more pungent.

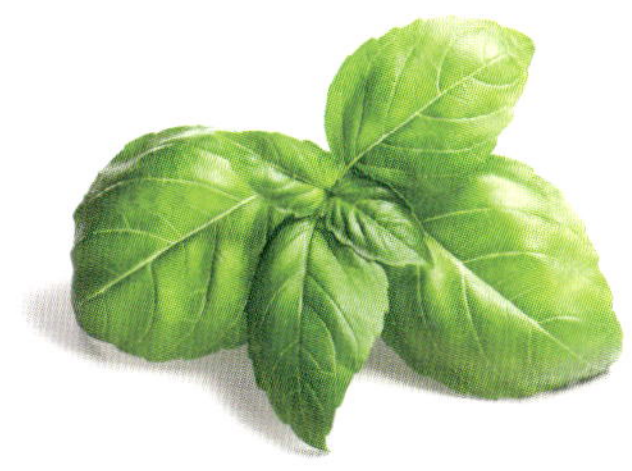

1. Preheat oven to 400°.
2. Remove excess papery skin from outside of garlic bulb, but do not completely peel. Place on a square of heavy-duty aluminum foil or two sheets of regular foil. Drizzle with oil, and wrap foil around garlic. Place in a small cast-iron skillet, if desired. Bake for 40 minutes or until golden brown and center is very tender. Remove from oven; allow to cool.
3. Reduce heat to 375°.
4. Squeeze garlic cloves into a large bowl, discarding peel. Stir in butter, parsley, basil, pepper, and salt.
5. Roll dough out onto a lightly floured surface into a 10x14-inch rectangle. Spread garlic mixture evenly on top, and sprinkle evenly with cheeses. Roll into a log, starting at long side and pinching long edge into dough to seal. Cut into 12 pieces.
6. Place rolls, cut side down, in a 12-inch cast-iron skillet. Bake for 25 to 30 minutes or until golden brown. Let stand for 5 minutes before serving. Serve with warm Pizza Sauce.

GRIDDLED HAM, BRIE, AND ARUGULA SANDWICHES

MAKES 4 SERVINGS

EQUIPMENT: *10- or 12-inch cast-iron skillet*

PAN SAVVY: *It's easier to turn the sandwiches over when they're cooked in batches rather than crowded together in the skillet.*

- ⅓ cup mango chutney, apricot preserves, or orange marmalade
- 8 slices sourdough bread
- 1 cup loosely packed baby arugula leaves
- 8 ounces Brie cheese (with or without rind), thinly sliced
- 1 green or red apple, cored and thinly sliced
- 9 to 12 ounces spiral-sliced ham or other deli ham
- 3 tablespoons salted butter, softened

A grill press is a heavy plate with a handle used to press bacon, sandwiches, or other foods down onto hot skillets, griddles, or grill grates. If you don't have one, you can carefully flip the sandwich over to cook the second side, taking care because the sandwich is piled high with fillings. You can also use a smaller cast-iron skillet to press down on the sandwich. If you happen to have any of the Baked Brie with Chutney appetizer (page 61) leftover, use it instead of plain Brie cheese.

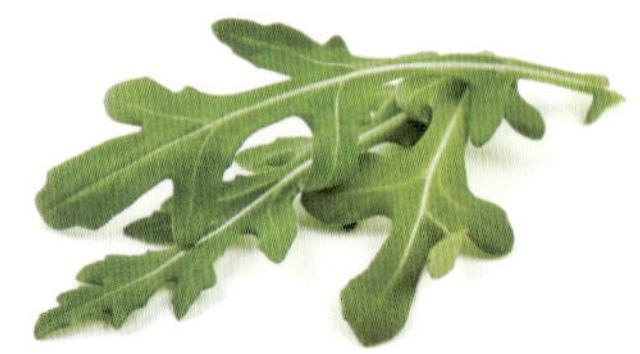

1. Spread chutney evenly on one side of bread slices. Arrange arugula, cheese, apple, and ham on 4 slices. Top with remaining 4 slices.
2. Spread outside of sandwiches with butter.
3. Heat a cast-iron grill pan over medium-low to medium heat. Add sandwiches, in batches if necessary. Weigh down with a grill press, smaller skillet, or press with a metal spatula. Cook for 3 to 4 minutes on each side or until cheese melts and outside is golden brown.

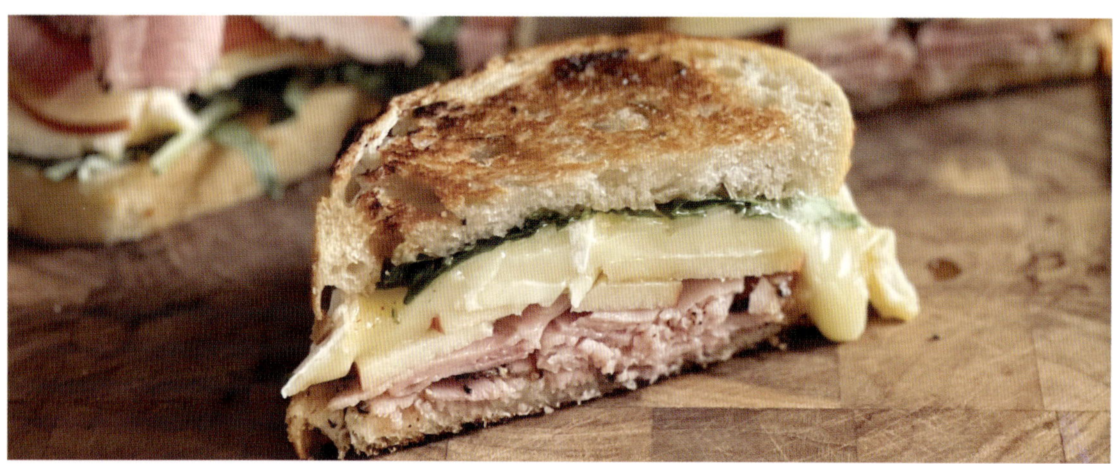

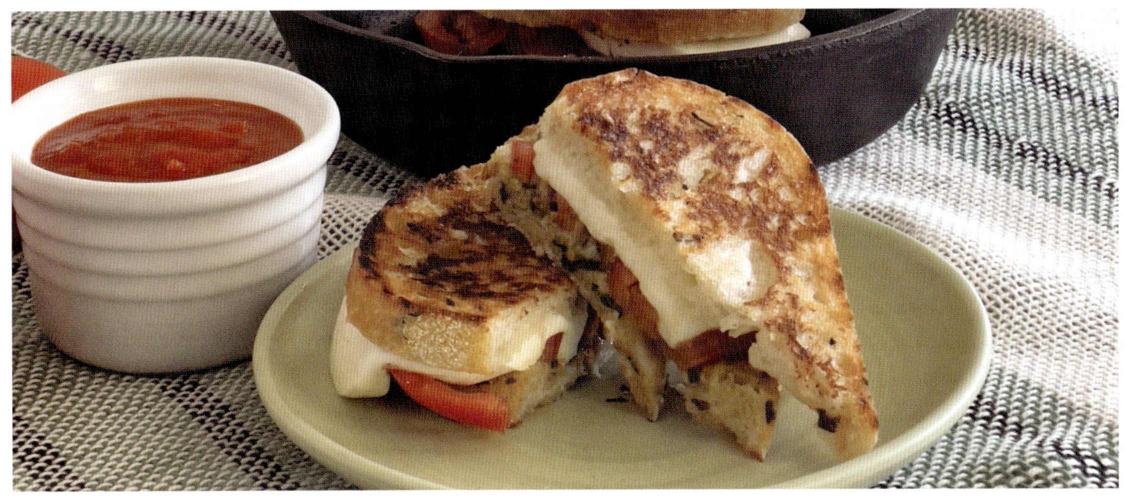

CAPRESE GRILLED CHEESE WITH PESTO

MAKES 2 SERVINGS

EQUIPMENT: *cast-iron grill pan*

PAN SAVVY: *The raised grill lines add color and extra-toasted flavor. You can also use a flat-bottomed skillet, if desired.*

4 slices sourdough, rosemary-Parmesan, or olive bread

1½ tablespoons salted butter

3 tablespoons Pesto Sauce (recipe at right) or store-bought refrigerated pesto sauce

2 ripe Roma or plum tomatoes, sliced

4 to 6 slices fresh mozzarella cheese

Pizza Sauce (page 109) or store-bought marinara sauce (optional)

Griddled between two slices of savory sourdough bread, fresh mozzarella makes a delicious pairing with ripe tomatoes and fresh pesto. Look for fresh, locally made artisan bread at bakeries or upscale markets for the best flavor.

1. Spread one side of each piece of bread with butter. On unbuttered side of two slices, layer evenly with Pesto Sauce, tomato, and cheese. Top with remaining bread, butter side out.
2. Heat a cast-iron grill pan over medium-high heat. Add sandwiches; weigh down with a grill press, smaller skillet, or press with a metal spatula. Cook for 3 to 4 minutes on each side or until cheese melts and outside is golden brown. Serve with Pizza Sauce, if desired.

Pesto Sauce: Combine **1 (4-ounce) container fresh basil, 2 coarsely chopped garlic cloves, ½ cup shredded Parmesan cheese, ½ cup extra-virgin olive oil, ½ teaspoon lemon zest, 1 tablespoon fresh lemon juice,** and **¼ teaspoon salt** in a food processor. Pulse until evenly and finely chopped. Add **¼ cup toasted pine nuts or walnuts.** Pulse until finely chopped. Cover and refrigerate for 1 week or freeze small portions up to 3 months. Makes 1 cup.

FALAFEL SANDWICHES

MAKES 4 SERVINGS

EQUIPMENT: *Dutch oven or deep cast-iron skillet*

1 cup dried chickpeas or garbanzo beans

½ teaspoon baking soda

⅓ cup chopped onion

1 cup lightly packed chopped parsley

½ cup lightly packed chopped cilantro

1 large garlic clove, roughly chopped

½ teaspoon grated lemon zest

1 teaspoon ground cumin

1 teaspoon ground coriander

1 teaspoon salt

¼ teaspoon coarsely ground black pepper

⅛ teaspoon ground cayenne pepper

½ teaspoon baking powder

1 tablespoon chickpea or all-purpose flour

1 tablespoon fresh lemon juice

Vegetable oil

Grilled Skillet Flatbread (page 28) or store-bought flatbread

Tzatziki Sauce (recipe at right)

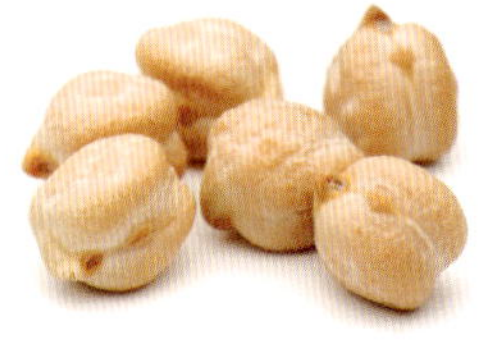

One of the most surprising things about falafel is that it's made from dried-and-soaked chickpeas that are not cooked—do not use canned chickpeas! You may see packages labeled garbanzo. Chickpea and garbanzo are different names for the same variety of seed (pulse) from a legume plant. Don't squeeze the falafel balls too tightly when rolling or they may fall apart. A gently held-together falafel will be tender after frying. For consistent portions, use a small ice-cream scoop.

1. Rinse beans and place in a large bowl. Cover with water by at least 3 inches. Stir in baking soda (this raises the pH, which tenderizes the beans). Soak for 24 hours, checking and adding water, if necessary, to keep beans submerged.
2. Drain beans and place in a food processor. Add onion, parsley, cilantro, garlic, zest, cumin, coriander, salt, black pepper, cayenne pepper, and baking powder. Pulse, stopping to scrape down sides, until bean mixture is minced and the texture of coarse sand. Add flour, pulsing until well blended. Add juice, pulsing until well blended. Mixture should hold together when gently squeezed. If mixture is too dry, add water by tablespoons. If mixture is too damp, add an additional 1 tablespoon chickpea flour or all-purpose flour.
3. Pour oil to depth of 2 to 2½ inches in a Dutch oven or deep cast-iron skillet. Heat to 350°.
4. Portion falafel mixture by heaping tablespoonfuls and form into 1½-inch balls. Fry for 2 to 3 minutes, turning occasionally, until they are a deep golden brown. Drain on paper towels. Serve with Skillet Flatbread and Tzatziki Sauce.

Tzatziki Sauce: Grate **½ seedless English cucumber** and squeeze dry. Transfer to a bowl and stir in **1¼ cups Greek yogurt, 1 finely grated garlic clove, ¼ teaspoon lemon zest, 2 tablespoons fresh lemon juice, 2 tablespoons extra-virgin olive oil, 1 tablespoon chopped fresh dill, ¼ teaspoon salt,** and **¼ teaspoon coarsely ground black pepper.** Makes 1¾ cups.

BLUE CHEESE-AND-ONION BURGER

MAKES 4 SERVINGS

EQUIPMENT: *10- to 12-inch cast-iron skillet*

PAN SAVVY: *I'll pick my least-seasoned pan for this recipe because there's a lot of butter and oil from the burgers to help re-season a sticky pan.*

¼ cup Caramelized Onions (recipe at right)
4 brioche, onion, poppy seed, or other burger buns, split
1 pound ground beef
1 tablespoon Worcestershire sauce
1 teaspoon hot sauce
½ teaspoon salt
¼ teaspoon coarsely ground black pepper
1 tablespoon avocado or extra-virgin olive oil
½ cup (2 ounces) crumbled blue cheese
4 slices provolone cheese
Arugula or other lettuce
4 slices crisp cooked bacon

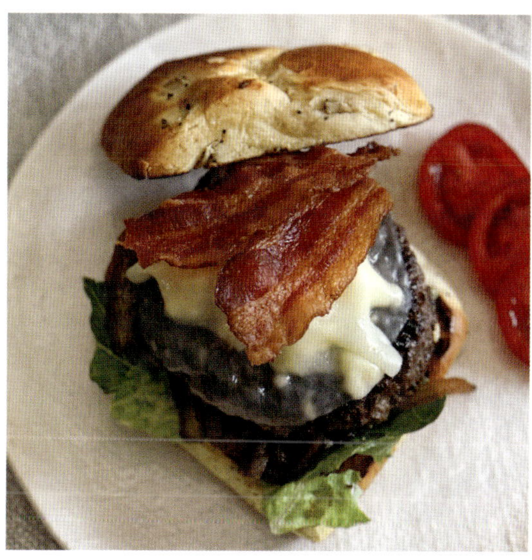

The sharp, piquant flavor of blue cheese is a surprisingly delicious complement to earthy beef burgers and sweet caramelized onions. The blue cheese crumbles tend to fall off the burger, so put a slice of provolone on top to hold the blue cheese in place.

1. Prepare Caramelized Onions. Transfer to a small bowl and set aside. Do not wipe skillet clean.
2. For toasted buns, heat skillet over medium-high heat. Place buns, cut side down, in skillet and cook for 1 minute or until golden brown. Keep warm.
3. Combine beef, Worcestershire sauce, hot sauce, salt, and pepper in a large bowl. Divide beef mixture and form into 4 patties.
4. Heat a large skillet over medium to medium-high heat. Add oil and allow to heat. Add patties and cook for 3 minutes for medium-rare or 4 minutes for medium. Turn patties over and cook for 2 minutes or until desired degree of doneness. Remove from heat; top evenly with blue cheese. Top with provolone, and allow cheese to melt.
5. Layer bottom buns with arugula, reserved Caramelized Onions, and bacon; add patties and top buns.

Caramelized Onions: Melt **1 tablespoon butter** in a large heavy skillet over medium heat. Add **1 large onion, halved and chopped.** Cover and cook for 10 minutes. Uncover and cook, stirring frequently, for 20 minutes or until golden brown and tender. Store leftovers in refrigerator for a week or freeze up to 3 months.

DUTCH OVEN PULLED PORK

MAKES 8 TO 10 SERVINGS

Pork shoulder is sometimes labeled as pork butt or Boston butt. I like using boneless in this recipe because it's easier to cut and brown smaller pieces of meat, rather than one large, heavy piece.

EQUIPMENT: *7-quart cast-iron Dutch oven*

PAN SAVVY: *The heaviness of a cast-iron lid is ideal for keeping a tight seal on the pan while the pork cooks. Make sure the knob is ovenproof, as some pans are sold with plastic knobs.*

1 (6- to 7-pound) piece of boneless pork shoulder

3 tablespoons dark or light brown sugar

1½ tablespoons kosher salt or 2 teaspoons fine sea salt

2 tablespoons paprika

1½ tablespoons chili powder

1 tablespoon coarsely ground black pepper

2 teaspoons garlic powder

2 teaspoons onion powder

1 tablespoon avocado or vegetable oil

½ cup chicken broth or water

Sandwich buns

Coleslaw (recipe at right)

Simple Barbecue Sauce (recipe at right) or store-bought barbecue sauce

1. Trim pork of excess fat, leaving a thin layer; cut into large pieces.
2. Stir together brown sugar, salt, paprika, chili powder, pepper, garlic powder, and onion powder in a shallow baking dish. Roll pork in spice blend to cover. For convenience and more flavor, cover and refrigerate for 8 hours or overnight.
3. Adjust oven rack to lower one-third position. Preheat oven to 300°.
4. Heat oil in a large Dutch oven over medium heat. Add pork, in batches, and sear for 2 minutes on each side or until golden brown. Transfer to a plate and repeat with remaining pork.
5. Remove from heat and add broth, scraping up any bits stuck on bottom of pan. Add pork, fat side up.
6. Cover with lid, and bake for 3 hours or until pork is tender. Remove lid and continue to bake until a dark bark forms on top of pork and meat is easily shredded with a fork.
7. Transfer meat to a cutting board set inside a rimmed baking sheet to catch any juices. Shred with two forks, discarding any fatty pieces. Place shredded meat in a large bowl, drizzling with enough pan juices to keep moist. Serve with buns and Coleslaw, drizzling with Simple Barbecue Sauce.

Coleslaw: Stir together **½ cup mayonnaise, ¼ cup sour cream, 3 tablespoons granulated sugar, 3 tablespoons apple cider vinegar, 2 teaspoons celery salt,** and **2 teaspoons grated sweet onion (optional)** in a large bowl. Add **8 cups lightly packed shredded green cabbage** and **5 cups lightly packed shredded purple cabbage,** tossing to blend. Makes 8 to 10 servings.

Simple Barbecue Sauce: Combine **1 cup tomato sauce or ketchup, ½ cup firmly packed dark brown sugar, ¼ cup apple cider vinegar, 2 tablespoons Worcestershire sauce, 1 tablespoon Dijon mustard, 1 teaspoon chili powder, 1 teaspoon fine sea salt, 2 teaspoons hot sauce, 1 teaspoon liquid smoke, ½ teaspoon garlic powder,** and **½ teaspoon black pepper** in a saucepan over medium heat. Bring to a boil, reduce heat, and simmer for 5 minutes or until mixture is reduced and slightly thickened. Makes 1¾ cups.

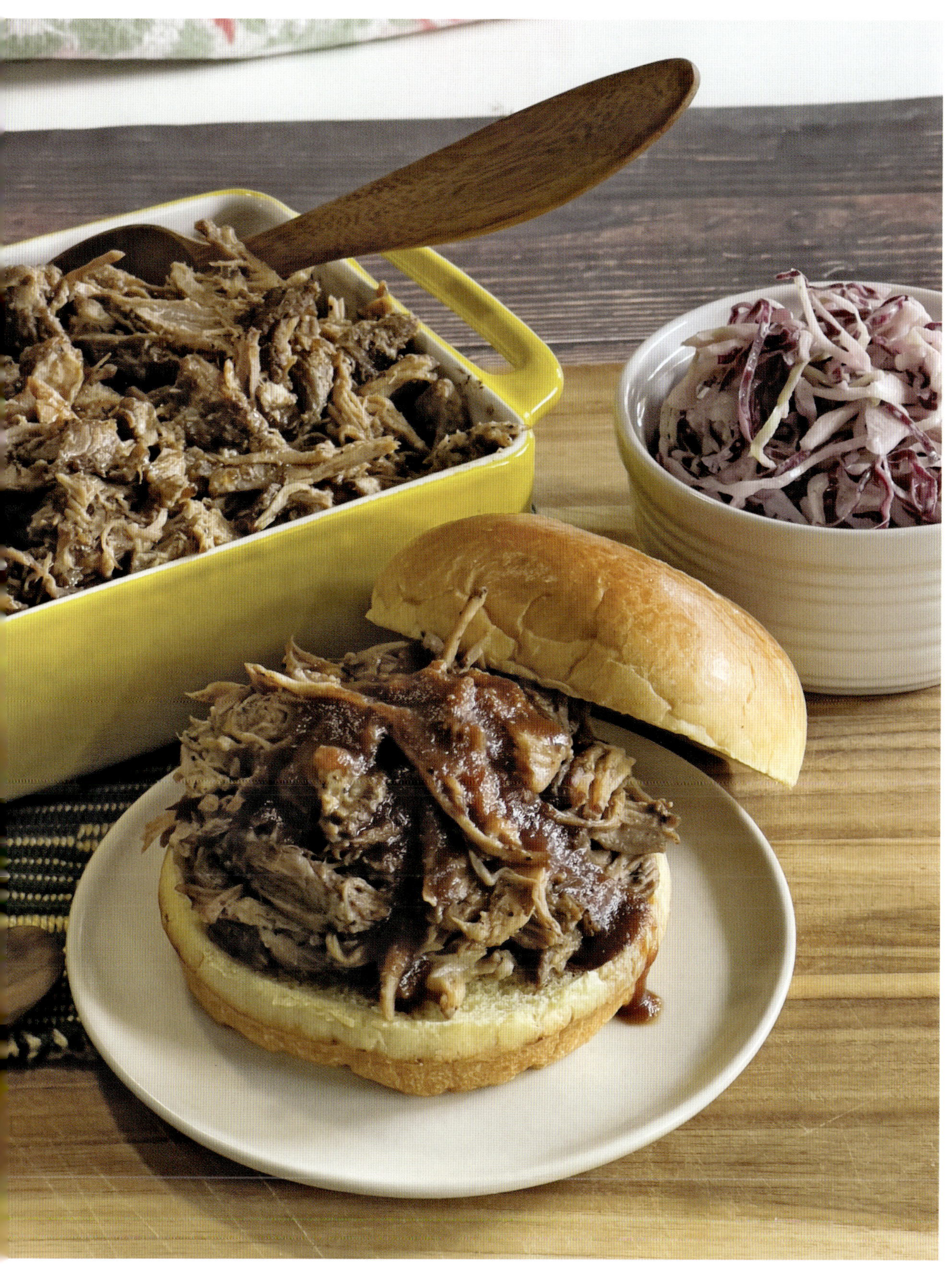

STEAK STREET TACOS WITH AVOCADO CREMA

MAKES 6 TO 8 SERVINGS

EQUIPMENT: *cast-iron grill pan*

PAN SAVVY: *Square or round grill pans work the same, but make sure the pan is not larger than the stove eye.*

2 tablespoons chili powder
1 teaspoon paprika
1 teaspoon garlic powder
1 teaspoon onion powder
1 teaspoon dark brown sugar
1 teaspoon kosher salt
1 teaspoon coarsely ground black pepper
1 (1¼- to 1½-pound) skirt or flank steak
12 to 16 small Homemade Corn Tortillas (page 29) or store-bought corn tortillas
Avocado Crema (recipe at right)
Charred Tomato Salsa (page 46) or store-bought salsa
Fresh cilantro

Tender, well-seasoned steak is the highlight of this no-fuss meal. Street tacos differ from typical tacos in that they use small, soft corn tortillas that surround a simple meat filling. Try the marinated steak without the taco fixings with corn on the cob for a different meal. Add leftover steak to salads for a hearty, protein-rich dinner.

1. Combine chili powder, paprika, garlic powder, onion powder, brown sugar, salt, and pepper. Rub over steak. Cover and refrigerate for 1 to 8 hours.
2. Heat a grill pan or large cast-iron skillet over medium-high to high heat. Cook steaks for 4 minutes on each side or until internal temperature registers 130° for medium-rare or to desired degree of doneness. Let rest on a cutting board for 10 minutes.
3. Slice steak thinly against the grain. Place in Homemade Corn Tortillas with Avocado Crema and Charred Tomato Salsa. Sprinkle with cilantro.

Avocado Crema: Combine **2 ripe avocados, ½ cup mascarpone or sour cream, 1 minced garlic clove, ½ teaspoon grated lime zest, 1½ tablespoons fresh lime juice,** and **½ teaspoon salt** in a food processor or blender. Process until smooth. Pulse in **2 tablespoons finely chopped fresh cilantro.** Makes 2 cups.

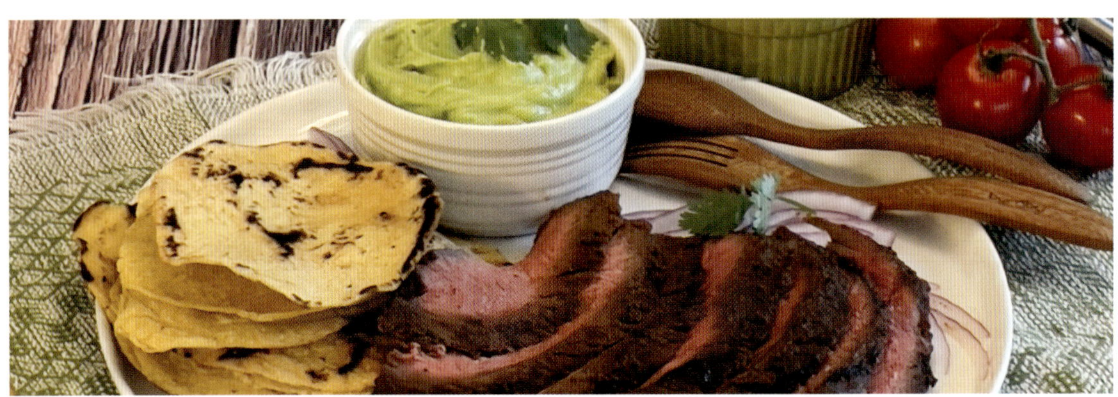

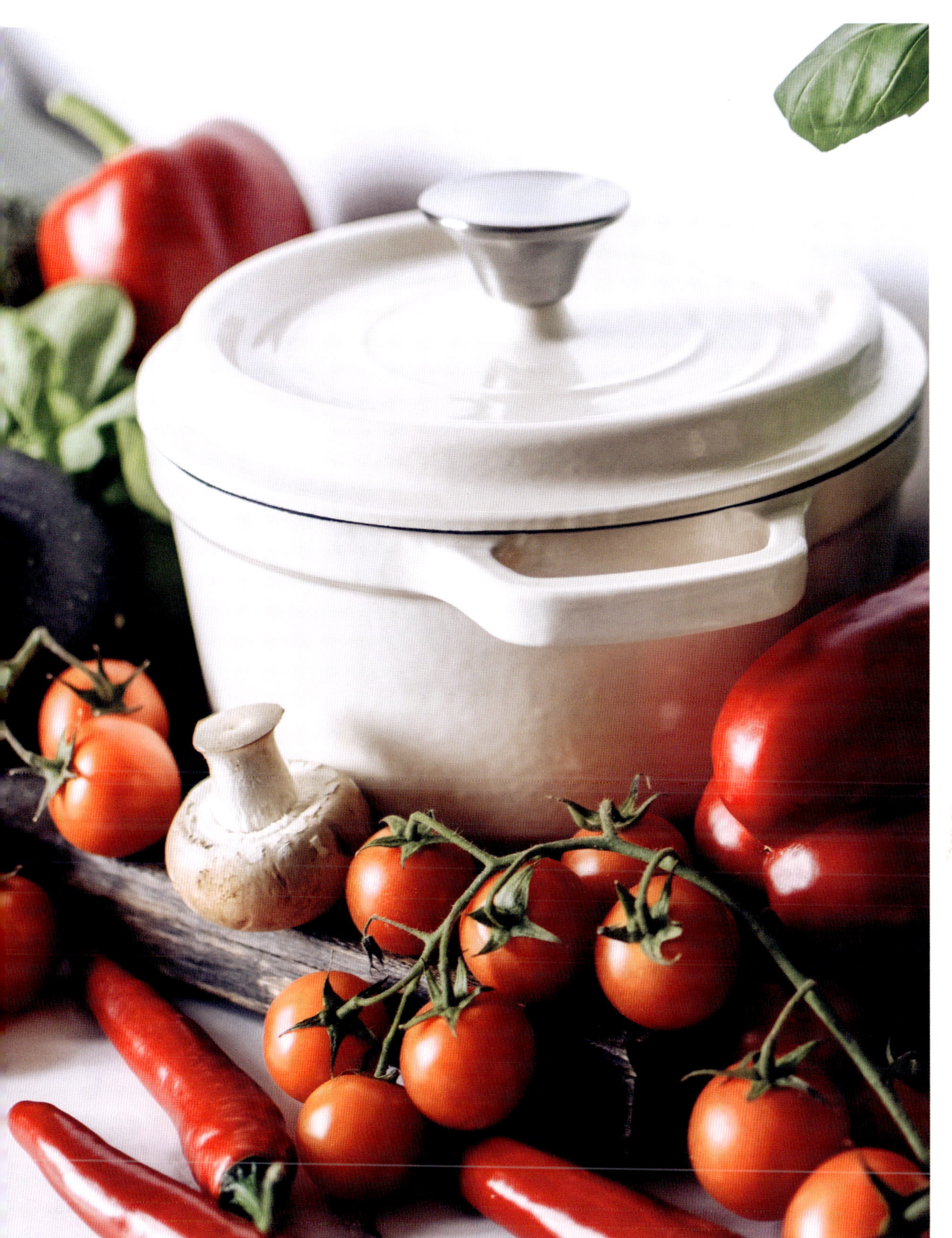

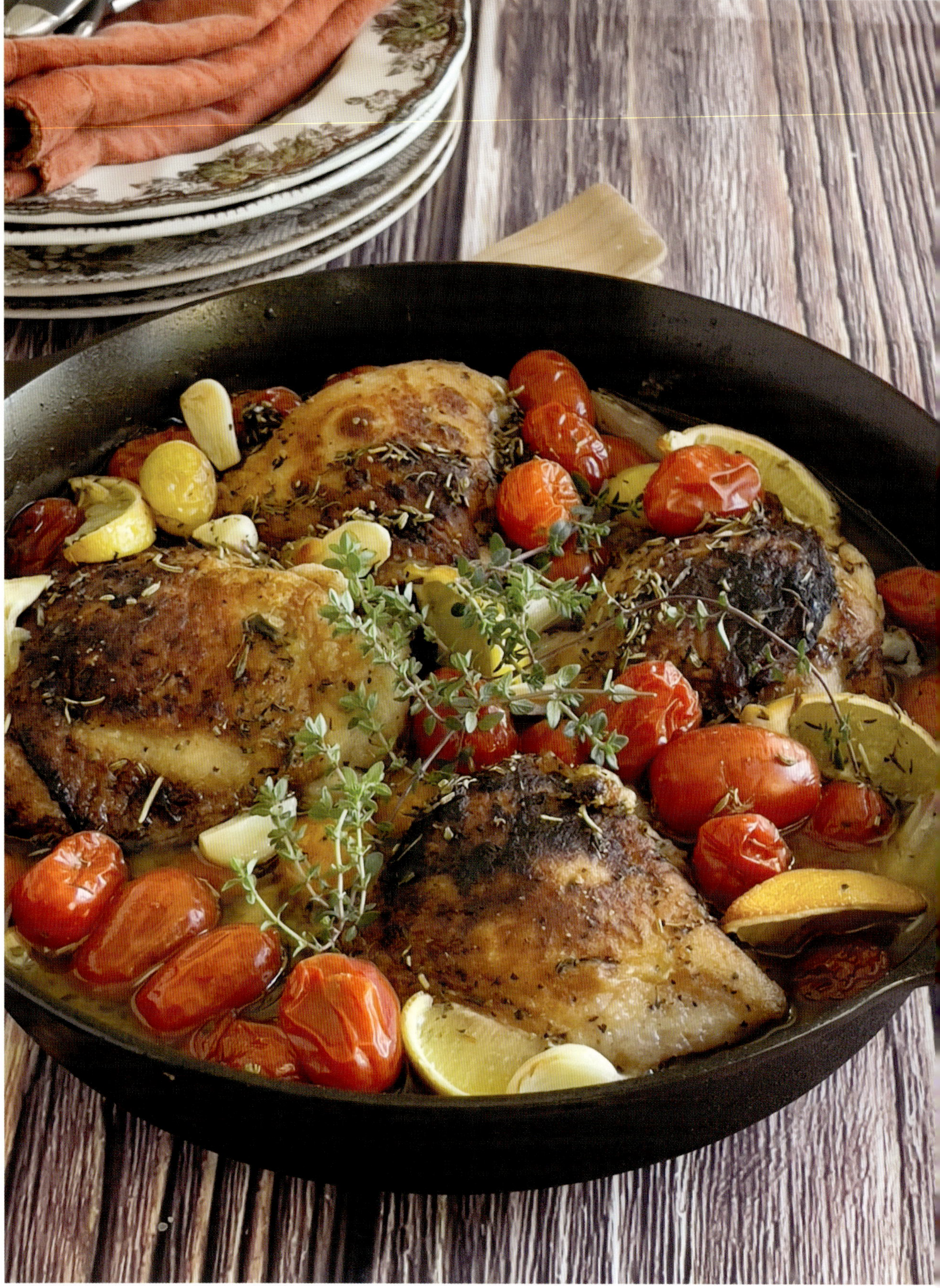

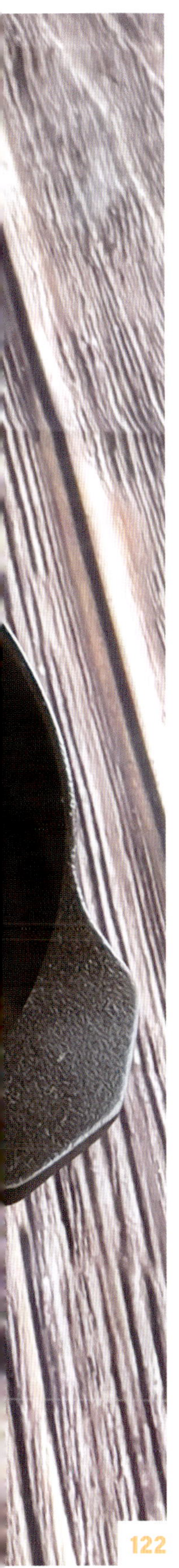
122

MAINS

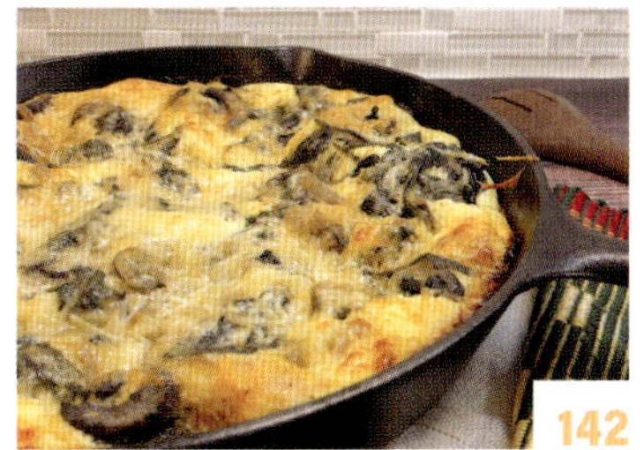
142

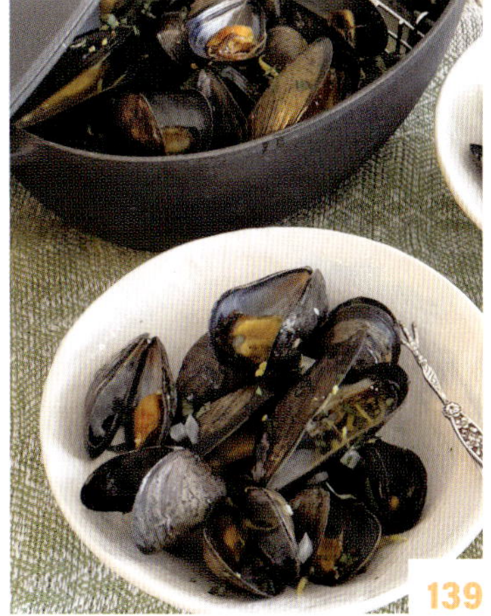
139

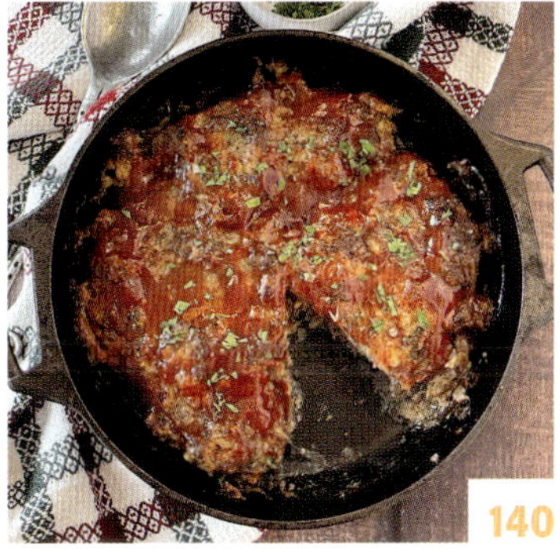
140

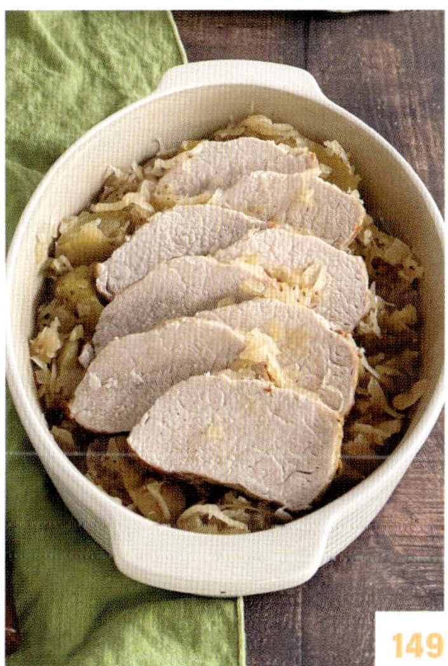
149

PAN-ROASTED CHICKEN PROVENÇAL

MAKES 4 SERVINGS

EQUIPMENT: *12-inch cast-iron skillet or braiser*

PAN SAVVY: *A brasier, with its deep sides, is also ideal for preparing this dish. (The lid won't be needed in this recipe.) A 10-inch skillet can be used as long as it has deep sides to contain the broth that's created during baking. You may also need to brown the chicken pieces in batches, but it's okay if they nestle tightly while they bake in the oven.*

2 tablespoons all-purpose flour

1 teaspoon fine sea salt, divided

½ teaspoon coarsely ground black pepper, divided

2½ pounds bone-in, skin-on chicken thighs or other pieces

2 tablespoons avocado or extra-virgin olive oil

3 shallots, quartered

8 whole garlic cloves, halved

1 pint cherry tomatoes

1 lemon, cut into wedges

½ cup chicken broth

½ cup white wine

2 to 3 teaspoons herbes de Provence

Garnish: fresh thyme sprigs

Herbes de Provence is a classic French blend consisting of dried herbs such as thyme, basil, rosemary, tarragon, savory, marjoram, oregano, and sometimes culinary lavender. Italian seasoning blend is a good substitute. If you prefer chicken breasts, cut them in half using sharp kitchen shears, as they tend to be oversized. The flavorful broth is delicious when sopped up with French bread or served with hot rice.

---

1. Preheat oven to 375°.
2. Combine flour, ½ teaspoon salt, and ¼ teaspoon pepper in a small bowl. Dredge chicken pieces in flour mixture, shaking off excess.
3. Heat oil in a 12-inch cast-iron skillet over medium-high heat. Add chicken, skin side down, and cook for 3 to 4 minutes or until golden brown. Remove from heat.
4. Turn chicken over and arrange in skillet. Add shallots, garlic, tomatoes, and lemon wedges to skillet. Combine broth, wine, herbes de Provence, remaining ½ teaspoon salt, and remaining ¼ teaspoon pepper in a glass measuring cup. Pour over and around chicken.
5. Bake for 30 to 35 minutes, basting occasionally with pan juices, until chicken is golden brown with crispy skin and internal temperature reads 165° when measured with a meat thermometer. Garnish, if desired.

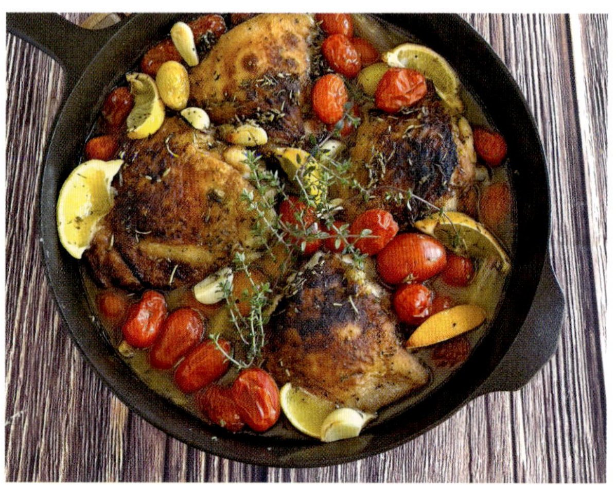

GOLDEN CHICKEN

MAKES 4 SERVINGS

EQUIPMENT: *brasier or Dutch oven*

PAN SAVVY: *Brasiers are shorter and wider than Dutch ovens and have flared sides, giving them more cooking surface. Both have heavy lids that seal well. You can cook this dish in a large skillet, but it's less convenient because most skillets don't come with lids.*

1 teaspoon fine sea salt
1 teaspoon ground cinnamon
1 teaspoon ground cumin
1 teaspoon ground coriander
½ teaspoon coarsely ground black pepper
½ teaspoon ground turmeric
¼ teaspoon ground allspice
¼ teaspoon ground nutmeg
⅛ teaspoon ground cardamom
Small pinch of ground cloves
4 to 6 bone-in, skin-on chicken thighs
1 tablespoon extra-virgin olive oil
1 onion, chopped
1 cup uncooked basmati rice
3 garlic cloves, coarsely chopped
3 cups chicken broth
2 tablespoons chopped, toasted sliced or slivered almonds or pistachios
1 tablespoon chopped fresh cilantro or parsley

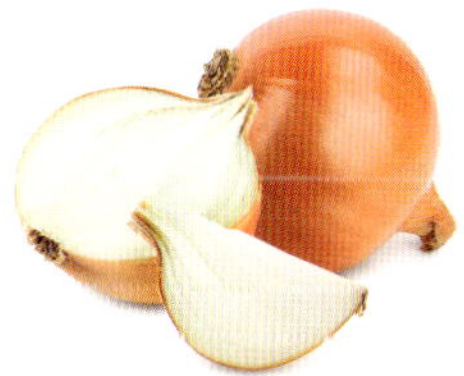

While there are a lot of ingredients in this dish, it's quick to put together and requires very little hands-on cooking. The Persian-inspired combination of spices adds a warm, rich flavor to basic chicken thighs. The turmeric adds a lovely golden hue to the chicken and is a healthful, lower-cost alternative to saffron.

1. Combine salt, cinnamon, cumin, coriander, pepper, turmeric, allspice, nutmeg, cardamom, and cloves in a small bowl. Rub chicken with spice blend on all sides. Let stand for 15 to 30 minutes.
2. Preheat oven to 400°.
3. Heat oil in a large brasier or Dutch oven over medium heat. Add chicken, and cook for 3 to 5 minutes on each side or until golden brown. Transfer to a plate and set chicken aside.
4. Add onion to pan. Cook, stirring constantly, for 5 to 7 minutes or until tender and golden. Add rice and garlic. Cook, stirring constantly, for 1 minute. Add broth and bring to a boil. Reduce heat, and simmer for 5 minutes.
5. Nestle reserved chicken in rice mixture. Cover and bake for 15 minutes. Uncover and bake for 10 minutes or until rice is tender and chicken is cooked through. Sprinkle with almonds and cilantro.

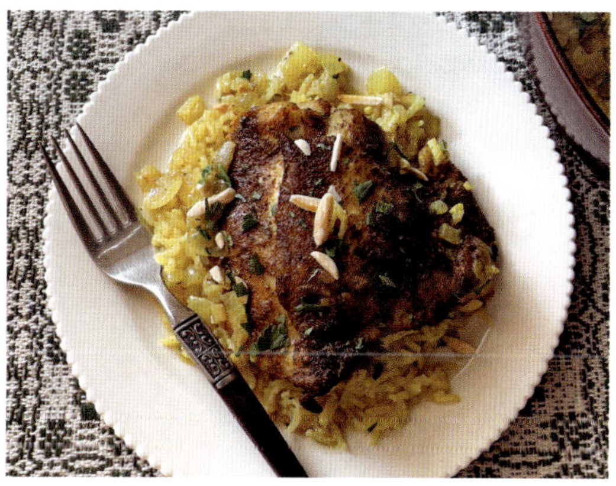

CHICKEN-AND-CHARD SKILLET POT PIE

MAKES 6 SERVINGS

EQUIPMENT: *12-inch cast-iron skillet*

1 tablespoon avocado or extra-virgin olive oil

1½ to 1¾ pounds boneless skinless chicken thighs, cut into bite-size pieces

1 teaspoon salt, divided

½ teaspoon coarsely ground black pepper, divided

2 tablespoons salted or unsalted butter

1 sweet potato, peeled and diced

1 onion, chopped

2 carrots, diced

2 parsnips or carrots, diced

2 garlic cloves, minced

½ teaspoon dried thyme

⅓ cup all-purpose flour

2 cups chicken broth

1½ cups half-and-half or whole milk

1 (9- to 10-ounce) bunch Swiss chard, tough stems removed and leaves chopped

½ (17.3-ounce) package frozen puff pastry, thawed

1 large egg, lightly beaten

Swiss chard is a leafy veggie related to spinach and beets, with a texture and flavor similar to kale. It's commonly seen with red or white stalks, but it also comes in vibrant shades of yellow and orange. Trim and discard the ends from the chard. You may see fibrous strings along the center stem (not unlike those found on celery). Pull those and discard. The center stem is edible but takes longer to cook. Thinly slice and cook it along with the sweet potato and other veggies.

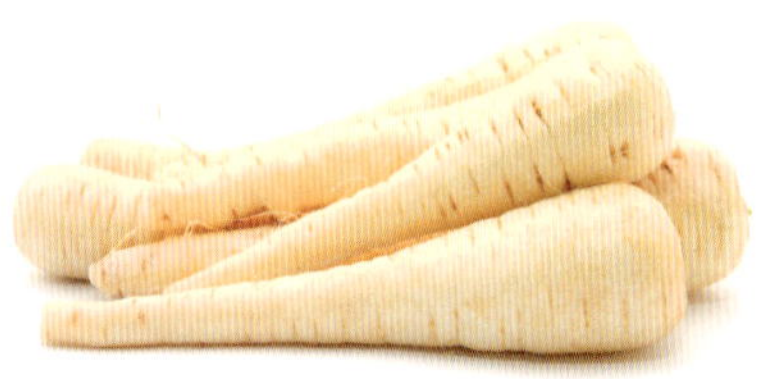

1. Heat oil in a 12-inch skillet over medium-high heat. Sprinkle chicken with ½ teaspoon salt and ¼ teaspoon pepper. Cook chicken, stirring often, for 6 minutes or until well browned. Transfer to a plate; set chicken aside.
2. Add butter to skillet and let melt. Add sweet potato, onion, carrots, parsnips, garlic, thyme, remaining ½ teaspoon salt, and remaining ¼ teaspoon pepper. Cook, stirring often, for 5 to 7 minutes or until vegetables are softened.
3. Add flour and cook, stirring constantly, for 1 minute. Whisk in broth and milk. Cook, whisking constantly, for 3 to 5 minutes or until mixture comes to a boil. Reduce heat and stir in reserved chicken and chard. Simmer for 4 to 5 minutes or until chard is tender and mixture is thickened. Remove from heat.
4. Preheat oven to 400°.
5. Unfold puff pastry on a lightly floured surface. Cut into strips, then rectangles. Arrange pastry over top of chicken mixture, overlapping as necessary. Brush top with egg.
6. Bake for 20 minutes or until pastry is golden.

CHICKEN MARSALA

MAKES 4 SERVINGS

EQUIPMENT: *10-inch cast-iron skillet*

1½ to 1¾ pounds boneless, skinless chicken breasts

¼ cup all-purpose flour

1 teaspoon fine sea salt, divided

½ teaspoon coarsely ground black pepper, divided

2 tablespoons extra-virgin olive oil

2 tablespoons salted or unsalted butter, divided

8 ounces cremini or button mushrooms, sliced

2 garlic cloves, minced

1 large shallot, finely chopped

½ cup Marsala, port, or white wine

¾ cup chicken broth

2 tablespoons chopped fresh parsley

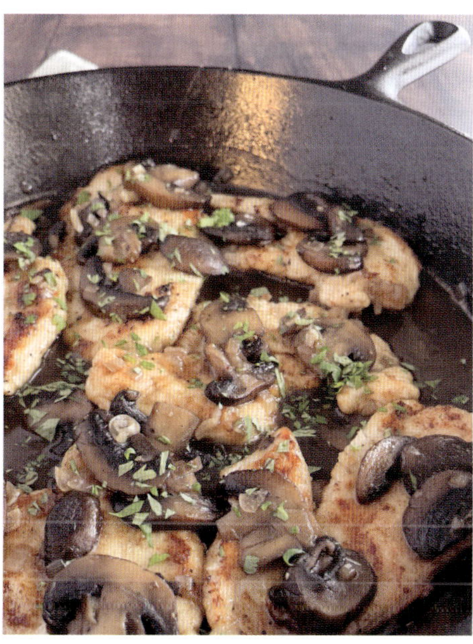

A recipe ubiquitous on Italian restaurant menus, this delicious standard can be made easily at home. Slicing the chicken breasts lengthwise creates cutlets that can be flattened to an equal thickness that cooks evenly. If your skillet isn't large enough to hold the chicken without packing it in, sauté the breasts in batches so they brown instead of steam.

1. Cut chicken breasts in half lengthwise. Place between plastic wrap and pound until about ⅓-inch thick.
2. Combine flour, ¾ teaspoon salt, and ¼ teaspoon pepper in a large, shallow dish. Set aside 1 tablespoon flour mixture. Dredge chicken in remaining flour mixture, shaking off excess.
3. Heat a large cast-iron pan over medium-high heat until hot. Add oil and 1 tablespoon butter to skillet and heat until butter melts. Add chicken and cook, in batches, for 2 to 3 minutes on each side or until golden brown. Remove pan from heat. Remove chicken from skillet and transfer to a plate; cover and keep warm.
4. Reduce heat to medium, and add remaining 1 tablespoon butter to skillet. Stir in mushrooms. Cook, stirring occasionally, for 3 minutes. Add garlic, shallot, remaining ¼ teaspoon salt, and remaining ¼ teaspoon pepper. Cook for 2 minutes or until mushrooms are browned and excess liquid evaporates.
5. Add Marsala wine to skillet over medium heat. Cook, scraping bits from bottom of pan, for 2 minutes or until wine reduces by half.
6. Whisk together broth and reserved flour mixture, and stir into mushroom mixture. Cook, stirring frequently, for 3 to 5 minutes or until mixture thickens slightly. Return chicken to skillet and reheat gently, if necessary. Sprinkle with parsley.

CHICKEN FAJITAS

MAKES 6 SERVINGS

EQUIPMENT: *12-inch cast-iron skillet or large griddle*

PAN SAVVY: *I like the chicken well seared and golden brown, so I cook it (and the veggies) in batches. To serve, I combine the ingredients in the skillet, which holds flavorful liquid that I stir back into the mixture. You can prepare it all at once on an extra-large cast-iron griddle, but a skillet is more convenient for serving portions. In summer, I will occasionally put the cast-iron griddle on the grill to get the nice smoky flavor of grilling without all the veggies falling through the grates.*

Southwestern Chicken Marinade (recipe at right)

2 pounds boneless, skinless chicken breasts, thinly sliced

1 tablespoon avocado or extra-virgin olive oil, divided

3 bell peppers (any color), sliced

1 large red or yellow onion, sliced

Homemade Corn Tortillas (page 29) or store-bought tortillas

Charred Tomato Salsa (page 46), store-bought salsa, or store-bought salsa verde

Toppings: sliced avocado, sour cream, shredded cheddar cheese, chopped fresh cilantro

With planning, you can make this festive dinner on a busy weeknight. While the chicken marinates, chop the vegetables. Prepare the salsa and tortillas ahead.

If you're looking for a quick-and-colorful meal, this straightforward recipe includes marinated chicken that is tender and packed with flavor. Corn tortillas make this a gluten-free option.

---

1. Place Southwestern Chicken Marinade and chicken in a large bowl or baking dish, tossing to coat. Cover and refrigerate for 30 minutes to 2 hours, stirring occasionally.
2. Heat ½ tablespoon oil in a large skillet over medium-high heat. Add half of chicken and cook, stirring occasionally, for 2 to 4 minutes or until chicken is golden brown. Transfer to a plate and repeat with remaining ½ tablespoon oil and remaining half of chicken. Discard marinade.
3. Add sliced bell peppers and onion to skillet. Cook, stirring occasionally, for 3 to 5 minutes or until vegetables are crisp-tender. Add chicken to vegetable mixture and cook, stirring frequently, until hot.
4. Serve chicken-and-vegetable mixture in warm tortillas with salsa and desired toppings.

Southwestern Chicken Marinade: Combine **¼ cup extra-virgin olive oil, 3 tablespoons lime juice, 2 tablespoons water, 2 minced garlic cloves, 1 teaspoon ground cumin, 1 teaspoon paprika or smoked paprika, 1 teaspoon chili powder, 1 teaspoon granulated sugar, ½ teaspoon dried oregano, ½ teaspoon salt,** and **¼ teaspoon coarsely ground black pepper.** Makes ½ cup.

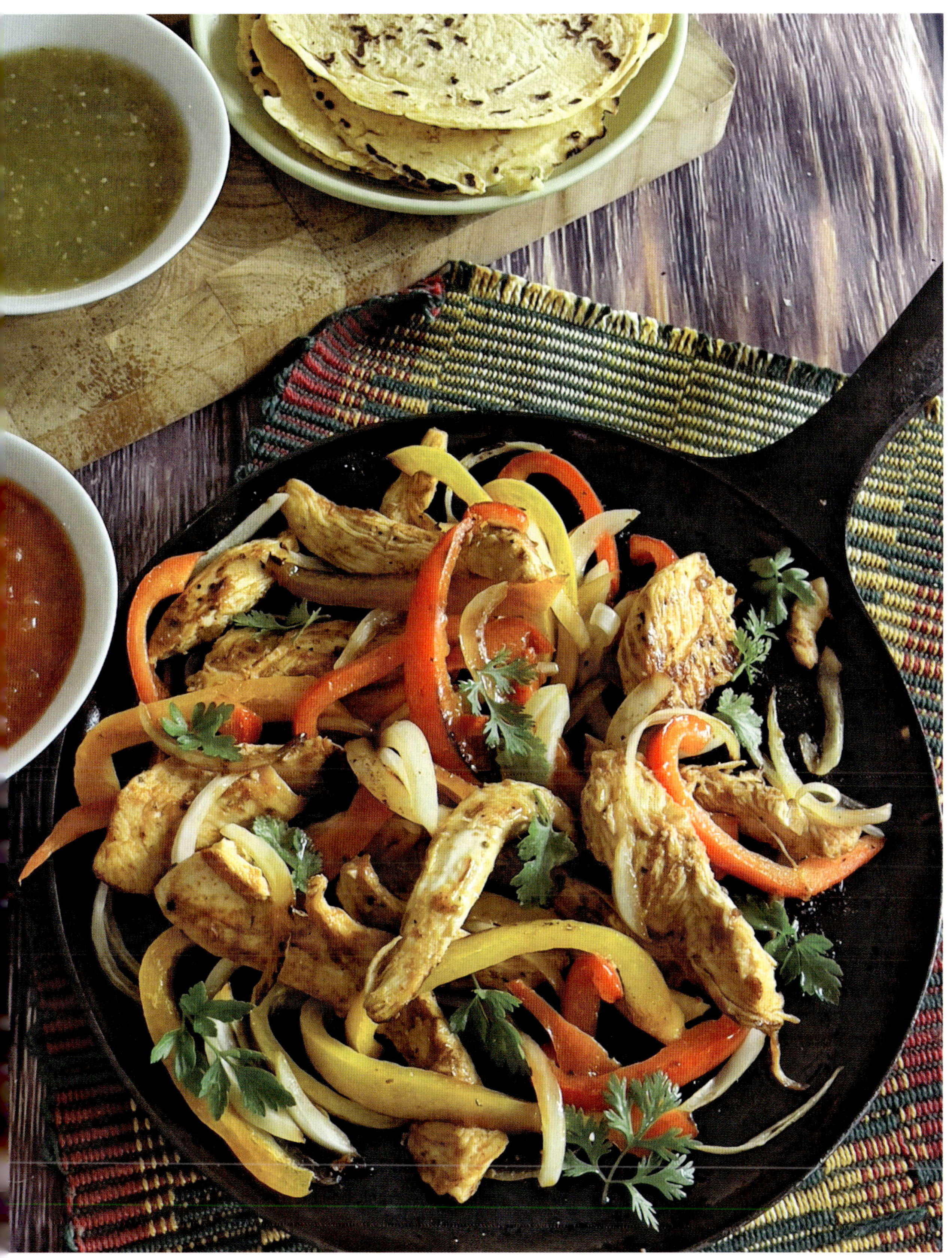

COQ AU VIN

MAKES 4 SERVINGS

EQUIPMENT: *7-quart Dutch oven or brasier*

PAN SAVVY: *Brasiers have lower sides and a bit more surface area, allowing bone-in chicken pieces to nestle easily. For even cooking, cut bone-in breasts in half crosswise (they tend to be oversized).*

4 slices thick-cut bacon, chopped or sliced (⅓ package)

1 (4-pound) whole chicken, cut into 8 pieces

1½ teaspoons fine sea salt, divided

1 teaspoon coarsely ground black pepper, divided

3 tablespoons salted or unsalted butter, divided

1 (8-ounce) container cremini or button mushrooms, sliced

1 celery rib, finely chopped

2 garlic cloves, chopped

3 tablespoons Cognac or brandy

2 cups red wine

1 cup chicken stock or broth

1 tablespoon tomato paste

1 teaspoon fresh thyme leaves

1 bay leaf

8 ounces small white boiling or pearl onions, peeled,* or ½ (14.4-ounce) bag frozen pearl onions, thawed

1½ tablespoons all-purpose flour

2 tablespoons chopped fresh Italian parsley

This is a more-streamlined variation on Julia Child's famous versions. You can serve it with mashed potatoes or rice, plus crisply toasted sourdough bread slices to sop up the amazing sauce. If you have any leftovers, remove the bones and use the chicken in griddled sandwiches with Swiss cheese—yum!

---

1. Cook bacon in a Dutch oven over medium heat for 5 to 7 minutes or until crispy. Remove with a slotted spoon and set bacon aside, reserving 1½ tablespoons drippings in pan.
2. Sprinkle chicken with 1 teaspoon salt and ½ teaspoon pepper. Add 1 tablespoon butter to Dutch oven and heat over medium to medium-high heat. Add chicken, in batches, and cook for 3 minutes on each side or until golden brown. Transfer to a plate; set chicken aside.
3. Add 1 tablespoon butter to Dutch oven and melt over medium heat. Add mushrooms, celery, and garlic. Cook, stirring frequently, for 5 to 7 minutes or until tender.
4. Stir in Cognac. Cook, stirring constantly and scraping bottom of pan, for 1 minute or until most of liquid evaporates. Stir in wine, broth, tomato paste, thyme, bay leaf, remaining ½ teaspoon salt, and remaining ½ teaspoon pepper. Add reserved bacon and chicken. Stir in onions.
5. Bring to a boil, reduce heat, and cover. Simmer for 40 minutes or until chicken is cooked through. Transfer chicken to a plate. Remove and discard bay leaf. Bring liquid to a boil; cook for 8 to 10 minutes or until reduced a bit.
6. Combine remaining 1 tablespoon butter and flour, mashing with a fork into a paste. Add to Dutch oven, stirring until well blended. Simmer for 1 to 2 minutes or until sauce thickens.
7. Return chicken and vegetables to Dutch oven. Cook, basting chicken with pan sauce, for 2 to 5 minutes or until chicken is thoroughly heated. Sprinkle with fresh parsley.

* To peel fresh boiling onions, place in boiling water for about 2 minutes, then plunge into ice water. Slip off skins.

CHICKEN PUTTANESCA

MAKES 4 SERVINGS

EQUIPMENT: *brasier or 12-inch cast-iron skillet*

PAN SAVVY: *Brasiers are enamel coated and the best option. If using a regular skillet, use a well-seasoned one because this dish contains acidic tomatoes. If using bare cast iron, wash in hot water promptly. Coat with a thin layer of oil, and re-season.*

6 boneless, skinless chicken thighs or 4 chicken breasts

¼ teaspoon salt

¼ teaspoon coarsely ground black pepper

2 tablespoons avocado oil, divided

1 onion, chopped

3 garlic cloves, minced

¼ to ½ teaspoon crushed red pepper flakes

1 (28-ounce) can fire-roasted or Italian-seasoned diced tomatoes, undrained

⅓ cup Kalamata olives, pitted and halved

1 tablespoon capers, drained

1 teaspoon dried Italian seasoning

Hot cooked pasta

¼ cup chopped fresh parsley

Parmesan cheese

This dish is known for its bold, spicy flavor from a combination of tomatoes, olives, and capers, along with a healthy amount of crushed red pepper flakes. Serve it over pasta for a filling main dish.

---

1. Sprinkle chicken pieces evenly with salt and black pepper.
2. Heat 1 tablespoon oil in an enameled brasier or well-seasoned cast-iron skillet over medium-high heat. Add chicken, skin side down, and cook for 2 to 3 minutes on each side or until golden brown. Set chicken aside.
3. Preheat oven to 375°.
4. Reduce heat to medium. Add remaining 1 tablespoon oil to skillet (no need to wipe clean). Add onion, garlic, and crushed red pepper flakes. Cook, stirring frequently, for 3 to 5 minutes.
5. Add tomatoes, olives, capers, and seasoning, stirring until well blended. Add reserved chicken to tomato mixture. Transfer skillet to oven and bake, uncovered, for 20 to 25 minutes or until chicken is cooked and reaches an internal temperature of 165° to 170°.
6. Serve over hot cooked pasta; sprinkle with fresh parsley and Parmesan cheese.

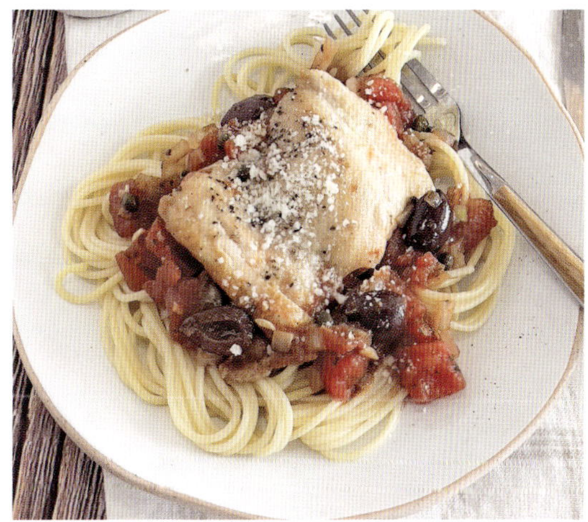

CHICKEN SHAWARMA

MAKES 4 TO 6 SERVINGS

EQUIPMENT: *12-inch cast-iron skillet*

PAN SAVVY: *If you don't have a pan or griddle large enough to cook the chicken in a single layer, cook it in batches. If crowded, the chicken will steam and not get a flavorful exterior sear.*

2 teaspoons ground cumin
2 teaspoons ground coriander
1 teaspoon fine sea salt
1 teaspoon ground turmeric
1 teaspoon paprika
¼ teaspoon ground cinnamon
¼ teaspoon coarsely ground black pepper
¼ teaspoon ground cayenne pepper
⅓ cup plus 1 tablespoon extra-virgin olive oil, divided
¼ cup lemon juice
3 garlic cloves, finely minced
2 pounds boneless, skinless chicken breasts or thighs
Store-bought hummus or Tzatziki Sauce (page 114)
1 red onion, halved and sliced
1 tablespoon chopped fresh parsley
Skillet Flatbread (page 28) or store-bought pita bread, warmed

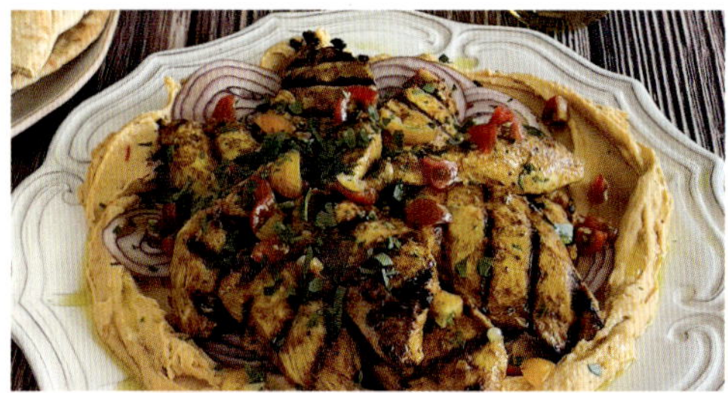

One of my favorite restaurants serves chicken shawarma with a powerful garlic sauce. While not as authentic, I enjoy a milder version that uses hummus or even tzatziki sauce, along with soft, warm pita bread. Round out the meal with a tomato-and-iceberg salad served with a simple vinaigrette.

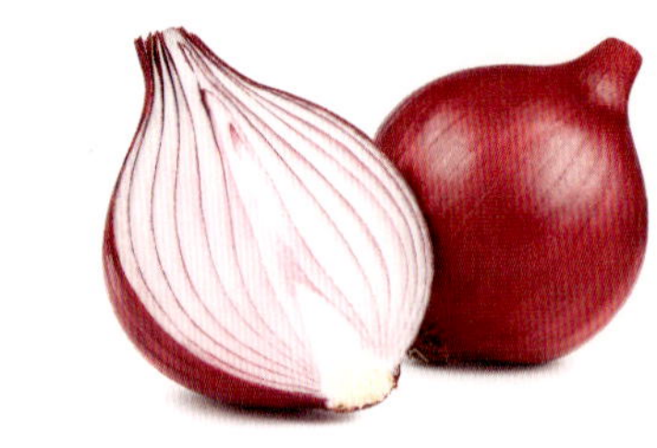

1. To make marinade, combine cumin, coriander, salt, turmeric, paprika, cinnamon, black pepper, and cayenne pepper in a large bowl, stirring until well blended. Stir in ⅓ cup olive oil, lemon juice, and garlic.
2. If using chicken breasts, slice in half lengthwise and crosswise to create thin cutlets. Add chicken to marinade, tossing to coat. Cover and refrigerate for 1 to 4 hours.
3. Preheat oven to 425°.
4. Heat remaining 1 tablespoon oil in a large cast-iron skillet over medium to medium-high heat. Drain chicken, discarding marinade. Add chicken to hot skillet and cook for 2 to 3 minutes on each side or until golden brown and cooked through. Cook in batches, if necessary.
5. Spread hummus on a platter or individual plates. Top evenly with onion and chicken. Sprinkle with parsley. Serve with Skillet Flatbread. For a sandwich, spread hummus on flatbread, then top with chicken and onion.

SEMI-TRADITIONAL CASSOULET

MAKES 6 SERVINGS

EQUIPMENT: *Cast-iron brasier*

PAN SAVVY: *Brasiers are similar to Dutch ovens but are shorter with flared sides that give them a large cooking surface. They are enamel coated and make a great choice when simmering recipes with acidic ingredients like tomatoes or tomato sauce. Cooking a cassoulet requires a lengthy cooking time and a large cooking surface, making brasiers ideal. Substitute a 7-quart Dutch oven or 12-inch-deep skillet.*

1 pound dried cannellini beans
3 quarts water
4 whole cloves
1 onion, halved
4 garlic cloves, halved
2 carrots, cut into pieces
1 sprig fresh rosemary
1 bay leaf
2 quarts chicken stock
1 pound bacon, diced
4 to 6 bone-in, skin-on chicken thighs or legs
1 (5-ounce) boneless, skin-on duck breast (optional)
1 pound chicken sausage or other firm sausage, sliced
Coarsely ground black pepper

Traditional cassoulet is a multiday affair that includes homemade duck confit. Instead, I use easy-to-find chicken thighs, plus a duck breast. Because this dish is already heavy, I use a lighter chicken-and-apple sausage rather than the pork-and-duck version. Keep the sausages whole, or slice to distribute well in multiple servings.

---

1. Place beans in a large bowl; add about 3 quarts water, covering beans by several inches. Cover and let stand for 8 hours. Rinse and drain beans.
2. Place beans in a large cast-iron brasier. Poke whole cloves into onion halves and place in pot. Add garlic, carrots, rosemary, and bay leaf. Add stock. If liquid doesn't cover beans by 2 inches, add water. Bring mixture to a boil, reduce heat, and simmer gently, partially covered, for 45 to 60 minutes or until beans are somewhat tender and almost cooked through. Skim off any scum that forms on top.
3. Meanwhile, cook bacon in a large skillet over medium heat for 7 minutes or until crisp. Transfer to a large plate, reserving 2 tablespoons drippings in skillet; set bacon aside.
4. Cook chicken in drippings for 3 to 4 minutes on each side or until browned. Transfer to a baking dish (to catch any liquid). If desired, cook duck breast for 4 minutes on each side or until browned. Transfer to baking dish. Cook sausage for 2 to 3 minutes on each side or until browned. Transfer to baking dish, reserving 1 tablespoon drippings.
5. Preheat oven to 325°.
6. Drain beans, reserving liquid. Remove and discard onion, carrots, and bay leaf. Stir reserved bacon and sausage into bean mixture. Pour in enough reserved liquid to just cover bean mixture. Do not discard remaining liquid (it may be needed later). Arrange chicken thighs, skin side up, on top. Arrange duck breast slices, skin side up, on top. Sprinkle with black pepper.
7. Bake, uncovered, for 1 hour. If a crust forms on the top, break it and spoon some of the cooking liquid on top of it. (This is a good thing—the crust is very flavorful.) If beans become dry, add a small amount of reserved liquid to just cover beans.

COCONUT-CURRY STIR-FRY

MAKES 4 SERVINGS

EQUIPMENT: *12-inch cast-iron skillet or wok*

1 (14-ounce) can coconut milk
2 to 3 teaspoons curry powder
1 tablespoon light brown sugar
¾ teaspoon fine sea salt, divided
1 to 1½ pounds boneless, skinless chicken breasts, cut into strips
¼ teaspoon coarsely ground black pepper
2 to 3 tablespoons avocado or vegetable oil, divided
1 onion, quartered and sliced
1 red bell pepper, thinly sliced
1 cup fresh (or frozen and thawed) thin green beans
1 tablespoon minced fresh ginger
½ cup salted cashews, chopped
¼ cup lightly packed fresh basil leaves, torn
Hot cooked rice

Curry powder is a blend of spices that varies by country. Indian curry powder can be mild or quite spicy. Look for Madras curry if you enjoy the heat. You can also substitute a Thai curry paste. Red and panang curry paste are spicy, while massaman is milder and sweeter. Create your sauce and taste, adding more curry, if desired. Vegetarians will enjoy this high-flavor dish using a firm or baked tofu as the protein.

---

1 Whisk together coconut milk, curry powder, brown sugar, and ½ teaspoon salt. Set milk sauce aside.

2 Sprinkle chicken with remaining ¼ teaspoon salt and black pepper. Heat 1 tablespoon oil in a large skillet or wok over medium-high to high heat. Add half of chicken to skillet and cook, stirring frequently, for 3 minutes or until browned on all sides. Repeat with remaining chicken, adding up to 1 tablespoon oil, if necessary. Transfer to a platter; set chicken aside.

3 Heat remaining 1 tablespoon oil in skillet over medium-high to high heat. Add onion, bell pepper, and green beans. Cook for 3 to 5 minutes or until just tender. Add ginger and cook, stirring constantly, for 1 minute.

4 Add reserved chicken to skillet and pour in reserved milk sauce. Bring to a simmer over medium heat. Cook for 10 minutes or until vegetables are tender and chicken is cooked through. Stir in cashews and basil. Serve over hot cooked rice.

BAD WEATHER BARBECUE CHICKEN

MAKES 4 TO 6 SERVINGS

EQUIPMENT: *12-inch cast-iron skillet*

PAN SAVVY: *Use the largest skillet you have. If crowded in the pan, the chicken won't get a good sear on the skin, so cook it in batches. It's okay to stack all the chicken together in the skillet when it bakes.*

1 teaspoon salt
1 teaspoon garlic powder
1 teaspoon onion powder
1 teaspoon chili powder
1 teaspoon paprika
½ teaspoon ground cumin
½ teaspoon coarsely ground black pepper
1 (4½-pound) whole chicken, cut into pieces, or 6 bone-in, skin-on chicken pieces
2 to 3 teaspoons avocado oil
1 small onion, finely chopped
¼ cup red wine vinegar
⅓ cup ketchup
¼ cup firmly packed light brown sugar
1 tablespoon molasses
1 tablespoon yellow mustard
¾ teaspoon liquid smoke (optional)

Seared on the stove, then baked in the oven, whole bone-in chicken pieces are easy to cook. I usually cut a chicken breast in half crosswise for more evenly sized portions. It's not difficult to do with a pair of good poultry scissors. The coating of sweet-and-zesty barbecue sauce has a hint of liquid smoke to give the sauce its outdoor flavor. Because the sauce is made from drippings from bone-in chicken, it'll contain natural gelatin that will thicken as it cools. Add hot sauce, if desired, for a bit of heat.

---

1. Combine salt, garlic powder, onion powder, chili powder, paprika, cumin, and pepper in a small bowl. Rub spice mixture over chicken. For added flavor, cover and refrigerate for 2 to 6 hours or until ready to cook.
2. Preheat oven to 450°.
3. Heat oil in a 12-inch cast-iron skillet over medium-high to high heat. Add chicken, skin side down, and cook for 3 minutes or until golden brown. (Cook chicken in batches if pieces don't fit in a single layer.) Turn chicken over, and transfer skillet to oven. Bake for 25 minutes or until breasts register 160° and thighs register 175° with a meat thermometer.
4. Remove skillet from oven and transfer chicken to a serving platter, reserving drippings in pan. Cover chicken with aluminum foil to keep warm.
5. Add onion to drippings, and cook over medium heat for 5 minutes or until onions are tender. Stir in vinegar, ketchup, brown sugar, molasses, mustard, and, if desired, liquid smoke. Bring mixture to boil, reduce heat, and simmer for 5 minutes or until thickened. Return chicken to skillet, turning to coat with sauce.

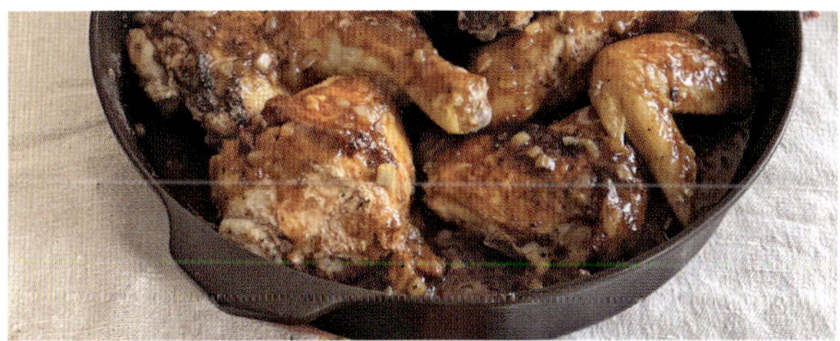

CHICKEN TAGINE WITH LEMON AND OLIVES

MAKES 4 SERVINGS

EQUIPMENT: *Cast-iron tagine*

PAN SAVVY: *A tagine is a cooking vessel with a conical lid that lets condensed liquid return to the pan to braise food or keep it very moist. Clay tagines are only used for baking, while those with iron or steel bottoms can be used on a cooktop. If unavailable, use a 5-quart Dutch oven, brasier, or a 10- to 12-inch cast-iron skillet with a heavy lid.*

1 tablespoon Moroccan Seasoning Blend (recipe at right) or store-bought Ras al Hanout

2 pounds chicken breasts or thighs, cut into pieces

Pinch of dry saffron threads, crushed

2 tablespoons hot water

2 tablespoons extra-virgin olive oil

1 onion, halved and sliced

4 garlic cloves, finely chopped

½ cup green olives, pitted and halved

½ to 1 large Preserved Lemon, thinly sliced (recipe at right) or store-bought preserved lemons

1 cup chicken stock or broth

Hot cooked couscous

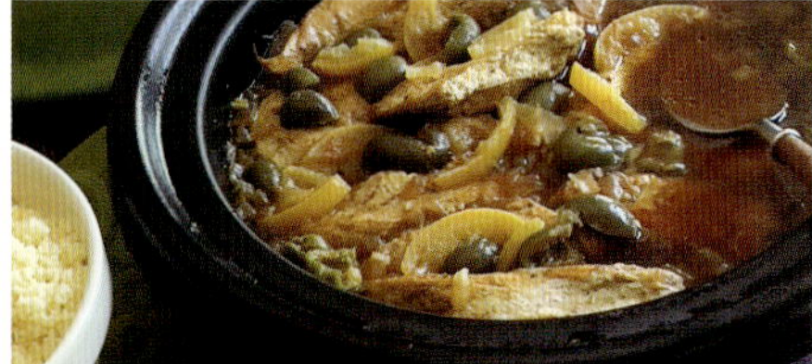

Preserved Lemons are heavily salted and cured for weeks, softening the texture of the skin, making it completely edible. The green olives used here are not the pickled pimiento-stuffed kind. Find them in the deli.

---

1. Sprinkle Moroccan Seasoning Blend evenly over chicken. Cover and marinate in the refrigerator for 2 to 6 hours.
2. Combine saffron and 2 tablespoons hot water in a bowl. Set saffron mixture aside.
3. Heat oil in a cast-iron tagine over medium-high heat. Add chicken and cook for 1 to 2 minutes or until brown on all sides. Transfer to a platter.
4. Reduce heat to medium. Add onion to skillet; cook, stirring frequently, for 5 minutes or until tender. Add garlic and cook, stirring often, for 1 minute. Place chicken and any liquid on top of onion mixture. Arrange olives and Preserved Lemon slices around chicken.
5. Combine broth and reserved saffron mixture. Pour over chicken. Bring to a boil, then reduce heat to low. Cover with tagine and simmer for 15 to 20 minutes or until chicken is cooked through. Serve over couscous.

Moroccan Seasoning Blend: Combine **3 tablespoons paprika, 2 tablespoons ground cumin, 1½ tablespoons ground coriander, 1 teaspoon ground turmeric, 1 teaspoon ground ginger, 1 teaspoon salt, ½ teaspoon ground cinnamon,** and **½ teaspoon coarsely ground black pepper** in a bowl. Store in an airtight container. Makes ½ cup.

Preserved Lemons: Scrub **6 organic lemons** well. Cut off about ¼ inch from ends. Cut each into quarters, almost all the way through, so they remain connected on one side. Combine **⅓ cup kosher salt** and **2 tablespoons granulated sugar** in a small bowl. Stuff each semi-quartered lemon with salt mixture. Pack lemons into a canning jar, including any remaining salt mixture. Add **fresh lemon juice** to cover lemons. Seal jar and store in refrigerator for at least 3 weeks before using. Store in refrigerator for up to 6 months. Makes 6.

ROSEMARY-THYME ROAST TURKEY BREAST

MAKES 6 SERVINGS

EQUIPMENT: *12-inch cast-iron skillet*

1 (6-pound) bone-in turkey breast
¼ cup unsalted or salted butter, softened
3 garlic cloves, minced
1½ teaspoons salt
1 teaspoon lemon zest
½ teaspoon coarsely ground black pepper
1 tablespoon chopped fresh rosemary and thyme
1 large onion, sliced
¼ cup all-purpose flour
2 cups turkey or chicken stock or broth

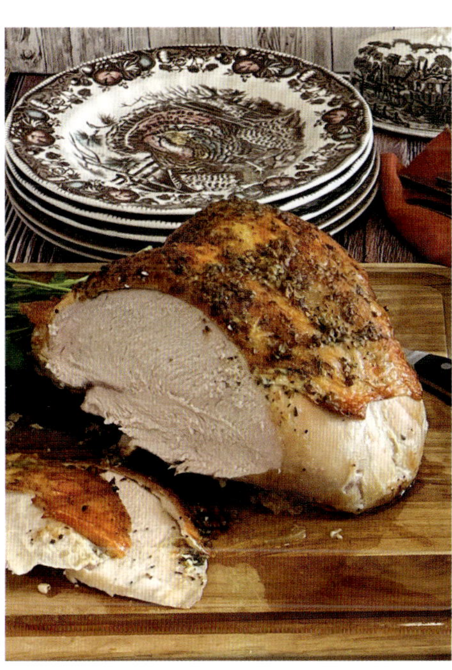

Turkey breasts are ideal for small Thanksgiving meals or whenever a turkey-and-gravy craving hits. Because they are much smaller than whole birds, they fit nicely in a large cast-iron skillet that can be used to create a gravy without using another pan. In general, turkey requires 20 minutes of baking per pound, so adjust accordingly. Patting the turkey dry with paper towels is the secret to golden-brown skin, along with using high heat for the first 15 minutes.

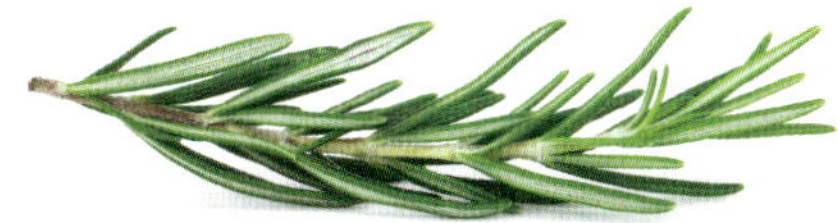

1. Preheat oven to 450°. Drain any liquid from turkey and pat dry.
2. Combine butter, garlic, salt, zest, pepper, and herbs in a small bowl. Using fingers, separate skin on turkey breast and legs; spread a little more than half of butter mixture under skin. Rub remaining half of butter mixture over entire top.
3. Layer onion slices in bottom of a 12-inch cast-iron skillet. Place turkey on top of onion slices.
4. Roast turkey for 15 minutes. Reduce heat to 325° and bake for 1 hour and 30 minutes or until cooked through and thermometer reads 155° (turkey will continue to cook with residual heat to 165°). Transfer turkey to a platter, reserving drippings in pan; let stand for 15 minutes.
5. Whisk flour into pan drippings. Bring mixture to a boil, whisking until smooth. Whisk in stock. Boil, whisking constantly, for 2 to 3 minutes or until thickened and smooth. Taste and add additional salt and pepper, if desired.
6. Slice turkey across the grain and serve with pan gravy.

TURKEY-CORNBREAD BAKE

MAKES 6 TO 8 SERVINGS

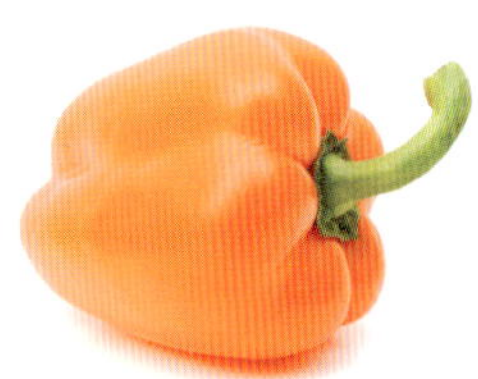

EQUIPMENT: *12-inch cast-iron skillet*

PAN SAVVY: *If a 12-inch skillet is unavailable, you can sauté the vegetables in a smaller skillet, mix the ingredients in a large bowl, and transfer it all to a 13x9-inch baking dish.*

1 tablespoon extra-virgin olive oil
1 onion, chopped
1 bell pepper (any color), chopped
1 celery rib, chopped
2 garlic cloves, minced
1 teaspoon paprika
¾ teaspoon poultry seasoning
¾ teaspoon salt
½ teaspoon coarsely ground black pepper
½ recipe Basic Skillet Cornbread (page 16), cubed
3 cups shredded or cubed roasted turkey or chicken
1 cup turkey or chicken broth
1 (14.75-ounce) can creamed corn
1 large egg, lightly beaten
1 cup (4 ounces) shredded cheddar or other cheese
¼ cup chopped fresh parsley
½ cup packaged fried onions

This dish is a fantastic way to use holiday leftovers, but its ease and comforting flavors make it something you'll want to make year-round. There's no need to roast a whole turkey—you can buy roast turkey at the deli in ½-inch-thick slices. You can also substitute leftover rotisserie chicken. The topping can be doubled if you're so inclined—here's a chance to use that giant bag of fried onions you bought at the warehouse store, even though you'll never make enough green bean casserole to use it up!

1. Preheat oven to 375°.
2. Heat oil in a 12-inch cast-iron skillet over medium heat. Add onion, bell pepper, and celery. Cook, stirring frequently, for 5 to 7 minutes or until tender. Stir in garlic. Cook, stirring constantly, for 1 minute. Stir in paprika, poultry seasoning, salt, and black pepper.
3. Add cornbread and turkey, tossing gently until well blended. Combine broth, corn, and egg in a bowl. Stir into turkey mixture. Stir in cheese and parsley. Top with fried onions.
4. Bake for 30 minutes or until golden brown and thoroughly heated. Let stand for 5 minutes before serving.

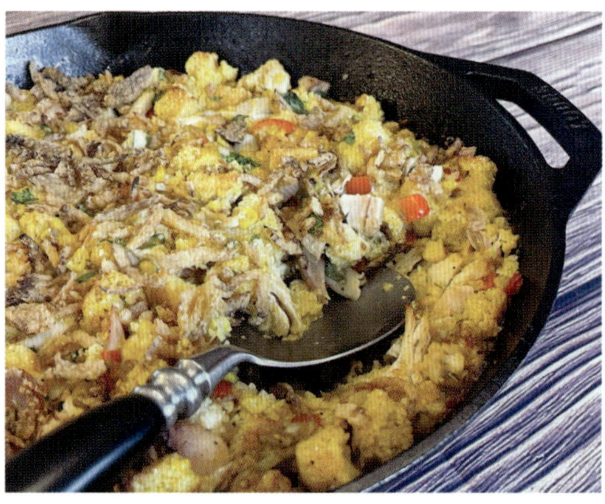

BLACKENED REDFISH

MAKES 4 SERVINGS

EQUIPMENT: *10- or 12-inch cast-iron skillet*

PAN SAVVY: *Cast iron is the perfect pan for cooking blackened fish, and I wouldn't cook it in anything else. High heat can warp some steel skillets, and it's never recommended for nonstick. Use a skillet that's large enough to hold all 4 fillets at once. You can cook in batches, but I recommend cooking them all at once to reduce the amount of time spent smoking up the kitchen.*

¼ cup salted or unsalted butter, melted
1 tablespoon sweet paprika
1½ teaspoons salt
1 teaspoon onion powder
1 teaspoon garlic powder
½ to ¾ teaspoon ground cayenne pepper
½ teaspoon black pepper
½ teaspoon dried thyme
½ teaspoon dried oregano
⅛ teaspoon white pepper
4 (6- to 10-ounce) skinless redfish, drum, yellowtail snapper, or other firm fillets
Garnish: blackened lemon slices

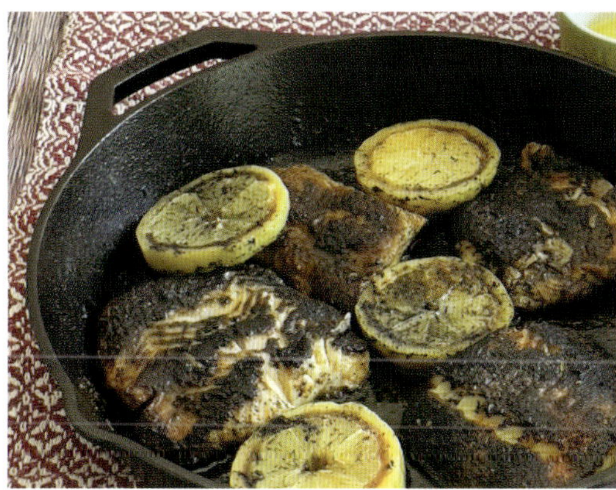

Paul Prudhomme's blackened redfish dish was my introduction to the great food of New Orleans, although I met the celebrity chef while I was living in Los Angeles. His book was a nationwide hit, and I was excited to try many of his recipes. This adaptation isn't as spicy as his, but it's still bursting with flavor. The ability of cast iron to get very hot is the trick to this recipe. It will smoke, so turn on that exhaust fan and crack a window. The flavor is worth any alarm you might set off! If you have a barbecue grill with a burner feature, cook this delicious recipe outside and don't worry about the smoke. The recipe cooks quickly, so have side dishes prepared and the table set before you start. You can use clarified butter—ghee—but I prefer the toasted milk solids in regular butter. This recipe works best with fillets no thicker than 1 inch.

---

1. Pour melted butter into a shallow dish or bowl.
2. Combine paprika, salt, onion powder, garlic powder, cayenne pepper, black pepper, thyme, oregano, and white pepper in another shallow dish.
3. Heat an empty, large cast-iron skillet over high heat for 5 to 10 minutes or until very hot.
4. Dip fish fillets into melted butter, turning to coat. Dredge in spice blend on both sides.
5. Place fillets in skillet and cook, uncovered, for 2 minutes. Turn over, and drizzle with any remaining butter. Cook for 1 to 2 minutes or until fish is cooked through. Garnish, if desired; serve immediately.

OVEN-ROASTED BLACK COD

MAKES 6 SERVINGS

EQUIPMENT: *10- or 12-inch cast-iron skillet*

2 tablespoons salted butter, softened
1 tablespoon chopped fresh parsley
1 large garlic clove, minced
1 shallot, minced
¼ teaspoon Dijon mustard
2 teaspoons all-purpose flour
¼ teaspoon lemon zest
1 tablespoon fresh lemon juice
2 slices bacon
6 (4- to 6-ounce) black cod, Chilean seabass, or halibut fillets
¼ teaspoon fine sea salt
⅛ teaspoon coarsely ground black pepper
Garnishes: lemon slices, chopped fresh parsley

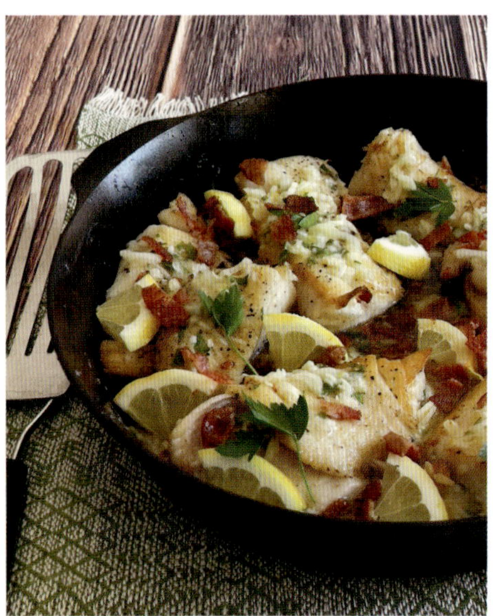

This fish dish is one of my favorites, adapted from Chef Alfred Portale of Gotham Bar and Grill in New York City. Fish and seafood are more often eaten at restaurants than cooked at home, but this recipe might change minds. It's so easy, yet it's elegant enough for company. Only ¼ teaspoon of mustard may not seem like enough to make a difference, but you can taste it—using more might overpower the mild-flavored seafood.

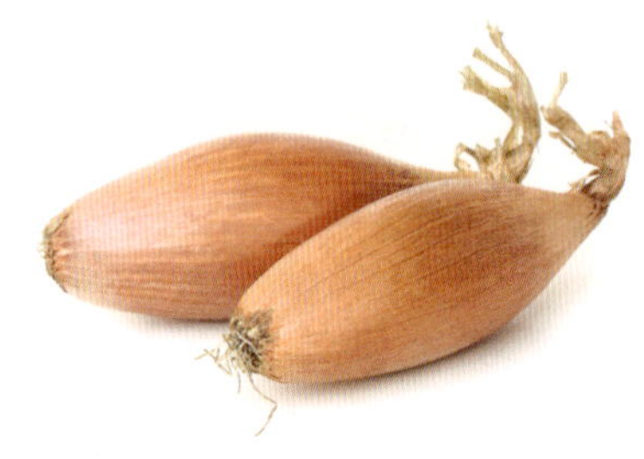

1. Preheat oven to 450°.
2. Combine butter, parsley, garlic, shallot, mustard, flour, zest, and lemon juice in a small bowl; set butter mixture aside.
3. Cook bacon in a large skillet over medium heat until crispy. Remove to paper towels, reserving 2 or 3 teaspoons drippings in skillet, and set bacon aside.
4. Sprinkle fish with salt and pepper. Heat skillet over medium-high heat. Cook fish, skin side up, for 2 minutes or until golden brown. Remove skillet from heat.
5. Turn fish over and spread three-fourths of butter mixture evenly over top of fillets. Transfer skillet to oven, and bake for 5 to 7 minutes or until fish is opaque and cooked through.
6. Remove from oven. Add remaining one-fourth of butter mixture to skillet, allowing butter to melt. Crumble reserved bacon and sprinkle over top. Garnish, if desired.

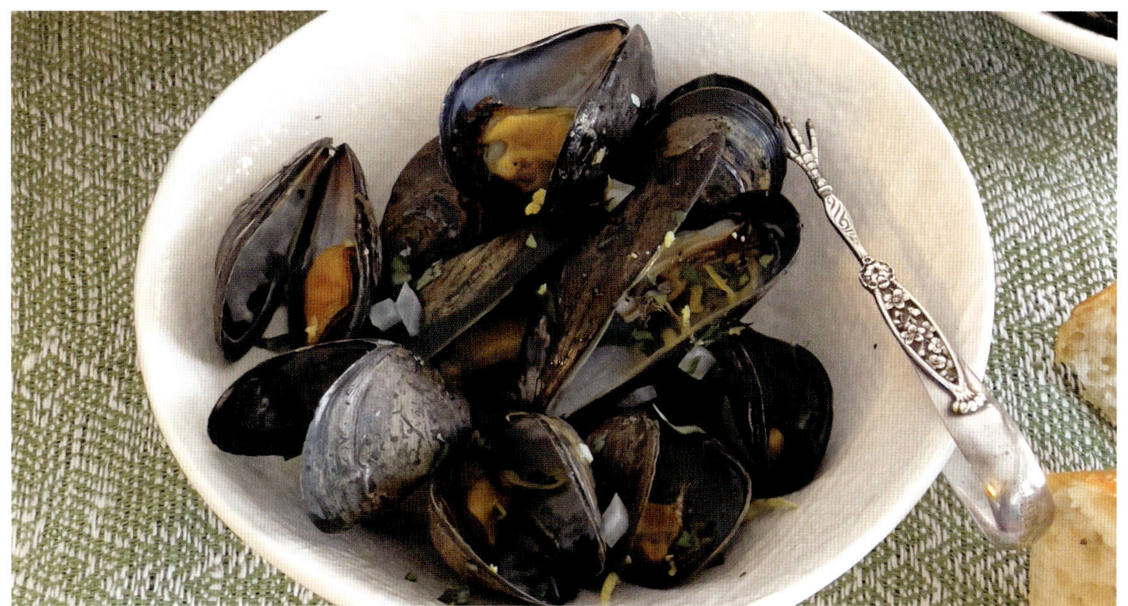

WINE-STEAMED MUSSELS

MAKES 2 MAIN-DISH OR 4 APPETIZER SERVINGS

EQUIPMENT: *Cast-iron mussels pan*

PAN SAVVY: *A Dutch oven makes an excellent substitution for a spendy specialty mussels pan.*

2 pounds fresh mussels
1 tablespoon extra-virgin olive oil
2 tablespoons salted butter
1 large shallot, minced
3 garlic cloves, minced
1 cup white wine
2 tablespoons chopped fresh basil
1 teaspoon lemon zest
¼ teaspoon coarsely ground black pepper
Toasted French bread slices

I have owned an oval-shaped cast-iron mussels pot for a long time, and I love how the inside is designed so there is space to dip bread into the delicious cooking liquid. It's not inexpensive, but it's worth it if you cook seafood regularly.

1. Scrub mussels under cold running water and remove "beard" or fibers. Discard any mussels that remain open. Set mussels aside.
2. Heat oil and butter in a mussels pot or small Dutch oven over medium heat. Add shallot and garlic. Cook for 1 to 2 minutes or until shallot is tender. Stir in wine.
3. Bring wine mixture to a boil. Add reserved mussels and cover. Cook, shaking pot periodically, for 3 to 5 minutes or until shells open. Discard any mussels that do not open after cooking.
4. Sprinkle with basil, zest, and pepper. Dip bread slices into broth mixture.

SKILLET MEAT LOAF

MAKES 6 SERVINGS

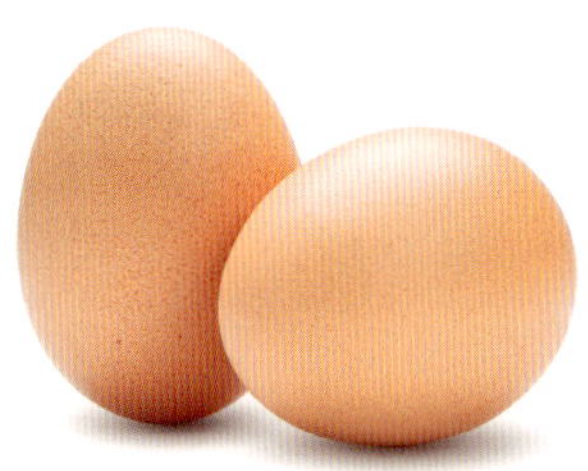

EQUIPMENT: *10-inch cast-iron skillet*

PAN SAVVY: *You can use a 12-inch skillet, but check for doneness 5 to 10 minutes earlier because the meat loaf will be thinner.*

2 teaspoons extra-virgin olive oil

1 small yellow onion, finely chopped

¼ teaspoon crushed red pepper flakes

2 large eggs, lightly beaten

¼ cup whole milk

1 tablespoon Worcestershire sauce

2 teaspoons dried Italian seasoning

1 teaspoon salt

½ teaspoon freshly ground black pepper

⅓ cup seasoned fine breadcrumbs

1½ pounds lean ground beef

½ pound ground pork, chicken, or turkey

⅓ cup ketchup

1 tablespoon dark or light brown sugar

1 teaspoon apple cider vinegar

Garnish: chopped fresh parsley

Baking meat loaf in a skillet means there's more of the crispy, browned pieces, arguably the best part of the dish. Place the meat mixture gently into the pan without packing down.

1. Preheat oven to 400°.
2. Heat oil in a 10-inch cast-iron skillet over medium heat. Add onion and red pepper flakes; cook, stirring frequently, for 4 to 5 minutes or until tender. Cool slightly.
3. Combine eggs, milk, Worcestershire, Italian seasoning, salt, and black pepper in a large bowl. Add breadcrumbs, stirring until well blended. Let stand for 5 minutes. Stir in onion mixture, ground beef, and ground pork. Use hands to blend mixture just until combined. Do not overmix. Spoon meat mixture gently into skillet (no need to wipe skillet clean).
4. Bake for 30 to 35 minutes or until the meat loaf is cooked through and a meat thermometer registers 160°. If excess oil collects on the side, drain carefully or spoon away, if desired.
5. Stir together ketchup, brown sugar, and vinegar in a small bowl. Spread ketchup glaze over top of meat loaf.
6. Heat oven to broil. Broil for 3 to 5 minutes or until dark and bubbly. Let stand for 5 minutes. Garnish, if desired.

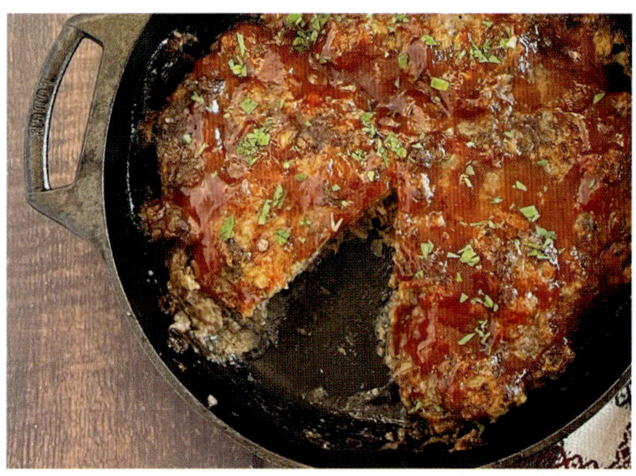

CAST-IRON SKILLET BEEFY LASAGNA

MAKES 6 SERVINGS

If you enjoy the crispy, cheesy edges of lasagna, then try this version baked in a cast-iron skillet. You can make this vegetarian with plant-based sausage and beef, but add 1 tablespoon olive oil when cooking.

EQUIPMENT: *12-inch cast-iron skillet*

PAN SAVVY: *Some people never cook tomato sauces in cast iron because the acidity of the tomatoes can leach out a metallic flavor. The key is to use a well-seasoned pan, making sure to re-season it after cleaning. You can also use an enamel-coated skillet instead.*

1 to 2 tablespoons olive oil

1 small onion, chopped

12 ounces (¾ pound) lean ground beef or plant-based crumbles

12 ounces (¾ pound) uncooked spicy Italian sausage or plant-based sausage

2 garlic cloves, minced

1 teaspoon dried Italian seasoning

1 (15-ounce) container ricotta cheese

1 large egg, lightly beaten

1 (8-ounce) packaged shredded mozzarella cheese, divided

½ cup (2 ounces) shredded or grated Parmesan cheese, divided

1 (24-ounce) jar pasta or marinara sauce

½ (12-ounce) box oven-ready lasagna noodles, cracked into 2-inch pieces

Vegetable cooking spray

¼ cup chopped fresh basil

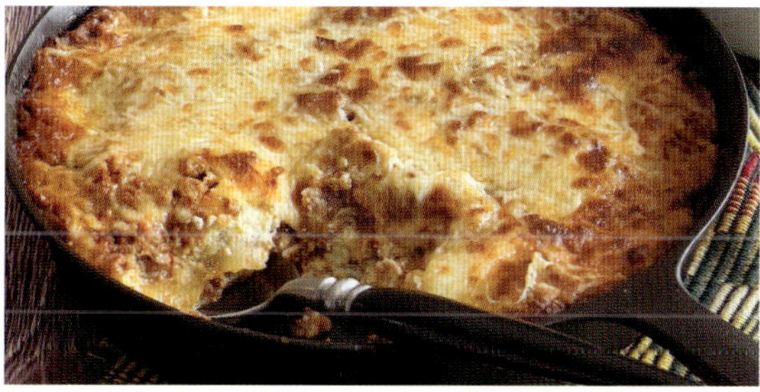

1. Heat 1 tablespoon oil in a 12-inch cast-iron skillet over medium heat. Add onion and cook, stirring occasionally, for 5 minutes. Add beef, sausage, garlic, and seasoning. (If using plant-based crumbles and sausage, add 1 tablespoon olive oil.) Cook, stirring occasionally, for 10 minutes or until meat is browned and crumbly. Drain any excess oil, if necessary.
2. Combine ricotta, egg, half of mozzarella, and half of Parmesan in a bowl.
3. Preheat oven to 375°.
4. Stir pasta sauce into cooked meat mixture. Transfer two-thirds of sauce mixture to a bowl, leaving one-third in skillet. Spread half of broken noodles over sauce mixture and dollop with half of ricotta mixture. Repeat with one-third sauce mixture, remaining half noodles, and remaining half ricotta mixture. Spread remaining one-third sauce mixture over ricotta mixture; sprinkle with remaining half of mozzarella and Parmesan cheeses.
5. Cover with a lid, nonstick aluminum foil, or foil lightly coated with cooking spray (to keep tomato sauce from touching aluminum). Bake, covered, for 45 minutes. Remove foil, and broil for 3 to 5 minutes or until golden brown. Cool for 5 minutes; sprinkle with basil before serving.

CREAMED SPINACH-AND-MUSHROOM SKILLET LASAGNA

MAKES 4 SERVINGS

EQUIPMENT: *12-inch cast-iron skillet*

PAN SAVVY: *Fresh spinach, best for flavor, is very fluffy and easier to manage in a large, 12-inch skillet. Once cooked down, it will all fit in a 10-inch skillet, if that's what you have. In that case, add spinach in batches.*

2 tablespoons extra-virgin olive oil
½ sweet onion, finely chopped
1 (8-ounce) container cremini or button mushrooms
½ cup white wine
½ teaspoon fine sea salt
½ teaspoon freshly ground black pepper
1 (16-ounce) package fresh baby spinach
1 (8-ounce) package mascarpone or softened cream cheese
1 cup (4 ounces) shredded Parmesan cheese, divided
9 oven-ready lasagna noodles
Ricotta Filling (recipe at right)

Oven-ready or no-boil lasagna noodles work well in this dish. The spinach-and-mushroom mixture tends to release liquid, and these types of lasagna noodles require plenty of sauce to cook properly. Feel free to use traditional boiled noodles, but drain them well. Mascarpone melts easily and creates a rich, delicious sauce. You may substitute very soft cream cheese. You can also substitute a 9- or 10-ounce package of frozen spinach (thawed). It must be drained well and squeezed very dry.

---

1. Heat oil in a 12-inch cast-iron skillet over medium heat. Add onion, mushrooms, wine, salt, and pepper. Cook, stirring frequently, for 7 to 9 minutes or until mushrooms are tender and most of liquid evaporates.
2. Add spinach in batches, and cook, tossing with tongs, for 5 minutes or until spinach wilts. Reduce heat to medium low. Stir in mascarpone and ½ cup Parmesan. Cook, stirring constantly, until cheese melts and mixture is well blended. Transfer to a bowl.
3. Preheat oven to 350°.
4. Spread one-third spinach mixture in bottom of skillet. Top with 3 noodles, breaking edges to fit pan. Top with one-third Ricotta Filling. Repeat layers twice.* Sprinkle top with remaining ½ cup Parmesan.
5. Cover skillet with aluminum foil, and bake for 45 minutes or until noodles are cooked and tender. Uncover and bake for 10 more minutes or until top is golden brown.

Ricotta Filling: Combine **1 (15-ounce) container ricotta cheese, 2 large eggs, ½ teaspoon fine sea salt, ¼ teaspoon ground nutmeg,** and **⅛ teaspoon coarsely ground black pepper** in a bowl. Makes 2 cups.

*The spinach mixture will not spread evenly across the ricotta mixture. It's okay to arrange the filling in any order. Just make sure all the noodles are covered by either the spinach or the ricotta mixture.

SKILLET PASTITSIO

MAKES 6 SERVINGS

EQUIPMENT: *12-inch cast-iron skillet*

PAN SAVVY: *The tomato sauce is acidic; with its lengthy cooking time, it could remove insufficient seasoning. Use a well-seasoned or enamel-coated skillet.*

8 ounces uncooked penne pasta
1 tablespoon extra-virgin olive oil
1 onion, chopped
¼ teaspoon crushed red pepper flakes
½ pound lean ground beef
½ pound ground lamb or lean ground beef
2 garlic cloves, minced
½ cup red wine
2 teaspoons ground cinnamon
1 teaspoon fine sea salt
¾ teaspoon coarsely ground black pepper
¾ teaspoon dried oregano
½ teaspoon dried thyme
3 cups seasoned or plain tomato sauce
Yogurt Béchamel Sauce (recipe at right)

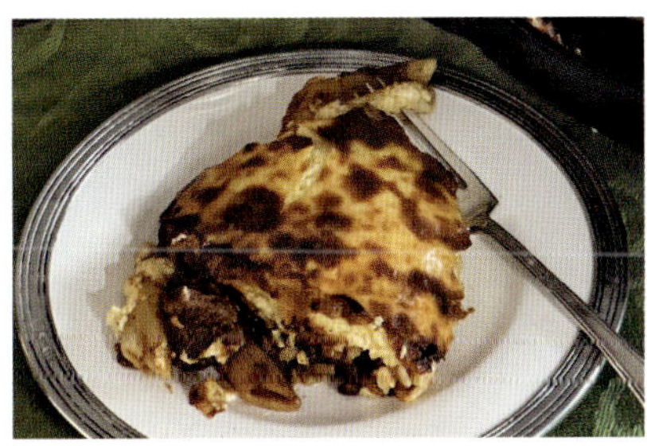

Pastitsio is a flavorful Greek dish made with a spiced ground lamb sauce and a creamy Béchamel sauce, which you'll want to prepare first. This version isn't completely authentic, but it's my take on the traditional casserole. Feel free to substitute ground chicken or turkey for a lighter flavor. Lean poultry may require a tablespoon of olive oil to brown.

---

1. Cook penne according to package directions; drain and set pasta aside.
2. Preheat oven to 350°.
3. Heat oil in a 12-inch cast-iron skillet over medium heat. Add onion and red pepper flakes. Cook, stirring frequently, for 3 to 5 minutes or until tender. Add beef, lamb, and garlic. Cook, stirring frequently, for 5 minutes or until meat is browned and crumbly. Stir in wine, and cook for 3 minutes or until liquid evaporates. Stir in cinnamon, salt, black pepper, oregano, and thyme. Stir in tomato sauce. Cook over medium-low heat, stirring occasionally, for 5 minutes or until thickened. (If making ahead, stop at this point. Cover and refrigerate meat sauce separately from pasta, which should be cooked just before assembling.)
4. Stir reserved pasta into meat sauce. Spread Yogurt Béchamel Sauce evenly over top.
5. Transfer skillet to oven and bake, uncovered, for 1 hour or until golden brown. Let stand for 10 minutes before serving.

Yogurt Béchamel Sauce: Melt **4 tablespoons butter** in a skillet or saucepan over medium heat. Whisk in **¼ cup all-purpose flour.** Cook, stirring constantly, for 1 minute. Whisk in **2 cups half-and-half, ¼ teaspoon ground nutmeg,** and **½ teaspoon fine sea salt.** Cook, stirring frequently, for 3 minutes or until thickened. Remove from heat. Stir in **¾ cup shredded Parmesan cheese.** Whisk together **2 large eggs** and **1 cup plain Greek yogurt** in a small bowl. Stir about ½ cup of warm sauce mixture into yogurt mixture, then add yogurt mixture back into sauce mixture (this keeps the eggs from curdling). Makes 3½ cups.

ROSEMARY BUTTER-BASTED STEAK

MAKES 2 TO 4 SERVINGS

EQUIPMENT: *10- or 12-inch cast-iron skillet*

PAN SAVVY: *While grill pans cook meats well and deliver pleasing grill marks, the ridges in the pan will make it too difficult to scoop up the butter for basting. Use a large skillet with room around the sides of the steaks so they are not crowded.*

2 (1¼-pound) bone-in ribeye or strip steaks

½ teaspoon kosher salt

½ teaspoon coarsely ground black pepper

1 tablespoon avocado oil

2 tablespoons unsalted or salted butter

2 rosemary sprigs, leaves removed from stems

Aim for a steak about 1 to 1¼ inches thick, especially if you prefer it cooked medium-rare. If you prefer meat more cooked, it's okay to use a thinner piece. If the thin steaks are wide, cook one at a time.

---

1. Sprinkle steaks with salt and pepper. Let stand at room temperature for 30 to 45 minutes.
2. Heat a large cast-iron skillet over medium-high heat until hot. Add oil to pan, swirling to coat.
3. Add steaks and cook for 1½ to 2 minutes on each side or until browned and crusty. Add butter and rosemary to skillet. Reduce heat to medium. Cook, basting with butter mixture and flipping steaks every 30 seconds to 1 minute, for 3 minutes or until desired degree of doneness. (A thermometer should register 120° to 125° for medium-rare, 130° to 135° for medium.)
4. Transfer steaks to a cutting board, reserving butter mixture in skillet; let rest for 10 minutes (steaks will continue to cook about 5 more degrees). Slice meat across grain. Drizzle with remaining butter mixture, if desired.

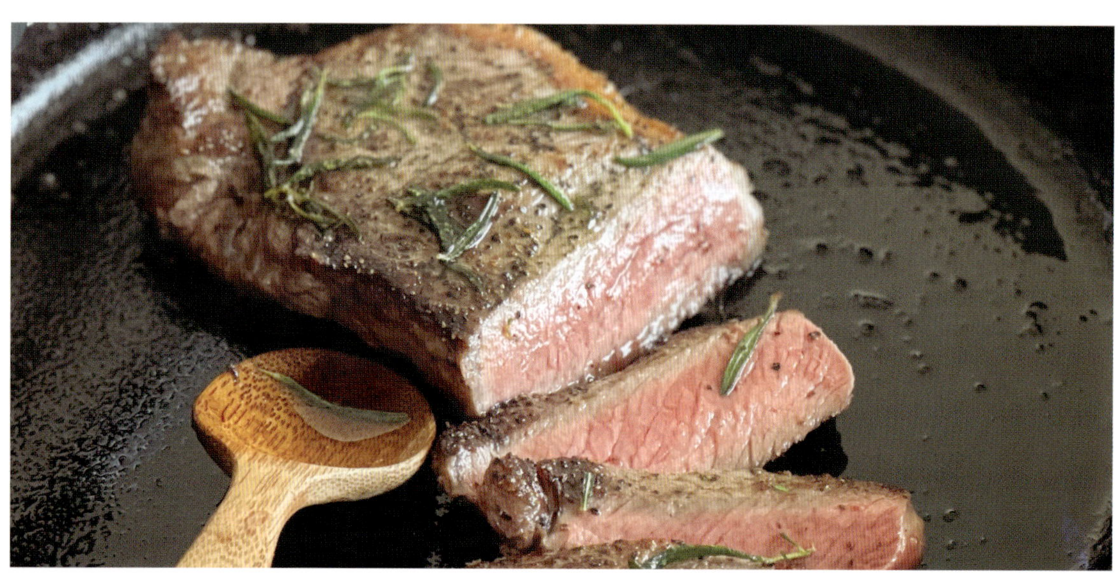

BRAISED POT ROAST

MAKES 6 TO 8 SERVINGS

EQUIPMENT: *7-quart Dutch oven*

- 2 tablespoons avocado or vegetable oil
- 1 (3- to 4-pound) beef chuck roast
- 1 tablespoon kosher salt or 1 teaspoon fine sea salt
- 1 teaspoon coarsely ground black pepper
- 2 onions, chopped
- 2 celery ribs, chopped
- 4 garlic cloves, chopped
- 2 tablespoons tomato paste
- ¾ cup red wine
- 2½ cups beef broth
- 1 tablespoon Worcestershire sauce
- 1 bay leaf
- 3 sprigs fresh rosemary
- 2 sprigs fresh thyme
- 5 carrots, cut into 2-inch pieces
- Simple Mashed Potatoes (recipe at right)

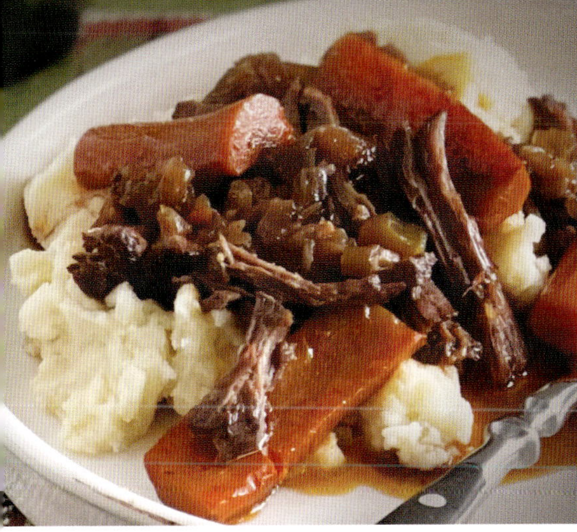

Braising means to cook foods in a moist environment, submerged in liquid and covered to trap steam. It's often done with large, tough cuts of beef that require lengthy cooking time to become tender. Before braising, sear the outside of the meat until it reaches a deep golden brown. The resulting crust seals in juices and adds color and flavor to the homey comfort dish.

---

1. Preheat oven to 325°.
2. Heat oil in a Dutch oven over medium to medium-high heat. Sprinkle beef evenly with salt and pepper. Add beef and cook for 3 minutes on each side or until golden brown. Remove meat to a plate; set meat aside.
3. Reduce heat to medium-low. Add onion and celery. Cook, stirring occasionally, for 5 minutes or until tender. Add garlic and cook, stirring frequently, for 1 minute. Stir in tomato paste. Cook for 1 minute.
4. Add wine and cook, scraping bottom of pot with a wooden spoon, for 2 to 3 minutes or until wine is reduced by half.
5. Stir in broth, Worcestershire, and bay leaf. Add reserved meat with any juices left on the plate. Arrange rosemary, thyme, and carrots around meat.
6. Cover and transfer to oven. Bake for 3 to 3½ hours or until meat is tender and falls apart with pulled with a fork. Remove and discard bay leaf.
7. Slice or shred pot roast, and serve over Simple Mashed Potatoes.

Simple Mashed Potatoes: Peel **3 pounds russet potatoes** and cut into 1½-inch chunks. Place in a soup pot and cover with cold water at least 1 inch above potatoes. Stir in some **1 to 2 teaspoons of broth paste or 2 bouillon cubes** for extra flavor. Add 1 to 2 teaspoons fine sea salt. Bring to a boil, reduce heat, and simmer for 15 minutes. Drain and return to pot. Mash and stir in **½ cup whipping cream** to create desired texture. Add 1 tablespoon butter, if desired, and stir until melted. Makes 8 servings.

PEPPER STEAK STIR-FRY

MAKES 4 TO 6 SERVINGS

EQUIPMENT: *12-inch cast-iron skillet*

- 1 tablespoon avocado or vegetable oil
- 2 teaspoons sesame oil
- ½ cup beef broth or water
- 1 tablespoon granulated sugar
- 1 tablespoon cornstarch
- 3 tablespoons low-sodium soy sauce
- 1 tablespoon rice wine vinegar
- 3 bell peppers (any color), cut into strips
- ½ white onion, sliced
- 1 tablespoon minced fresh ginger
- 2 garlic cloves, minced
- 1 to 1½ pounds lean flank or sirloin steak, very thinly sliced
- ⅛ teaspoon salt
- ¼ teaspoon coarsely ground black pepper
- Hot cooked rice
- Sriracha sauce or hoisin sauce (optional)

Put some sizzle and spice on the table tonight. Choose your color palette when you pick your trio of bell peppers.

The heat of cast iron creates a delicious crusty-edged steak, but it doesn't reduce quickly. To avoid scorching the meal, have all your ingredients and sauce mixture prepped ahead. Make sure the beef is very cold, as it's easier to thinly slice meat that's chilled to semi-frozen. While this dish is mild and universally appealing, I like a bit of spice, so I'll drizzle sriracha and hoisin sauce over my serving.

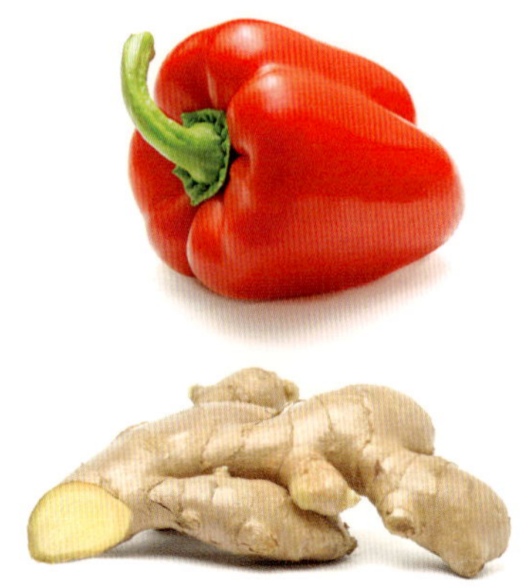

1. Combine avocado oil and sesame oil in a small bowl. Combine broth, sugar, cornstarch, soy sauce, and vinegar in another small bowl; set broth mixture aside.
2. Heat half of oil mixture in a cast-iron skillet over medium-high heat. Add bell peppers and onion. Cook, stirring constantly, for 3 to 4 minutes. Add ginger and garlic; cook, stirring constantly, for 1 minute. Transfer bell pepper mixture to a platter.
3. Heat remaining half of oil mixture in skillet over medium-high heat. Sprinkle steak with salt and black pepper. Add steak and cook, stirring constantly, for 2 minutes or until browned on all sides. Stir in reserved broth mixture. Bring to a boil, reduce heat, and cook for 1 minute or until sauce thickens. Stir in bell pepper mixture.
4. Serve over hot cooked rice, and drizzle with sriracha sauce, if desired.

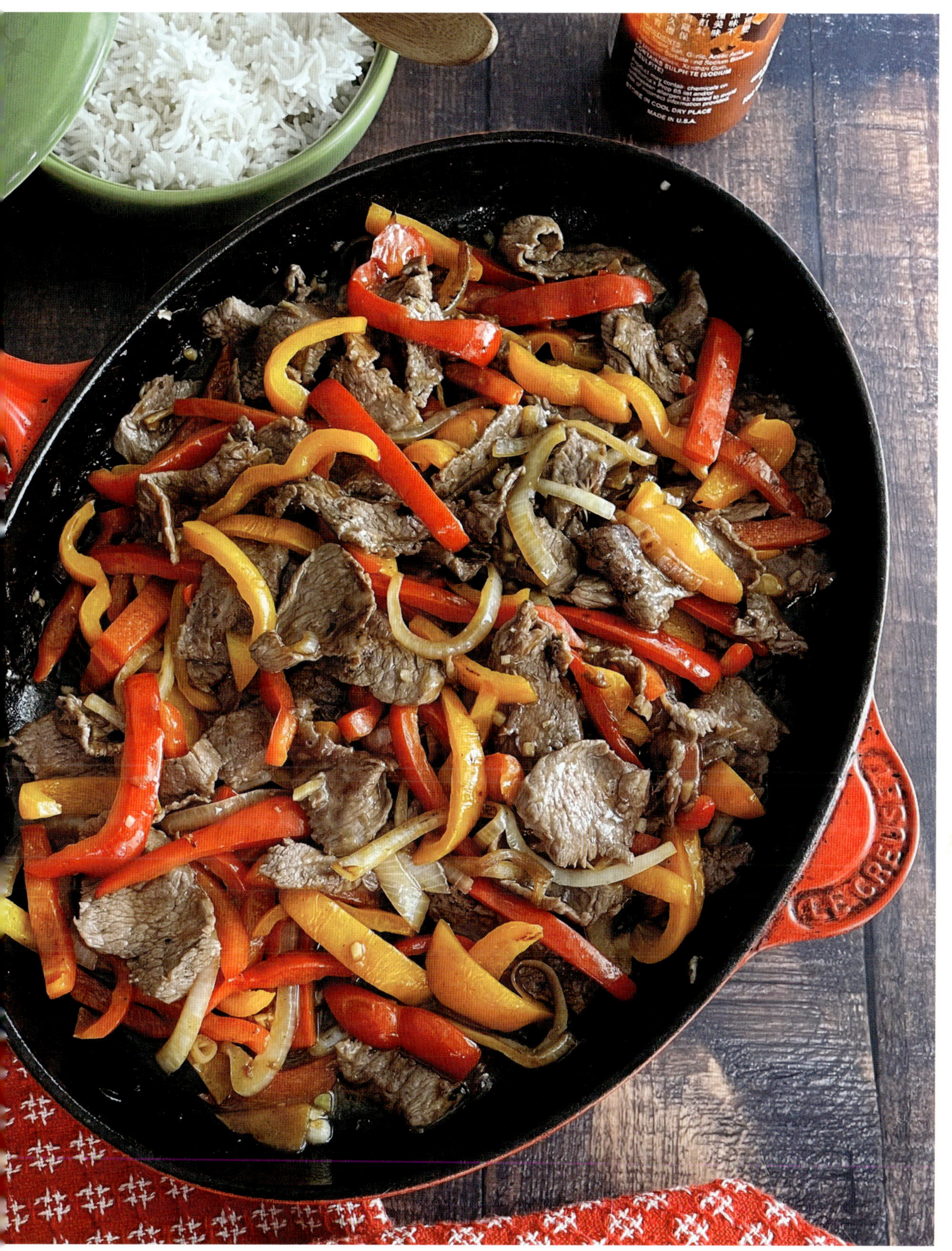
STORE IN COOL DRY PLACE
MADE IN U.S.A.
LE CREUSET

ASIAN SPICED SHORT RIBS

MAKES 4 SERVINGS

EQUIPMENT: *5- to 7-quart Dutch oven*

1 tablespoon avocado or olive oil
2½ to 3 pounds beef short ribs
2 cups beef broth
⅔ cup low-sodium soy sauce
¼ cup dark brown sugar
3 tablespoons finely chopped fresh ginger
3 garlic cloves, sliced
2 (3-inch) pieces fresh lemongrass
2 tablespoons toasted sesame oil
1 to 2 tablespoons gochujang or sriracha sauce
2 tablespoons rice vinegar
Hot cooked rice

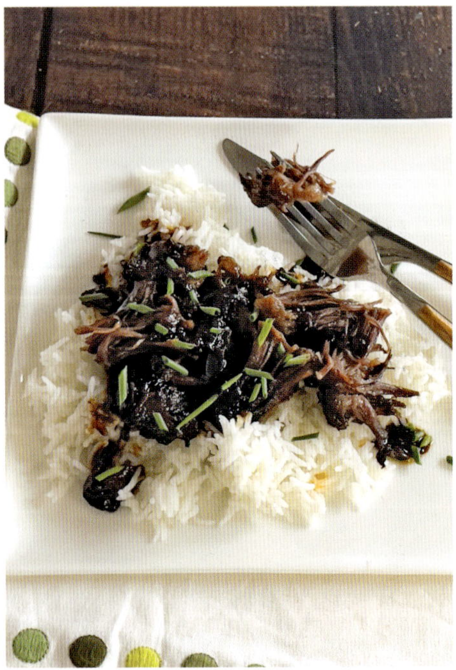

Check international markets if fresh lemongrass isn't available at your store (it's easy to grow, by the way!). It freezes well: Remove tough outer leaves and cut fresh lemongrass into 2½- to 3-inch lengths; place in a zip-top plastic storage bag and freeze until ready to use. You can also substitute a teaspoon of lemongrass paste (sold in the herb section in the produce department). Use low-sodium soy sauce because it condenses while cooking; otherwise, the sauce will be too salty.

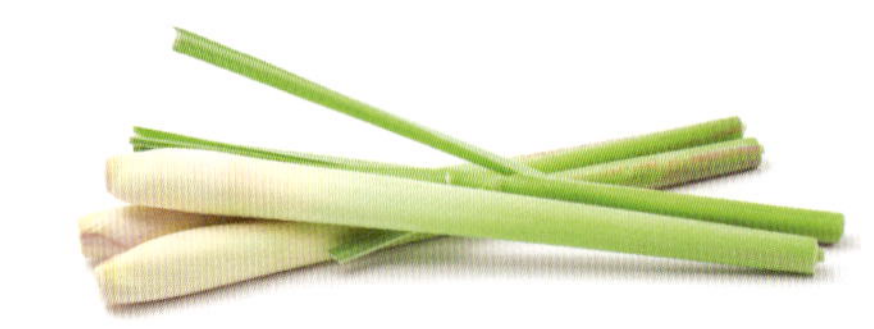

1. Heat oil in a large Dutch oven over medium-high heat. Add short ribs and cook for 3 minutes on each side or until browned. Transfer to a plate, and set ribs aside; drain off excess oil (no need to wipe pan clean).
2. Add broth, soy sauce, brown sugar, ginger, garlic, lemongrass, sesame oil, gochujang, and vinegar to Dutch oven, stirring until well blended.
3. Preheat oven to 350°.
4. Add reserved ribs to Dutch oven, bone side up. Cover and bake for 3 hours or until meat is very tender and falling off the bone.
5. Transfer meat to a platter and let stand until cool enough to handle. Remove bones and tough inedible pieces. Shred meat into bite-size pieces. Cover with aluminum foil to keep warm.
6. Drain liquid into a fat-separating measuring cup or a glass measuring cup. Skim away excess oil.
7. Serve meat over hot cooked rice, and drizzle with cooking liquid, if desired.

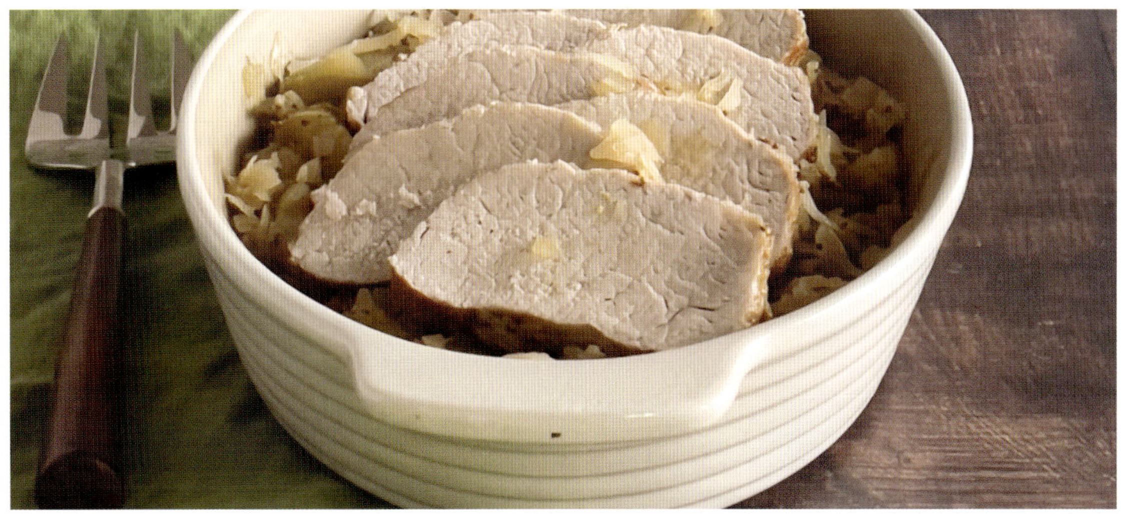

ROAST PORK LOIN WITH SAUERKRAUT

MAKES 6 SERVINGS

EQUIPMENT: *7-quart Dutch oven*

- 2 tablespoons avocado or extra-virgin olive oil
- 1 (2- to 2½-pound) boneless pork loin roast
- 1 onion, chopped
- ½ cup chicken or vegetable broth
- 1 (32-ounce) package refrigerated sauerkraut, undrained
- 3 tablespoons light brown sugar
- 1 tablespoon whole-grain mustard
- 2 teaspoons caraway seeds
- ¾ teaspoon fine sea salt
- 1 teaspoon coarsely ground black pepper
- 2 baking apples such as Golden Delicious, Granny Smith, or Fuji, cut into wedges

Pork roasts make a great pairing with sauerkraut. Although the apples cook to a point where they are almost falling apart, their sweet flavor contributes to balancing the tangy sauerkraut. Cooking pork to 145° ensures that it is safe to eat yet remains deliciously moist. The temperature of the meat will continue to rise slightly after it's removed from the oven due to carryover cooking.

---

1. Heat oil in a Dutch oven over medium-high heat. Add pork and cook, turning occasionally, for 6 to 8 minutes or until browned on all sides. Remove from pan and set pork aside.
2. Reduce heat to medium. Add onion and cook, stirring constantly, for 3 minutes or until tender. Add broth, and cook for 1 minute, scraping up any bits stuck on bottom of pan.
3. Remove from heat and stir in sauerkraut, brown sugar, mustard, caraway seeds, salt, and pepper. Stir in apples.
4. Preheat oven to 325°.
5. Transfer reserved pork and any liquid back to pan, nestling in center. Cover and bake for 1 to 1½ hours or until pork reaches an internal temperature of 145°.
6. Let rest for 10 minutes. Remove pork and cut into thick slices. Serve over sauerkraut mixture.

PORK CHOPS WITH APPLES AND ONION

MAKES 4 SERVINGS

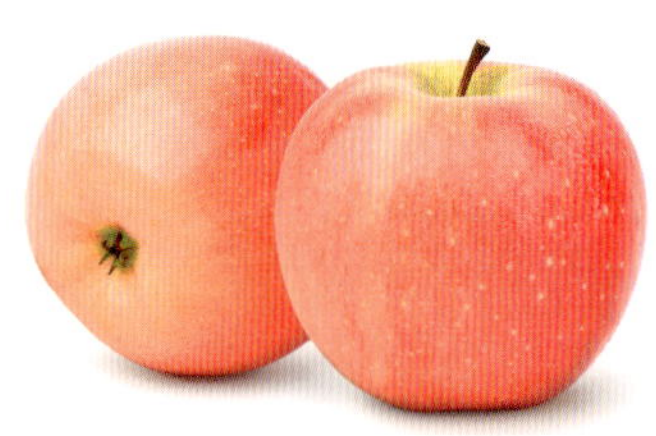

EQUIPMENT: *12-inch cast-iron skillet or brasier*

PAN SAVVY: *Most skillets do not come with lids, but you can top yours with a baking sheet because this dish is cooked solely on a cooktop. You can use a 10-inch skillet as long as the chops fit in the bottom in a single layer; pile the apples and onion on top of the chops when cooking.*

4 (1-inch-thick) boneless pork chops
½ teaspoon fine sea salt
¼ teaspoon coarsely ground black pepper
3 tablespoons avocado oil, divided
1 sweet onion, halved and sliced
2 apples, cored and sliced
2 tablespoons salted butter
2 small garlic cloves, minced
1 tablespoon chopped fresh sage or 1 teaspoon dried sage
½ teaspoon chopped fresh thyme or ¼ teaspoon dried thyme
½ cup chicken stock
2 teaspoons whole-grain mustard
Garnish: chopped fresh sage

You can use whatever you have on hand, but you want a baking apple that holds its shape when cooked. I eat the peel on foods whenever possible; therefore, I usually pick Gala, Fuji, or Granny Smith. Save the expensive Honeycrisp for noshing with cheese or for apple pies.

1. Trim excess fat from pork chops and sprinkle evenly with salt and pepper. Heat a 12-inch cast-iron skillet over medium-high heat.
2. Add 2 tablespoons oil to skillet. Add chops and cook for 3 minutes on each side or until golden brown. Transfer to a platter; set pork chops aside.
3. Heat remaining 1 tablespoon oil in the same skillet (no need to wipe clean) over medium heat. Add onion. Cook, stirring occasionally, for 5 minutes or until tender. Add apples, butter, garlic, sage, and thyme; cook, turning gently, for 3 minutes or until apples are slightly tender.
4. Stir together stock and mustard, and pour into skillet. Return reserved pork chops to skillet. Cover and simmer over low heat for 10 minutes or until internal temperature of pork chops reaches 145°. Garnish, if desired.

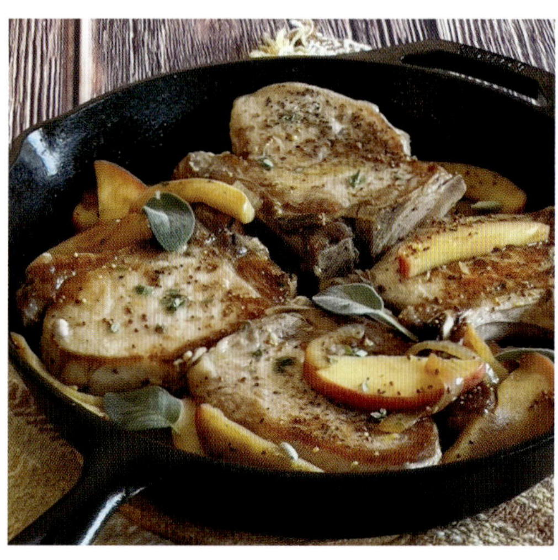

LAMB CHOPS WITH MINT CHIMICHURRI

MAKES 4 SERVINGS

EQUIPMENT: *12-inch cast-iron skillet*

3 tablespoons extra-virgin or avocado oil, divided
½ teaspoon grated lemon zest
2 tablespoons fresh lemon juice
2 garlic cloves, minced
1 teaspoon fine sea salt
½ teaspoon ground cumin
¼ teaspoon coarsely ground black pepper
8 (1-inch-thick) lamb rib chops
Fresh Lemon-Mint Chimichurri (recipe at right)

Lamb rib chops take just a few minutes to cook and are best medium-rare to medium. Check temperature and aim for 135°, then allow meat to rest for 3 to 5 minutes to allow for residual cooking for a final internal temperature of 145° for medium-rare. For medium, remove lamb at 150° to reach 160°.

---

1 Combine 2 tablespoons oil, zest, juice, garlic, salt, cumin, and black pepper in a baking dish or zip-top plastic storage bag. Add lamb, turning to coat. Cover and refrigerate for 1 hour.

2 Heat remaining 1 tablespoon oil in a large skillet over medium-high heat. Remove chops, discarding marinade. Add chops to skillet, in batches if necessary to avoid overcrowding. Cook for 2 to 3 minutes or until golden brown. Turn chops over and cook for 2 minutes for medium-rare or longer, if desired.

3 Transfer to a platter and let rest for 3 to 5 minutes. Serve with Fresh Lemon-Mint Chimichurri.

Fresh Lemon-Mint Chimichurri: Combine **¼ cup extra-virgin olive oil, ¼ teaspoon lemon zest, 3 tablespoons fresh lemon juice, 1 cup lightly packed fresh mint, ½ cup lightly packed fresh cilantro, 1 coarsely chopped garlic clove, 1 teaspoon granulated sugar, ¼ teaspoon crushed red pepper flakes, ¼ teaspoon salt,** and **1 tablespoon water** in a food processor. Process until finely chopped. Makes ½ cup.

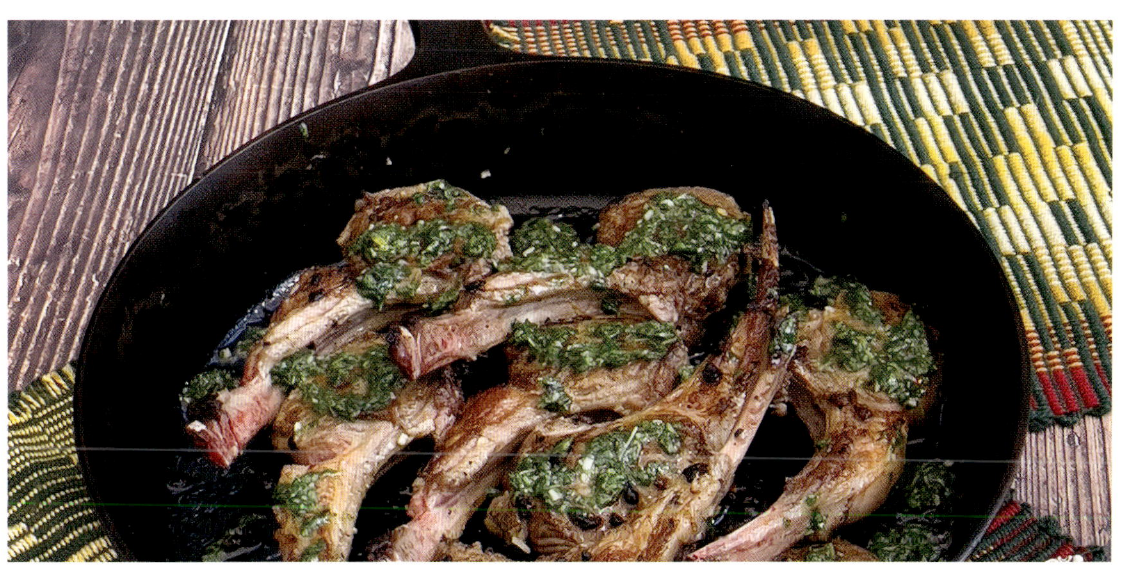

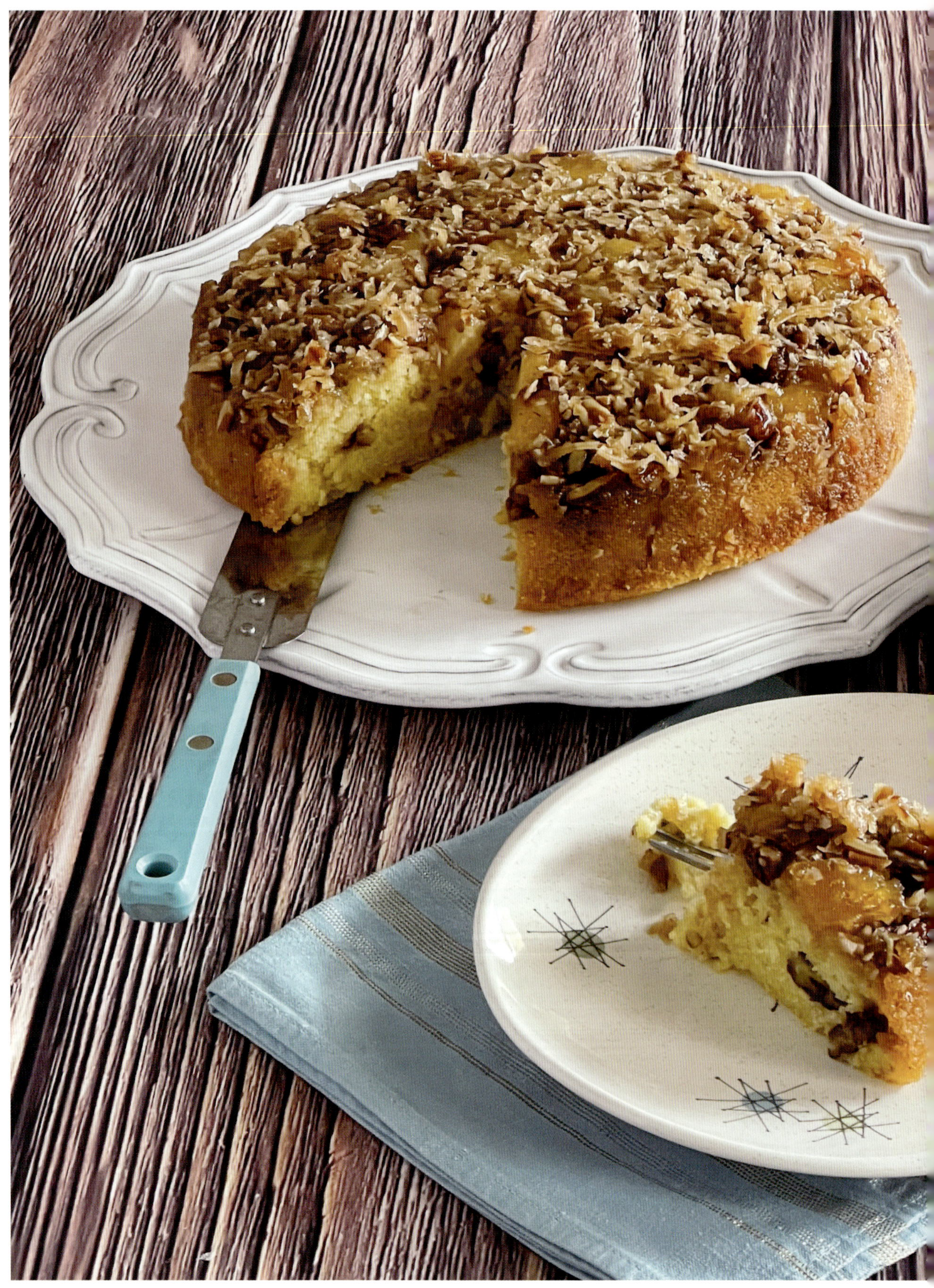

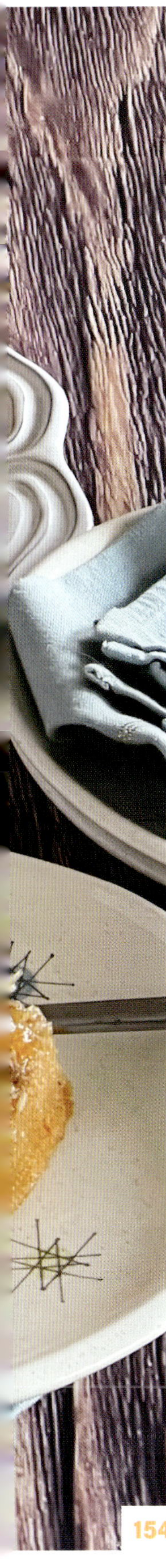

154

DESSERTS

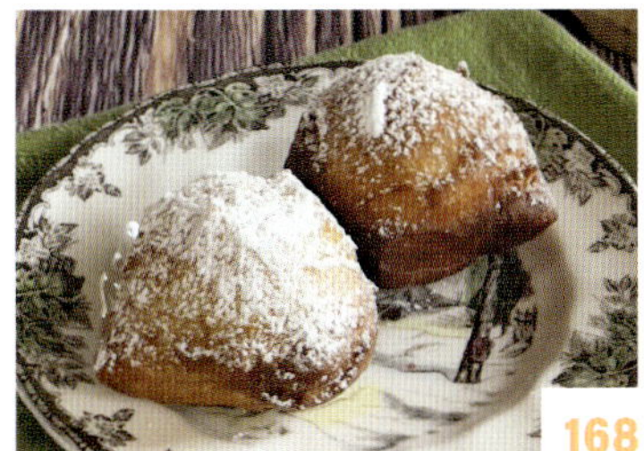

168

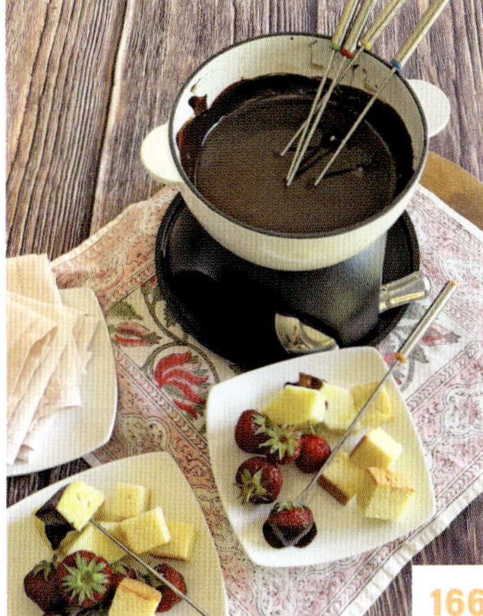

166

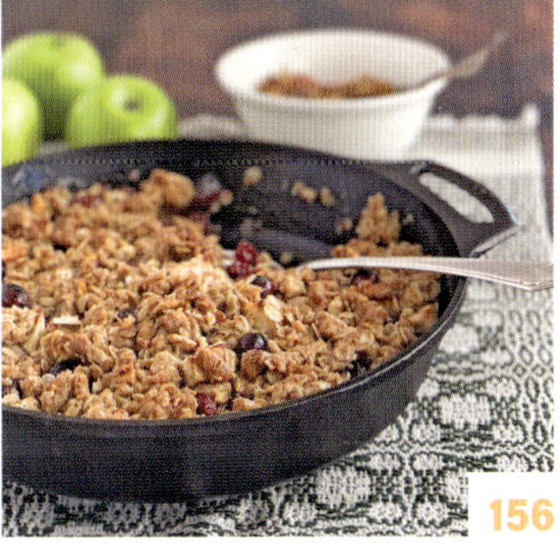

156

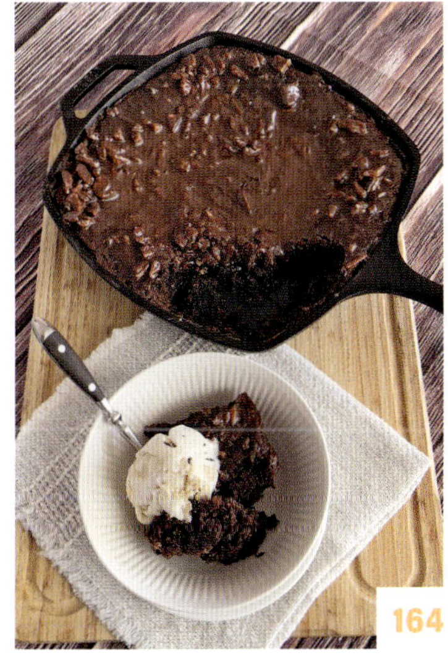

164

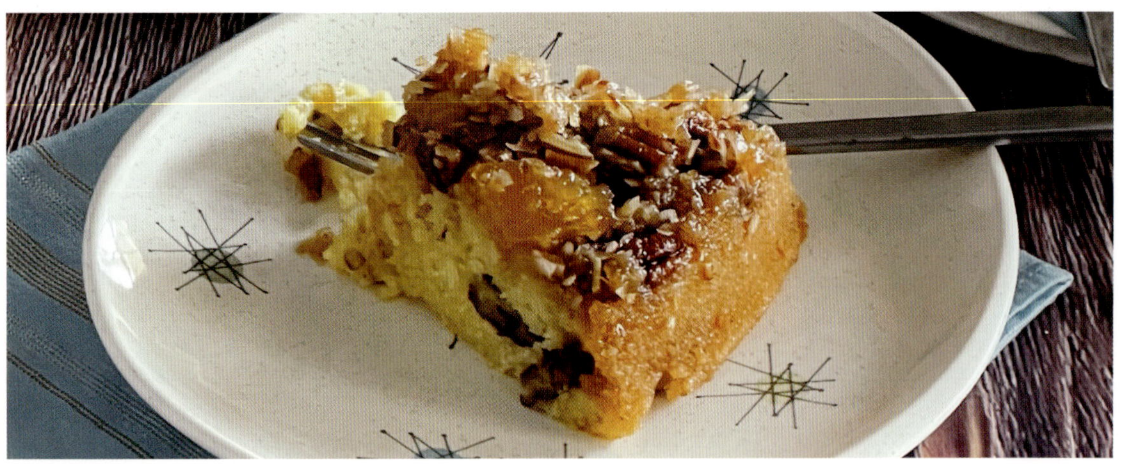

COCONUT–PECAN FLIP CAKE

MAKES 8 TO 10 SERVINGS

EQUIPMENT: *10-inch enamel-coated cast-iron skillet*

PAN SAVVY: *The acidity of the pineapple might react with bare cast iron, creating very dark areas on the cake. It's fine to eat but appears burned. To avoid discoloration, bake in an enamel-coated skillet.*

⅓ cup plus ½ cup unsalted butter, softened and divided
½ cup firmly packed light brown sugar
1 (8-ounce) can chopped pineapple, drained
½ cup sweetened coconut flakes
½ cup chopped pecans
½ cup granulated sugar
2 large eggs
1 teaspoon vanilla extract
1½ cups all-purpose flour
2 teaspoons baking powder
½ teaspoon salt
1 (13.5-ounce) can coconut milk

This is a delightful twist on refreshing tropical flavors. There's no need for frosting because the topping of caramelized pineapple, coconut, and pecans adds sweetness.

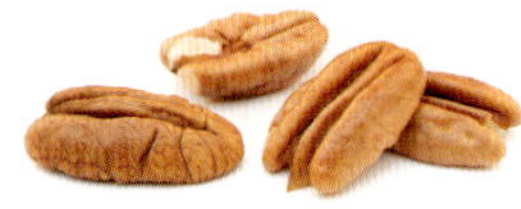

1. Preheat oven to 350°.
2. Melt ⅓ cup butter in a 10-inch cast-iron skillet over medium heat. Stir in brown sugar, pineapple, coconut, and pecans. Remove from heat.
3. Beat remaining ½ cup butter and granulated sugar in a mixing bowl until light and fluffy. Beat in eggs and vanilla.
4. Stir together flour, baking powder, and salt in a small bowl. Add flour mixture to egg mixture, alternating with coconut milk, beating just until combined. Pour batter over coconut mixture in skillet.
5. Bake for 40 minutes or until a toothpick inserted in center comes out clean.
6. Cool in pan for 10 minutes. Run a knife around edge, place a large plate or platter on top, and carefully invert cake. Let cool to room temperature.

ORANGE-BERRY CORNMEAL CAKE

MAKES 8 SERVINGS

EQUIPMENT: *10-inch cast-iron baker's skillet or long-handled skillet*

PAN SAVVY: *A baker's skillet with two short end pieces is easier to transfer in and out of an oven. Although there's a slight bit of acidity with the fruit and orange juice, there is not enough to make an enamel-coated pan a necessity.*

1 cup all-purpose flour
1 cup granulated sugar
¾ cup yellow cornmeal
2 teaspoons baking powder
1 teaspoon fine sea salt
2 large eggs
2 teaspoons orange zest
½ cup fresh orange juice
½ cup melted plus 1 tablespoon cold salted or unsalted butter
2 cups frozen mixed berries, mostly thawed
Powdered sugar (optional)

This is another treat that falls between a breakfast coffee cake and dessert, and I've placed it in the latter chapter only because my family tends to eat more of this tasty snack after dinner. I tend to keep leftover summer berries in the freezer, so I've always made this from frozen fruit. Use any type you enjoy, but cut strawberries into quarters so the different berries are around the same size. A 10-ounce bag of frozen mixed berries from the grocery store is about 2 cups.

1. Preheat oven to 375°. Place a 10-inch baker's skillet in oven to preheat.
2. Combine flour, granulated sugar, cornmeal, baking powder, and salt in a large bowl.
3. Whisk together eggs, zest, juice, and ½ cup melted butter in another bowl. Stir egg mixture into flour mixture.
4. Place remaining 1 tablespoon butter in skillet and allow to melt, swirling pan to coat bottom. Pour in batter and sprinkle evenly with fruit.
5. Bake for 40 to 45 minutes or until golden brown. Transfer to a wire rack to cool. Sprinkle with powdered sugar, if desired.

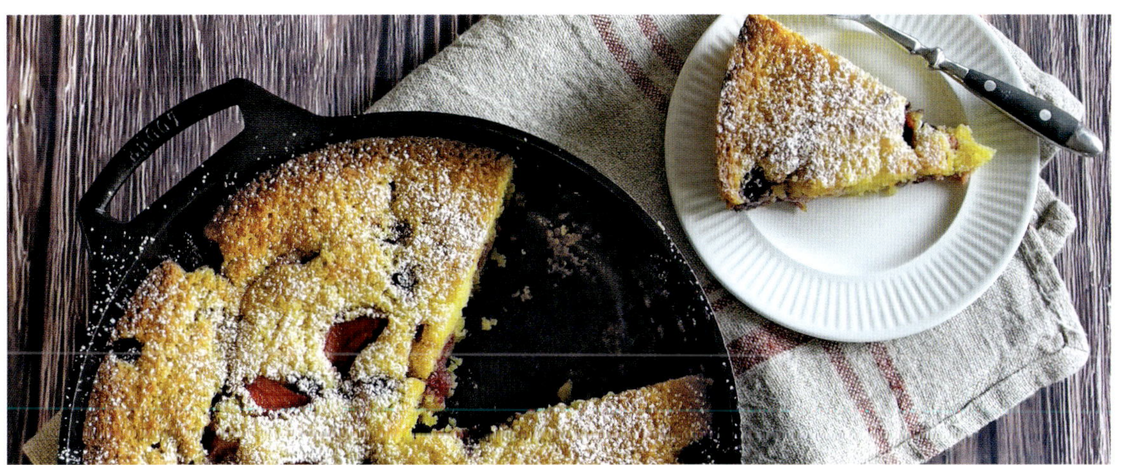

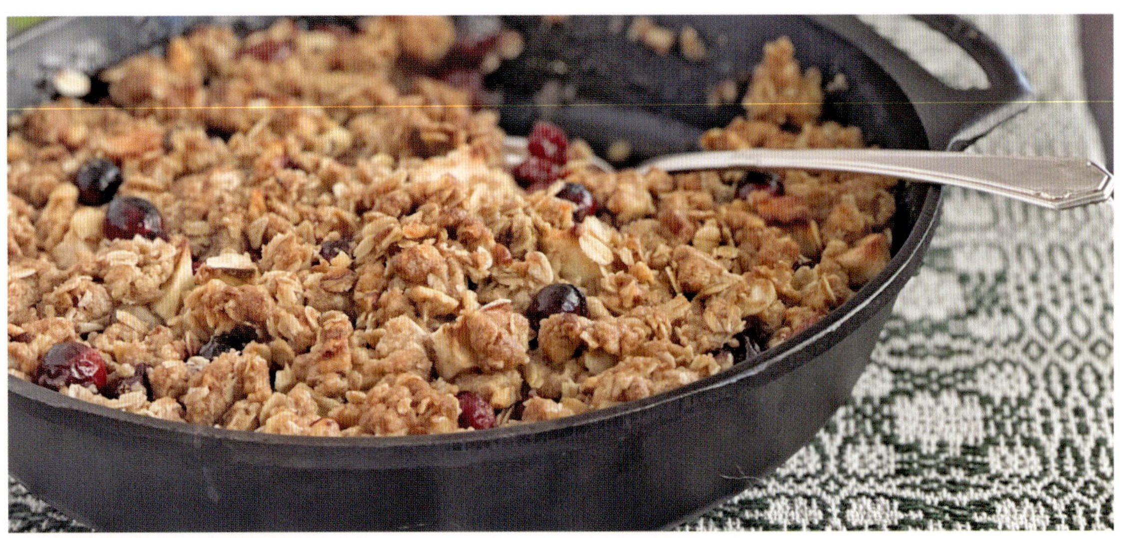

CRANBERRY-APPLE CRUMB SKILLET CRISP

Topped with a crispy, buttery crumble, this fall-to-winter dessert features tart seasonal cranberries and sweet apples. Serve it in a bowl with a scoop of simple vanilla ice cream.

MAKES 8 SERVINGS

EQUIPMENT: *10-inch cast-iron skillet*

PAN SAVVY: *Substitute a 10-inch baker's skillet for easier handling.*

3 tablespoons unsalted butter, divided

6 large baking apples, such as Granny Smith, Honey Gold, Fuji, or Gala, peeled and cut into pieces (2¼ pounds or about 5 cups)

2 cups fresh (or frozen and thawed) cranberries

⅓ cup granulated sugar

2 tablespoons all-purpose flour

1 tablespoon lemon juice

⅛ teaspoon fine sea salt

Walnut-Oat Topping (recipe at right)

1. Preheat oven to 350°. Generously grease a 10-inch cast-iron skillet with 1 tablespoon unsalted butter.
2. Combine apples, cranberries, sugar, flour, lemon juice, and salt in a large bowl, tossing until well blended. Let stand for 10 minutes. Meanwhile, prepare Walnut-Oat Topping.
3. Stir fruit mixture, then transfer to prepared skillet. Cut remaining 2 tablespoons butter into pieces; dot onto top of fruit. Sprinkle evenly with Walnut-Oat Topping.
4. Bake for 50 to 60 minutes or until golden brown, hot, and bubbly.

Walnut-Oat Topping: Combine **¾ cup all-purpose flour, ¾ cup old-fashioned oats, ½ cup chopped walnuts, ½ cup firmly packed light brown sugar, ¾ teaspoon ground cinnamon, ½ teaspoon ground ginger,** and **½ teaspoon fine sea salt** in a bowl. Cut in **½ cup unsalted butter** with a pastry blender or with fingers until mixture resembles coarse, evenly sized crumbs. Makes 2 cups.

PEAR UPSIDE-DOWN GINGERBREAD CAKE

MAKES 8 TO 10 SERVINGS

EQUIPMENT: *10-inch cast-iron skillet or baker's skillet*

PAN SAVVY: *A baker's skillet with two small handles is easier to transfer in and out of the oven—as well as to flip over onto a serving plate.*

¾ cup unsalted butter, divided

1½ cups firmly packed light brown sugar, divided

1 large ripe pear, cored and thinly sliced

1½ cups all-purpose flour

2 teaspoons ground ginger

1 teaspoon ground cinnamon

¾ teaspoon baking soda

½ teaspoon fine sea salt

¼ teaspoon ground cloves

½ cup hot water

½ cup molasses

1 large egg

Sweetened whipped cream or vanilla ice cream

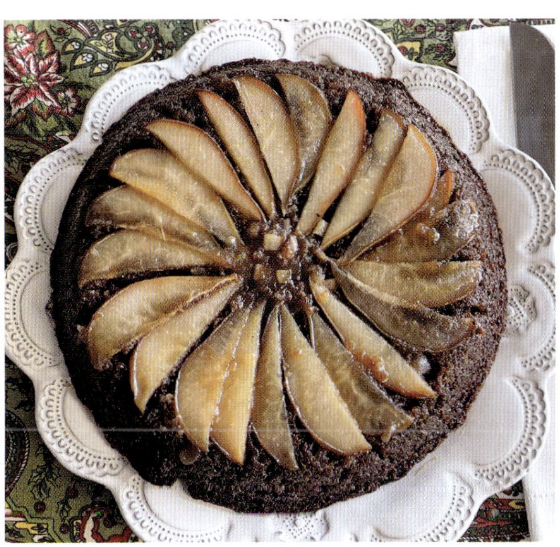

Rich with fragrant spices, gingerbread makes an ideal holiday or winter treat. The moist, dense texture is delicious on its own but sublime with a bit of whipped cream or ice cream.

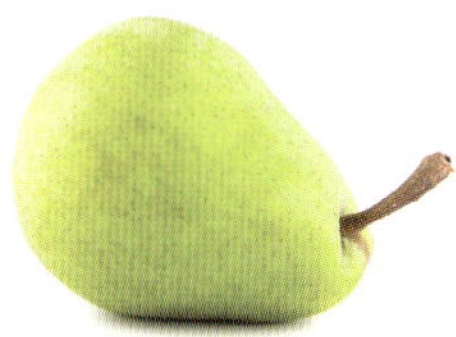

1. Preheat oven to 350°.
2. Heat a cast-iron skillet over medium heat until hot. Add 6 tablespoons butter and melt, tilting pan to coat sides. Add 1 cup brown sugar, stirring just until well blended. Remove from heat and arrange pear slices on top of sugar mixture.
3. Combine flour, ginger, cinnamon, baking soda, salt, and cloves in a large bowl.
4. Melt remaining 6 tablespoons butter in a small pan. Remove from heat and stir in ½ cup hot water, molasses, and remaining ½ cup brown sugar. Whisk in egg.
5. Add butter mixture to flour mixture, stirring until well blended. Pour batter into skillet, being careful not to disturb pear slices.
6. Bake for 35 minutes or until a toothpick inserted in center comes out almost clean. Cool in pan for 10 minutes. Place a round platter on top and carefully turn over (pan will be hot). Scrape any remaining sugar mixture out of skillet and pour on cake. Serve warm or at room temperature with whipped cream or ice cream.

UPSIDE-DOWN STICKY TOFFEE CAKE

MAKES 10 TO 12 SERVINGS

Melted butter and oil contribute to this cake's softness, but the key to the dense, butterscotch-sweet dessert is the sauce that is infused into it. Use a thick skewer to poke many holes and pour the sauce in batches to avoid overflow. If your cake rises above the rim, take care to move it away from the sides of the pan while drizzling, to keep the sticky sauce inside the pan. You can serve the cake in the pan, or flip it upside down onto a platter. Serve the remaining sauce on the side. The Maple-Rye Sauce adds a spicy adult flavor, but feel free to skip it or substitute plain bourbon or whiskey plus ¼ teaspoon maple extract, if desired.

EQUIPMENT: *10-inch cast-iron baker's skillet*

PAN SAVVY: *A 10-inch baker's skillet results in a domed cake that's easier to flip over onto a platter, but be careful, as the sauce may spill over the sides. A 12-inch skillet will create a flatter, wider cake, and you won't have to worry about the sauce dribbling over.*

8 ounces pitted dates (about 12 large), chopped
1 cup hot coffee or boiling water
1 teaspoon baking soda
½ cup unsalted butter, melted
½ cup vegetable oil
1½ cups firmly packed dark or light brown sugar
2 large eggs, lightly beaten
2½ cups all-purpose flour
1 teaspoon baking powder
¼ teaspoon salt
Maple-Rye Sauce (recipe at right)

1. Combine dates, coffee, and baking soda in a large bowl. Let stand for 15 minutes.
2. Preheat oven to 350°. Butter and flour a 10-inch cast-iron skillet.
3. Blend date mixture with a fork or in a food processor until very finely chopped or pasty. Stir in butter, oil, and brown sugar. Whisk in eggs, one at a time. Combine flour, baking powder, and salt in a bowl. Stir flour mixture into date mixture.
4. Spoon batter into prepared pan. Bake for 40 to 45 minutes or until a wooden pick inserted in center comes out almost clean. Meanwhile, prepare Maple-Rye Sauce.
5. Poke holes in cake with a skewer; drizzle about ½ cup warm Maple-Rye Sauce over cake, allowing sauce to seep into holes. Return cake to oven and bake for 5 minutes. Cool cake in pan for 15 minutes. Turn out onto a serving plate. Serve warm with remaining sauce.

Maple-Rye Sauce: Melt **½ cup unsalted butter** in a saucepan over medium heat. Stir in **¾ cup brown sugar, ¾ cup heavy whipping cream,** and **salt.** Bring mixture to a boil. Reduce heat and simmer, stirring frequently, for 5 minutes or until mixture slightly thickens. Remove from heat and stir in **1 to 2 tablespoons maple-flavored or plain rye whiskey** and **¼ teaspoon maple extract,** if desired (mixture will bubble). Cover and set aside in a warm place. Makes 2 cups.

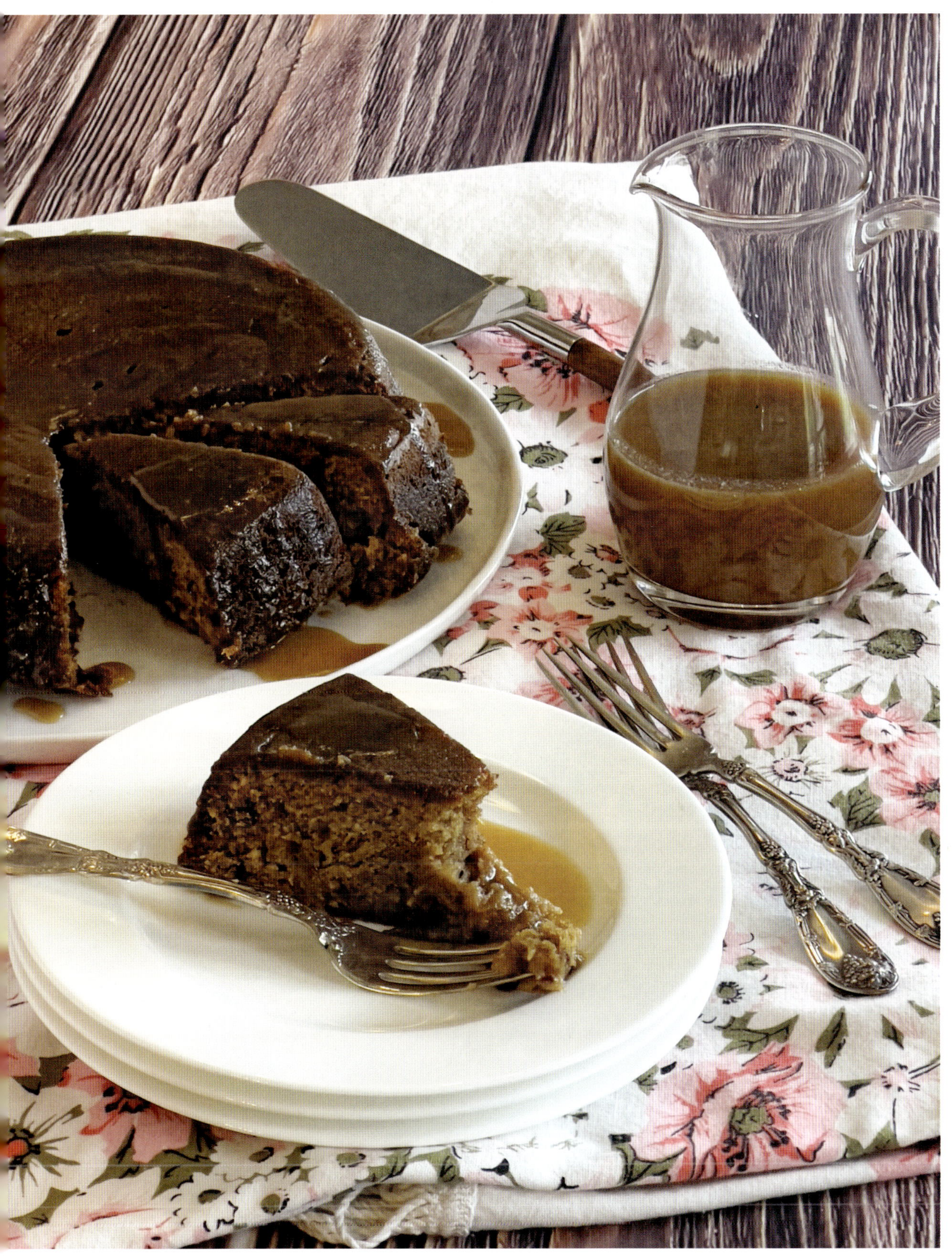

BLACKBERRY COBBLER

MAKES 8 SERVINGS

EQUIPMENT: *10-inch cast-iron skillet*

PAN-SAVVY: *There's enough acid in the berry mixture to possibly cause a reaction with the iron in the skillet if it's not well seasoned. Butter well if you have a new pan, or use an enamel-coated skillet.*

⅓ cup plus 1 tablespoon unsalted butter, cut into pieces
4 cups fresh (or frozen and thawed) blackberries
½ cup granulated sugar, divided
1½ cups plus 1 tablespoon all-purpose flour
½ teaspoon grated lemon rind
2 teaspoons baking powder
½ teaspoon salt
¾ cup heavy whipping cream
Vanilla ice cream (optional)

If you keep some blackberries in the freezer, coming up with a comforting, easy dessert in little over an hour's time isn't just a dream. For faster defrosting, spread berries out in a single layer on a platter or baking sheet. If you have tart berries, you can add up to ¼ cup more sugar to the berry mixture, but it's probably not necessary if you're serving the cobbler with vanilla ice cream.

---

1. Preheat oven to 375°. Spread 1 tablespoon butter on bottom and sides of a 10-inch cast-iron skillet.
2. To make filling, combine berries, ¼ cup sugar, 1 tablespoon flour, and lemon rind in a large bowl. Stir until well blended. Set filling aside.
3. To make dough, combine remaining 1½ cups flour, remaining ¼ cup sugar, baking powder, and salt in a bowl. Cut in remaining ⅓ cup butter with a pastry blender or fork until mixture resembles coarse meal. Add cream, stirring just until dry ingredients are moistened.
4. Place reserved filling in prepared skillet. With floured hands, form dough into individual biscuits and place over berries, or dollop dough with a large spoon.
5. Bake for 35 to 40 minutes or until top is golden brown and filling is thick and bubbling.
6. Cool for 5 to 10 minutes before serving with ice cream, if desired.

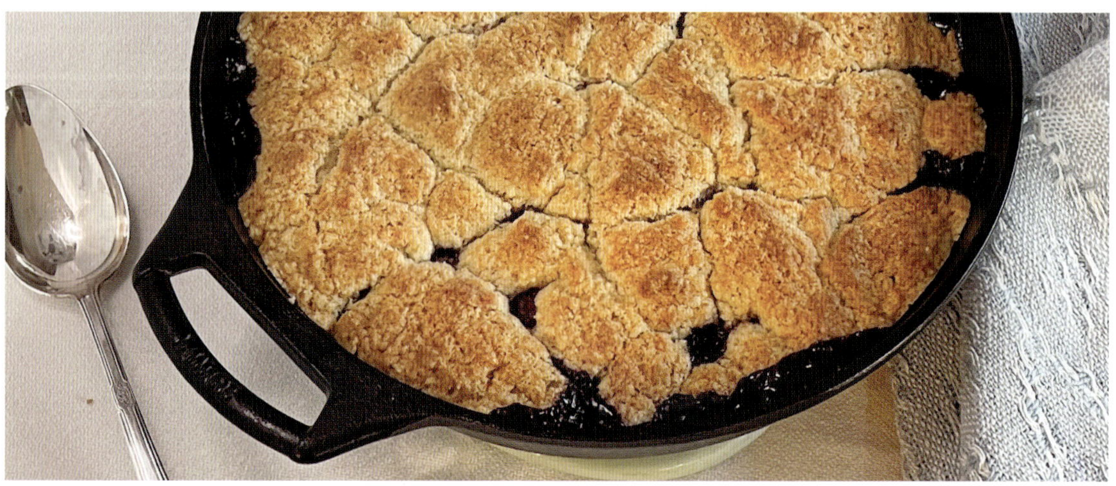

DOUBLE-CRUST BLUEBERRY PIE

I want to keep the bottom crust as flaky as possible, so I cook the blueberry filling first. Add some uncooked berries to the mixture to give it a nice texture.

MAKES 8 SERVINGS

EQUIPMENT: *10-inch cast-iron skillet*

PAN-SAVVY: *There's enough acid in the berry mixture to possibly cause a reaction with the iron in the skillet if it's not well seasoned. Butter well if you have a new pan, or use an enamel-coated skillet.*

5 cups fresh (or frozen and thawed) blueberries, divided

¾ cup granulated sugar

1 teaspoon lemon zest

¼ teaspoon salt

2 tablespoons fresh lemon juice

3 tablespoons cornstarch

2 tablespoons water

1 tablespoon unsalted or salted butter

Double-Crust Pastry Dough (recipe at right) or 1 package store-bought refrigerated piecrusts

1 egg, lightly beaten

Sparkling or turbinado sugar (optional)

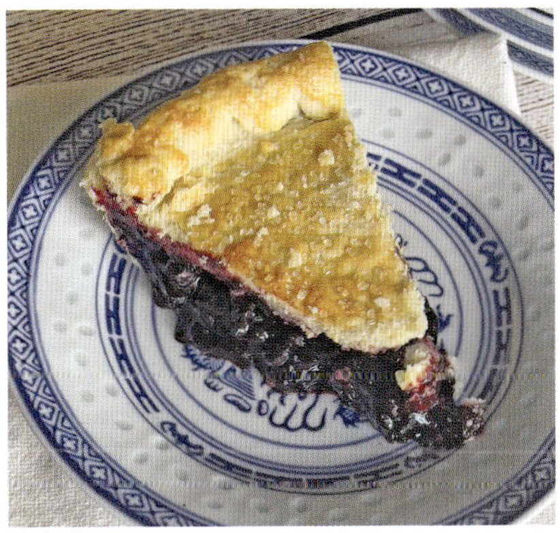

1. To make filling, combine 4 cups blueberries, granulated sugar, zest, salt, and juice in a small saucepan. Cook over medium heat for 8 to 10 minutes, pressing berries against pan with back of a spoon or spatula to crush. Combine cornstarch with 2 tablespoons water in a small bowl; stir into berry mixture. Bring to a boil; reduce heat and simmer for 2 minutes or until thickened. Stir in remaining 1 cup berries. Set filling aside.
2. Preheat oven to 375°. Generously grease a 10-inch cast-iron skillet on bottom and sides with 1 tablespoon butter.
3. On a lightly floured surface, roll 1 Double-Crust Pastry Dough disk into an 11-inch circle. Fit into prepared skillet. Spoon reserved filling into crust.
4. Roll remaining dough disk into a 9- or 10-inch circle. Fit top crust over filling, and pinch to seal top and bottom crusts. Make cuts into top crust for steam vents. Brush top with egg and sprinkle with sparkling sugar, if desired.
5. Bake for 35 to 40 minutes or until golden brown, shielding crust with aluminum foil after 20 minutes if edges get too brown. Cool completely.

Double-Crust Pastry Dough: Combine **2½ cups all-purpose flour** and **1 teaspoon salt** in a food processor; pulse until well blended. Add **1 cup unsalted butter,** cut into small pieces, and pulse until well blended and finely textured. Do not overprocess. Mixture should have lumps of butter the size of peas throughout. With processor running, gradually add **⅓ to ½ cup water,** and process until dough just begins to stick together. Turn dough out onto a lightly floured surface and squeeze gently until it sticks together in a ball. Divide dough in half, and wrap each dough disk in plastic wrap. Cover and chill for 30 minutes or up to one day ahead. Makes 2 piecrusts.

APPLE PIE WITH LATTICE CRUST

MAKES 8 SERVINGS

EQUIPMENT: *12-inch cast-iron skillet*

PAN SAVVY: *I like this recipe in my larger 12-inch skillet because the ingredients fit nicely without any oven spills; it also creates a somewhat flat dessert that's easy to slice and serve. A 10-inch skillet will hold all the ingredients and the pie will have a lovely domed shape. However, it will bubble over, so place the pan on a parchment- or aluminum foil-lined baking sheet. Increase baking time by 15 minutes.*

3½ pounds peeled and thinly sliced baking apples (about 9½ cups)

2 tablespoons lemon juice

⅓ cup granulated sugar

⅓ cup firmly packed light brown sugar

2 tablespoons all-purpose flour

2 tablespoons cornstarch

1 teaspoon ground cinnamon

Pinch of salt

Double-Crust Pastry Dough (page 161) or store-bought refrigerated piecrust dough

1 tablespoon unsalted or salted butter, cut into small pieces

1 egg white, lightly beaten

1 teaspoon sparkling, turbinado, or coarse-grain sugar (optional)

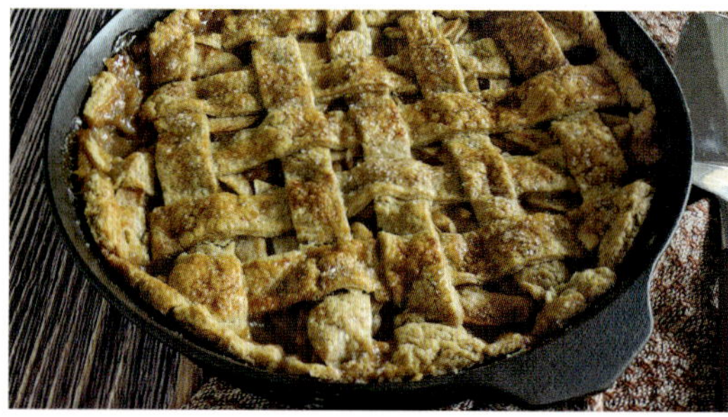

Sometimes, a pie will have what is called "apple pie gap." This occurs when the fruit has cooked down while the pastry has firmed up and stayed in place, leaving a gap between the two. To prevent it, thinly slice apples and nestle them into the pastry to avoid air gaps between pieces of fruit. If a gap occurs, gently press the lattice down on the filling when the pie is removed from the oven. It's not a typo—I use both flour and cornstarch to help thicken the pie filling.

---

1 Preheat oven to 425°. Place oven rack in lower third of oven.

2 Combine apples and juice in a large bowl, tossing to coat. Combine granulated sugar, brown sugar, flour, cornstarch, cinnamon, and salt in a small bowl. Sprinkle fruit mixture with sugar mixture, and toss gently until well blended.

3 Roll 1 Double-Crust Pastry Dough disk into a 12- to 14-inch circle on a lightly floured surface. Place in a 10-inch cast-iron skillet. Roll remaining dough disk into a 12-inch circle. Cut into 1½- to 2-inch strips.

4 Pour fruit mixture into crust. Sprinkle top with pieces of butter. Place pastry strips in a lattice pattern over top of pie; pinch edges to seal. Use any pastry scraps to decorate top, if desired. Brush with egg and sprinkle with sparkling sugar, if desired.

5 Bake for 15 minutes; reduce heat to 350°. Bake for 1 hour or until golden brown and bubbly. Shield edges of crust with aluminum foil, if necessary, to prevent overbrowning. Cool on a wire rack. For the cleanest slices, refrigerate until ready to serve; heat individual slices, if desired.

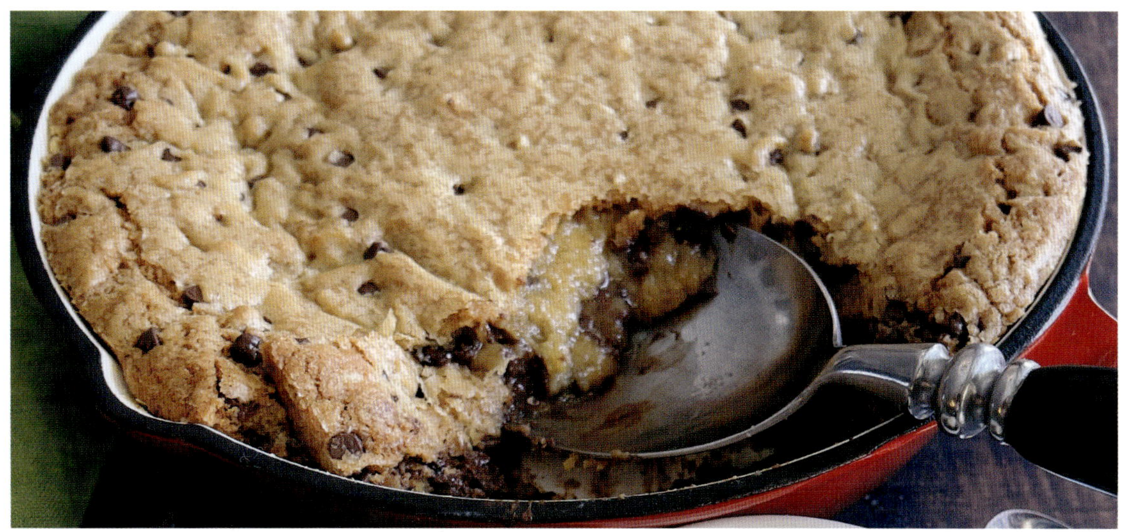

CHOCOLATE CHIP SKILLET COOKIE

MAKES 10 TO 12 SERVINGS

EQUIPMENT: *10- or 12-inch cast-iron skillet*

PAN SAVVY: *The batter will fit in either skillet. Use a 10-inch pan for a cookie that's thick and very soft in the center or a 12-inch pan for a thinner dessert that can be cut into more servings.*

1 cup unsalted butter, softened

1 cup firmly packed light brown sugar

½ cup granulated sugar

2 large eggs

1 teaspoon vanilla extract

2¼ cups all-purpose flour

1 teaspoon baking soda

½ teaspoon fine sea salt

1 cup semisweet chocolate chips

Vanilla ice cream

Baking a giant chocolate chip cookie in a skillet is a fun twist on the classic. The edges get crisp, while the inside stays warm and slightly gooey—safe to eat as long as the interior reaches at least 160° so the raw eggs will be cooked. It will bake faster in a 12-inch skillet, so check on it earlier. Scoop pieces into small bowls and top with vanilla ice cream, or simply enjoy with a glass of chilled milk.

1. Preheat oven to 325°.
2. Melt butter in a 10- or 12-inch skillet over low heat. Remove from heat and let cool for about 5 minutes.
3. Whisk together brown sugar, granulated sugar, eggs, and vanilla in a large bowl. Pour in melted butter, leaving a light coating of butter in bottom of skillet.
4. Combine flour, baking soda, and salt in a bowl. Stir flour mixture into sugar mixture. Stir in chocolate chips. Spoon dough into skillet, spreading to edges and smoothing top.
5. Bake for 35 to 40 minutes (10-inch skillet) or 30 minutes (12-inch skillet) or until edges are golden brown and center is almost set. Serve warm with ice cream.

GOOEY CHOCOLATE SKILLET CAKE

MAKES 6 SERVINGS

EQUIPMENT: *10-inch cast-iron skillet*

PAN SAVVY: *For a soft cake that is spooned into a bowl, use any shape skillet. For evenly portioned servings, try baking in a 10-inch square skillet.*

1½ cups all-purpose flour
3 tablespoons cocoa powder
¾ teaspoon baking soda
½ teaspoon salt
1 cup unsalted or salted butter
1½ cups lightly packed brown sugar
½ cup whole or other milk
2 large eggs
1 teaspoon vanilla extract
½ cup semisweet chocolate chips
Chocolate-Pecan Frosting (recipe at right)
Vanilla ice cream (optional)

Sort of a cobbler with a flavor reminiscent of Texas sheet cake, this yummy dessert satisfies any chocolate craving. Your choice—bake until it's done in the center or very soft. You can underbake a few minutes and make it very gooey, but just make sure the temperature reaches 160° for adequate food safety.

1 Preheat oven to 350°.
2 Combine flour, cocoa powder, baking soda, and salt in a large bowl.
3 Heat butter in a 10-inch cast-iron skillet over medium heat just until melted. Remove from heat. Stir in brown sugar and milk. Whisk in eggs and vanilla. Add flour mixture, whisking until well blended. Stir in chocolate chips.
4 Bake for 25 minutes or until edges are set and center is almost done. Cake will get firmer as it cools.
5 Meanwhile, prepare Chocolate-Pecan Frosting. Spread over warm cake. Serve with vanilla ice cream, if desired.

Chocolate-Pecan Frosting: Combine **¼ cup milk, 2 tablespoons cocoa powder,** and **4 tablespoons butter** in a small saucepan. Bring just to a boil. Remove from heat and whisk in **2 cups powdered sugar** and **½ teaspoon vanilla extract.** Stir in **½ cup chopped pecans.** Makes 1 cup.

DOUBLE CHOCOLATE DUMPLINGS

MAKES 6 SERVINGS

Chocolate lovers, cheer! Here's another dessert for your repertoire! It's not pretty—it kinda looks like lumpy pudding—but the flavor is rich and delicious. Keep the heat low enough so it just barely simmers, and make sure to cover the pan tightly with a lid or a sturdy layer of aluminum foil.

EQUIPMENT: *5- to 7-quart Dutch oven*

1½ cups firmly packed light brown sugar
⅓ cup plus 2 tablespoons cocoa powder, divided
1 tablespoon cornstarch
1¼ teaspoons fine sea salt, divided
3 cups water
6 tablespoons unsalted butter, divided
1 teaspoon vanilla extract
1¼ cups all-purpose flour
½ cup granulated sugar
2 teaspoons baking powder
1 egg, lightly beaten
⅓ cup whole milk
Vanilla ice cream

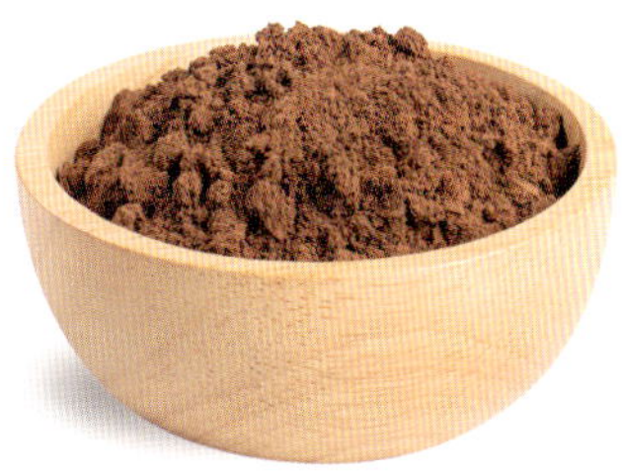

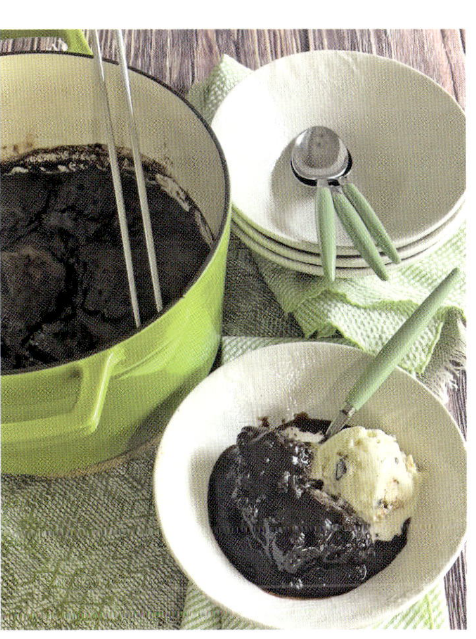

1 To make sauce, combine brown sugar, ⅓ cup cocoa powder, cornstarch, and ¼ teaspoon salt in a cast-iron Dutch oven. Stir in 3 cups water. Bring mixture to a boil, reduce heat, and simmer until smooth and slightly thickened. Add 3 tablespoons butter, stirring until it melts. Stir in vanilla. Remove from heat; set sauce aside.

2 To make batter, combine flour, granulated sugar, baking powder, remaining 2 tablespoons cocoa powder, and remaining 1 teaspoon salt in a large bowl. Cut in remaining 3 tablespoons butter with a pastry blender or fork. Stir in egg and milk.

3 Return Dutch oven to medium heat and bring reserved sauce to a simmer.

4 Drop heaping tablespoonfuls of batter into chocolate sauce in a single layer. Cover tightly and simmer very gently for 10 minutes (do not boil or chocolate may scorch on bottom of pan). Uncover and continue to cook for 5 minutes or until cooked through. Serve dumplings and sauce with vanilla ice cream.

CHOCOLATE-ALMOND FONDUE

MAKES 2 CUPS

EQUIPMENT: *5-cup cast-iron fondue pot*

PAN SAVVY: *Because of the chocolate and dairy (whipping cream) that might stick, I prefer an enamel-coated fondue pot or saucepan.*

1 cup heavy whipping cream
2 tablespoons granulated sugar
8 ounces bittersweet or semisweet chocolate, chopped
1 tablespoon salted or unsalted butter
2 to 3 tablespoons almond liqueur
Fruit, pound cake, marshmallows

Circle up to enjoy this dessert that's easy to make and exciting to eat! You can experiment with a variety of fruits (berries and pineapple) and types of pound cake (lemon and sour cream) to find your favorite flavor combinations.

Strawberries and chocolate are an exquisite pairing, but you can also dip pound cake, angel food cake, or artisan marshmallows. If you prefer, substitute ¼ teaspoon (or more to taste) of almond extract for the almond liqueur. If using unsalted butter, add a small pinch of salt to enhance the flavor. Make sure to save any leftovers. It firms up to be a luscious truffle consistency.

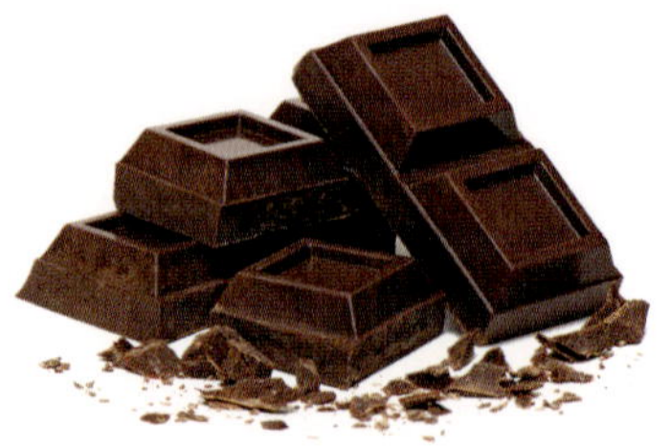

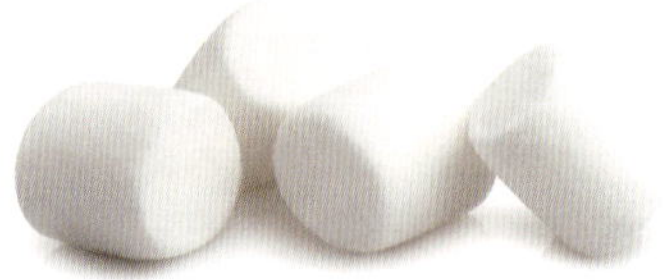

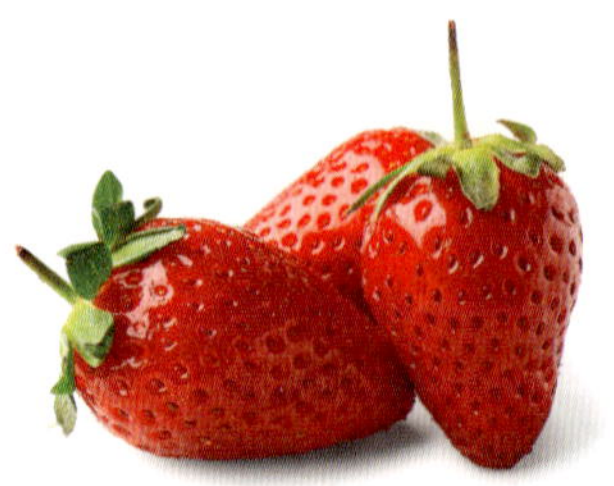

1. Combine cream and sugar in a cast-iron fondue pot or small heavy saucepan over low heat. Cook, stirring constantly, until sugar dissolves. Add chocolate and butter; cook, stirring constantly, until mixture is smooth. Remove from heat; stir in liqueur.
2. Keep warm in a fondue pot heated over a candle (canned fuel is too hot). Serve with fruit, pound cake, and marshmallows.

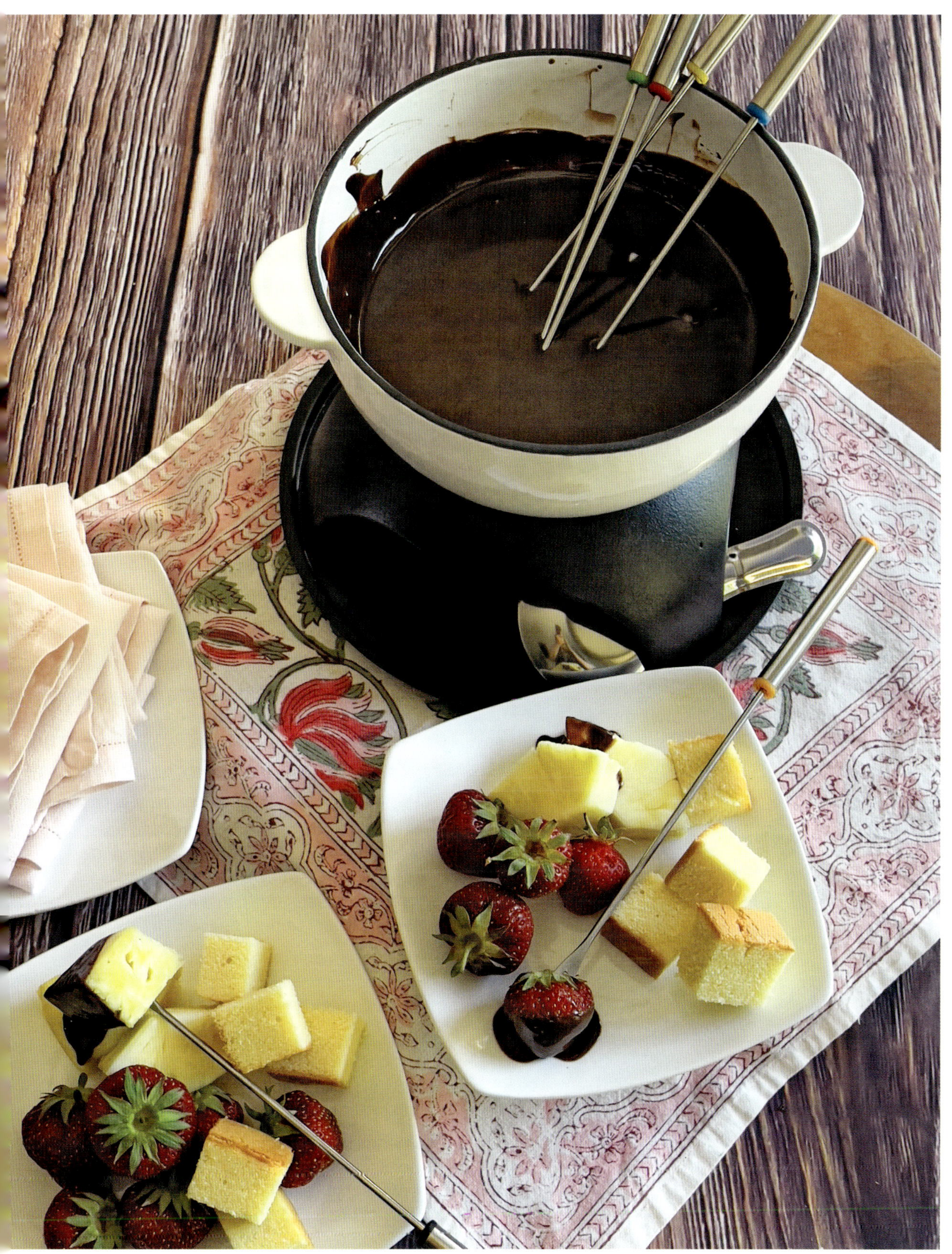

HOMEMADE BEIGNETS

MAKES ABOUT 2½ DOZEN

EQUIPMENT: *Dutch oven or deep cast-iron skillet*

PAN SAVVY: *Cast iron makes an ideal pan for frying because it maintains heat, requiring less fiddling with the temperature on the stove. Beignets are flat, so they won't require as much oil for frying, and a deep skillet works fine. However, the higher sides of a Dutch oven minimize splattering.*

¾ cup warm (105° to 110°) water
1 (0.25-ounce) package or 2¼ teaspoons active dry yeast
¼ cup granulated sugar
1 large egg
½ cup milk, at room temperature
2 tablespoons unsalted butter, melted
3½ cups all-purpose flour
½ teaspoon salt
Vegetable oil
Powdered sugar

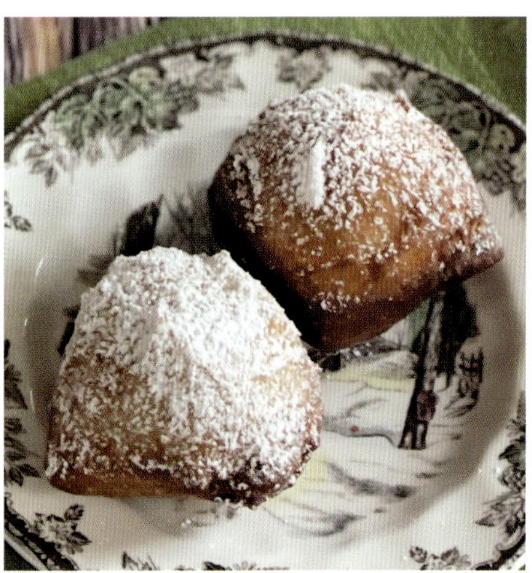

Pronounced "ben-yay," this iconic New Orleans treat is best eaten warm. No worries—they are delicious and won't last long! It's a great dessert for a party. To make the dough ahead, prepare as directed, but instead of letting it rise in a warm place, cover the dough and refrigerate it overnight. Remove from the refrigerator and allow it to warm to room temperature before rolling and cutting.

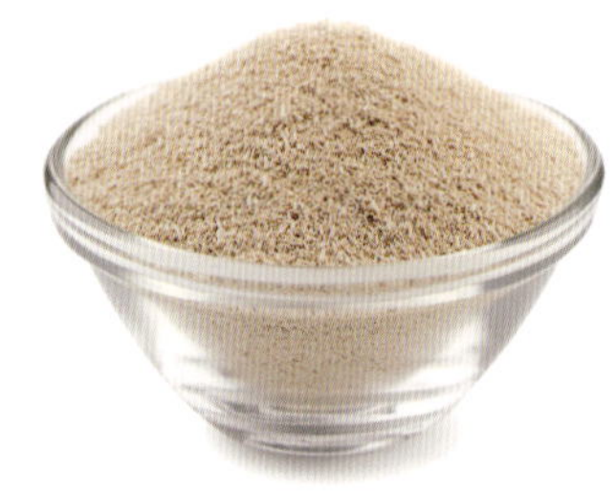

1. Combine ¾ cup warm water, yeast, and granulated sugar in a large mixing bowl. Let stand for 5 minutes.
2. Stir in egg and milk. Stir in butter.
3. Combine flour and salt in a large bowl. Stir flour mixture into milk mixture, and beat with an electric mixer until well blended (dough will be sticky). Cover and let rise in a warm place (85°), free from drafts, for 1½ to 2 hours or until doubled in size.
4. Roll dough out, on a floured surface, into a rectangle or square about ½- to ¾-inch thick. Cut into 1½-inch squares.
5. Pour oil to a depth of 2 inches in a Dutch oven or deep skillet. Heat to 375°. Place a wire cooling rack over a rimmed baking sheet.
6. Fry dough pieces, in batches, turning occasionally, for 3 minutes or until golden brown on all sides. Transfer to a wire rack and let drain. Sprinkle warm beignets with powdered sugar.

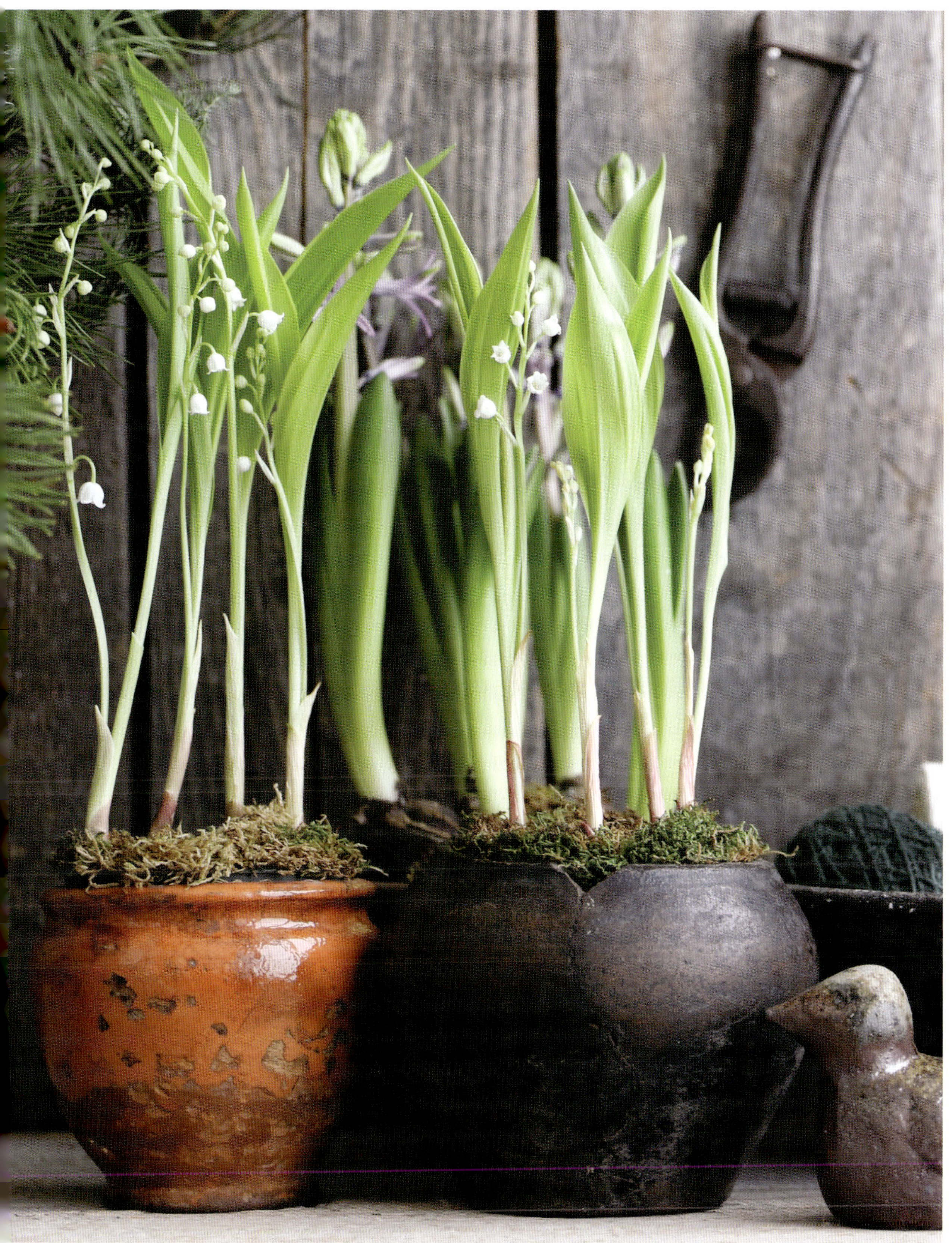

EQUIVALENTS

Almonds	1 pound shelled	4 cups slivered	
Bacon	1 slice bacon	1 tablespoon crumbled	
Beans (Black)	1 pound dried	2⅓ cups uncooked	4¼ cups cooked
Beans (Black)	1 (15½-ounce) can	2 cups cooked	
Beans (Green)	1 pound fresh	3½ cups	
Beans (Green)	9 ounces frozen	1½ cups	
Beans (Green)	1 (15½-ounce) can	1¾ cups	
Bell Peppers	1 large	1 cup chopped	
Blueberries	1 pint fresh	2 cups	
Blueberries	10 ounces frozen	1½ cups	
Butter	1 stick	½ cup	8 tablespoons
Butter	2 sticks	1 cup	½ pound
Butter	4 sticks	2 cups	1 pound
Carrots	1 pound fresh	2½ cups grated	
Celery	2 medium ribs	½ cup chopped	
Cheese	4 ounces	1 cup shredded	
Cheese (Blue, Feta)	¼ pound	1 cup crumbled	
Cheese (Cheddar, Swiss, Jack)	8 ounces	2 cups shredded	
Cheese (Parmesan, Romano)	4 ounces	1 cup grated	
Corn	2 medium ears	1 cup kernels	
Crackers	28 soda or saltine crackers	1 cup crumbs	
Crackers	15 graham squares	1 cup crumbs	
Garlic	1 clove	½ teaspoon minced	
Lemon	1 medium	2 tablespoons juice	
Lemon	1 medium	2 teaspoons zest	
Lime	1 medium	1½ tablespoons juice	
Lime	1 medium	1 teaspoon zest	
Nuts	1 pound shelled	4 cups chopped	
Onion	1 large onion	1 cup chopped	

Orange	1 medium	⅓ cup juice	
Orange	1 medium	2 tablespoons zest	
Pasta	2 ounces uncooked	1 serving cooked	
Pasta	1 cup uncooked small macaroni	2 cups cooked	
Pasta	4 ounces uncooked spaghetti	4 cups cooked	
Rice	1 cup long-grain uncooked	3 cups cooked	
Sour Cream	8 ounces	1 cup	
Strawberries	1 pint	2 cups sliced	
Tomato	1 large	1 cup chopped	
Whipping Cream	1 cup	2 cups whipped	

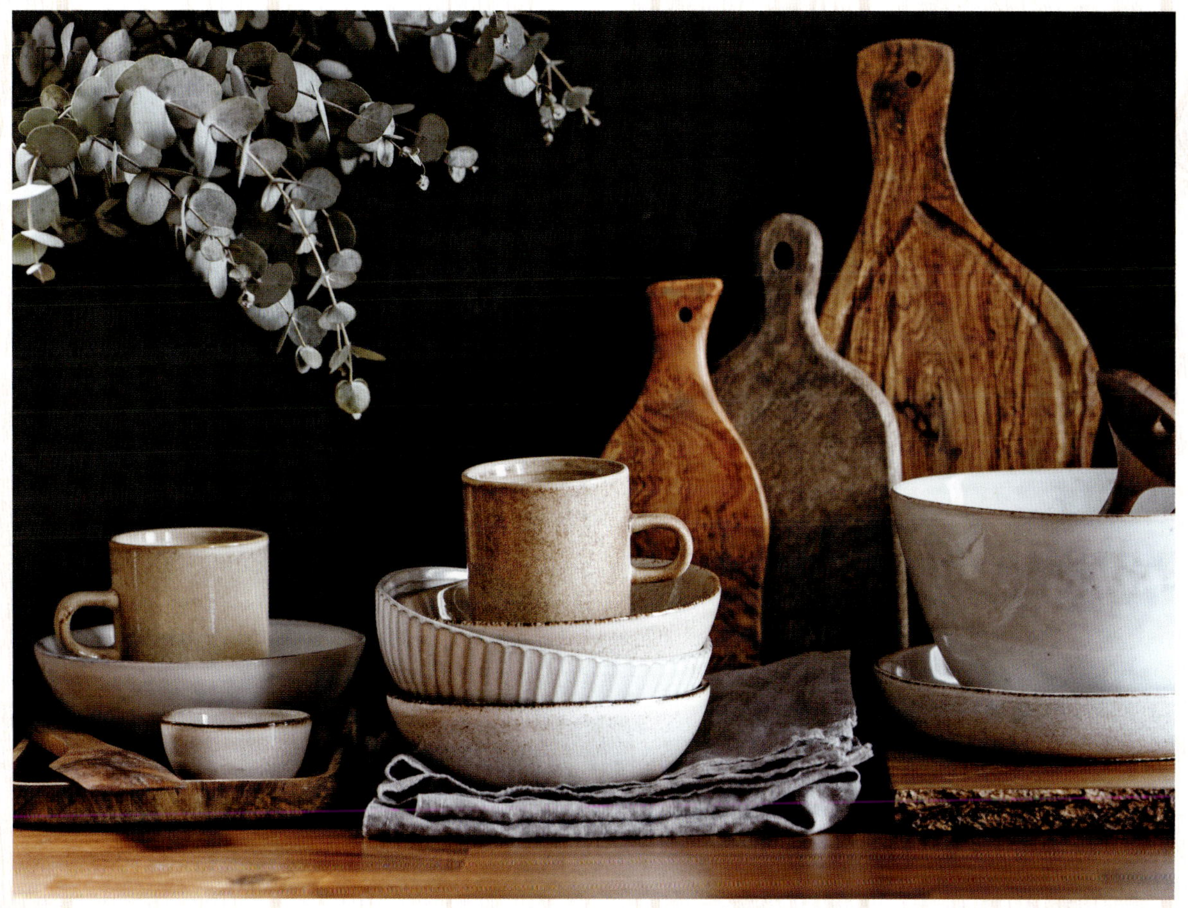

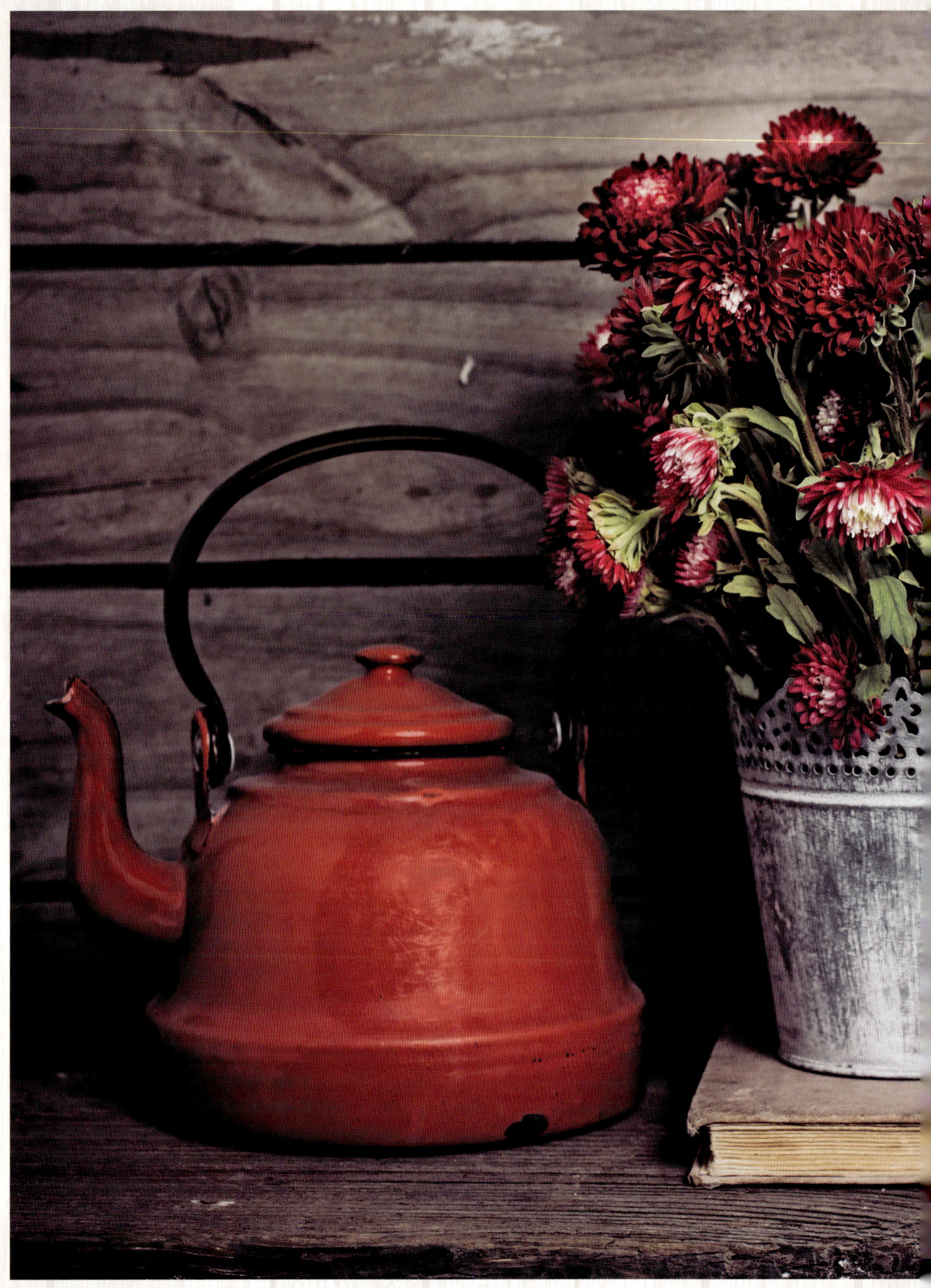

MEASUREMENT CONVERSIONS

Pinch	less than ⅛ teaspoon
3 teaspoons	1 tablespoon
2 tablespoons	⅛ cup
4 tablespoons	¼ cup
5⅓ tablespoons	⅓ cup
8 tablespoons	½ cup
16 tablespoons	1 cup
1 tablespoon	½ fluid ounce
2 tablespoons	1 fluid ounce
¼ cup	2 fluid ounces
½ cup	4 fluid ounces
1 cup	8 fluid ounces
2 cups	16 fluid ounces
4 cups	32 fluid ounces
½ cup	¼ pint
1 cup	½ pint
2 cups	1 pint
4 cups	1 quart
4 quarts	1 gallon
16 cups	1 gallon

BAKING DISH CONVERSIONS

ROUND	
8x1½-inch	4 cups
8x2-inch	6 cups
9x1½-inch	6 cups
9x2-inch	8 cups
SQUARE	
8x8x1½-inch	6 cups
9x9x1½-inch	2 quarts
9x9x2-inch	2½ quarts
RECTANGLE	
11x7x2-inch	2½ quarts
13x9x2-inch	3 quarts
LOAF	
8½x4½x2½-inch	1½ quarts
9x5x3-inch	2 quarts
BUNDT—1 QUART	
9x3-inch	9 cups
10x3-inch	12 cups

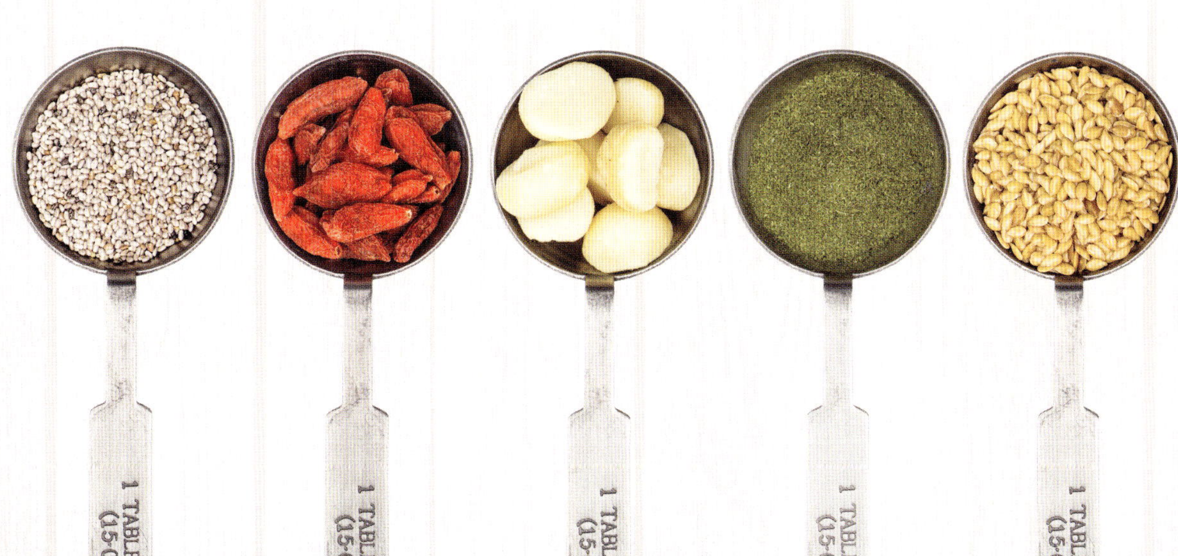

SUBSTITUTIONS

BAKING POWDER	
1 teaspoon	¼ teaspoon baking soda + ½ teaspoon cream of tartar
BISCUIT MIX	
1 cup	1 cup all-purpose flour + 1½ teaspoons baking powder + 2 tablespoons shortening or butter
BREADCRUMBS	
1 cup	¾ cup cracker crumbs
BROTH	
1 cup	1 cup boiling water + 1 bouillon cube or 1 teaspoon granules or paste
BUTTERMILK	
1 cup	1 cup milk + 1 tablespoon lemon juice or vinegar
1 cup	1 cup plain yogurt
CHOCOLATE	
1 ounce unsweetened	3 tablespoons cocoa powder + 1 tablespoon butter or vegetable oil
1 ounce unsweetened	1½ ounces semisweet and remove 1 tablespoon sugar from recipe
1 ounce bittersweet or semisweet	⅔ ounce unsweetened chocolate + 2 teaspoons sugar
1 ounce bittersweet	1 ounce semisweet
1 ounce semisweet	1 ounce unsweetened + 1 tablespoon sugar
1 ounce sweet baking chocolate	3 tablespoons cocoa powder + 4 teaspoons sugar + 1 tablespoon butter or vegetable oil
CORN SYRUP (LIGHT)	
1 cup	¾ cup sugar + ¼ cup additional liquid in recipe
CORN SYRUP (DARK)	
1 cup	¾ cup light corn syrup + ¼ cup molasses
FLOUR, ALL-PURPOSE FLOUR (FOR THICKENING)	
2 tablespoons	1 tablespoon cornstarch
2 tablespoons	2 tablespoons quick-cooking tapioca
FLOUR, CAKE	
1 cup	1 cup - 2 tablespoons all-purpose flour + 2 tablespoons cornstarch

FLOUR, SELF-RISING	
1 cup	1 cup all-purpose flour + 1½ teaspoons baking powder + ⅛ teaspoon salt
HALF-AND-HALF	
1 cup	½ cup milk + ½ cup whipping cream
HERBS	
1 tablespoon fresh	1 teaspoon dried
LEMON JUICE	
1 teaspoon fresh juice	½ teaspoon vinegar
MOLASSES	
1 cup	1 cup almond butter
PEANUT BUTTER	
1 cup	1 cup almond butter
SUGAR (LIGHT BROWN)	
1 cup	½ cup dark brown sugar + ½ cup granulated sugar
SUGAR (GRANULATED)	
1 cup	1¾ cups powdered
1 cup	1 cup firmly packed light brown sugar
TOMATO SAUCE	
2 cups	1 cup tomato paste + 1 cup water

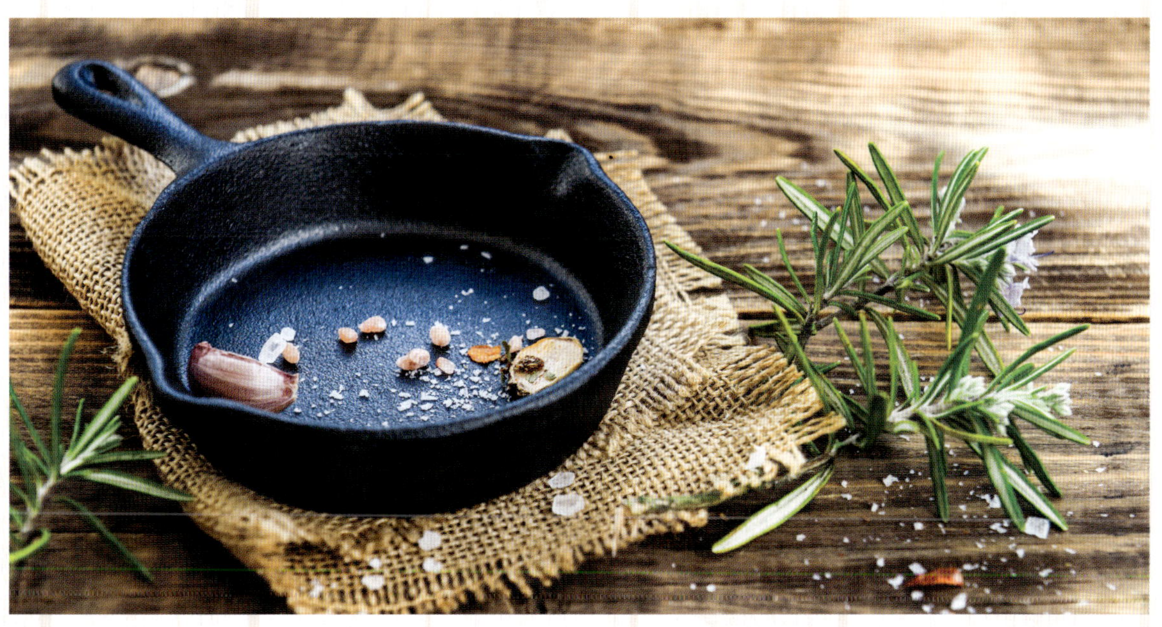

INDEX

C

D

M

N

O

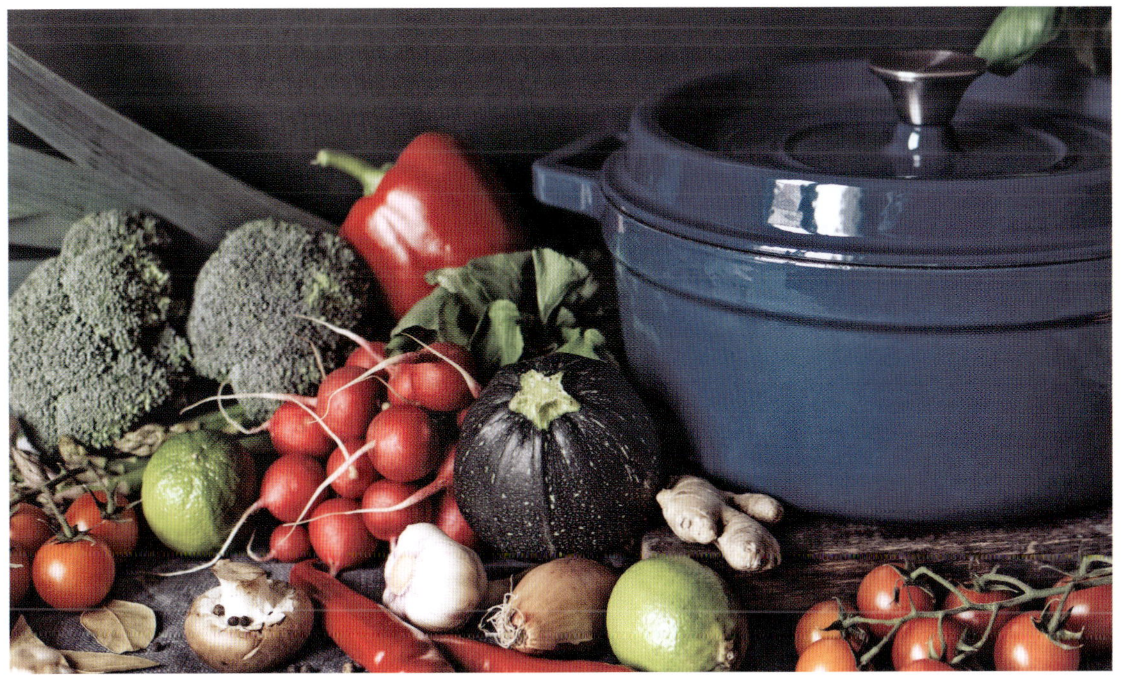

Q

R

S

T

U

V

W

Y

Z

Cover design by Jonathan Norberg
Book design by Hilary Harkness
Edited by Emily Beaumont

Cover images: All photos copyright by **Julia Rutland** unless otherwise noted.
Wachiwit/Shutterstock.com: back cover brick background

All photos by **Julia Rutland** unless otherwise noted.

Field Company: 5 (round griddle, baker's skillet, long handled skillet); and **Lodge Cast Iron:** 7 (fluted cake pan).

This image is used under CC 1.0 Universal (CC0 1.0) Public Domain Dedication, which can be found at creativecommons.org/publicdomain/zero/1.0/: **Lazychris2000/English Wikipedia:** 7 (aebleskiver pan)

Images used under license from Shutterstock.com:
Andrey Eremin: 157 (pear); **Anna Mente:** 175 (cast iron pan and burlap); **Anton Starikov:** 168 (yeast); **Arlee.P:** 140 (eggs); **ArtKio**: grainy background on pages 170, 171, 173–175; **Bjoern Wylezich:** 2 (iron, silicon); **Bowonpat Sakaew:** 72 (swiss chard); **chyworks:** 185 (watercolor); **cristi180884:** 54 (emmentaler cheese); **Daria Minaeva:** 172; **den781:** 146 (red pepper); **Dewin ID:** 5 (grill pan); **Dyfrain:** 88 (zucchini); **Edalin Photography:** 171 (dishes); **Ermak Oksana:** 82 (kidney beans); **Fattyplace:** ii–iii; **Fernati2007:** 25 (blueberries); **Food Impressions:** 64 (shrimp); **Galina Grebenyuk:** 169; **Gandhi_V:** 80 (green beans); **George3973:** 154 (pecans); **GSDesign:** 21 (eggs), 112 (arugula); **Halil ibrahim mescioglu:** 135 (rosemary); **Hong Vo:** 55 (cheddar cheese), 90 (yellow squash), 136 (bell pepper); **Hortimages:** 111 (basil); **ifiStudio:** 138 (shallots); **irin-k:** 166 (dark chocolate); **JIANG HONGYAN:** 92 (green tomatoes); **Jiri Hera:** 48 (bruschetta); **Jit-anong Sae-ung:** 58 (black beans); **Jr images:** 165 (cocoa powder); **Kaiskynet Studio:** 94 (oyster mushrooms); **Kanokkarn Machaiwong:** 18 (green chilies); **Kelvin Wong:** 124 (parsnips); **Luke SW:** 12; **mahirart:** 114 (dried chickpeas); **MaraZe:** 61 (brie); **MarcoFood:** 36 (oranges); 48 (garlic); **marekuliasz:** 173 (measuring spoons); **mikeledray:** 8; **nafterphoto:** v (red checked napkin); **Natalia Klenova:** 1; **NataliaZa:** 110 (spinach); **Nataly Studio:** 68 (cloves), 123 (yellow onion); **Nelli Kovalchuk:** 119, 181; **New Africa:** 2 (carbon), 25 (butter), 39 (spinach), 51 (bacon), 58 (cilantro), 60 (parmesan wedge), 76 (tortillas); **NUM LPPHOTO:** 148 (lemongrass); **Oleksandr Lytvynenko:** 184; **Olesia Bech:** 73 (tomato); **Olga Guchek:** 100 (sweet potato); **photogal:** 102 (yukon gold potato); **Photoongraphy:** 146 (ginger), 150 (fuji apples); **Pinkyone:** woodgrain on pages 15, 45, 71, 87, 107, 121, 153, 170–175; **Pisut chounyoo:** 84 (butternut squash); **Pixel-Shot:** 166 (strawberries); **posteriori:** i; **pukao:** 78 (celery); **RESTOCK images:** 34 (mascarpone in bowls); **Roman Samokhin:** 37 (lemon); **StudioPixs:** 68 (lemon); **studiovin:** 55 (mustard in bowl); **Tanya_mtv:** 53 (eggplant); **Tiger Images:** 17 (plum tomato), 101 (russet potato); **Timmary:** 105 (cabbage); **Ton Bangkeaw:** 22 (yellow onion); **Uswatun des:** 16 (corn on the cob); **Valentyn Volkov:** 28 (olive oil); **warat42:** 30 (cinnamon/sticks); **Washdog:** 186 (frame); **Yeti studio:** 89 (corn kernels), 130 (red onion), 166 (marshmallows); **yulyamade:** 7 (wok); **ZOOM-STUDIO:** 7 (cauldron)

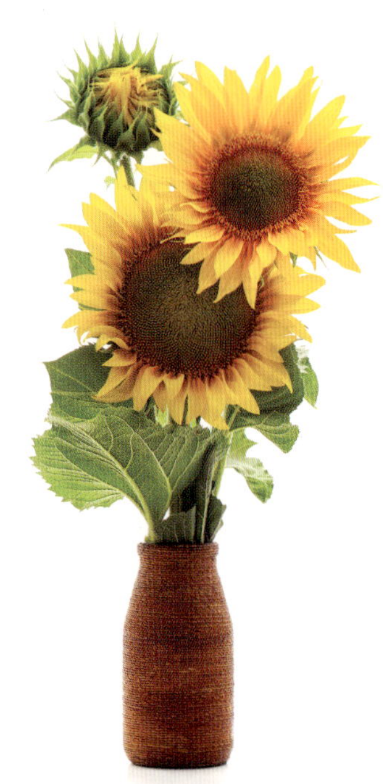

10 9 8 7 6 5 4 3 2

Cast-Iron Cooking

Published by Adventure Publications
An imprint of AdventureKEEN
310 Garfield Street South
Cambridge, Minnesota 55008
(800) 678-7006
www.adventurepublications.net

Printed in China
LCCN 2024056428 (print), 2024056429 (ebook)
ISBN 978-1-64755-470-5 (pbk.); ISBN 978-1-64755-471-2 (ebook)

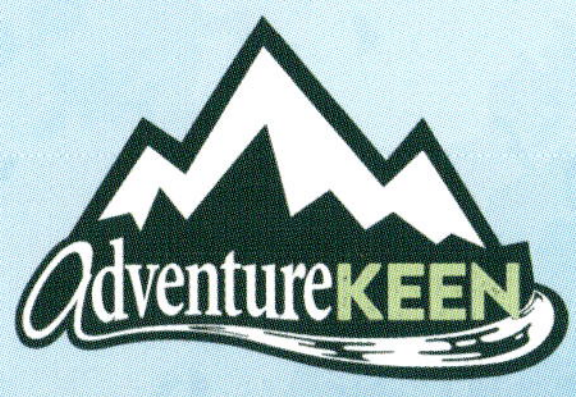

The Story of AdventureKEEN

We are an independent nature and outdoor activity publisher. Our founding dates back more than 40 years, guided then and now by our love of being in the woods and on the water, by our passion for reading and books, and by the sense of wonder and discovery made possible by spending time recreating outdoors in beautiful places.

It is our mission to share that wonder and fun with our readers, especially with those who haven't yet experienced all the physical and mental health benefits that nature and outdoor activity can bring.

In addition, we strive to teach about responsible recreation so that the natural resources and habitats we cherish and rely upon will be available for future generations.

We are a small team deeply rooted in the places where we live and work. We have been shaped by our communities of origin—primarily Birmingham, Alabama; Cincinnati, Ohio; and the northern suburbs of Minneapolis, Minnesota. Drawing on the decades of experience of our staff and our awareness of the industry, the marketplace, and the world at large, we have shaped a unique vision and mission for a company that serves our readers and authors.

We hope to meet you out on the trail someday.

#bewellbeoutdoors

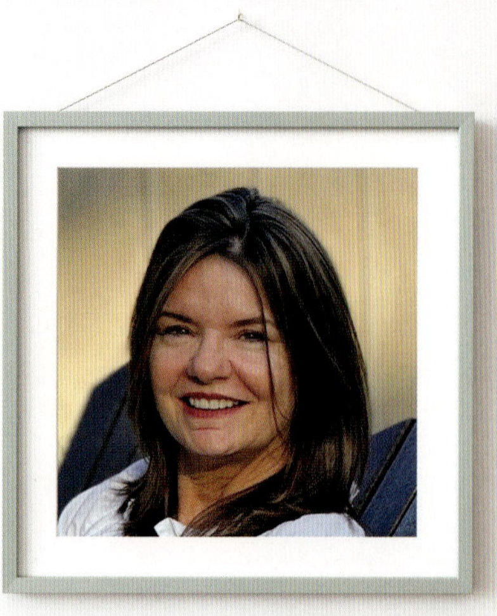

ABOUT THE AUTHOR

Julia Rutland is a writer and author with 25 years of experience in the food, publishing, travel, and marketing industries. She is the author of more than a dozen cookbooks, including *The Campfire Foodie Cookbook, On a Stick, Blueberries, Squash, Apples, Honey, Tomatoes, Eggs, Foil Pack Dinners, 101 Lasagnas, The Christmas Movie Cookbook, and Homestyle Kitchen*. Before moving to the Washington, D.C., area and developing her own business, Julia worked at *Coastal Living* magazine as senior food editor, with Wimmer Cookbooks as a sales and marketing consultant, and in the test kitchens of *Southern Living* magazine. Julia has a deep knowledge of cooking principles; she is passionate about consumer education and skilled in savvy story packaging. She is a member of Les Dames d'Escoffier, an international philanthropic organization of women leaders in the fields of food, fine beverage, and hospitality. Julia is also a trained volunteer and serves on the board with the Virginia Cooperative Extension Master Gardener program in Loudoun County. Julia lives in the D.C. wine-country town of Hillsboro, Virginia, with her husband, two daughters, and many furred and feathered friends.